AFTER THE FUTURE

A volume in the series

Critical Perspectives on

Modern Culture

Edited by David Gross

and William M. Johnston

AFTER THE FUTURE

THE PARADOXES OF

POSTMODERNISM

AND CONTEMPORARY

RUSSIAN CULTURE

Mikhail N. Epstein

Translated with an introduction by Anesa Miller-Pogacar

THE UNIVERSITY OF MASSACHUSETTS PRESS   Amherst

Copyright © 1995 by
The University of Massachusetts Press
All rights reserved
Printed in the United States of America
LC 94–40289
ISBN 0–87023–973–2 (cloth); 974–0 (pbk.)
Designed by Mary Mendell
Set in Melior and Futura by Keystone Typesetting, Inc.
Printed and bound by Thomson-Shore, Inc.
Library of Congress Cataloging-in-Publication Data
Ėpshteĭn, Mikhail.

    After the future : the paradoxes of postmodernism and contemporary
Russian culture / Mikhail N. Epstein ; translated with an
introduction by Anesa Miller-Pogacar.

      p. cm. — (Critical perspectives on modern culture)
    Includes bibliographical references and index.
    ISBN 0–87023–973–2 (cloth : alk. paper). — ISBN 0–87023–974–0
(pbk. : alk. paper)

    1. Russia (Federation)—Intellectual life. 2. Postmodernism—
Russia (Federation) I. Miller-Pogacar, Anesa, 1954– . II. Title.
III. Series.
DK510.32.E67   1995
947.084—dc20

                                94–40289
                                    CIP
British Library Cataloguing in Publication data are available.

032095-2285H3

In memory of my parents

CONTENTS

NOTE ON TRANSLITERATION

Every effort has been made to use Thomas Shaw's System II consistently in transliterating Russian terms employed in this book. Personal and place names, however, have been westernized for ease of reading. Spellings used in *Webster's Biographical Dictionary* are followed here for the names of those Russian cultural figures sufficiently well known in the West to be included. It is hoped that this practice will appropriately reflect an increasing familiarity with Russian culture, in that the name of a nineteenth-century writer such as Aleksandr Pushkin retains an exotic aura, while that of contemporary poet Alexander Eremenko is immediately recognizable. Spellings preferred by contemporary cultural figures with established reputations in the West have been used insofar as we were aware of them. Thus the reader will encounter Vassily Aksyonov rather than Vasily (or Vasilii) Aksenov and Ilya Kabakov rather than Ilia.

PREFACE

The semantic shift contained in the title of this book indicates the paradoxical nature of contemporary Russian culture. If the future always comes *after*, at the end of time, what can come after the future itself? This is the main question of the book, and the answer can hardly be unproblematic. It would seem that Francis Fukuyama proposed the most radical interpretation possible: the collapse of Soviet communism *is* the "end of world history." But for Russia itself, this was something even more radical than the end; it meant, rather, turning back in our tracks, or turning ourselves inside out. An end, after all, is still an end—a normal point in the progression of time. But for Russian consciousness, the collapse of communism was not simply the end, but rather an inversion of beginning and end, an almost impossible anomaly of time. The "communist future" has become a thing of the past, while the feudal and bourgeois "past" approaches us from the direction where we had expected to meet the future. The historical perspective, once so confidently described by Marxism, has been turned inside out, not only for Russia, but for all of humankind, insofar as it had been drawn into the communist project in one way or another, even if only to oppose it.

The term *postmodernism* ("after-time") suits the given situation only in part, although it is coming into increasingly frequent use among Russian writers and critics. Actually, we are experiencing a kind of post-futurism, insofar as it is not the present that turns out to be behind us, but the future itself. Nonetheless, if we consider communism an extremist form of modernism—with its utopian emphases, the avant-garde breakup of reality and mania for infallible truth—then Western commentators on postmodernism will find more than a few common features in the postmodern West and postcommunist Russia. One of these is the disappearance of "the present." Crucial to contemporary Russian culture is that it is least of all "con-temporary" in the narrow sense of "modern." It contains far more elements of the archaic and the postmodern than it does properly "modern" ones. A number of the more peculiar features of Western post-modernism find heightened expression here, because of this tendency to abide *not* in the mode of the contemporary, but in the pre- and postcontem-porary, in a kind of futuristic archaism. Having outlived our future, we find ourselves suddenly in the arrière-garde of world culture, making a distant approach to capitalism, if not an incipient departure from some slaveown-ing system: such is the shock of confronting one's own past, the like of which, perhaps, no other contemporary culture has experienced.

In the trinary system of time, the present normally represents authentic reality, whereas the past and future appear as its long-distance projections. Not so in Russia. Here, the present has almost never enjoyed its own worth, but rather was perceived as an echo of the past or a step toward the future. When Diderot was corresponding with Catherine the Great and began to despair of making Russia grow accustomed to the fruits of the Enlighten-ment, he wrote that this country was "a fruit that rots before it ripens." In other words, the future of this fruit turns out to be in the past. Later Russian thinkers expressed a similar idea: "Russia's fate is one of needless ventures based on being born soon and soon collapsing" (Prince M. Shcherbatov); "We grow but don't ripen" (Petr Chaadaev); "We were born well, but grew up very little" (Vasily Rozanov).[1] If the past corresponds to youth, the pres-ent to maturity, and the future to old age, then Russia is at once a young and an old country, that managed to bypass maturity unnoticed.

Iury M. Lotman and Boris A. Uspensky have substantially revealed the operation of dualistic models in their work on the semiotics of Russian culture, which tends to avoid a third, neutral member in any semantic op-position. Thus, the pagan deities of Russian antiquity were either reinter-preted as personifications of unclean powers, or they merged with images of Christian saints, but they were never shifted into a neutral value zone. Sim-ilarly, Russian religious consciousness recognized the existence of heaven and hell, but not of purgatory. Russia's relations with the West passed through alternate stages of lauding the "new Russia" over the "decrepit West" and of humbling "decrepit Russia" before the "new West," but the two societies have almost never been considered on one and the same value-neutral plane.[2] This prevailing pattern explains why present time figures weakly in Russian culture: the present is a middling, neutral member in the historical opposition of "past" and "future." According to Lotman and

Uspensky's dualistic model, Russian culture operates not by equalizing and mediating oppositions, but through their diametrical reversal.[3] Recent examples affirm this. What was perceived as the future only yesterday—the classless society of communism—suddenly, without ever becoming the present, is already the past that one wants to be rid of as quickly as possible, like a burdensome and outdated legacy. On the other hand, what seemed a relic of the distant past—the monarchy, the division of society into "estates," a constituent assembly—suddenly moves into the zone of a possible and desirable future.[4]

In this book, however, Russian culture is of interest to me not as an exotic other, but as a magnifying glass through which one can look at Western culture as a whole. Those paradoxes that have become so tragically acute in contemporary Russia constitute, in one way or another, the essence of cultural dynamics, in that any progressive movement turns out to be at once a modernization and an archaization—a leap into both the future and the past. As Thomas Mann once remarked, "life's interesting phenomena appear to always have a double face, turned toward the past and future; they appear to always be at once progressive and regressive."[5] The birth of the new bears within it the traces of rebirth of the old, and however radical an innovation may be, just as deep are the archaic layers it resurrects.

Culture differs from history in its movement along the axis of time in both directions simultaneously, as in the classical dance of "one step forward and one step back." Pirouettes of time, describing circles around a central axis of "the present"—this is culture. In one sense, culture is an anti–time machine built into history.

Thus, in art, the movement from realism to symbolism, and further on to cubism, surrealism, and abstractionism, was not only a movement from the nineteenth century into the twentieth, but at the same time a movement from the nineteenth century into the world of medieval icons, of ancient Egyptian and Chinese hieroglyphics, of primeval cave paintings. In philosophy, the movement from Kant to Hegel and further on to Nietzsche and Heidegger was at the same time a movement from Cartesian rationalism to Platonic idealism and beyond to the pre-Socratics.

But if culture moves forward and back at the same time, at an increasing amplitude of fluctuation, then what remains in the middle? Where is that reality that might be known as the present? Within the expanding boundaries of culture, from remote archaic times to the postmodern, there remains less and less room for established modernity, for the ambitious middleground. In this way, Russian culture, with its meaningful lack of the present and its inversion of future and past, sharpens the paradoxes proper to contemporary culture in general. After all, the very terms "contemporary" and "modern," so recently synonymous, are now becoming antonyms before the eyes of a single generation. The more culture today is contemporary, the less it is modern.

ACKNOWLEDGMENTS

First of all, I want to express my deep gratitude to Anesa Miller-Pogacar whose thoughtful work as a translator and commentator made publication of this book possible. She provided the Introduction and translated the Preface, Chapters 1, 2, 7, 8, and 10, and the Conclusion. She carefully edited other chapters as well, both those that I wrote in English (Chapters 4, 6, and 9, and the third section of Chapter 5) and those translated by Andrew Wachtel of Northwestern University (the first and second sections of Chapter 5) and Gene Kuperman of Duke University (Chapter 3), who in his translation made use of an earlier one by Jamie Gambrell and Catherine Nepomnyashchy, which had been sponsored by the Wheatland Foundation. I am thankful to all these people for their valuable contributions.

I am especially indebted to Dale E. Peterson of Amherst College for his interest in and encouragement of this project from its earliest stages; as a consulting editor for the book, he has been an invaluable source of helpful commentary. I am also grateful to Gerald J. Janecek of the University of Kentucky for his attentive reading of the final draft of the manuscript. The insightful recommendations of Professors Peterson and Janecek contributed significantly to the refinement of the book's contents, composition, and style.

As a Fellow of the Kennan Institute for Advanced Russian Studies at the Wilson Center in Washington, D.C., from August 1990 to August 1991, I enjoyed privileges that made it possible to write the fourth chapter and to prepare the rest of the project. I am grateful to Blair Ruble, Mark Teeter, and the staff of the Kennan Institute for their comprehensive support of my research on Soviet ideological language. Special thanks go to Steve Garber who served as my research assistant and helped enormously in typing and editing my manuscripts, and to Peggy McInerny, editor of my "Occasional Paper" on Soviet ideological language.

I was assisted in my work on Chapters 6 and 9 by the generous financial support of the National Council for Soviet and East European Research (Washington, D.C.), which has sponsored my research in the field of contemporary Russian philosophical thought. I am also grateful to the Research Committee of Emory University, whose awards allowed me to concentrate on my study in the summer of 1992 and to take an academic leave in the spring semester of 1993. Special thanks are due to Juliette Apkarian and my other colleagues at Emory University for their moral and organizational support.

I am grateful to Ellen Berry, Tatiana Kaledina, Sally Laird, Walter Laqueur, Albena Lyutskanova, Priscilla Meyer, and Donald Weber for their generous help and kind advice during various stages of this project.

Some sections of this book have been previously published and are reprinted here with permission: portions of Chapter 1 first appeared in *Third Wave: The New Russian Poetry,* edited by Kent Johnson and Stephen M. Ashby (Ann Arbor: University of Michigan Press, 1992), © The University of Michigan; Chapter 3 first appeared in *Late Soviet Culture: From Perestroika to Novostroika,* edited by Thomas Lahusen with Gene Kuperman (Durham, N.C.: Duke University Press, 1993); Chapter 4 first appeared as Occasional Paper #243 of the Kennan Institute for Advanced Russian Studies, Washington, D.C., and is published now with the permission of the Woodrow Wilson International Center for Scholars; Chapter 5 originally appeared in *Common Knowledge* 1, no. 3 (1992) © 1992 by Oxford University Press.

I wish to express my gratitude to Clark Dougan, senior editor of the University of Massachusetts Press, for his continuous encouragement of this project, to Pam Wilkinson, managing editor, and to Betty S. Waterhouse, who helped to edit the manuscript.

And, finally, special thanks are due to my wife, Helen, who read the manuscripts more than once and made penetrating comments that led to substantial improvements in the initial drafts.

AFTER THE FUTURE

INTRODUCTION · Mikhail Epstein's Transcultural Visions

Literary Theory and the New Focus on Culture

In the 1960s a new trend began to emerge in Russian literary philology and criticism, originating in a variety of schools that stood in tacit opposition to socialist realism, established by the Communist Party as an official methodology in the early thirties. Such writers as Iury Lotman, Viacheslav Ivanov, Georgy Gachev, Sergei Averintsev and others, while not overtly hostile to socialism as a governmental system, insisted on discussing artistic and other cultural phenomena in terms of immanent laws and functions that cannot be formulaically derived from economic structures or class relations. Drawing upon work by the Russian Formalists and their archopponents in the school of Mikhail Bakhtin, as well as the theories of structural semiotics, these thinkers developed a view of art as inseparable from the total cultural and communication system of a community.

The Russian Formalists, operating in small discussion groups centered in Moscow and St. Petersburg in the late 1910s and through the 1920s, succeeded in establishing in the hearts and minds of intellectuals for generations to come recognition of the autonomy and internal integrity of art as a sphere of creative activity that must be studied independently of political, philosophical, religious, and psychological considerations. Under the oppressive circumstances of their time, which silenced all critics failing to espouse socialist realism, they were not able to establish the autonomy of literary studies as a discipline. Nonetheless, they convinced many of their detractors of the need to devote attention to the internal devices and techniques that make literature a unique cultural institution.[1]

Mikhail Bakhtin and his followers strongly criticized the Formalists' early disregard of the role social and ideological factors play in shaping artistic expression. These charges were motivated by a recognition of the strengths of the Formalists' approach and a desire to engage in debate with a more thoughtful opposition than any the orthodox Marxist critics could then offer. Before their decimation in the course of the thirties, the Bakhtin circle advanced socialistic alternatives to the increasingly rigid Bolshevik view of culture as an inert superstructure on the dynamic base of economic relations. Deemphasizing the role of individual psychology, these thinkers posited a thoroughly social ontology of language, which existed for them solely in the "interindividual territory" between and among participants in specific speech acts, or utterances. Similarly, in discussing the verbal arts, Bakhtin emphasized the mode of existence of these forms in the specific performance practices of a given community.[2]

Between the late 1950s and the late 1970s, the Moscow-Tartu school of semiotics integrated methods of textual analysis such as those begun by the Formalists into a comprehensive theory of linguistic and cultural meaning. Structural analyses of literature were readily extended to other social phenomena, including the visual arts, myths and folklore, and games, such as chess. Gradually the semioticians developed a conception of culture as a massive network of symbolic systems that structure our perceptions of and relations to reality. This marked a decisive shift away from the isolationism of formalistic "literariness" and toward the common signifying properties of all cultural enterprises.

The term "culturology" was coined in the sixties to designate the scholarly orientation of theorists who realized the significance of uniquely artistic structures while situating them firmly within a specific cultural (and sometimes sociocultural) context. Literature took its place within the "system of systems," which could be accurately described only with reference to the interactions of many operational levels, from phonetics through stylistics and on to cultural history or, for some thinkers, even spirituality.[3] While promoting the most rigorous traditions of classical European philology, culturologists also tend to espouse a poststructuralist skepticism of objectivity. Recognizing that all cultural activity, including scholarship, entails subjective and evaluative processes, many culturologists feel justified in allowing their work to express their advocacy of various cultural policies, such as tolerance of diversity or reverence for religious traditions.

Mikhail Epstein (born in 1950) is a leading representative of the young generation of thinkers who developed the culturological orientation into a loosely affiliated movement that transformed the Russian intellectual scene during the perestroika years. Despite a variety of professional setbacks, attributable to prejudice against his Jewish ethnicity and his affinity for avant-garde literature, Epstein was active in Moscow cultural life throughout the seventies and eighties. He felt that an important step toward revitalization must be to bring people together, entirely outside of institutional contexts, for collaborative reflection on all types of ideas. One of his first efforts in this direction was to organize a small group of intellectual acquaintances into an "Essayists' Club" that met regularly over a six-year period beginning in the early 1980s. The varying group of five to twenty participants would select a topic for the evening, either whimsical or serious, and, after discussing it, would spend an hour or two writing down their perspectives, producing a compendium of responses to the topic that would later be shared and discussed further.

In 1986, while still involved in the Essayists' Club, Epstein helped initiate another interdisciplinary association, known as "Image and Thought." This was also a group of artists and intellectuals of various professions who gathered on a regular basis to share ideas on social and cultural issues. Rather than focusing on collaborative essays, however, this group chose as its main project the establishment of a "Bank of New Ideas and Terms," which publicized its willingness to accept for discussion and evaluation new ideas extrapolated from any field of the humanities. Those ideas found to be genuinely innovative and possessed of significant potential for productive development in society would be enrolled in the "bank" for preservation, as a type of intellectual capital. This group's activities are described in Chapter 10 of this volume.

Perhaps Epstein's largest undertaking was the organization (beginning in 1988) of the Laboratory of Contemporary Culture. He advanced the notion that culture itself is a laboratory in which intellectual research should enjoy perfect freedom. Thus, new cultural movements for the future should be initiated in a laboratory setting, as a proper place to mix together diverse, even seemingly incompatible substances, or, less metaphorically, people with the various types of consciousness appropriate to their diverse walks of life. Old habits, cultural stagnation, and the repression of honest interaction enforced by the political regime had tended to keep these representatives of Russian culture's multiple viewpoints isolated from one another. In order to counteract these inhibiting factors, this forum sponsored a monthly program of lectures, readings, and discussions on topics ranging from the Stalin cult to world religions and contemporary poetry. Numerous Moscow artists and thinkers of various backgrounds participated in these events. The Laboratory of Contemporary Culture was both an expression and a stimulus of the intellectual ferment that characterized the halcyon days of glasnost.

In his speech at the opening of the new center, Epstein asserted that "the proper place for developing new cultural directions is in a laboratory."[4] This statement highlights what might be called the "futuristic" perspective that Epstein brings to bear on culture itself and on culturology as a discipline. The apocalyptic quality of Epstein's thought, evident in the very title of this book, expresses itself in his emphasis on the need for creative individuals to develop new levels of consciousness and effect a renewal of cultural production, necessary in a new historical era. His writings persistently urge us to consider what cultural actions are appropriate to the end of an epoch, a millenium, or even the end of time. In this regard, it is worth noting that, in addition to the scholarly inspirations culturologists have drawn from the literary theories of the second and third decades of the twentieth century, many have looked to Russian philosophical traditions of the early century. Epstein, for example, avows an affinity with the thought of Nikolai Berdiaev, who commented that "the Russian people, by its metaphysical nature and by virtue of its vocation in the world, is a people of the End. Apocalypse always played a great role on the popular level and on the high cultural level as well, among Russian writers and thinkers."[5]

Epstein's early publications, following his graduation from the Philological Faculty of Moscow State University, were on Russian modernist poetry, Western literature, and semiotic theory; he also catalogued a "system of landscape imagery," developed over three centuries of the Russian poetic tradition. In the mid-eighties he became the critic-champion of what he calls the first "whole generation of poets" to coalesce in Russia since the 1960s. He wrote ardently and often about the conceptualist poets, attempting to explain to readers the theoretical and aesthetic significance of verse that seemed trivial yet shocking to some, offensive and blasphemous to others. At a time when Russian traditionalists were gathering public support for the preservation of churches and other monuments of the past, Epstein came out in favor of experimentation and the creation of new monuments, worthy of preservation for the future. Members of the nationalistic Pamiat movement came to heckle and threaten Epstein at several of his public lectures. In early 1990 he was invited to teach at Wesleyan University and the following year received a research fellowship at the Woodrow Wilson International Center for scholars. Thereafter he moved to a position at Emory University which has allowed him to remain in the United States on a permanent basis.

On Soviet Ideology: Context for a Second World Postmodernism

Mikhail Bakhtin was at the height of his belated influence on the Moscow in-telligentsia when Epstein was a university student in the early seventies. Like many culturologists, Epstein credits Bakhtin with a great contribution to the new understanding of culture; citing, for example, Bakhtin's emphasis on borders as an essential category in discussions of cultural phenomena, an elusive yet vital feature of any nation's (and, in another sense, any individual's) identity, establishing its distinction from all others. Epstein focuses on the internal borders that differentiate a culture from its own predominant tra-ditions, dividing it into various age and ethnic groups, religions, economic classes, political parties, and numerous other competing worldviews. As the essays in this book illustrate in an impressive variety of contexts, Epstein is concerned with the ways in which a phenomenon diverges *from itself,* be it a personality, a genre or style, a phase of time, even an entire national culture.

One area in which Epstein differs sharply from Bakhtin, however, is on the controversial question of culture and ideology. *The Formal Method in Literary Scholarship* (attributed to Bakhtin and his colleague Pavel Med-vedev) presents a view of ideology as both ubiquitous and political, in that it plays a key role in all acts of "social evaluation." Art is said to embody values that reveal its fundamentally ideological nature, whose relation to political and economic determinants is implicit. Culture is confined within a broad domain defined by ideology, as the following remarks indicate:

> The bases of the study of ideologies (in the form of a general definition of ideological superstructures, their function in the whole of social life, their relationship to the economic base . . .) have been profoundly and firmly established by Marxism. However, the detailed study of the dis-tinctive features and qualitative individuality of each of the branches of ideological creation—science, art, ethics, religion, etc.—is still in the embryonic stage.[6]

Statements like these, which emphasize the social and materialist stance of the Bakhtin school, have naturally served to bolster Marxian applications of Bakhtinian theory, as pursued in the Western cultural studies movement. A different view prevails in Epstein's culturology. He argues for an alternative delineation of spheres:

> . . . what is ideology? Perhaps it is a level of culture where cultural signs lose their freedom, their looseness.[7]

The scope of culture is much broader and deeper than that of society as such. While society encompasses all living people in their combined activity and the interrelations of their roles, culture embraces the activity of all previous generations accumulated in artistic works, scientific discoveries, moral values, and so on. The social level is but one horizontal section of culture.[8]

Taking exception to Lenin's pronouncement that "one cannot live in a society and be free of it," Epstein argues, "but this is exactly what culture is designed for: to liberate a person from that very society in which he is doomed to live. Culture is not a product of society, but a challenge and alternative to society."[9] He proposes restricting the term "ideology" to evaluative views expressed in specific uses of language as a calculated tactic for obtaining or enhancing political power. Such a definition serves to confine the potentially dangerous monster of ideology within the optimal field for its evenhanded investigation and management, namely culture.

Epstein outlines his theory of ideological language in his study "Relativistic Patterns in Totalitarian Thinking: The Linguistic Games of Soviet Ideology" (Chapter 4 of this book). Here he asserts that the only value of concern to ideology properly so-called is power: the ability to control people and events. In other words, ideology is not ubiquitous, as in Bakhtin and Medvedev's usage, but it *is* always political. Epstein argues that "if every evaluative component of speech is classified as ideological, then the distinction between different modes of evaluation is lost." In order to isolate and study the usage of language as a tool in the pursuit of power, he puts forth the premise that "the mission of ideology is to rule the process of communication and organize people into communities governed by specific ideas." Implicit in this delineation is his assessment that evaluations based on "personal judgments, desires, preferences, and whims" seldom enter into these processes; to regard them then as ideological statements only serves to obscure the workings of true power relations in language. The type of "ideolinguistic" analysis he proposes would ultimately enable scholars to identify ideological, or power-oriented, components and intentions in any type of discourse—artistic, journalistic, scientific, rhetorical—with a high degree of objectivity.

As a consequence of his views on ideology, Epstein takes a controversial position on the question of global postmodernism, presented in Chapter 6, "The Origins and Meaning of Russian Postmodernism." These views put him at odds with some Western theorists who consider the endemic decline of capitalist systems an essential determinant of the truly postmodern condition. According to this outlook, the commodity status of all products of art and culture is a result of capitalist expansion, which is not comparable to the developmental patterns of Eastern Europe, where consumerism, cultural reification, and related phenomena of late twentieth-century economy presumably did not occur, or began very recently.[10] Epstein, however, asserts that despite vast differences in economic conditions, the underlying cultural situation in the late Soviet Union and post-Soviet republics is analogous to that of commodified Western societies.

This assertion hinges on the premise that, while consumer demand, access to capital, and other market factors appropriate to capitalism were of little relevance in the planned Soviet economy, ideological considerations acquired paramount importance in all spheres of material and cultural production. Epstein maintains that when Marxist ideology became established as the driving force of all Soviet society, it gradually relativized all possible political positions, just as Stalin opposed and then absorbed both Trotsky's leftism and Bukharin's rightism. As power was consolidated into a totalitarian system, the specific positions proper to genuine Marxism were eroded. With the same self-propelling energy exhibited by capital in its expansionist stage, totalitarianism commodified culture and ideas, bending them to serve its ideological affirmation. As a result, Epstein claims, mature Soviet ideology absorbed such a diversity of ideas that it devolved into a postmodern pastiche of political positions. Moreover, he theorizes a reversal of the classic Marxian positions of base and superstructure, arguing that in the Soviet system ideology became the base that determined a superstructure of economic activity. For this reason, Epstein advocates the culturological investigation of Soviet ideology and Western capitalist economies as analogous determinants in relation to the production of culture.

On Literature: The Aesthetics of Ideological Deconstruction

The new developments in Russian poetic language of the eighties and nineties attracted Epstein's particular attention. In Chapter 1, "New Currents in Russian Poetry," he states that poetry serves a purifying function in culture, sloughing off deadened layers of linguistic cliché either by repeating catchwords and slogans ad nauseum, until their lack of true meaning becomes blatantly apparent, or by restricting the poetic lexicon to archetypal terms proper to ancient civilizations. In his many articles on the conceptualist aesthetic that predominated in Soviet underground art of the 1980s, Epstein argued that this was a quintessentially postmodern movement. In comparison with other literary trends, conceptualism provided a uniquely apt response to the hyperideologized environment of a late communist society, as Epstein describes it. Conceptualist painters and writers recognized that ideological concepts, clothed in aesthetically acceptable trappings, were omnipresent in socialist realist artworks. They saw that the mission of such art was to make ideology appear true and appropriate to some external "reality," whereas, in the terms of postmodern theory that Epstein borrows from Jean Baudrillard, these works merely participated in the creation of an ideological "simulacrum"—a simulated copy of reality that had lost all reference to the original. By pursuing an anti-aesthetic that favors the least sophisticated modes of depiction, this movement offers, as Epstein explains, "in place of a 'work with a conception' . . . a 'conception as the work.'" Blatant rendering of the concept, as opposed to its meticulous concealment, provides a glimpse of ideological constructions in all their contrived pretentiousness.

Epstein suggests that the appeal of realistic art, which portrays the world with comprehensible clarity, as opposed to conceptual absurdity, is similar to the appeal of "metanarratives" such as Freudianism or Marxism, which purport to explain a vast array of phenomena by relating (or reducing) them to a universal principle, such as the Oedipus complex or economic class struggle. In the case of contemporary Russian literature, Epstein feels that while the noble aims of such writers as Solzhenitsyn and Shalamov are beyond reproach, their declamatory and moralistic style places their works within the tradition that produced socialist realism. This approach to writing has come to seem contaminated, even prostituted, by its former complicity with the totalitarian system. In reaction, many contemporary writers tend to favor what has been called "decentered" or "unresolved" prose, which eschews the traditionally didactic function of Russian literature.[11]

Epstein points out that conceptual art indeed defies the criterion of truth in the relationship between ideology and reality, because ideology re-creates reality in its own image, precluding the possibility of appealing to "objective facts." Conceptual art confronts the viewer or reader with the virtual impossibility of evaluating reality, given the independence of human evaluations from any objectivity beyond themselves. Epstein sees this position as serving an important function, claiming that conceptualism actually demystifies evaluative, ideological concepts and breaks their viselike grip on the mind as a necessary first step toward revitalizing artistic culture.

The essay on "Avant-Garde Art and Religion" (Chapter 2) points out that conceptual artists, like the Russian futurists before them, forsake the elevated social position of "high" art, by deliberately provoking ridicule, incredulity, and scandal, through an anti-aesthetic practice that, in Epstein's view, closely resembles the self-humiliation and mockery of medieval holy fools. Epstein claims that the rejection of graceful forms and logical exposition expresses the ascendency of eternal spiritual values over the transient pleasures of beauty. In contrast to the didactic moral statements of writers like Solzhenitsyn, however, such values cannot be proclaimed in the manner of an ordained religious leader whose tone underscores his position of authority. Rather, purported truths are ironically intoned and symbolically pantomimed in such a way as to appear to mock their own moral practice: "the art of the avant-garde renews in all its sharpness the sense of crisis that casts away aesthetic and moral values before the Supreme Value of something strange and unthinkable." Epstein identifies this higher value as the spiritual awareness of an apocalyptic reality portrayed in visual art through the loss of material form and beauty, and in futurist "trans-sense language" or conceptualist verses as a lapse of logic and harmony, presaging the end of the world as we know it. Thus, the dross of bankrupt beliefs and prejudices is jettisoned, as if for a voyage to the shores of an as yet unknown era, although, as Epstein points out, conceptualism is virtually devoid of any utopian impulse, in contrast to the old avant-garde.

Epstein suggests that reading works of conceptual literature can have an effect almost like that of religious chanting or meditation. The "automation of perception" afforded by repetitions of banal words and phrases, or by the excessive accumulation of petty details allows not only for a "parodic deflation" of lofty, ideological notions, but also gives a sense of the unnamed reality beyond linguistic meaning. According to this view, political evaluations and stereotypes, such as those lampooned by poet Dmitry Prigov, the acknowledged master of conceptual verse, represent but the first layer of deadened consciousness that is endemic to the survivors of totalitarian stagnation. Everyday speech clichés and social conventions also dominate our thinking to a great extent, regardless of how free we believe our society to be. As Epstein says, in a statement reminiscent of the French poststructuralists, "it is not we who speak this way, this is how 'they' speak 'us.' " He suggests that postideological conceptual poetry, as practiced, for example, by Lev Rubinshtein, or the absurdist prose of Vladimir Sorokin or Ruslan Marsovich allow for contemplation of the silence that underlies all language. As the reader's immediate perception chants through page after page of conceptualist verbiage, the higher levels of consciousness are freed to float at liberty above the text.

In keeping with what we have called his culturological approach to literary analysis, Epstein links conceptual and other avant-gardist techniques with the spiritual climate of a postatheist society. He points out affinities between the lapses of meaning evident in contemporary art (and in the postcommunist era generally) and the quietism of Taoist and Buddhist beliefs. The appearance of such Eastern philosophical views in Russian literature is symptomatic, he believes, of a "contemporary religious need, culturally and geographically directed from West to East." In this culturological interpretation, religious inspiration may not be the poet's conscious intent, but his aesthetic (or anti-aesthetic) aspirations naturally shape the channel carved out by larger cultural forces.

Furthermore, Epstein argues in Chapter 6 that Russia has historically occupied a pivotal position in this global cultural shift. Tracing a long pattern of broadly conceptual tendencies, from Peter the First's "great idea" of erecting a modern city on the swamps of northern Russia, to Prince Potemkin's showcase villages, to Soviet "hyperreality," Epstein proposes that the Russian predisposition to grant symbolic systems total freedom from material reality corresponds to Russia's balance between the Western religious outlook (which emphasizes God's active presence) and Eastern perspectives on absence and nothingness. Offering a new interpretation of the Scythian, or Eurasian, theme in Russian culture, Epstein theorizes that the importance of positive appearances coupled with negligible physical results represents the coexistence of Western material and institutional constructs with Eastern belief systems. The result is a culture that tends to subversively "hollow out" its own attainments. In this view, even though Russia counts numerous genuine achievements among its cultural creations, these works represent "the self-erasure of a positive form"; not "primordial and pure, 'Eastern' emptiness," but a worldly self-negation that includes a reminder of otherworldly nothingness.

Implicit in these discussions is the notion that literary analysis inevitably sheds light not only on the works under immediate discussion, but on the larger cultural system as well. Culture is treated as a complex of tightly interconnected levels or types of activity, each of which is separable from the others in theory, but woven with them in one cloth of actual practice. One might well ask, Is the aim of a given research project to discover facts about culture or about literature? Epstein shows that the two cannot be definitively separated; only the researcher's self-imposed limitations restrict the topic to one focus rather than another.

The Elusive Spirit of Culture

In his discussion of art and religion, Epstein does not neglect to mention a trend in Christian theology known as the "apophatic tradition," which, he explains, eschews describing the positive qualities of the deity in favor of enumerating what it is *not,* thereby emphasizing the unique and incomparable nature of the divine. By outlining God's nonidentity through negated attributes, such mystics as Dionysius the Areopagite left a theoretical "open space" in which the astute believer could discern something of the undefinable. The same type of procedure serves Epstein as a model not only for conceptual poetic techniques, but for larger cultural facts as well.

In Chapter 10, "Theory and Fantasy," Epstein foresees the emergence of a remarkable range of intellectual procedures in the aftermath of restrictive Marxist practices. He argues that methodologies developed in one subject area may find fruitful application in another, just as linguistic, psychological, and philosophical methods of analysis have been successfully applied to the study of literature. He feels that this trend should be extended to other fields, in recognition that, like cultures, life's phenomena are manifold and cannot be fully elucidated in terms of any one aspect alone. "Thus," Epstein explains, "at any given moment of cognitive inquiry, the mathematical 'highlight' may fall on literature, while the poetical one falls on the star chart, and the astronomical one falls on the genetic code, etc."

While such practices might well sacrifice the pristine orderliness of existing academic fields, they do so for the cause of bringing them into closer contact with each other. Epstein gives this "metamethodology" the name *continualism* because it is premised on the notion of an indivisible continuum of existence that intellectual culture strives to comprehend. Rather than dividing reality into discrete elements and defining fields of inquiry as restricted territories of narrow specialization, continualism would encourage scholars to focus on the contributions their areas could make to other fields. Without abolishing the depth of expertise necessary to each given discipline, such an approach would focus on broad questions demanding multiple perspectives, so that, in the apophatic manner, each could contribute a segment of the outline within which reality might manifest increasingly comprehensible attributes.

In pondering the relevance of theology to the study of culture and to

Epstein's thought in particular, it may be worthwhile returning to the question of Mikhail Bakhtin's influence on the development of Russian culturology. The ongoing controversy in Western Slavistics and cultural studies over the relevance of Bakhtin's religious beliefs for his theoretical work testifies to the subtlety of expression Bakhtin was able to give his most pervasive ideas. Epstein follows a similar strategy of appealing to broadly "spiritual" values that lend themselves to a variety of interpretations. For example, where Bakhtin meditates on a "unified truth that requires a plurality of consciousnesses," which lends itself to being read as a metaphor for God's creation of thinking human beings,[12] Epstein discusses the potential "transcultural world," which he describes as a collective state of awareness involving a plurality of cultural expressions.

Epstein has explained that he was among a small group of students in Vladimir Turbin's literary seminar at Moscow University who had an opportunity to meet with Bakhtin in the early 1970s. Recalling this meeting, Epstein comments that the elderly Bakhtin seemed determined to turn away from all "serious questions about life" and specifically about religion, which, in Epstein's opinion, should have been addressed as a matter of course in discussing Dostoevsky's poetics, for example. Instead of responding directly to questions on such matters, Epstein reports that Bakhtin answered "apophatically," translating such issues "into professional matters, into literature."[13] This tactic of deflecting one topic onto another was successful not only in avoiding the religious controversies of the difficult decades that Bakhtin managed to survive, but clearly increased the semantic potential of his works, giving them "variable interpretability" (to borrow a term from Victor Shklovsky) to the extent that today Bakhtin's thought inspires scholars of diverse persuasions in Russia as well as the West.

Several points of contact between Epstein's thought and Bakhtin's are readily apparent, for instance, the discussion of "outsideness" (*vnenak-hodimost*) in Chapter 9. A subtle but more pervasive example is the notion of "potential," on which Bakhtin focused in the last years of his life, explaining that great artistic works accrue more profound meaning over time, thanks to their innate semantic potential. Bakhtin said that such works "live . . . in great time," acquiring a kind of cultural immortality.[14]

In Chapter 7, "At the Crossroads of Image and Concept," Epstein focuses on the significance of potential as a special quality of certain kinds of writing, particularly what he calls the "self-substantiation" of the author in essayistic genres. Here, he feels, we observe the writer in a process of unfolding a unique and singular intellectual existence. Refering to Montaigne's works as prototypical of the genre, Epstein observes that the essayist's contemplations on a chosen subject are intrinsically relativistic, as a variety of bases for a given opinion are explored, interlarding the essay with rich potentials for alternative lines of thought. In his view, "essayization" offers a more radical type of creative potentiality than does "novelization" as discussed in Bakhtin's well-known works.

Epstein also argues for the significance of potential as an element in all cultural enterprises, deserving of recognition and investigation virtually on a par with accomplished fact. He suggests, for example, that the interdisciplinary approach of cultural studies has the potential to foster hitherto unsuspected interconnections among the traditional disciplines. Further, he asserts that heightened cultural consciousness offers awareness of "the unity of all cultures and all noncultures, of all possibilities that have never been realized in existing cultures."

Here again is a schematic expression of the apophatic procedure whereby a sum of nonidentities helps to describe an elusive phenomenon. As Dionysius the Areopagite allowed a hint of the divine to resonate in the empty space between God's negative attributes, so does a sense of something universal emerge from the potential space that Epstein calls transculture.

Culturology and Transculture

Epstein proposes continualism as a metamethodology for interconnecting the humanitarian disciplines and unifying their intellectual missions under the rubric of culturology. In his seminal exposition of this "umbrella" discipline in Chapter 9, "Culture—Culturology—Transculture," he emphasizes that although culturology investigates numerous specific and specialized areas, it is primarily "called upon to realize the ideal of cultural wholeness." This ideal is seen as providing the integrating matrix within which isolated parts congeal by extending their arenas of self-consciousness to incorporate one another into a collective entity. Furthermore, Epstein believes that—not unlike essayism in writing—this integrative cultural self-consciousness can serve as a prophylactic against the monomania of totalitarianism and the schizophrenia of atomized individualism. In other words, the interdisciplinary practice of cultural studies should allow the diverse compartments within a single culture to overcome their limitations and negative potentials through awareness of their common aspirations and interdependencies.

Culturology discloses gaps within an established culture, as Epstein's analysis of conceptual poetry discloses the gaps between ideologically colored portrayals of life in Soviet society and the actual material conditions that people experienced. In anthropological terms, such gaps exist, for example, among diverse marital practices, such as American and European serial monogamy, Islamic polygyny, and Tibetan polyandry. Epstein calls culturology an "egalitarian science," because it generates knowledge of these alternatives as equally valid creative solutions to the problem of organizing human life; it records the range of their variability.

He introduces another concept to account for the ideal of cultural wholeness. Transculture, described as "a multidimensional space that appears gradually over the course of historical time," is a notion that lays claim to both material and ideal embodiments in the real world, according to Epstein's system of thought. Transculture is presented not as a field of knowledge, but as a type of consciousness or mentality capable of envisioning the as yet unrealized potentials of existing cultures. A realm accessible only to thought, the transcultural world is nonetheless present "within all existing cultures." It might be defined as the set of all real cultural achievements, past and present, along with all of their potential developments.

In discussing the origins of transcultural consciousness as a type of postmodern mentality, Epstein focuses on the internal splits occasioned by countercultural movements both in the industrialized West and behind the Iron Curtain. Dissidents, sectarians, and underground artists in the former Soviet Union, as well as hippies, punks, and other disaffected youth groups in both the East and West attempted to locate themselves outside established norms, creating through their life-styles and artistic practices "zones of emptiness," that had no place in the predominant systems of their societies. The very possibility that such zones could exist, rendered aspects of the dominant culture "meaningless," weakening its hold on the minds of its people by demonstrating the viability of alternative ways of life. As more and more individuals, in various parts of the world, find themselves outside the obsolescent categories accepted in their societies, unable to identify themselves fully with standard models of behavior, the ideal condition of transculture obtains its being, in Epstein's understanding, through the fullness of newly conceived potentials. For the new Russian society, this is one manifestation of what Epstein identifies as the growth of new spiritual perspectives in a postatheist society.

Epstein indicates that the self-awareness that culturology offers to culture, which in turn allows for the development of transcultural consciousness, also provides protection from "totalitarian temptations": no individual culture can claim to offer the "only way" to live or to think when its members are well informed about alternatives. This contrast with totalitarianism is tempered by a similarity, however: while totalitarianism makes all cultural practices and political positions relative with respect to its own lust for power, Epstein explains that in the transcultural world, "all specific cultures [are] relative with regard to something transcendental."[15] So while both totalitarian and transcultural modes of thought challenge absolutist beliefs, the former destroys culture by restricting its creative arena, but the latter safeguards it by "opening gaps" in the will to power that presses culture into compliant ideological service. Transcultural awareness allows us to conceive alternatives to the lockstep mechanisms of totalitarian thinking with its black-and-white judgments; it implies a suspension of judgment, in that it favors no one tradition over another. In Epstein's description, transculture preserves an attitude of respect and even love for earthbound, traditional cultures, while liberating individuals from the compelling, often chauvinistic attachment to native ways that totalitarian consciousness retains and exploits. We have the option of realizing unity and wholeness in the freedom of transcultural consciousness, just as we have the ability to enshrine one way of life above all others in the restrictive obsessions of totalitarianism.

The importance of imaginable potentials is nowhere more evident in Epstein's thought than in his vision of a spiritualized human ecology transformed through the detached yet reverent attitudes of transculture. In Chapter 8, "Thing and Word: On the Lyrical Museum," Epstein explores the fates of such cultural by-products and rejects as candy wrappers, broken toys, and other everyday objects that have lost their original usefulness. In the process of lavishing descriptive and contemplative attention on such items, he suggests that even the world's most humble objects have the potential to develop a unique and undefinable identity of their own, while simultaneously serving to establish the cultural and personal identity of the human subject who makes use of them. In a remarkable recasting of Freud's ideas about an ego and its objects as the fundamental opposition that institutes selfhood, Epstein conveys a tangible sense of the intimate connections between a person and the material things in his or her immediate environment. This view echoes the proposed definition of culture as "everything humanly created that simultaneously creates a human being"; it invests the humblest objects with a significance far beyond the recognition they normally receive. Indeed, Epstein accords physical objects such a central role in creating our humanity that he argues they possess an integrity of being perhaps as remotely comparable to that of a person or a society as these are to the integrity of a divine being. It would seem that we are equally free to endow the objects around us in cultural settings with soulful animacy as we are to commodify them, erasing all self-sufficient value from their being. The respect toward things that Epstein outlines here would be capable of redefining the ecology of our physical and social environment.

Rather than disposable products of alienating labor, things can thus become participants in transcultural consciousness, as our human subjectivity overflows to encompass the very objects which for Freud's modernist psychology were the inaugural other. Astonishing as such ideas may well appear, it is not my intention to overemphasize their visionary character at the expense of their practical and scholarly value. New conceptions of identity, difference, and unity are essential to describe the new world order in which basic understandings of self and other have been cast in doubt on global and personal levels. In Mikhail Epstein's words, "To define the patterns of . . . *unity* based on *pluralistic* values should be . . . the most immediate aim of the contemporary humanities." Such an assertion clearly calls on scholars to broaden the scope of serious inquiry even as we advocate a cultural life worthy of a future in the new millennium.

PART I LITERATURE

CHAPTER 1 · New Currents in Russian Poetry:
Conceptualism, Metarealism, and Presentism

As the century ends, we are amazed to find ourselves returning to its beginnings. The poetic currents that were formed in Russia at the beginning of the twentieth century—symbolism, acmeism, futurism—have unexpectedly reemerged as a new poetic triad: metarealism, presentism, conceptualism. This is not to say that those original movements have simply been renewed; rather, there has occurred an expansion of poetic boundaries, a restructuring of the figurative space of sign systems. In their time, symbolism and futurism delineated two opposing means of relating the word to its signification. In the case of symbolism, the signifier is almost withdrawn, giving full precedence to the signified. This is a poetics of suprasignification, through which the mythological nature of the image comes to indicate another world, a world that is eternal and whole. Futurism, on the other hand, was the world of the signifier itself, where the word, the "self-sufficient word" (Khlebnikov), is the authentic reality, rescinding everything otherworldly, everything beyond the bounds of its own sound properties. Between these two movements, or rather stylistic boundaries, we find acmeism, which stands for the golden mean, for the customary and direct meanings of words.[1]

And now, we find before us another three poetic movements, located at the same historical distance from the end of the century that those were from the beginning. It seems as if the new developments have transcended a flat, quasi-realistic, social realistic picture of the world, restoring the former breadth and depth of poetic space that once prevailed in Russia. At the risk of oversimplification, we can nonetheless trace paths of succession from symbolism to metarealism, from futurism to conceptualism, while presentism makes a new attempt to define the mean. Metarealism endeavors to return to the word the fullness of its figurative and transcendent meanings.

To the same degree, conceptualism tries to wrench out of the word any meaning whatever, leaving an empty, echoing shell: a senseless cliché that says nothing.

Presentism, like acmeism before, strives to sail between Scylla and Charybdis, the excessive pretentiousness of archetype and the excessive banality of stereotype, by turning to the world of visible, tangible surfaces that are, in their own right, the ultimate depth. Thus, we do observe a process of succession, but I describe it as such only to show more clearly the striking shifts and ruptures manifest within this very process. It is these changes that radically distinguish the end of the poetic century from the middle years; precisely for that reason, the end becomes a link to the beginning.

A Time of Ripening

For quite some time, almost since the end of the 1960s, criticism has been searching our poetry for a new generation, has awaited and summoned it. But it did not appear. There were greater and lesser individual talents: Alexander Kushner, Iury Kuznetsov, Oleg Chukhontsev, Igor Shkliarevsky, and others, but in no way did there come about a commonality, or rather, mutuality, as when an idea originating with one poet finds its echo and augmentation with another, when the poetic air takes on that certain resonance, a broad responsiveness, that indicates the presence of a whole generation.

Criticism had become accustomed to the "pointal" or "intermittent" reality of the seventies, that impelled us to delve into the poets' individuality, but freed us from the need to search for a unifying idea. Has the situation changed since the mid-eighties, with the appearance of books and large selections of poetry by such authors as Alexander Eremenko, Ivan Zhdanov, Aleksei Korolev, Ilya Kutik, Marina Kudimova, Aleksei Parshchikov, Mikhail Sinelnikov, Oleg Khlebnikov, and others? Can it be that the generation long-awaited through the seventies has finally found itself in the eighties and is now searching in turn for a criticism to grasp and receive it as a whole?

Unfortunately, in considering the creative work of young poets, our criticism is often inclined to restrict itself to didactic tasks of pointing out what is good and what is bad in their poems, making assessments in relation to some normative standard. Meanwhile, the young poetry—if it has emerged from the apprenticeship of versification to be worthy of that name—is primarily a new poetry, whose youth is determined not only by the ages of its authors, but by its creative freshness, its position at the forefront of literature. What is wanted is to look at this poetry not from the standpoint of "still" unripened, not yet achieved and trudging along toward finality, but rather from the standpoint of "already": as having risen above the level of yesterday's ripeness, and, precisely for that reason, young today. It seems to me that the poetry of our 30-year-olds (roughly speaking) is not just a promise for the future but already an embodiment deserving of scholarly investigation, whose object must be the creative metamorphosis, the succession of aesthetic precepts, that has gradually unfolded throughout our poetry, but that shows itself with the young poets as a shift or break in the slow evolution of styles.

It is no simple matter to define the conditions of life that formed the new generation and summoned it forth into poetry. There is no one event that could easily be recognized as determining the fate of poets, as there was for the war generation or the generation that came of literary age after 1956.[2] Perhaps it was not a single event, but the very pace of day-to-day existence in the seventies, so oppressively measured and retarded, that exerted a defining impact on the poetry of those who were young then, setting down in that "ordinariness" a moral and aesthetic significance, whose value they found themselves ready to defend, albeit with a stoical sadness. Precisely this experience of the stubborn, patient flux of days through a particular historical period brought the new poets into literary activity; because of this they have entered the field as a rule, when not so very young themselves, and literature has had to wait so long for the emergence of their generation. What matters, however, is the enriching result of this drop-by-drop accumulation of experience, the readiness to sink down into the slow flux of life, its fitfully ripening meaning. The new sense of life is highly sympathetic to past epochs, as it lovingly reaches through the thickness of historical time to reveal life even in time's most stultified layers. Mikhail Sinelnikov has created a significant image for the new generation in "Excavation":

As a fish with spawn, the overlayerings of the earth
With damp bitterness are full down to their very grounding.

The friable night of a long vanished ethos
Is packed to its depth with the implosiveness of soils.

And the broken banks of ravines and shoals,
Like layers of words, spring back, recoil.

The experience of living through a retarded and saturated elongation of time has conditioned not only the thematic turn toward history, but also a historical approach to contemporary times; it has lain down in our poetry as a series of images, compacted into polysemy, as though pressed down beneath the weight of time like "implosive soils," packed to the limit with different cultural layers. The works of many new poets do recall excavations into the depths, where beneath one layer of meanings there lies another, still more ancient, reaching down to the eternal foundations of life. Revelation of the most enduring, recurring patterns from which "ordinary life" is made, has become one of the main endeavors of the new poetic generation that has grown up under the "normal" conditions of direct cultural succession, without the disruptions of wars, revolutions, mass repressions, and other historical upheavals. The accumulated layer of culture laid down in the soil of reality itself comes to the surface in complex, reflexively saturated, poetic images.

The Self-Awareness of Culture

At different times the life of our poetry has been accompanied by various batteries of critical bywords. In the late fifties and early sixties we heard a preponderance of such words as "sincerity," "openness," "the confessional," "boldness," "freedom from inhibition." Behind the use of such terms stood the discovery of the individual as a subject with full rights—the hero of creative works and the most interesting and inexhaustible element in the self-expression of reality ("I in great diversity can be seen by myself"—Evgeny Evtushenko). But then this self-sufficient "I" began to irritate, to seem empty and proud, and poetry was drawn to the bosom of fields and meadows, to the humble wisdom of nature in order to contemplate that pure and distant "star of the fields" (Nikolai Rubtsov). At that time a new group of key words came into use: "memory," "origin," "nature," "warmth," "kinship," "nativity." However shifting these half-concept, half-images may be, they clearly delineate the boundaries of periods and generations.

If one had to trace out such a group of terms for the new poetic generation—and in my opinion it has indeed matured to the point of requiring such critical thought and formulation—one could include the following: "culture," "meaning," "myth," "custom," "mediation," "reflexivity," "polysemy." Reality, as it has repeatedly been felt and lived through in its "ordinary" manifestation, comes to be perceived as the sum total of customs, rules, and habits that regulate the behavior of man and even nature; not so much as physical data or emotional conditions, but rather as a system of culturally established significations.[3]

And what is the sea?—a dumping ground for handlebars,
and the earth beneath your feet rides away.
The sea—it's a dumping ground for all dictionaries,
only the land has swallowed its tongue.

For Aleksei Parshchikov, the author of these lines, even the simplest and
most ancient things, such as the earth and sea, enter into a sign system of
representational coordinates—the tongues of waves recall multilingual dictionaries as well as the wavelike shape of bicycle handlebars—that fill the
whole world to its very horizon. The heaving first element from which life
emerged is reinterpreted as secondary in relation to culture, the site of
concentration of vast material and verbal supplies or more precisely, by-
products. This type of "secondary," culturally mediated vision had already
been formed by certain poets of the first half of this century: Khlebnikov,
Mayakovsky, Pasternak; and yet, at that time, this was as yet only relatively
"originary," as in Pasternak's "Waves" (1931):

Before me are the waves of the sea.
There are so many. They are countless.
They are a swarm. They roar in a minor key.
The surf bakes them like waffles.
All the shore is trampled as by cattle.
They are a swarm, the skyscape drove them out.
In a herd, he set them down to pasture
And went to bed beyond the hill, belly down.

Pasternak's waves are a part of production, but still, so to speak, on the level
of "cottage industry," inseparable from the doings of nature itself that bakes
them like waffles or herds them like cattle. Half a century later a young poet
sees waves as sediment from the cultural activity of man; billows are transformed into the ridges of a worldwide garbage dump. Not a word is said here
about the ecological revolution or the ecological catastrophe, but these notions enter into the image system of contemporary poetical thinking, forming the basis of many clusters of metaphors.

If one were to search for a common artistic idea, uniting the new poets on
a level above all of their stylistic differences, then the closest approximation
might be precisely this idea of culture. Needless to say, this is not an abstract
idea, but the primary, self-evident reality through which the young poets
cast their ideas of nature and man. The principal innovation lies in the fact
that this poetry is enriched by a second, self-reactive layer of perception

directed at that cultural matter of which poetry itself is a part. Previously, poetry had developed by assimilating all possible new levels of reality: society, individuality, nature, and so on; but suddenly a leap of self-awareness, self-doubling, occurred when a powerful system, such as culture, embracing all sides of reality, entered into the realm of assimilation. All that culture can take in and refract within itself—and that is, in fact, everything—is now reflected and interpreted anew by poetry, this time transfigured as an intra-, rather than an extracultural reality. Poetry becomes a form of self-consciousness for culture, reflecting the relativity and diversity of sign systems. Here, for example, is a sonnet by Alexander Eremenko:

> . . . In the dense metallurgical forests,
> where chlorophyll production was in progress,
> a leaf fell. Autumn had already arrived
> in the dense metallurgical forests.

> And stalled up in the skies forever
> are a tank truck and drosophila fly.
> Pressed down by the resultant force,
> they're stranded in a flattened clock.

> The last hawk-owl is broken and sawed up.
> And with an office push-pin he's been tacked
> to an autumnal bough, head-down,

> he hangs and ponders in his head:
> why, with such an awful force,
> have binoculars been mounted into him!

A poem like this one could hardly have come into being in the previous poetic epoch; it is contemporary to the extent that it demands of criticism an understanding of its language, rather than a discussion of whether or not it is well written in that language. In the seventies it was common to counterpose nature, chaste and unfortunate, with the rapaciousness of technology, to delight in the primordial, pristine purity that cried out for preservation. This was a predictable reaction to the excessive demands of a rapidly developing technological civilization. In Eremenko's work we find neither the single-minded cult of nature, nor wild enthusiasm for the power of technology. For him both one and the other are essential elements of culture, parts of a single whole, that can be translated from one language to another, so that signs belonging to nature (a leaf, a fly, an owl) enter into an indissoluble combination with technological signs (metal, a tank truck, binoculars), forming a sort of flickering picture: now it seems to be about a natural forest, now about industrial scaffolding.[4]

At the same time, we hear in this sonnet a note of irony on this strange blend of elements, as when the hawk-owl ponders the binoculars mounted in his head in place of eyes, and indeed, when it embraces so much, culture cannot and must not try to hide its own "seams"—the artificial and eclectic overlayerings, by which it tries to achieve unification—and the paradoxes without which it could not move. This irony of pure doubling is emphasized by the odd rhymes "forests/forests" and "head/head," where, contrary to our usual expectation, words rhyme with themselves, as if demonstrating the duality of every object, the state of belonging, at one and the same time, to two opposing worlds.

Eremenko is generally a highly ironic poet, although he does not resort to blatant mockery; he stands firm on the border of the serious, casting a somewhat skeptical glance at irony itself. In this way, poetry begins to pass through a stage of cultural introspection unheard of even in the recent past. One could name several poets, harking to the traditions of the Oberiuty[5]— Dmitry Prigov, Lev Rubinshtein, Vsevolod Nekrasov, Mikhail Sukhotin, Timur Kibirov—who achieve effective imagery through the artificial and distinctly ironic pressure of cultural signs or conventional codes that weigh upon contemporary consciousness. Technological, aesthetic, social, and everyday stereotypes are all the superficial shell of culture, blocking off its complex, living content; thus conceptual-grotesque poetry carries out an important task by sweeping culture clean, turning up and sloughing off its dead layers of cliché and kitsch.

But there is also another current in the new poetry. It makes its revelation of culture not in the conventionality of persistent stereotypes, but in the deepest archetypal foundations of culture that cast their light through daily life and concerns even as they are one with the organic existence of soul and nature. To comprehend these foundations is perhaps the archtask of poet Ivan Zhdanov, whose collection A Portrait (1982) drew numerous complaints for being puzzling and indecipherable. If Eremenko specifically demonstrates the artificiality of various cultural codes, incorporating them into a context of anomalous, heterogeneous material, then Zhdanov searches for a natural coplacement of material and code that seems to sink down to the level of a deep subtext, nowhere directly manifest, but making way for careful reading and a slow but striking solution.

> There, behind the window, is a shabby little room,
> and with scarlet thunder on the throne
> of the floor plays an infant, and the gray abyss
> languishes like dry brush in a corner.

As a literary theme, reminiscences of childhood have been popularized, almost trivialized, in contemporary poetry, but here the theme acquires a new scope. Through the worn, tiresome scene of daily life ("shabby little room"), there suddenly appears the reality of a higher power and significance: a child as god of thunder sits on his "throne of the floor" and, playing with a shiny rattle, scatters thunderclaps. Who among us has not felt this majesty of childhood? Zhdanov does not bring to the surface of the text those specific mythological names and plot formulas that his treatment brings to mind: the infant Zeus and his father Cronus, the grey "abyss" of all-consuming time. All of these images remain in the depths of intercultural memory, where reader meets poet on equal ground and is not subjected to enforced associations. Here lies the distinction between "culture," which has always nourished poetry, and "culturedness," that settles out in a heavy sediment of names, allusions, and bookish borrowings in need of a spiritual sorting-out. Here the main criterion is how organically the "eternal" combines with our "own," the past with the present.

Many of the new poets use a particular cultural prism, akin to their own sense of life, through which they recast images of the reality around them. For Mikhail Sinelnikov, author of the collections *Clouds and Birds* and *Argonautics,* it is the East: Mongolia, Kazakhstan, Georgia. His gift is to re-create the dry tangibility and entrancing, ethereal quality of this world, where "clouds are as of stone" and "mountains are of air." For Elena Shvarts of St. Petersburg, the lyrical heroine takes on an image of the ancient Roman Cynthia, whose antique surroundings now and then let filter through traces of a northern city with its damp winds, frost, and hoarfrost on the walls of classical-style buildings—altogether a successful attempt to resurrect "maiden Rome on the banks of the Neva" (Mandelshtam). Olga Sedakova finds kindred the world of the European classics: Tristan and Iseult, Francis of Assisi, Dante, and Petrarch, whose passionate and long-suffering aspiration to higher things brings measure to her own lyrical concerns, leading to the symbolic depths of such images as "garden," "rose," "road," or "gates."

The scope of imagery displayed by contemporary poetry has considerable breadth. It extends from extreme conventionality on one end, to total unconditionality on the other, from ironic play to high pathos, from the grotesque to the mystical. Somewhere in the middle of this scale lies the work of those poets—Aleksei Parshchikov, Aleksei Korolev, Ilya Kutik—who strive to reduce as far as possible the distance between lofty and low, the everyday and the triumphant, to endow with the poetic importance of odic or elegaic mood such phenomena and words as "anthracite" and "motorcycle," "foam rubber" and "tile floor," "breaststroke" and "barge." In so doing they attempt to reveal within a new, untraditional, and strictly technical materiality an appropriate weight of unchanging meaning, to elevate terminology to metaphor. Kutik devotes his "Ode" to ultracontemporary impressions of the Sea of Azov; Korolev writes his "Stanzas" on cinematography; Parshchikov, an elegy on coal, and another on the toads that live in the estuary of the Dnieper:

> In girlhood, they knit; in married life, they go about with roe,
> suddenly, they join in fatal battle, and again the rustling dies down.
> Or, as in Dante, they freeze in the ice in winter,
> Or, as in Chekhov, they talk the night away.

Some may see in this an abolition of hierarchical values, but it is essential first to grasp the positive meaning of such equalization as movement through all levels of culture for the purpose of their momentary contact and interpenetration, for bringing into being that highest principle of poetic thought: "everything in everything."

In the work of the young poets we also see a striving to make maximal use of words in their culturally saturated, enduring aspect. Aleksei Korolev carries this tendency to its extreme; the basic element of his poetic language is the turn of phrase, the saying, the idiom: a closed linguistic unit seemingly ready-made by speech traditions themselves. The titles of his collections are prime examples: *The Apple of the Eye* (*Zenitsa oka*) and *A Bird in the Bush* (*Sinitsa v nebe*). Needless to say, these idioms and colloquialisms are not at all the language we hear at home and on the streets; rather, it is precisely the *culture* of conversational speech, embodied as a phenomenon of contemporary poetic language. This is in no way intended as a reproach to the poet, for whom language is as much an integral part of the reality around him as are buildings or trees, not only a means of expression but also an object for depiction. Outside of language man could not live any more than he can live without shelter: speechlessness and homelessness become the indicators of extreme degeneration. The orientation toward language in its culturally stamped, traditionally worked-out forms, a striving to speak not only in it, but also about it, as one would speak about the "house" of memory, hearing, thought—all of this is essential to the young poetry for the fullest exploitation of the semantic potential that lies in its most basic verbal material. At the same time, of course, moderation is needed in such work to guard against lapsing into ornamental exercises, arranging well-cast and minted, yet hollow, rhetorical figures.

One could name other poets as well who assimilate the full range of culture from the borders of the profane to those of the sacred: Iury Arabov, Vladimir Aristov, Evgeny Bunimovich, Sergei Gandlevsky, Faina Grimberg, Alexander Lavrin, Tatiana Shcherbina, Alexander Soprovsky. For all the variety of manner and inequality of talent represented among them, the style of a generation is nonetheless worked out: a fabric of imagery so tangible it cannot be dissolved in an outpouring of emotion or a lyrical sigh—that songlike romance or limerickal intonation found in many works by poets of the previous generation. Here one must disentangle the most intricate knot of associations harking back to different planes of culture, particularly those most sensitive to its mythological foundations. Each image has not one, but an entire "enumeration of reasons," behind which feeling itself often cannot keep pace as it longs for an immediate and unmistakable clue. This poetry is reserved, as a rule, unsentimental and tending toward an objective plasticity of forms, rather than subjective expression of moods; it demands material clarity, completion, and it calls upon reason more strongly than feeling, or, more accurately, it calls for discipline and interdistinction of feelings themselves.

In the poems of the young, times and countries enter into intense dialogue with one another; nature and technology, archaeology and astronomy, art and daily life are all component parts of culture, cast out across different epochs, habitats, origins, and genres, entering into cross-callings with each other, realizing that they are fated to unity. Needless to say, it was neither immediately nor suddenly that poetry ventured upon such a responsible and all-encompassing task; the generally high level of culturological research in our country has certainly been influential, particularly Bakhtin's idea that the essence of a culture lives on its borders with other cultures—an idea that has found many-sided affirmation and development in the works of Iury Lotman, Sergei Averintsev, Viacheslav Ivanov, Vladimir Toporov, Boris Uspensky, Vladimir Bibler, Georgy Gachev, and other scholars in the humanities. The fact that such growth in the cultural layer of poetry should find its stimulus or parallel in corresponding theoretical inquiry is in no way an embarrassment, precisely as—to give a classic example—Thomas Mann's *Magic Mountain* deserves no reproach on account of the author's prior acquaintance with Frazer's *Golden Bough* and other works on mythology. As if one could toss culture and intellect out of the spiritual life of mankind, reducing this life to the "gut level," of purely instinctive comprehension! How can one see lilacs in a new light if we forget that "Konchalovsky has been here before us, touched the twigs and narrowed his eyes" (Alexander Kushner)?[6]

The poetry of the young graphically demonstrates that when we attempt to bypass culture and inscribe directly, as it were, intuitively, the "world as such," while remaining, nonetheless, within culture ourselves, we tend to sink to its lowest level. For example, these lines (by a certain author, but essentially anonymous): "You were like a green grove along my path, / so long-legged, / so radiant" were clearly written with a sincere heart, in a state of lyrical outburst, when one wants to speak in the simplest of words. But banality rather than natural expressiveness is the result: a cut-rate romance or popular song—contemporary urban folklore. Life is not equal to itself; it grows insofar as it is transformed and made more complex by culture, and the most lively poetry of today is just that: cultural to the utmost, not in the sense of culturedness as evident knowledge, but in the sense of culture as the accumulated memory or spiritual continuity that broadens the content capacity of each image.

I must emphasize that culture today is not only memory, but also hope, the hope that nourishes poetry no less than life itself: the hope of survival. As we stand before the threat of destruction of worldwide civilization, the need is entirely natural for compression of all the layers of civilization into a profoundly indivisible nucleus of human spirit. Turning once again to Eremenko's lines that were presented above, we can better grasp why technology and nature, the tank truck and the drosophila fly should be collapsed into each other:

> Pressed down by the resultant force,
> Stranded in a flattened clock.

A flattened clock: the time of history at a standstill. Such is the threat before which culture cannot fail to reveal its unity as the "resultant" of all the forces of mankind.[7]

On Conceptualism

In the previous sections we spoke about tendencies common to all of the new poetry; now I wish to define more clearly some contrasts. Literature moves by internal contradictions, by the variety of its own stylistic currents. As a "single stream,"[8] to use the slogan that was current in our lexicon for quite some time with its attribution of total homogeneity and cohesion to all artistic groups, literature stops "flowing" altogether, contrary to expectations, and turns into stagnant waters despite their oceanic proportions.

It is a sign of our time that notions defining the heterogeneity of literature have returned, along with the precept of competitiveness: "stylistic currents," "artistic directions," "poetic schools," and "creative collectives." These notions do not erase such customary, tenacious categories as the "literary process" and "authorial individuality," but they do mediate them, filling a vacant, intervening area. An artistic direction is a collective individuality: "individual" in relation to the literary process as a whole, "collective" in relation to individual authors. The negative experience of the past decades shows that without such an intervening link creative individuality easily loses its special place in the literary process, which subordinates it to generally accepted standards, ideologically and aesthetically "socializes" and mediocritizes it, so that the process itself loses its dynamism, dependent as that is on the diversity and energy of the creative contradictions that constitute it.

By the seventies and early eighties, it was already impossible to contain the growing and essentially fertile stratification of our literature within a few ideological-stylistic currents. Deprived of the possibility of openly announcing themselves, however, of defining their creative positions, these currents often degenerated into short-lived groupings, brought together by mercantile or regional, rather than properly artistic, aspirations.

Only very recently have some of the "submerged" currents of our literature begun to surface and be favored with the attention and interest of society. Among the most clearly defined, artistically intentional, currents are conceptualism and metarealism; they are represented in the visual arts as well, but we will confine ourselves here to the sphere of poetry.

Virtually nothing has been written on conceptualism in our country,[9] although representatives of this current have, on several occasions, presented their works before large audiences that not only heard them out, but discussed them with great interest. I recall one evening in particular, 8 June 1983 at the Central House of Art Workers. It was officially called "Stylistic Searching in Contemporary Poetry: On the Dispute Over Metarealism and Conceptualism." At this event, for perhaps the first time since the 1920s, a vocal and theoretically formulated demarcation took place between two stylistic currents of our poetry. The process of artistic differentiation made itself clearly felt; and without this the threat of stagnation and repetition of generalities continues to hang over literature.

What is conceptualism? We will attempt to explain this without making evaluations, but rather by describing the principles that this stylistic current recognizes as pertinent to itself, and by which it must therefore be judged. Almost any artistic work (with the possible exception of the purely ornamental or decorative) is conceptual insofar as there lies within it a certain conception, or the sum of conceptions, which the critic or interpreter draws out. In conceptual art this conception is demonstrably separable from the live artistic fabric and even becomes an independent creation or "concept" in itself. In place of a "work with a conception," we see before us a "conception as the work."

It might seem that there have been and are being produced in our country more than enough of such pseudoartistic compositions from which the ideological formula protrudes like a bare stake from the back of a scarecrow. Conceptualists create precisely such a break between the idea and the thing, the sign and reality, but in this case with complete intentionality, as a stylistic principle. The petrification of language, which brings forth ideological chimeras, becomes nourishing soil for this process. Conceptualism is the workshop for making scarecrows, ideologically figurative formulas, that are hastily covered with a slovenly sackcloth of linguistic fabric.

> The outstanding hero—
> He goes forward without fear
> But our ordinary hero—
> He's also almost without fear
> But first he waits to see:
> Maybe it'll all blow over
> And if not—then on he goes
> And the people get it all.

Behind these lines by Dmitry Prigov we easily recognize the formula that lies at the basis of numerous pathetic works about the fearless, all-conquering hero and his slightly backward but devoted comrades in arms. The typical problem with such odic writings is how to reliably hide the formula under the clothing of linguistic beauty, so as to make it frighteningly similar to a live person. The poet-conceptualist, on the contrary, drags the formula out into the open from the sum of its aesthetic imprintings and changes of form, presenting it as an independent fact for the reader's perception.

From this there develops a peculiar aesthetic (or, if you prefer, anti-aesthetic) of tongue-tiedness. Since the detached formula turns out to be primary in relation to all of the "highly-low-artistic"[10] means of its embodiment, the more arbitrary, inorganic, unsanitary the language, the better for demonstrating the self-sufficiency of the formula, its extraneousness to art as such. Conceptualism in this sense comes forward as criticism of artistic reason, unmasking beneath the covering of lyrical soulfulness or epic picturesqueness, the skeleton of an idea-engendering construct.

> Here flows the beauty of the Oka
> Through the beauty of Kaluga[11]
> The beauty of the people
> Toasts its legs-arms in the sun
>
> By day it's off to work he goes
> To the beauty of his blackened lathe
> And in the evening he comes back
> Again to dwell by the Oka's beauty
>
> Perhaps this is, just incident'ly,
> That same beauty we've expected
> In a year—two at the most—
> To save the world through beauty

How many lyric songs and pompous poems have been composed along these plotlines, stunning in their monumental simplicity? Prigov's concept is a generalization of numerous stereotypes free-floating in mass consciousness, from the idyllic-benevolent "beautification" of our native landscape, to a parodic deflation of Dostoevsky's prophecy "beauty will save the world." Conceptualism puts together a primer, as it were, of these stereotypes, removing from them the aura of creative mist and lofty animation to reveal their vulgar nature as signs called forth to stimulate the most elementary reactions to love and hate, "for" and "against." In so doing, they use minimal linguistic means to demonstrate the depletion and deadening of language itself, degenerated to the formulation of best-selling ideas. Tongue-tiedness turns out to be the alter ego of grandiloquence, the exposure of its quintessential emptiness. Conceptualism unequivocally reflects the reality of that milieu from which it arose and spread, or, more precisely, its apparent, empty "idealness." Much of what Prigov was writing about in the late seventies and early eighties is now openly discussed in the press; back then, however, this was all kept quiet, and we must give the poet his due for such courage:

It doesn't matter that the dairy yield recorded
Is unequal to the dairy yield for real
Whatever's written down—is written on the skies
And if it doesn't come to pass in 2–3 days
Then in a few years it will surely come to pass
And in the highest sense it has already been
And in the lowest sense it soon will be forgotten
And in fact it's just about forgotten now

In these lines we see the characteristic conceptualist intergrafting of "jour-nalese" and "mystical" jargons: one grows over into the other ("written" in account books, "written on the skies"), revealing the very process of mystifi-cation as it takes place in everyday reality, which itself then turns into some-thing loftily incomprehensible, portentously unavoidable until what little that remains of actual reality is so negligible as to be easily forgotten. Many of Prigov's poems are constructed in precisely this way: starting out with some sort of ordinary, topical fact, they go on to exalt it wildly, raise it to the level of a rhetorically providential plan, while, along the way, exposing its basic typicality, its insignificance. Then they conclude with a rythmical faltering, a weak gesture of some sort, or a muttering of the initial fact within the frame of workaday consciousness for which it doesn't matter how or of what one thinks or speaks. Reality has already become so disembodied as to lose its significance and substance: "And in fact it's just about forgotten now."

Conceptualism draws upon the entirely respectable traditions of twen-tieth-century Russian literature: the poetry of the Oberiuty (Daniil Kharms, Nikolai Oleinikov, the early Nikolai Zabolotsky and others) and the prose of Mikhail Zoshchenko.[12] Nevertheless, we must also note a shift of the stylis-tic system that the conceptualists have achieved in contrast to their pre-decessors. In the works of Zoshchenko or Oleinikov, mass consciousness is personalized within a concrete social layer (the petty bourgeoisie, NEP-men,[13] and so on) and in the image of a concrete protagonist, who usually speaks in the first person. Conceptualism eschews this kind of localization, be it social or psychological. The structures and stereotypes that are singled out do not belong to any one concrete consciousness, but rather to con-sciousness in general—the author's as much as the character's. For this rea-son conceptualist works cannot be placed in the category of humorous or ironic pieces, in which the author maintains a certain distance between himself (or, which is the same thing, the realm of the ideal) and the reality that he is mocking.

While it may be seen as either a strength or a weakness of conceptualism, the values of its world are uniform and admit of no privileged points of view whatsoever, no zones free from conceptualization. This is a world of objects from which the subject is absent, or else he himself with all of his acute existential misery falls into line with the rest of the objects fabricated by the "existential" rubber stamps of language—as, for example, in Lev Rubinshtein's composition "Life is all around us," in which sayings are set down of the following type:

> —Life is not given to man in a hurry.
> He doesn't even notice it, but he's alive . . .
> —Right . . .

> —Life is given to man when he's barely alive.
> It all depends on the likes of his soul . . .
> —Hold it!
> —Gentlemen, by the way, the tea's getting cold . . .

> —Three—four . . .
> —Life is given to man for a lifetime.
> All our life we must remember this . . .

> —All right, next . . .

Various positions on life and sayings about life as such are used here as ready-made objects placed by the author in his museum of linguistic models. The author's own position is lacking, as something inappropriate, even impossible, quite as if a tour guide in the process of showing us around a museum should suddenly offer up his own personal things as part of an exhibit.

Rubinshtein has developed his own version of conceptualism, a much more rigid version than Prigov's. Prigov's poems are monocentric, pronounced by a single voice that sounds from the idiotic depths of the collective unconscious, while still preserving a certain gravitational lyricality, a dull-witted seriousness of worldview. Prigov intentionally reduces his poems to rhyme-scheming, graphomania à la Dostoevsky's Lebiadkin, beyond which emerges the tragedy of entire generations condemned to speechlessness, having swallowed their tongue; like the "cannibaless Ellochka,"[14] who demonstrates that cannibalism is at one and the same time "tonguebalism"—the destruction of language down to its elementary signal systems.[15] In Rubinshtein's works rhyme-scheming falls away like yet another, final mask with its frozen, aesthetic grimace, as the skeletal constructions of our daily language are uncovered in their almost algorithmical predictability. Rubinshtein writes his texts on cards, which he files through almost mechanically at his public readings, habitually, like a reference librarian filing through the card catalogue (this is, in fact, Rubinshtein's profession); a system of summarization, of enumeration prevails. Various linguistical misunderstandings and microdialogues arise, continually pointing to one final goal: to reveal that our words denote no one knows what, perhaps nothing, although they continue to be pronounced; the very habit of living boils down to this verbal persistence.

—The air burst aloud . . .
—What say? Allowed?
—Not allowed, aloud.
—But I heard "allowed." That sounds even better.
—Maybe it's better, but I said, "The air burst aloud."
—I already understood what you said, but "allowed" is still better.
  (*Pause*)[16]

This excerpt from the catalogue "A Little Nighttime Serenade" (1986) is only a tiny snag in the endless linguistic red tape that Rubinshtein draws out, now tangling it in petty paradoxes, now untangling it in tawdry tautologies, but always reproducing with diplomatically dispassionate precision the tirelessness of our verbal practice, ambling through "pauses" from laugh to laugh, from banality to banality. Rubinshtein is a master of displaying the tawdriness of tawdry speech formations, a certain lack of willfulness of our speech operations: no matter what is said, it all appears as merely an imitation of someone—no one—else's speech; it is not we who speak this way, this is how "they" speak "us." Ordinary conversations stand next to literature, penetrating judgments on life and everyday remarks; it's all drawn into a speech-engendering mechanism that stamps its clichés onto library file cards or punchcards.

After hearing Rubinshtein's catalogues, one begins to perceive one's own utterances differently; they seem to become a continuation of these phraseological enumerations, sloughing off dead layers one after the other, leaving them for catalogues yet to be written. Thus, there occurs a liberation from speech; it must now begin anew from a source as yet unknown, from which first arose the Logos. Rubinshtein's texts undermine our faith in the independence of our own judgments, by opening the door on another author who stands behind them, thereby posing the difficult question of our linguistic identity. In order to speak for ourselves, we must overcome "the Other" in ourselves, but this is not at all simple to do. "The Other" has already managed to say so much: all of our oral and written literature, teeming with self-repetition and multitudes of tautologies, all that has been accumulated over the millenia of "speaking man" belongs to him. In the flood of speech stretching from Homer to Rubinshtein, an authentic "I" can no longer find a place, except as another mask for the speaker.

It would be superficial to reduce all the work of conceptualism to the level of a social criticism of language. Both Prigov and Rubinshtein deal not only with the newly formed linguistic "stamps" of the past few decades, but also with the evaluative capability of language itself to stamp and register as it makes use of us, exploiting our speech organs for the production of "surplus value," filling up the world with ephemeral significances, pseudo-meanings, ideological garbage. Conceptualism is a canal system, draining off all of this cultural garbage and scrap into cesspool texts where the garbage can be filtered out from the nongarbage—a necessary function for any developed culture. Conceptualism is the autorepresentation and self-criticism of language, which, having lost the second dimension of being able to speak about itself, risks identifying itself with reality and proudly abolishing the latter—an entirely imaginable event, as our recent history shows with its rhetorical "achievements."[17] The culture that does not allow its conceptions to be brought out into the open and changed into "concepts," into the objects of conceptual art, is a one-dimensional culture, condemned to decay.

Finally, there is the question of answerability, which readers unaccustomed to such texts love to pose to conceptualist artists. "Here you are," they say, "writing and writing, but, after all, those are not your words. What is it you yourself wish to say? What is your authorial position, where is your answerability for the word, without which there can be no serious art?" At this point, one must recall that the realm of a writer's answerability is not some abstract "authorial word," but the object of concrete, writerly work. And if a writer, as in the case of Gogol, Leskov and the *skaz* writers[18] of the nineteenth century, works with someone else's—or no one in particular's—word, then he answers for its precise reproduction, in the same way that the compiler of a dictionary answers not for the "sincere expression of his own convictions," but for the fullest possible representation of the laws and potentials of the language itself. It is, in fact, the position of compiler that appears more productive, and therefore more morally responsible, as regards contemporary conceptualist texts, than does the position of a composer.

The dictionary is a genre no less significant and responsible than a text consisting of the direct utterances of an author. If contemporary literature is becoming increasingly "dictionaric" (not scientifically, but creatively dictionaric), then this has been conditioned by the laws of development of literature itself, which is entering upon the phase of self-description, self-interpretation. Conceptions are becoming concepts, artistic designs and objects of study; in this lies the essence of the conceptual revolution that confronts art with the need to analyze and criticize its own language.

On Metarealism

Along with conceptualism, another stylistic current has formed in our poetry since the beginning of the seventies, which also long remained unknown to the broader reading public. It did not fit into the normative framework of the "middle" style,[19] which alone was acceptable to publishing houses and editorial boards by virtue of moderately combining characteristics of "live conversational" style and "high poeticality." Any attempt to disturb this balance met with an administrative-aesthetic protest. A decidedly low style, incorporating elements of street slang in the tawdry, literarily unpolished manner of plebeian conversation, was classified as "hooliganism,"[20] calculated for shock effect. High style, conscientiously freed from conversationality and all marks of everyday life, oriented toward the most highly authoritative spiritual traditions, was regarded as "secondary" and "bookish." Poetry stays alive, however, precisely by going beyond the bounds of prevailing norms, through the counterbalances of its stylistic foundations. Establishing the middle style as a precept, in part conversational and in part literary, led to the dominance of mediocrity—a grayness that swallows up contrasts. The other two styles, the "low" and the "high," were pushed out into the realm of unofficial existence, where both gained popularity with a single audience, primarily the youthful readership that has been oriented toward alternative forms of artistic thought.

The stylistic current opposed to conceptualism and directed not toward simplification and primitivization, but toward the greatest complexity of poetic language, has become known in recent years under the name of metarealism. Metarealism is not a negation of realism, but its expansion into the realm of things unseen, a complication of the very notion of realism, revealing its multidimensionality, irreducible to the level of physical and psychological verisimilitude and including a higher, metaphysical reality, like that made manifest to Pushkin's prophet.[21] That which we are accustomed to call "realism," narrowing the breadth of that concept, is the realism of only one reality, the social reality of day-to-day existence that directly surrounds us. Metarealism is the realism of multiple realities, connected by a continuum of internal passageways and interchangeabilities. There is a reality open to the vision of an ant or the wandering of an electron, the reality which has been called "the lofty flight of angels,"[22] and all of these enter into the essence of Reality. The prefix "meta" would not be needed if "realism" were not understood in an abbreviated form. "Meta" merely returns to realism that which has been left out from the all-encompassing Reality, when it is reduced to any one of its many subspecies.[23]

Such a broadened and deepened contemplation of Reality appears in the works of Olga Sedakova, Elena Shvarts, Ivan Zhdanov, Victor Krivulin, Dmitry Shchedrovitsky, Vladimir Aristov, Arkady Dragomoshchenko, and other poets of both Moscow and St. Petersburg. Of particular significance for their work are the traditions of "sacred" and "metaphysical" poetry of the European Middle Ages and baroque styles. The image is reborn in its archetypal significance, penetrating through the density of cultural overlayerings, to mythological, originary foundations. If conceptualism consciously reduces the image to its simplest ideological scheme, tearing from it the mask of artistry, then metarealism raises the image to the level of supra-artistic generalizations, giving it the generality and semantic dimensionality of myth. In both instances there is a noticeable pull toward the construction of supratemporal models of reality that lower the veils of history to reveal the stereotypes of mass consciousness or the archetypes of collective unconsciousness. This generation, spiritually formed under the conditions of historical stagnation, cannot but feel the retarded flow of time and respond with a heightened sensitivity to the eternal, recurring patterns of being.

Olga Sedakova, author of several collections of poetry, achieves such a rupture with the standardized norms of contemporary "literary" language. Sedakova's poems are unusually dark, yet nonetheless transparent; their meaning slips away among a mass of details in order to then make clear the animation of the whole.

> Can it be, Maria
>   that frames alone do creak,
> that panes of glass alone do ache and tremble?
> If this is not the garden—
> then let me turn back,
> to the quiet, where things are thought out.

If this isn't the garden, if the frames are creaking
because it can't get any darker,
if this isn't The Garden,
where hungry children sit by apple trees
forgetting the fruit that they've tasted,

where no light can be seen,
but breath is more dark
and the healing of night is more trusty . . .
I know not, Maria, this sickness of mine.
It's my garden that rises above me.

It is impossible and scarcely necessary to offer one unified interpretation of these lines, but clearly they lead us toward the higher reality of which the human soul inquires, for which it sickens and by which it is healed. The soul stands on the eve of its embodiment in an earthly life that it sees as if through rippled glass. It tries to make out the distorted image of a sequestered garden—an allusion to the loss of paradise—while struggling but not daring to be born, now pulling back "into the silence, where things are thought out," now moving forward on the promise of bliss, now sinking down into the murkiness of being, as into an inescapable disease.

One recalls (no doubt according to Sedakova's design) Tiutchev's[24] poem "O clairvoyant soul of mine," in which the soul, "resident of two worlds," stands in turmoil on the threshold "of being as if doubled," then concludes with lines that evoke the name of Maria. The fact that in Christian legends Mary is the comforter of the sick, intercessor for sinners, and "opener of the gates of heaven," gives this image its supratemporal dimension, setting it in the context of an enduring spiritual tradition.

In several of their characteristics Sedakova's poems show an affinity with symbolism: their highly generalized verbal significations, abstract distance from mundane daily concerns, their striving toward the world of the spiritual and eternal. Nevertheless, the metarealist poetic differs from that of symbolism, even when they seem to approach each other most closely, as in the case of Sedakova's works. The artistic principle of "doubled worlds," the clear boundary between "this" and "that," between "here" and "the beyond," is lacking. For symbolist poets the symbol is a juncture of two sharply differing meanings, the literal and the figurative, with an emphasis on the very duality of these two planes, the gap and rupture between them. Each word is a clue pointing to the heights and the distance. A rose is not simply a flower; it is the idea of womanliness, the symbol of the world soul.

A boat does not simply sail along the river; it unites two shores and two worlds, appearing as the symbol of spiritual ascent.

Such duality is not acceptable to the contemporary poetic consciousness, which considers alien any intensification of the "otherly" in opposition to the "here and now." Metarealism arises from the principle of "one world," presuming an interpenetration of realities, not a dispatch from one "apparent" or "functionary" reality to another "authentic" one. The artist's contemplative powers are focused on a plane of Reality where "this" and "that" are one, where any clue or allegory becomes almost obscene, since everything of which it is possible to speak must be said; that which cannot be said, it makes no sense to talk about. In metareal images it is impossible to separate the direct from the figurative meaning, to relate them according to principles of metaphoric similarity or symbolic correspondence; the image means just what it means, and dividing it in two would contradict its artistic nature. Sedakova's garden *is* Eden, not a symbol of Eden.

Instead of symbol or metaphor, the metarealists put forward a different poetic figure, which is not easy to place in a traditional classification of tropes. This figure is close to that which the ancients understood as "metamorphosis": one thing is not simply similar or corresponding to another, which presupposes an indestructible border between them, the artistic contingency and illusory quality of such a juxtaposition; rather, one thing *becomes* the other. All of the similarities that poetry has loved to seek out—the moon and a frog, lightning and a photographic flash, birches and the keys of a piano (metaphors from poems by Esenin, Pasternak, and Voznesensky)—these are only the signs of metamorphoses that have not taken place, and in the course of which things *really,* not apparently, exchange their essences. Metarealist poetry seeks intently for that reality wherein metaphor is again revealed as metamorphosis, as an authentic intercommonality, rather than the symbolic similarity, of two phenomena. Metarealism is not only "metaphysical," but also "metaphorical" realism, insofar as it is the poetry of that reality which is hidden within the metaphor, uniting its divergent meanings; the literal and the figurative.

> You will unfold in the expanded heart of suffering,
>   wild rose,
>   oh,
>   wounding garden of earth's creation!
> Wild is the rose and white, whiter than any.
> He who will name you would outargue Job.

I am silent, I vanish in mind from the beloved gaze,
not lowering my eye
nor dropping my hands from the fence.
The wild rose comes like a gardener, stern and
        knowing no fear,
with the crimson rose,
with the hidden wound of care beneath a wild blouse.

In Sedakova's poem "Wild Rose" there are neither similarities nor correspondences, but there is the continuous flow and transformation of an image. The wild rose is an image of all the universe, in which a thorny path leads to the secret garden; suffering leads to salvation. The essence of the image grows through its own broadened being; it does not refer to something other than itself: the "wild rose" reveals simultaneously the neglected, "fallen" condition of the world's garden and the lofty nature of the gardener, whose sufferings, even worse than those of Job, till the soil of the garden and turn a "hidden wound" into a "crimson rose." The precise position of the lyrical heroine is also poetically defined: she is by the fence, awaiting a meeting that already transfixes her gaze and, at any moment, will seize all of her being. The unfolding of the image—planting, the garden, the gardener (for whom the risen Savior was mistaken, according to legend)—brings to mind the germination of a seed, within which the future plant is already contained, through the organics of transformation, rather than the technique of comparison. All of Sedakova's poetry could be called, if we select for it the most concise single term, poetry of transfiguration.

The world of Ivan Zhdanov's poetry is also metareal, extended into the realm of the transparent, where pure prototypes of things are made manifest. Wind, mirror, memory, atmosphere, melting, reflection—these are the motifs that pass all through his book, consistently disembodying the substance of objects:

Does a house die, if afterwards there remain
only smoke and space, only the immortal scent of habitation?
How the snowfalls protect it,
bending as before, above the roof
that is long gone,
parting at the point where the walls once stood . . .
More like itself in dying than in life.

The essence of a thing comes out in its return to the original or predetermined model; death utters the secret, all-clarifying word on life. Zhdanov is a master of depicting forms that seem already to have lost their substance, but regain themselves in memory, in times of waiting, in the depth of a mirror or the shell of a shadow. Often the essence that has survived its own existence is singled out in a crisp formula. We are accustomed to the fact that a river has depth, while objects have weight; but for Zhdanov, "depth floats on the autumn water / and weight flows on, washing things all around." Properties of things are more primary than the things themselves, and "flight flies without birds."

Zhdanov's poetic intuition emerges at the vanishing point of things and leads us away to a world of pure essences, but then these essences acquire a visible outline. The very first line of one of his collections presents the principle of a new vision: "and they're plowing the mirror." The field where his father is at work becomes a mirror that dissolves the past, while at the same time acquiring a substance in which memory can drive its plow. It would seem that Zhdanov is depicting nonbeing: shadow fading into darkness, wind fading into emptiness, a reflection fading into a semblance; but his depiction conveys the precision of some mathematically verifiable knowledge. After all, form itself has no body; nor does a number, but for this very reason it is precise. At the boundary of a disembodied state there arises high seriousness and absolute knowledge.

From "An Ode to the Wind":

> Your ripple delves the mirrors,
> branches changing places
> sketch you like a needle.
> And if a mirror falls
> it will pour out my face
> and into mortal veins will go
> a prescience of light.

Here, the melting of substance is described almost with the inexorability of a physical law: with their "place-changing," branches reveal the wind's flesh; with its rippling, the wind reveals the mirror's flesh; with its reflection, the mirror reveals the flesh of a face, and with its death, the face reveals the flesh of light. One flesh enters into something less fully embodied until, on the border of its own disembodiment, it reveals another, obviously resurrected flesh: the flesh of those essences in which it died.

Zhdanov's poetry draws a fully visible, multi-dimensional state of being for things that have faded away into their own reflection and then find themselves there with greater obviousness than in that passing state of being from which they came. The same act by which a thing sinks into the depth of its own essence brings this essence to the surface where it becomes apparent to us: death is equal to resurrection.

From Metaphor to Metabole

The special quality of this new stylistic current is sometimes seen in its penchant for metaphor; Zhdanov and Eremenko, for example, have been called "metaphorists." As we can see, this is not simply a terminological misnomer, but a misunderstanding of the essential nature of the new poetry. It was under the banner of metaphor that Voznesensky's generation entered poetry, adorning the dull fabric of everyday reality with the magical designs of likeness and similarities, leaving great numbers of refractive prisms and mirrors along the way.

Nonetheless, through metaphor reality merely finds its likeness in another reality; the two remain separated, mutually untransformed, like reality and some illusion that has cropped up within it. Here we see deer gliding through the forest, and suddenly, for just an instant, a ghost of city traffic flashes before our eyes, right there in the depths of nature, only to fade immediately: "deer, like trollies, draw their current from the skies" (Voznesensky). Metaphor or comparison is just such a flash, of varying brightness but inescapably fading, since it is brought into reality from somewhere outside, to illuminate it for just an instant, in order to inscribe it. The new poetry seeks the source of light in the illuminated object itself, expanding the borders of its reality from within, revealing its simultaneous and unconditional belonging to two worlds. A poetic image such as this, in which there is no division of the "real" and the "illusory," the "literal" and the "figurative," but rather an unbroken continuity from one to the other, given their authentic intercommonality—this we will call *metabole* (from the ancient Greek, "transference, transformation, turning over"), as something distinct from metaphor.

Let us juxtapose two images, outwardly similar in their material motivation, but profoundly different in structure—one metaphoric, the other metabolist. First, from Voznesensky's "Autumn in Dilizhan":

As cupolas are gilt
in the light scaffolds of construction,

the orange mountain stands
in its deserted forests.

Metaphor divides the world into comparing and compared, into a reflected reality and a reflective similarity. Voznesensky clearly announces the point of reference, the object to be described—the natural surroundings of Dilizhan ("the orange mountain"); in relation to this, the ascribed similarity— the towers of a church—are spectral and symbolic, seeming to float above reality without entering into it, remaining a separate layer as befits a colorful, picturesquely selected correspondence. The autumn foliage resembles a gold tower. The forests reaching up Dilizhan's mountain resemble scaffolding set up around a church. Voznesensky is a brilliant poet in the area of metaphoric similarities, of associative flashes between doubled, alternating groupings of images. But now let us consider how the same basic objects are transformed in the verses of Alexander Eremenko, one of the new poets quoted above:

In the dense metallurgical forests,
where chlorophyll production was in progress . . .[25]

Here we have a metabolist image: the "forests" show us now their natural, now their industrial side, without any division into "basic" reality and the "superstructure" of illusion; rather we confront a wholistic reality fraught with transformations.

The metabole is an image that cannot be divided into the two halves of literal and figurative meaning, of an object described and the similarity ascribed to it; it is the image for a doubled and yet unitary reality. Nature and industry are transformed one into the other through the medium of forest-like structures that grow according to their own incomprehensible laws; technology has its own organics, and they constitute, along with nature, a single reality, in which the traits of both plant life and metallurgy are recognizable, although frightfully intertwined. Is this not the reality in which we live—the reality of our industrial landscapes, where a wire can grow directly through the trunk of a gnarled tree, and a tree through a rusted girder? This is a fantastical, baroque reality à la Hieronymus Bosch, which is itself unreal, but the artist doesn't dare to specify within it a privileged point of reference, to derive technology from organics or organics from technology—or rather, he does not usurp that right. (Not coincidentally, Eremenko has dedicated an epic poem to Bosch.) Metabole works toward the self-discovery of reality in all the miraculousness or monstrosity of its transformations. If metaphor, reintroduced into our poetry by the generation of the sixties (Voznesensky, Okudzhava, Akhmadulina, Matveeva, Rozhdestvensky), is the willingness to believe in miracles, then metabole is the ability to feel them.

For the generation of the eighties, or at least for those poets who are called metarealists, a nondualistically structured image is characteristic. In place of a representational likeness of things, there comes about a complicity of different worlds, equal in their authenticity. Significantly, the movement from metaphor to metabole may develop within the bounds of a single poem, reproducing the general literary shift.

> This homey beast which came from rustlings
> and the forest path—here is a cozy table.
> In its heart it mixed the wild way of life
> with a jostling of roots, secret and obscure.

In the first two lines of this poem by Ivan Zhdanov, we find the hint of a traditional metaphor: a table resembles a four-legged animal. But this is only the visible similarity, behind which the poet makes out the deeper commonality of the table with the primeval life of forests, as that life is preserved in the wooden composition and makes itself known, now with a hollow creaking, now in the grain that shows from under a tablecloth.

> And sometimes from its surface,
> to the sounding of branches, tangled in a creak,
> as a cloth of hands, slips down a triumph
> of bears' eyes that stopped the lindens,
> their tender honey running down the trunks,
> through bees' feet, through the chilling scent.
> And in that instant live in all tables
> mute faces on bears' paws.

Simplifying somewhat, one can say that here the essential thing is not a likeness, but the direct contact, a state of actual belonging, which is absent in metaphor. The qualities of bear and bees and wood form a single world, united in the alluring smell of honey: thousands of "sticky" glances, touches that maul the surface of the trunk—these animate the essence of this world. Beasts large and small prowling near the roots, or swarming in the crown have entered into the being of the table, so that their primordial faces show through its clouded grain.

Metaphor is born of the mythological image of metamorphosis, which embodies the unity and interchangeability of all things. This unity breaks down as a result of the historically necessitated pattern of separation into "reflected" and "reflecting," "literal" and "figurative" meanings, between which a symbolic link of likeness is established. But this type of dualism, with its artificial isolation of the image from reality, ceases to satisfy contemporary creative consciousness, which strives for "realism in the highest sense." So now metaphor is itself being overcome from within, moving back from dichotomy to a complicated unity, from the external similarity of distant objects to their necessary copresence in one expanded reality. Of course, this is not to say that we have a return to ancient syncretism, but rather a striving to overcome the symbolism of metaphor in a progressive manner, by moving forward. Metabole as image is a path of searching for a kind of wholeness that is not reducible to the simple identity of all phenomena as in the case of metamorphosis; nor does it separate them through the contingency of similarity, as in the metaphor. The metabole brings us to a new level of poetic consciousness, where the truth of myth is soberly and almost scientifically founded by the fantastical nature of reality itself![26]

The Scale of Poetic Styles

In art, as in science, there occurs from time to time a replacement of creative paradigms, with the difference that in the case of art, the new does not cancel out the previous. Indeed, in searching for continuity we often overlook the birth of the new. In the sixties and seventies, a paradigm reigned throughout our poetry that was determined by the interrelation of symbolic-metaphoric and lifelike styles. On one flank stood Voznesensky and Sosnora; on the other, Rubtsov, Sokolov, Zhigulin and other "quiet" or "rural-style" poets. In the middle of the scale were found the poets who sought a harmonic interrelation of the symbolic and the lifelike, the intellectual and the emotional: Kushner, Chukhontsev, Leonovich.

In the eighties, a new paradigm enters poetry, one determined by the interrelation of the conceptual and metareal currents. Between their representatives there has developed that total opposition that occurs only between contemporaries. Time breaks down into extremes in order to reach the fullest extent of its potentials. Conceptualism is the poetic of bare ideas, of self-sufficient signs abstracted from the reality they would seem called to denote, the poetic of formulas and stereotypes, that shows the falling away of forms from substances, of words from things. Naive mass consciousness serves as the object for self-reflective reproduction and fission, for criticism and analysis. The "concept" (*kontsept*) is a devastated or perverted idea, one that has lost its real content and calls forth by its absurdity an alienating, ironic-grotesque effect.

Metarealism is the poetic of multidimensional reality in the full breadth of its potentials and conversions. The figurative nature of metaphor is overcome in the unconditionality of metabole as it uncovers the intercommonality—not merely the similarity—of different worlds. If metaphor is a shard of myth, then metabole is an attempt to restore wholeness: an individual image appointed to draw near to myth, to the interpenetration of idea and realia, insofar as this is possible in contemporary poetry.

Within one and the same cultural situation, conceptualism and metarealism fulfill two necessary and mutually supplementary tasks: they slough away the false, habitual, tenacious meanings of words while giving them a new polysemy and fullness of meaning. The verbal fabric of conceptualism is slovenly, artistically undervalued and torn to rags, because one of the tasks of this current is to show the dilapidation and infirm helplessness of the vocabulary through which we make sense of the world. Metarealism creates a solid and lofty verbal structure, seeking out the limits of transformation of things, of association in meaning. Therefore, it turns toward eternal themes or eternal prototypes in contemporary themes, and it is saturated with archetypes: word, light, death, earth, wind, night. It draws upon nature, history, high culture, and art of various periods as the material for its creative works. Conceptualism, on the contrary, reveals the deceptiveness of all value designations; it is overtly associated with the themes of today, of the ephemeral, the communal life-style of mass consciousness and the lower, vulgar forms of culture.

At recent public discussions disputes have broken out between metarealist and conceptual poets. From the viewpoint of the former, conceptualism is not even art, but simply a phenomenon that reflects the lower strata of contemporary culture, aesthetically impoverished and transitory; when the banal realia of contemporary life pass away, conceptual poems will likewise lose their meaning. From the conceptualists' viewpoint, metarealists merely repeat the artistic systems of past epochs, indulging in the bombastics of well-worn poeticisms, rather than groping their way to a new position, such as that of conceptualizing and objectifying the very language of poetry. The authorial personality behind a metarealist poem is nothing but a character in a poem by a conceptualist.[27]

I emphasize that metarealism and conceptualism are not so much closed groups as they are the poles between which contemporary poetry remains in motion: the stylistic boundaries, between which there exist as many intergradations as there are poetic individualities. The most consistent and extreme metarealism is that practiced by Sedakova; a transparent and almost disembodied archetypal foundation emerges through her poetry. Zhdanov, while sharing with Sedakova a striving for the eternal, "Platonic" prototypes of things, gives his image system dynamism by turning to contemporary realia. In such of his works as "Radiator Rhapsody," a tense relationship is created between traditional and pure archetypes such as "water," "rose," and "Orpheus," as well as the incongruous elements whimsically inserted into this transparent world as kenotypes,[28] the prototypes of a new age: "cast iron gutters," "newspaper," "can opener."

Farther along in the space of transition from metarealism to the opposite pole, one finds the stylistic realm of such poets as Aleksei Parshchikov, Ilya Kutik, Alexander Eremenko. They are similarly drawn to the kenotypal level of contemporary civilization, abounding as it is in new objects and ideas, whose starting point was not assigned by prehistory and mythology, but which demands an equally generalizing, structuring approach. In their poems, such technicisms as "dual molecular spirals," "tactile contact," "hypothetical medians" and "*Kronstein* construction" are used not only as details of daily life in the era of the nuclear technological revolution, but also as the mysterious prototypes of a world that is to come, like the signs of an unknown civilization, its eschatological indicators, arising out of darkness. While harking to the traditions of futurism, with its taste for contemporaneity and the technological plasticity of objects, this new poetic lacks social-aesthetic aggressiveness and evangelistic utopianism; delight in the future is excluded by an intent, visually gripping attention toward the present, toward data itself, the extent and endurance of objects. Such poetry cannot be considered futuristic; rather, it is presentistic: a poetry of presence, of the present (from the Latin, *praesens*).

Presentism affirms the presence of an object, its visibility and tangibility, as the necessary and sufficient conditions of its meaningfulness. Between the extremes of poetic monism (the merging of object and sense) and dualism (their separateness) a medial approach to reality is sketched out, close to a phenomenological description. A poetic work is built as a succession of different views of the object, different ways of perceiving and inscribing it that form in their totality the manifestations of its actual essence. Such is

Parshchikov's "catfish"—the sum total of ways it is perceived in water and on land, waking and sleeping:

It seems as if he's dug out in the water, like a trench.
Surfacing, he thrusts out a wave above his head.
Consciousness and flesh compress themselves more tightly.
He's altogether like a backway from the bedroom to the moon.

And if you dip your hand into the underwater byways
they'll turn and speak to you, telling fortunes by your palm.
A kingfish on the sand flounders ringingly
and goes cold, like a key in its thickening lock.

An object is the apparition of an object, the sum of its refractions through different visual media and signal codes. The thing is neither united with the idea nor opposed to it, but is an "idea" itself, that is, in the ancient Greek meaning of this word: "appearance," that which presents, "makes itself present." Parshchikov expresses the principle of such a view of the world, which from within itself is the world: "I became the habitation for vision of all the planet." And Kutik does something similar in his "Ode on Visiting the Belosaraisk Sandbar on the Sea of Azov": "designs and colors are shuffled, / while all are but a hypostasis of vision."

In this medial stylistic diapason between the poles of metarealism and conceptualism, we find the poetry of Alexander Eremenko, Mikhail Aizenberg, Tatiana Shcherbina, and Nina Iskrenko. Moving farther along the stylistic scale, we eventually cross over into the realm of conceptualism, where the shift has been demonstrated above on the example of Prigov's work, in which all of reality, even its deeply archetypal layers, becomes the field of a conceptual game, albeit one conducted according to the rules of a more or less traditional, vaudevillian-idiotic rhyme-scheming. Farther on in the direction of the conceptualist limit we encounter Rubinshtein, the most extreme and consistent representative, with his use not even of words but of ready-made verbal blocks, formulas like catalogue cards, points in a service manual, or commands in a computer program.

From archetype, through kenotype, to stereotype, through all the subtle shifts in the relation of idea and object, the new poetry covers a broad field of image potentials. Individual style is actualized not as membership in one or another group or trend, but as inclusion in the field itself, where the dialectic of the artistic image unfolds through an opposition that strives at

one end toward myth, at the other toward concept. Metarealism and conceptualism, along with the intermediary zone between them that can be
designated as presentism, together trace out new image formations, among
which there remains adequate open space for yet another, however greatly
talented poet.

The expression "ecology of culture" has gained popularity in recent times.
As a rule, it is understood as advocating the protection of the cultural heritage of the past, a worthy task that cannot be postponed, if we consider the
colossal lapses and destruction in the history of our culture that have already taken place, from the years of the Tatar-Mongolian invasion to the
Bolsheviks' devastation of our "tsarist past."

But ecology is more than a preservationist discipline. It is also a creative
one, a system of the interrelations of man with the living medium that
nourishes him—such is contemporary culture, in the given instance. The
greatest lesson to be learned from our latest losses is to be protective of the
present. Otherwise, in our delight over the monuments of the past, we might
fail to leave our descendants any monuments of our own time. Nihilism has
many faces: yesterday it demanded the destruction of ancient sacred treasures in the name of the bright future; today, having donned the face of
conservatism, it demands an end to "modernist outrage" and "avant-gardist
escapades" in the name of a bright past.

The ecology of culture demands the recognition of all types and varieties
of creativity as worthy of existence, since they form, in their interaction, a
multiply complex cultural system: if we remove some elements, others will
come apart, deprived of nourishment and meaning. The example of biocide
is telling: destroy the "harmful," and valued, "useful" species will also be
lost. If in relation to plants and animals our knowledge and power are not
omnipotent, then much less is it for us to decide who among ourselves is
"harmful" and who is "useful"—our descendants will figure this out, if only
we leave them the item and opportunity for figuring: the live cultural medium that we inhabit. If we throw out one or another contemporary current
from the sphere of readership, the channels will be broken that connect us
to symbolism, acmeism, futurism, the Oberiuty; without these our poetic
heritage would be irredeemably impoverished. The egocentrism of one or
another current wishing to squeeze out the others must be set against eco-
centrism, the self-preservation of culture in the fullest variety and comple-
mentarity of its components.

CHAPTER 2 · Avant-Garde Art and Religion

Marcel Duchamp, one of the founders and pillars of European avant-gardism, was once asked if he believed in God: "No, not at all. Don't ask me about this! This question does not exist for me. God is man's invention. . . . I simply don't want to talk about it. We don't discuss how bees spend their lives on Sundays, do we? Well, this is the same."

In Duchamp's words, we find a sort of summary answer from the entire twentieth-century avant-garde to the question of belief: No, and further-more, "I simply don't want to talk about it." Indeed, avant-garde artists seem to prefer to keep silent, as if avoiding an undesirable topic, but their disin-clination reveals a deeply hidden significance. In the foreword to his book of conversations with Duchamp, the interviewer comments, "He speaks in a calm, evenly-measured voice. . . . Only one question aroused in him a clearly phrased reaction—towards the end, when I asked if he believed in God."[1]

Why would a question deemed to lack essential meaning elicit a man's strongest reaction? Why is he so reluctant to talk about it?

Anti-Art: The Gesture of a Holy Fool

The avant-garde is often characterized as a realm for the self-destruction of art, as negation of the artistic. An official Soviet critic of avant-gardism once wrote, "Avant-garde works cannot stand up to artistic criteria at all, let alone great artistic criteria. Therefore, it is not possible to analyze them from the standpoint of art scholarship (the methods of such scholarship cannot be applied to an object that has, by its very nature, ceased to be art.)"[2] But if the avant-garde, as it has become customary to assume, represents an anti-art, then we should stop and think: What force can be capable of pushing art out of its proper area and taking its place? The claim that avant-gardism constitutes an "anti-art" requires further explanation of the social, religious, or other content implicit in this phenomenon.

Not all forms of destruction are identical. Let us compare two events that occurred at almost the same time and on the same material basis. In 1917, Marcel Duchamp attempted to arrange exhibition in New York of an artistic work consisting of an ordinary urinal, bearing the title "Fountain" (it was eventually rejected). In 1919, a congress of the poor peasantry was convened in Petersburg, and delegates were accommodated at the Winter Palace. Here are Maxim Gorky's recollections of the event:

> When the congress was over and the people had left, it was discovered that they had not only made use of all the bathtubs in the palace, but that an enormous quantity of valuable Sevres, Saxon, and Oriental vases had been used as chamber pots and left filthy. This was not done out of necessity; the palace facilities and plumbing were found to be in working order. No, this vandalism expressed a desire to spoil, to degrade beautiful things.[3]

In one instance, a urinal is displayed as an art object. In the other, an art object is used as a urinal. Clearly, there is a fundamental difference between the destruction of art and the creation of an anti-art. It is the same difference that exists between the actions of a bully and those of a holy fool.[4] The use of Sevres vases as chamber pots is an act of pure, socially based nihilism, expressing the attitude of ignorant, backward people toward the creations of "aristocratic" art. It is quite another matter when an artist "blasphemously" pushes back the boundaries of his art into the realm of the base and ugly. This is the way in which art throws itself down from its lofty pedestal, willingly humiliates itself, calling forth a scandalized reaction (rather than the typical piety and awe).

A. M. Panchenko, a specialist in old Russian culture, writes, "The life of the holy fool is a conscious negation of the beautiful, a rejection of the customary ideal of the beautiful, or, more precisely, an inversion of this ideal and an elevation of the ugly to an aesthetically positive level."[5] But the same is brought as an accusation against the avant-garde by its critics from the standpoint of "good taste" and "high ideals" (examples may be found in the work of Marxist and Orthodox religious writers alike). The avant-garde is a holy fool's art, consciously going forth to its own humiliation, to the mutilation of its own aesthetic face, even to the point that a urinal may take a sculpture's place on display, and a pathetic, twisted "dyr bur shchil ubeshchur" may take the place of beautiful poetic harmonies.[6]

Clearly, such holy foolery is an anti-aesthetic phenomenon, but may also be positively defined as a religious phenomenon. Panchenko suggests that "the ugliness of holy foolery is . . . possible only because the aesthetic element is absorbed by ethics. This is a return to the early Christian ideals, in accordance with which carnal beauty came from the devil. . . . In holy foolery that era seems to be preserved when Christianity and the fine arts were antagonistic categories" (80). In this context, the significance of the avant-garde as a religious negation of art by artistic means becomes clear. Art becomes impoverished, pathetic in order to partake of God's fate, to follow his path of degradation and mockery.

Of course, the avant-garde might not choose this religious aim for itself consciously, since it remains art, nonetheless, and only in the gesture by which it strips off all aesthetic definitions is its supra-aesthetic nature revealed. The religious aspect enters here not as a self-affirming goal, but as self-denial. Thus, the avant-garde does not set itself a task of religious preaching; it recalls not a priest reading sermons from the pulpit, but a holy fool lolling in the mud. Of primary importance here is the act of *self-annihilation*, thanks to which anti-art still remains art, while also incorporating a self-abolishing religious element. After all, this abolition is accomplished within art's own sphere, while a socially motivated force directed from the outside would abolish the sphere of art as such. One should distinguish two types of de-aestheticization: (1) the destruction of art as a social act (as in Gorky's example); and (2) the self-humiliation of art as a religious act, endowing art with the new, paradoxical qualities of anti-art.

This type of behavior on the part of an avant-garde artist reveals a rupture with the habits and conventions of the social milieu. Such concepts as the "pure" and "sacred" are subjected to derision. The artist bespatters his public with spit and abuse, so as to provoke its indignation and mockery in return. As for the holy fool, "he continually provokes the viewers, actually forces them to beat him, he casts stones, muck, and filth at them, spits at them, and outrages their sense of propriety" (90). This characterization of a holy fool may equally well be applied to the scandalous conduct of the Russian and Italian futurists, the French dadaists and surrealists. Scandal, a flagrant toppling of social norms, exposes a more deeply paradoxical system of values, wherein the high takes on the visage of the low. In essence, the behavior of Christ, considered within the worldview of Jewish law, was certainly a scandal: he who announced himself the Son of God had the appearance of a poor pilgrim and befriended publicans, fishermen, and wayward women. The phenomenon of holy foolery is based on this primal paradox of Christian religiosity, and the art of the avant-garde renews in all its sharpness the sense of crisis that casts away aesthetic and moral values before the Supreme Value of something strange and unthinkable.

This "foolishness" is not the negation of faith, but negation by means of faith. Even blasphemous statements that are often made in the avant-garde milieu can find a parallel in the deeds of holy fools. For example: "Before the eyes of stunned pilgrims, Vasily the Blessed took a rock and broke an icon of the Holy Mother on the Varvarsky gates, that from age-old times had been considered wonderworking. It turned out that on the board beneath the sacred image there was a drawing of a devil" (104). The theomachian impulses of avant-garde consciousness may be explained to a great extent as a conscious or unconscious battle against idolatry. Even the provocational declarations in Mayakovsky's early works, such as

> I thought you were a great big god almighty,
> but you're a dunce, a minute little godlet . . .
> I'll rip you, reeking of incense,
> wide open from here to Alaska![7]

simply do not fit the teachings of "scientific atheism": first, because a struggle with God entails the admission of him as living (recall Jacob's struggle with the mysterious stranger); and second, because the hero betrays his participation in the meaning of faith by offering himself in sacrifice:

> . . . I am where pain is—everywhere;
> on each drop of the tear-flow
> I have nailed myself on the cross.[8]

One must distinguish nihilistic negation, which annihilates the meaning of faith, from "protestant" negation, which aims to purify this meaning. Avant-gardism is closer to the latter. However haughty and challenging the avant-garde artist may appear, one senses in him the vulnerability of a willing sacrifice. He is rude to the public in order to humble himself before them:

> This led to my Golgothas in the halls
> of Petrograd, Moscow, Odessa, and Kiev,
> where not a man
> but
> shouted:
> "Crucify, crucify him!"[9]

The avant-garde often gravitates toward negative forms of expression: oblique speech, trans-sense language, and, in the extreme, to total silence and a liberation from symbolic language. The public, accustomed to traditional forms of audible, elegant, aesthetically formulated speech, may take all this as blasphemy, but here again, we can discern features of a religious use of language. Futurist trans-sense strips off all obligations for poetry to be comprehensible and demands instead that we "honor the rights of poets . . . to unconquerable hatred for all pre-existing language" (from the manifesto "A Slap in the Face of Public Taste" [1913]). By the same token, "in alienating himself from society, the holy fool and his language are estranged from language as it is generally used" (106). Alexei Kruchenykh's "dyr bul shchil ubeshchur" or Velimir Khlebnikov's "gzi-gzi-gzeo"[10] are akin to "glossolalia and oblique mutterings, comprehensible to the holy fool alone, those 'murky words' uttered by Andrei Tsaregradsky" (96). Obliqueness is a device for expressing the inexpressibility of the inexpressible—things that do not yield themselves to the tongue, but rather slide away from nomination. The avant-garde is an artistic assimilation of those invisible, intangible, and unspeakable realms of being, but the specific nature of art consists in the fact that the unspeakable must be spoken (and not preserved in silence), the invisible must be shown (and not hidden in darkness). The paradox of content negated by its own form draws the avant-garde close to holy foolery.

Art of the Second Commandment

One of the general characteristics of the avant-garde, proper to all of its various branches, is the rejection of artistic verisimilitude, a refusal to follow the forms of reality. Avant-garde art is nonfigurative, as a rule, and this is sometimes seen as a retreat into solipsism and agnosticism, an inability to cope with reality and an attendant rejection of its cognition and reproduction. However, one need not go far in search of arguments to show that the nonrepresentational tendency of the avant-garde brings it close to sacred art, which turns away from the likeness and duplication of reality, as from the production of counterfeit coins. Verisimilitude is a dangerous thing; it creates an illusion of permanence and completeness of depicted forms and, along with this, a temptation to deify them. For this reason the second commandment states: "Thou shalt not make unto thee any graven image, or any likeness of any thing that is in heaven above, or that is in the earth beneath or that is in the water beneath the earth" (Exod. 20:4).

Such depiction is an evil in the sight of God. Strict monotheistic religions, such as Judaism and Islam, carry out this commandment by forbidding, first and foremost, the depiction of living creatures. Thus, the avant-garde continues and develops the ancient principle of nonrepresentationalism. But since it arises on the soil of European culture, with its strong traditions of representational art, stemming from iconography with its attempt to imprint the face of the incarnate God, the avant-garde accepts representation as a ground, a premise established for direct erasure and destruction. The spectrum of avant-garde trends includes variably representational ones, from cubism's purely geometric view of nature, to abstractionism's more fantastical geometry. But abstractionism did not and could not become the predominant trend in avant-gardism, because it claimed victory too easily: by totally annulling the world of objects. Thus, it also annulled the paradox that holds the avant-garde canvas in a state of unified tension, giving a tormentingly tragic quality to the entire avant-garde worldview. The image wipes away from itself all traces of an image. The incorporeal must reveal itself in flesh, wounded and crucified.

Of course, in its refusal of the representational, or better still, in allowing it the role of sacrifice, the avant-garde draws inspiration not directly from the heritage of monotheistic culture, but from the living sense of crisis in contemporary civilization. In this context, no prohibition lies on the depiction of existing things, but these things lose their image, break down and fall to dust before the powerful breath of Spirit, as it cleanses the world of the scabs of matter. Artistry loses its erstwhile joyfulness: "O, could we but return the shame of sighted fingers, and the protrudant joy of recognition!"[11] This is the wail of a classicist who finds himself in the "Dark Ages," where the barbaric art of a disembodied afterlife holds sway. The world of objects is dismembered into energy flows that pour invisibly down conductive wires into the dashes and signs that emerge on computer screens. What has become of the surface that one might lovingly survey with an all-encompassing gaze?

At the beginning of this century, physics was precise and dry, but suddenly it raised an alarm over the loss of matter. The world of things fell away somewhere, into an abyss of pulsating fields and flowing energies. How could art not sense the fatal downward shifting of the platforms of matter into yawning emptiness?

Nikolai Berdiaev found in the crisis of the visual arts very subtle evidence for the material "disengagement" of the world:

> The world becomes disincarnate in its membranes, and is reincarnated again. Art also cannot be preserved in its old incarnation. . . . The true

meaning of the crisis in the visual arts lies in the convulsive effort to go beyond the material membrane of the world, to capture a more ethereal flesh, to overcome the law of impenetrability. . . . Thus the fate of the world's flesh comes to pass, leading to resurrection and a new life through death.[12]

Thus, the avant-garde is intimately linked to the apocalyptic worldview that achieved its zenith in early Christian times, but thereafter was pushed aside for many centuries by the traditions of secularized religiosity. These traditions affirmed attachment of the living to this world, and secular art appeared in direct response to the problems of setting the material house in order. From the Renaissance to the nineteenth century inclusive, art amassed itself on the surface of the world, becoming indistinguishable and inseparable from it. But inside the house itself, so beautifully inhabitable, a gust of wind rips the door from its hinges, bursts the windows open, and the darkness of the world to come falls across one's eyes.

It is especially difficult to recognize the features of religious art in avant-garde artworks, because these forms follow secular art, rather than preceding it in time. Avant-garde art is closer to the icon than to artistic painting, and still closer to the characters and signs found in monotheistic churches, than to the icon: its subject is the passing away of the world, rolled up and sealed like a scroll, on the eve of the great transfiguration. The apostle Paul said, "for the fashion of this world passeth away," (1 Cor. 7:31). Can there be any other way to leave an imprint of this world than in the process of its loss, of its disappearing image? The avant-garde is the art of building an Image to frame this world in the process of its passing away, as it sheds its apparent, worldly surface. This is the realism of an apocalyptic age that has realized the unstable and spectral nature of all worldly arrangements. This is apocalyptic realism.

Art is often considered religious when it depicts the concrete accoutrements of religious practice: crosses, cupolas, icons, candles (as, for example, in Ilya Glazunov's paintings). But it is quite obvious that art which so graphically portrays a specifically religious object, brings religion itself into the zone of objects, and may not necessarily be religious in essence. An artist may depict a cup on a table, or a candle on an altar as equally rich and brilliant details of the domestic or ecclesiastical worlds. Contemporary religious art, however, does not play with religious objects, does not objectify the sacred, but instead is present in them. Malevich's *Black Square* or Kandinsky's compositions contain as much a concentration of religious feeling, aimed beyond the boundaries of the sensuous world, as the religious objects of Vasnetsov or Nesterov contain a sensuous indulgence. It is not things that are holy, but Spirit, as it evades all likeness to things. *Black Square* is the absorption of depth on a white background, a visible image of a world passing away, and an open tunnel of passage to other worlds.

What is it that attracts suspicion, that links avant-gardism to the deviltry of our epoch, that wafts demonic cold and corruption from its direction? Is it that in avant-garde works the absurd overrules meaning; faces appear in estranged forms, in some sort of broken pieces with crooked edges; the individual is inimical to himself and displays something like the properties of a plant, a molecule, or a hole, but not a human being? Avant-garde art exposes the submolecular structure of matter, traces the plans of universal forces as they doze in the subconscious, goes further than the incarnate, further than beautiful appearances and the aesthetics of the middleground, and collaborates with imagination to the end—an end that cannot be contained within any historical perspective. Here is a crisis of reality that no longer fits into our humanly assimilated forms, that melts and disappears, becoming ever less tangible and comprehensible.

But it may well be more accurate to suppose that it is reality, brimming with health, full and round to the eye, that would rather serve the demonic seduction of humanity, turning it toward the earthly path and away from the celestial. Conservative consciousness, which coincides in many ways with religious tradition, is disinclined to part with that beloved reality wherein the organizational and ideological structures of traditional denominations abide in greater or lesser degrees of comfort. They have merged with the world that they once came to judge and to destroy; they have entered into its flesh, and have fallen in love with its roundness, its aesthetic appearances, so brilliantly displayed in traditional, "realistic" art.

The avant-garde, on the other hand, is much closer to the age-old eschatological spirit of these denominations, their expectations of the end of the world. A religious worldview is, by its very nature, not the least bit conservative. It is crisis-oriented, attuned to the collapse of all norms and the crack of all foundations, as a wave of new times and spaces breaks high over the top of all creation.

What sort of art might express the depth of this religious rebellion against the established and embodied? Traditional representations of lovely madonnas with lovely infants in their arms? But this art emerged from the sense of positive value and justification that pervades the world in its creaturely forms, inspired by the tales of a prior Revelation. As the sense of an approaching Revelation begins to grow, all sanctified and reliable images of the past crumble to dust, like plaster, beneath the blows of unseen outside forces. These dents in the walls, gaps and zigzags that grow before our eyes, are reproduced in avant-garde art. It is religious to the same extent that religion itself is avant-garde: it moves ahead of all the world's conclusive results, leaving behind all things of dominance and stability. Avant-garde belief finds its place not within the walls of a church, but beyond the borders of this world, from where a new earth and sky move toward humanity apace, showing through in fleeting shapes and gaps among the disintegrating layers of reality. Avant-gardism is an aesthetic of the end. It is to art what eschatology is to religion. The art of the second commandment is also an art of the final Revelation: do not depict that which is in the world, for the world is already losing this form.

Conceptualism and Apophatic Consciousness

Christian theology includes an affirmative, or "cataphatic" trend, which advances definite, positive assertions as to the nature of God and his characteristics; it also includes a negative, or "apophatic" trend, which in Eastern Christianity is considered to be more perfect.[13] Apophatic theology expresses the absolute transcendental nature of God, by stressing his nonidentity, his "elsewhere-ness" in relation to all visible manifestations and possible designations, by denying his names and attributes. Any definition proves incommensurable with that Absolute which must remain closed within itself. In its relation to higher reality, the avant-garde may also be divided into two trends that we will symbolically designate with these same terms.

The avant-garde of the second and third decades of the twentieth century, including expressionism, futurism, constructivism, and suprematism expressed primarily cataphatic impulses in that it aimed to create positive impressions of higher emanations from a kind of Spirit, as in the poetry and prose of Andrei Bely and Khlebnikov or in the painting of Kandinsky and Malevich. But this early avant-garde utopianism was compromised and abandoned precisely because of the realization of these utopias in historical practice, revealing the horror and poverty of such "higher realities," whose literal embodiment in the ethics and ontology of mystical communism was the cause célèbre of Mayakovsky and Malevich and, in another political version, of Marinetti. And in part for this reason, the second-generation avant-garde, of the sixties and seventies, was anti-utopian, as it discovered on the artistic horizon utterly nonsymbolic, purely commercial objects (pop art) or objectless, purely ideological signs (soc-art).

An influential trend in the contemporary avant-garde is conceptualism, which liberates things and signs from reciprocal responsibility, or rather releases them into a field of "irresponsible correspondence," where signs, overblown with significance, and things, impoverished in their objectness, are called to bear witness to each other.[14]

Let us consider, for example, the work of conceptual artist Ilya Kabakov: his *Trash Novel* and the installation *The Man Who Never Threw Anything Away*.[15] The novel is a series of albums, containing sewn-up and glued-in sheets of paper and documents, yellow with age: receipts, tickets, coupons, bits of cardboard and all manner of such trifling stuff. The installation consists of bits and pieces of everyday trash all attached to a massive wooden stand: an old knife, bits of tin, threads, broken glasses, pencil-shavings—whatever we might find on the floor, under the sofa, or in the bottom of a drawer. Looking through these trifles, one after another, you fail to understand at first why they were assembled, and what sort of artistic idea peers out from between them.

However, a label affixed to each object recalls when and in what circumstance it was purchased, picked up, utilized, or thrown away. Each bit of trash is strictly documented and woven by the author into the scrimwork of his life. In all of this there is not a hint of revelry, havoc, or chaos, as would befit a pile of trash; on the contrary, everything is painstakingly selected, arranged in graceful rows along the length and width of the stand, or glued neatly in the album. This ideal of orderliness would not be out of place in a government archive or the private museum of some stately person. Similarly, the important tone of the descriptions is in obvious contradiction to the insignificance of the objects themselves. Here is a string of some kind, there an apple seed, all with the drily circumstantial commentary appropriate to historically significant objects.

And suddenly you grasp the combined meaning of this orderliness and insignificance. Order is what our lives should become, what we try to make of them, and insignificance is what they really consist of. Each caption is a despairing surge toward meaning and eternity, spreading out in the transience and uselessness of trash so assiduously documented. Surging forward and guttering out: a handful of ashes. Carefully arranged and all in vain: a trash heap.

Trash, complete with labels that attach the full diversity of a personal life to these specks of dust, suddenly allows us to see this life as a whole. And just what is it? Does it not consist of these dust motes after all? What about meetings? Illnesses? Fear? Hope? But aren't these ultimately nothing but displacements, sweepings-up, accumulations, and rarifications of just such specks of dust? And suddenly, from all this trash, words from the Bible come into your heart: "ashes to ashes, dust to dust." By its own insignificance, this conceptual creation forces us humbly to experience the insignificance of life; if some further gesture is wanted, it might be to strike one's forehead to the floor, sob out loud, and pray: "Lord, have mercy!" For a man makes nothing more than dust in all his life, since he himself is made of this.

The theme of trash acquires for Kabakov a deeply eschatological meaning—like a farewell to the dusty materiality of this world. All of life, even filled with myriad details as it is, becomes but one of them—a lightly floating dust mote.

Conceptualism, only one of many trends in the Western avant-garde of the seventies, gained particular importance in Russia. The didactic, ideologically overloaded verbal style of Soviet literature and culture in general translated easily into a language of anti-artistic schemata: of concepts (*kontsepty*) flaunting themselves as conceptions of nonexistent and even unnecessary artworks. Why write yet another canticle of love for life or another ode to Pushkin, when Lev Rubinshtein has already written: "Life is given to man for his whole life" and Dmitry Prigov has added, writing of Pushkin, "a god of fertility, protector of the flocks, and father to the people"? And further, "Our youth have clear roads everywhere," "Heroes live beside us," "The happiness of future generations," "We were born to make fairy-tales come true," "When the party calls, the Komsomol answers 'Done!' " Read through a list of topics, suggested year after year to eighth-graders for their exam-compositions in literature, and you will get a clue not only as to the enigmatic method of socialist realism, but also a highly accurate guide to conceptual literature.

Socialist realism created an abundance of defective images illustrative of super-valuable ideas. Conceptualism, on the contrary, creates images that reveal the defectiveness of ideas themselves. If ideology counterfeits artistic creations, then artistry avenges itself by counterfeiting ideological concepts and presenting their absurd and hollow character. Pseudo-art, which occupies itself with fabricating images to suit ideas, gave birth to an anti-art that parts ways with ideas altogether, as it demonstrates their sterility and lack of form. A concept is the reverse side of an "ideal," utterly counterfeit and fatal for all vital ideas. Conceptualism gives us the satisfaction of parting with imaginary scarecrows as we laugh, having assured ourselves that these are not "men of the future," but simply overdressed mannequins that no customer would want in the least to resemble (in this, incidentally, can be found the difference between propaganda and advertising).

One of the traits of conceptual poetics is the use of well-known terms and phrases, the selection of precisely those things that have passed from hand to hand, retaining the mark of otherness, of having been used: a quotational quality. In Timur Kibirov's poem dedicated to the former Soviet leader Konstantin Chernenko, a full assortment of ideologemes from the past epoch is arrayed in the canonical genre of heroic biography, from his barefooted boyhood and fervently irreconcilable enmity toward the kulaks (an archetype of Pavlik Morozov), to his solemn speech at the plenum of Soviet writers on the topic of creative freedom, which brought tears and delight to all, beginning with Rasul Gamzatov and ending with Homer himself (the archetype of "Thanks to the Party!"). This is not to say that only sociopolitical ideas enter into conceptual works. This is the sphere of "ideological meaning" as such, manifesting itself in all the typical prejudices of common thought, be they humanistic, moralistic, nationalistic-patriotic, everyday-popular, philosophico-cosmic, and so on.

Conceptualism can boast of few works executed in masterly fashion, in the traditional sense of the word. Its language is impoverished, primitive, pompous; its pictures are underdrawn, any which way, by an artist who was obviously lazy. But the absence of imagery is the only way to reveal these ideas whose image has long since passed away, like the image of a world spoiled by sin. Ideal and concept form a single whole, like a bagel and its hole—an emptied form and formed emptiness—or separated ends of one historical epoch that began with "ideological meaning" and ends with "conceptuality." Conceptualism entails something akin to Buddhism, even Zen: reality reveals its illusory, spectral quality and gives way to the perception of emptiness itself. Conceptualism is the tsardom of tiresome, petty trifles beyond which opens a vast, summoning emptiness.

One of the most effective devices of avant-garde art today is automation and its result, "sloughing off" (*otslaivanie*). Here it is helpful to draw a parallel with the device common to late realism and early avant-garde art that Victor Shklovsky called "estrangement," or "making it strange" (*ostranenie*). A well-known, familiar object that one has seen time and again suddenly reveals a strangeness, holding back our attention (for example, Mayakovsky's line "the muzzle of the rain sucked round every passer-by"). Shklovsky believed that art in general was founded on this principle, which has as its aim the removal of our perception from its automatic regime, in order to allow for a more complete experience of the world in its unusual, unpredicated state.

Virtually the opposite device operates in the late avant-garde: the automation of perception. Using an example from nature, as above, we find the following lines in Rubinshtein's poetry:

Nightingale, my nightingale
He appeared here in the dale!

Like a phantom in the dale
There appears a nightingale!

Nightingale, my nightingale,
Where are you, where in the dale?

In the leafy hills and dale
Sang his song the nightingale![16]

The aim here is not to underscore and "make strange," but to have done with and cross out. Not to see the world in more detail and beauty, but to make evident its recurring repetitions, to read and have done with reading, to turn the page more quickly. It may take one page or many to drive perception on until it flies from line to line, so that the already overfamiliar comes to flash past all the faster. All of existence is translated into the mode of banality, whereby each utterance is taken as if in quotation marks: "someone said as much," "it goes without saying," "that's what they say."

Recitation of such verses calls for a special vocal style: one poet grumbles, another jabbers, while a third hums and mumbles. Each is immediately recognizable and distinct in his manner and intonation, but the verbal trash that this manner ruminates and spits out is all basically the same. Not only ready verbal clichés are put to use, but entire worldviews become clichéd in consciously masterful ways, as do situations, characters, plot elements, and judgments on life. All verbal activity is translated into an automated regime of fast-talking mumblings and ready-made phrases—an unadulterated mass of idioms. Rather than a difficult birth of speech laden with amazement, we find rumination and a bolting of words arousing boredom. Everything that is said should be noted, tired of, and tossed aside as quickly as possible; any topic whatever, from lofty to low, including love, faith, and life, is subject to this rule.[17] A characteristic example from the work of Vsevolod Nekrasov reads as follows:

well
I live
I wait

for what
that

I say that
I think that
I want to say

I keep silent

And, indeed, such poetic speech as this staggers through its own words and tends toward silence.

Such is the negative aesthetic of the contemporary avant-garde[18] as it comes to take the place of the affirmative aesthetic of earlier trends. But what is the purpose of this banalization of things that in and of themselves are far from always banal? Can we call it nihilism and leave it at that? But nihilism would be self-satisfied and self-assured in its negation of higher values. Conceptualism, with its sense of inadequacy, of the shortage of meaning in each sphere of being it addresses, is diametrically opposed to nihilism. Nihilism announces itself in cruelly ringing words, slogans, resolutions, verdicts: "Let's fire a bullet into Holy Russia!" Conceptualism uses flat, jingling, somewhat stupid words:

People are so necessary,
Even if they're solitary!

People are not solitary,
If they're really necessary!

People surely get th' idea,
If they're just not idiots!

People are not idiots,
Even if they miss th' idea![19]

But why is it that they sound so flat and clumsy? Is it not because we sense behind them a load of meaning on whose backdrop (and in contrast to which) they appear flat? A humbling of speech, a deflation of meaning— these are ways of pointing to another, silent reality for which there are no and can be no words. Any value is made small, when we assume the Supreme Value. The latter cannot itself be made manifest; only that can be manifested which this value is not.

Nihilism affirms the strength, pride, and truth of negation. Conceptualism drapes negation in the tattered rags of mediocrity and senselessness, showing its own negation of itself. Nihilism *affirms negation*. Conceptualism *negates affirmation*. Such is the difference between satanic laughter, which destroys belief, and the laughter of a holy fool, as he unmasks an idol.

Any assertions whatever, be they lofty, true, sacred, or eternal, become mediocre in conceptual poetics and are subject to erasure:

> It [the Cause of all] cannot be grasped by the understanding since it is neither knowledge nor truth. It is not kingship. It is not wisdom. It is neither one nor oneness, divinity nor goodness. . . . There is no speaking of it, nor name nor knowledge of it.[20]

Thus wrote Pseudo-Dionysius the Areopagite, founder of apophatic theology, in the fifth century A.D. This tradition, which rejected all names theretofore applied to God, did not even preserve the proper name of its founder.

In similar fashion, conceptualism brings out the absurdity of what we know, for the sake of a fuller knowledge of what we do not know. "I pray we could come to this darkness so far above light . . . so as to see, so as to know, unseeing and unknowing, that which lies beyond all vision and knowledge."[21] For this same reason any enlightening ecstasy is closed off and erased by conceptual devices, as a technique for getting rid of the viselike grip of ideology on consciousness and thereby healing socioneuroses, in order to carry us into the depth of a darkness surpassing light, of an obscurity surpassing clarity. Even "truth," "goodness," "wisdom," and "divinity," must be placed in quotation marks in conceptual space as they are sloughed off in the form of sayings that belong to someone else. After all, the Supreme Value (which is also non-Value) keeps silent, and the more words about it we quote, the sooner we will approach its "authorial" word about itself: silence within itself, where we, too, may abide. Listening to conceptual works means to experience a boredom and soul-wrenching emptiness that erases all artistic "categories" and "pathos" as mediocre and alien. While listening intently to muteness, looking deeply into darkness, going deaf and blind, you approach the Absolute negation of all assertions. Such an approach to the Absolute, "rises from what is below up to the transcendent, and the more it climbs, the more language falters, and when it has passed up and beyond the ascent, it will turn silent completely."[22]

Perhaps the device of "getting rid," or, to use Pseudo-Dionysius's term, "clearing aside," is just as common in great art as is that of "making strange." Indeed, it seems they often operate in tandem: certain aspects of reality are driven into the automatic regime of perception, while others are lifted out of it. Some acquire acuity at the expense of others. Thus, in *Eugene Onegin* (chap. 1, stanza 22), Pushkin dulls our perception with a hasty enumeration of typical accoutrements from theatrical life:

> Still amors, devils, serpents
> on the stage caper and make noise;
> still the tired footmen
> sleep on the pelisses at the carriage porch;
> still . . .
> still . . .

The very syntax contributes to automating certain elements, in order to make strange and emphasize another: Onegin's premature departure from the theater, a violation of aesthetic convention. The most ordinary words

> and yet Onegin has already left;
> he's driving home to dress.[23]

appear estranged on the background of the preceding, automating, words. In essence, this is art's primary occupation: the creative transformation of reality, accentuating some elements, retouching others, so that first and foremost emerges the very contrast between reality and art. A good eraser is as indispensable in this process as is an underlining pencil. I would call this law the contrastive quality of art in relation to reality. After all, the viewer or reader, who lives in this reality and speaks its language, has a great need for such artistic contrast as can compensate for reality's shortcomings and "get rid" of its excesses, "restating" it in the "foreign" language of aesthetic being.

If "making strange" allows us to sense the material world anew, then "sloughing off" removes the layers of matter one after another, leaving us alone with universal emptiness. Such emptiness can readily become the object of religious experience, in that it is the visage of the most Absolute, as it is turned toward us on this plane, or rather, as it is always averted. It is present in the world through its absence. It affirms itself through denial of all affirmations pertaining to itself. Peeling back is a device expressive of the contemporary religious need, culturally and geographically directed from West to East, from the positive forms of Epiphany to the empty forms manifesting pure Nothingness, as in Taoism and Buddhism.[24]

When reality lacks definition, art makes it strange; when it imposes an overactive intensity upon the person, art begins to remove it. Or, in the terms of information theory: if there is noise in the environment, the message must be enunciated very clearly; but if one and the same voice blares out of every loudspeaker, then it should be toned down by passing over its wave with a ripple and a splash. Conceptualism is the droning of our consciousness, which drowns out blaring voices and lets us be, at least briefly, in the quiet, to hear other, mysterious, barely audible sounds.

Soil of the Russian Avant-Garde

There is a commonly held opinion that in Russia, with its strong tradition of realistic literature and painting, avant-garde art had to be borrowed whole from the West and lacked firm soil in the native culture. Russia is, indeed, indebted to other cultures for many things, but this very indebtedness, however paradoxical it may seem, indicates Russia's organic inclination toward avant-garde thinking, which runs ahead to unestablished, impossible, non-existent territories.[25]

What went by the name of realism, especially in Soviet Russia of the thirties through the fifties, was, in fact, itself a derivative aesthetic, borrowed from various cultures of the past and perpetuating their preconceptions about reality and its proper representation. This involved an assortment of obligatorily connected elements: where there are cows, there must be a cowherd; where there is a sunset, there must be a rosy glow on the cowherd's face, and so on. Meanwhile, back in actuality, the cowherd's face was no more, having long since passed from the scene along with the cows, leaving only a "skeleton" crew and a "skeleton" herd, and the only thing that could still reflect the rosy glow of sunset was the hard, glinting hilt of the whip. In other words, any realism of the reality surrounding us was altogether forced out of art; instead, only a realism of long-past realities was allowed. In this given instance, realism became the foundation for illusionism.

The peculiarities of Russian civilization themselves provoke avant-garde thinking, which does not grow out of actuality, but, as it were, deducts certain elements from it and adds others until the system gets out of kilter. But if such an inorganic form of thought and action ever did become organic, it did so precisely in Russia, where actuality seems to lack a firm basis and constructs inventions capable of supplanting itself. A kind of "masochism" in our way of life led to a "sadism" of ideas.

Subordination to an assigned and, no doubt, beautiful and lofty idea has defined all of our literary, artistic, and scientific constructs, each of which was obliged to "teach," "build character," "instill morals," "strengthen," and "breathe-life-into." The quest for truth, creation of beauty, and enactment of the good were ideologized and made to serve the "idea," which was conceived as preceding everything else and setting the course for those cultural enterprises whose mission was to affirm the "idea" among the masses. The phases of what might be called the "conceptual dominant" of Russian culture may be traced through such a series of terms as "edification" and "good for the soul," "intentionality" and "the fantastical," "ideals" and "Utopias," "party loyalty" and "tendentiousness," "ideological spirit" and "devotion to the plan." In essence, it is the conception that comes to the fore and marches ahead of reality, like a proper avant-garde. Our avant-garde art is born of precisely this real-life avant-gardism that continually takes flight, leaving the native soil behind. Or, as soil for life's endeavors, these conceptions prove so unstable that the only structures they will support are castles in the air. Thus, "conceptualism" may be considered yet another term in the series of phases enumerated above, proceeding naturally, if not altogether organically, from the tendencies of Russian culture.

The one service that sets it apart from all previous forms of conceptuality, is that conceptualism becomes conscious of its own nature and advances itself for open observation, whereas "devotion to the plan" and "party loyalty" attempted to conceal the ideational nature of their constructs in an attempt to pass them off as properties of reality itself, as historical laws. Conceptuality is that stage in the development of "ideological spirit" at which there is no longer any question of passing off its projections as anything other than what they are. Instead, their forced and artificial, their counterfeit character, is blatantly exposed.

Conceptualism does not so much criticize a specific ideology as ideologism at large: as they leave reality behind, going off into an abstract-utopian distance, ideas gradually effect a concrete historical rupture by cutting life off at the roots. It is no simple matter to struggle against ideology while looking it straight in the eyes—its gaze is perfectly controlled and unblinking. Truth appears to be its staunch ally, as witnessed by such self-evident ideological statements as "we must struggle for peace" (who would oppose it?) and "study, study, study" (not at all a bad idea). How can you argue? You have to agree! But if we can only see these truths in their multiple conceptual refractions, their righteousness and power are reduced to those of automatic "magic" formulas.

Conceptualism does not quarrel with ideology's wonderful assertions;

rather, it fans their flame to the point that they go out by themselves. In this sense it constitutes a *continuation* and *transcendence* of all the utopian-ideological traditions of Russian culture. Contemporary conceptualism reproduces these traditions and casts them off, like Perseus's sly tool in his struggle against the Medusa. The mythological monster of our age flies high in Utopian guise but turns all living things to stone. Only by looking to the side, coming in close, and exposing the monster to an exact reflection of itself did Perseus win out. The all-comprehensive totalitarian Ideology cannot be defeated by another, better ideology, but by repetition of its own signs: this was conceptualism's principal discovery. Brave challengers from both the left and the right had tried to defy the Medusa but eventually stopped dead, bewitched by its power. The novelty was to use a mirror, not a sword, to conquer Ideology, bewitching it with its own reflection.

The epoch that is now typically called the "time of stagnation" actually manifested an internal dynamic of its own: life, indeed, came to a standstill as if frozen, but all the more brightly there shone through it and all the more sharply there protruded the same old ideas, now in the process of petrification, leading to an increasing stiffness, a flattening to one-dimensionality and self-reflection throughout society, a peeling back from the fabric of reality. It would be naive to attribute all of these half-idea/half-myths to sources of the past seventy years, be they official in character, like the "class struggle" and "classless society"; or quasi-official, like the "veneration of relics" and the "personality cult"; or even unofficial, like "nothing can be sold, but everything can be bought" and "nothing is allowed but everything is permitted." These ideas date back much farther. The simple fact that time had stopped during stagnation allowed us to see more clearly what had always been with us: the idea-engendering model of Russian national history stepped out of its temporal framework and ceased to propel history forward. History itself, driven to the end, finally refused to follow the idea's lead, and the iron bit brought in at the finish not a proud charger, but only his slinking shadow.

Let us trace briefly the evolution of "the steed" as a favorite literary symbol of Russia's headlong progress into a glorious future. In 1833, Pushkin asked, "Where are you galloping, proud steed, where do you set your swift hoof?" Even then one could detect a note of warning, a direct hint of cruel potentials, as "He raised Russia onto her hind legs." But Gogol's whirlwind steeds raced on in 1842, "straining their bronze chests," outstripping all foreign peoples and states. Dostoevsky had accurately scented the air by 1875, when he described Peter the Great's mount (in reference to the "Bronze horseman") as "a hotly breathing, hard-driven steed." But the more this erstwhile steed deteriorated into a nag, the greater was the desire to drive it to the bitter end: the rider is the Idea, the horse is our history. But who is holding the reins?[26]

"Let's drive the nag of history," was another old-style avant-garde battle cry of 1918, this time from the pen of Mayakovsky. Sixty years later, history finally collapsed on the shining summit, and only its ideas rode on, whooping and whistling, holding the stern whip on high. Indeed, something did come to an end at the very border post, 1980, where the third Communist Party program had promised the conclusion of all human prehistory and a decisive leap into the tsardom of communist freedom. History bared its own anatomy, its ideological skeleton that had once been obscured by luxuriant flesh. Then the bare bones began to dance, just as if unseen hands played a tattoo for them on a taut horseskin drum.

Thus dawned the conceptualist epoch. It becomes clear that the role of the contemporary avant-garde and of conceptualism in particular is to aid in the process of self-purification that Russian culture must undergo. The tendency toward avant-gardism in our sociopolitical history is both underlined and crossed out by avant-gardism in art. Finding itself on the same swampy soil where our "proud steed" set its swift hooves, avant-garde art pulls back from ideas and reaches for reality instead.

Conceptualism is the gloomy but gay funeral procession of all the ideas that tormented the soul of the people for centuries, with their mania for power, unity, victory, and obligatory happiness. But as it sends false faith down to defeat, conceptualism declines to utter its own. Without making any assertions about God, it acknowledges deviation from him. Deviation, failure, ignorance. This, in fact, is why one need not ask avant-garde art about its faith. It speaks of faith by rejecting the question.

CHAPTER 3 · After the Future: On the New Consciousness in Literature

From a Superfluous Person to a Superfluous World

The summer of 1989 through the summer of 1990 cannot possibly fit into the interval of a single year, and this is not only because it marks the passing of a decade, thereby opening ample space for generalizations and predictions. In the course of this year, our past and future have exchanged places. The principal problem posed by this year is no longer a (derivative) social or a political one, but rather an eschatological one: how to live after one's own future, or, if you like, after one's own death.

Suddenly it became evident that all possible and sufficient communism had already been achieved in our country and well within the promised time frame—by approximately 1980. The subsequent ten years were an attempt to rid ourselves of this oppressive fact—to put the triumph of communism somewhere further off, in order to retain at least a semblance of historical perspective, through a sequence of sociopolitical periods: "actual socialism," "developed socialism," "acceleration," and—the longest of all— "perestroika."

Nonetheless, with the quickening breath of imminent suffocation, it suddenly became clear that the end had already arrived. Historical perspective collapsed, and we felt ourselves carried off into some kind of Beyond. At the zenith of development, we crashed into the rear guard of all humanity: a communal-tribal structure in the thick of a civilization turned savage. And all the while, the same question: how to tame, how to domesticate this civilization gone wild, this premeditated barbarism?

Once again we experience the peculiar nausea associated with social concerns: What is to be done? This question, posed by the radical democratic writer Nikolai Chernyshevsky in 1863, was anticipated by that writer of the

people, Aleksandr Pushkin, in the latter's favorite verdict: "there's nothing
to be done." (The experts might count the number of times this expression
appears in *The Captain's Daughter* alone.) While everyone sought to outwit
all others in deciding what must be done, only Pushkin concisely disposed
of this false question, by showing that a man truly becomes himself and
matures morally when there is *nothing* to be done. But having escaped the
trap of historiography-biography, this man finds himself in a strange, to-
pologically inverted space, where there is no imminent horizon, no left or
right, front or rear. Despair forces him to taste the tea served up by Dostoevsky's underground man, beside the ruins of all the world's future crystal
palaces—when, meanwhile, there is no longer any light left in the world.[1]
An eschatologically pure Beyond has already opened up, tasteless, colorless, and soundless. To paraphrase Mandelshtam, the word is in delirium
amid transparent graves.[2]

In 1989, Victor Erofeev cast his paper "The Wake for Soviet Literature," in
the optimistic genre of a celebratory epitaph. But it must be noted that the
bell tolls for all those who remain alive; the word "Soviet," with its gloomy,
owl-like, sepulchral symbolism, does not depart from the lexicon, but extends itself far and wide: institutions of power and everyday mores become
not less, but more and more "Soviet." And it is not in spite of, but rather
because of this, that one feels a growing sense of the gaping grave and
a widespread shamelessness at the festival of the dead: "Bobok! Bobok!
Bobok!"[3] is heard on all sides. Everyone is overcome by a sense of ultimate
outrage; not only do people revel in the excess of insanity and hopelessness,
but the very image of the world seems to be passing away. Or, as they joke in
the streets of Moscow, we are witnessing apocalypse in a single country.[4]

This is why, in reflecting on the literature of the recent period, one wants
to pause precisely on the category of "the last." It may well turn out that
history will once again close up in waves around the realm of the beyond.
Yet the eternal island of Patmos is currently populated as never before, since
it encompasses a sixth of the entire earth.[5] "The Last" cannot be defined in
terms of the category of time: it is *after* time, and remains last even if the
flow of history is eventually renewed. The new literature is "of the last," not
so much because it has appeared at this point in time, as because of its own
essential "beyondness." Devoid of signs of time, it is precisely this literature
that is now perceived as genuinely contemporary.

Above all, this literature has no attachment to the image of this world, or
to attempts to re-create it. One image of the "last" or "final" phase of world
history is that of the Antichrist—and all so-called anti-totalitarian prose

gravitates toward this image, framed in terms of the coordinates of historical time and space. In the works of Grossman, Bek, Dudintsev, Rybakov, as well as their lesser-known followers,[6] the Antichrist is the overt subject, along with the soldiers and marshals of his army, and the suffering of his victims. Yet with the Antichrist, history ends and we enter a region where structures dissipate, and reality evaporates; the lyrico-epic imagery, which functioned to exalt and then to expose the Antichrist, has also been exhausted. Along with the reality it studiously reflected, literature loses the representational quality common to both "socialist realism" and "social criticism" (of Solzhenitsyn's type): this is the first distinction between a "last" literature and the previous, realistic style. A last literature is dishonorable and arbitrary: like Proteus, it is capable of almost anything; like Narcissus, it desires only itself.

Another distinction: it becomes impossible for a last literature to work in an "anti-" genre, whether antitotalitarian, anti-utopian, anticommunist, or antimilitarist. Literature finds itself in the beyond, without a top or a bottom, without a left or a right; any orientation "for" or "against" is entirely alien. This is a tired literature that would like "to fall asleep like this forever," regretting nothing, desiring nothing.

Finally, there is no longer any positive backdrop against which a last literature might be contrasted. Even the notion of apocalypse fails to yield the alarming, catastrophic mindset with which one could awaken the conscience of a slumbering generation, or presage an ominous future to an unrepentant people. Today's Patmos is devoid of all pathos and is more akin to a tea party in Chekhov than in Dostoevsky. Black humor, absurdity, a surreal act, futuristic shock—at one time, these were symptoms of revolt *against:* against one's environment, gluttony, reason, well-being. In our last literature, the beyond is akin to indifference, so equally otherworldly is everything in this, the most impossible of worlds.

Not long ago, in the spirit of classical traditions, Soviet Russian literature was preoccupied with the tragedy of superfluous people who felt alien to the world of socially useful homogeneity: this was the grand theme of the best writers, from Iury Olesha to Andrei Bitov.[7] But the Kavalerovs and the Odoevtsevs—those enfeebled descendants of the Onegins and Pechorins— had actually become extinct in the Soviet world.[8] This is not because that world had assimilated and consumed them for its own purposes—as might still have been feared not so very long ago. No, the surrounding world itself had become so completely superfluous that the superfluousness of an individual had become a trait of widespread general indifference. It is impossible to stand out or be ennobled by superfluousness when one is surrounded by rootless things, nonrepayable money, maladapted dwellings, and unpassable roads. Superfluous people stand in lines and crowd into packs, but this does not enable them to take root in existence; on the contrary, existence itself becomes transparently peopleless and superfluous.

Somnambulism is the last phase in this course of development. "It is only the appearance of us that is left," writes contemporary author Valeria Narbikova, whose novella is called just that, *The Appearance of Us*. Somnambulists are predominant in a last literature: characters who have not managed to accomplish anything or think anything through, who immediately drown in apocalyptic fog. We may recall the stories of Tatiana Tolstaia—"Peters," "The Circle," "The Okkerville River"—about the fates of people who are not simply failures, but who no longer count: failure would even be a reward, a status of some sort. At times such people are aggressive, they strive, bustle, acquire, but all the same somehow manage to be absent from life: touch their shoulder, give them a good shake, and they won't even notice. It is as if all their activity comes from some lunar magic, while on earth they have already long been asleep, whether blissful or troubled. "Night blows in his sleeping face," is said about a running man in Tolstaia's "Sleepwalker in the Fog." Such is our present race along impassable paths: this terrifying, involuntary acceleration, not by the strength of our legs, but as if drawn to a rupture in the soil, an attraction to imminent voids. "Could it really be that he won't make it to the light?" The kind of light that is meant here—after the pitch-dark and the black void—needs no explanation. A dying man dreams of resurrection.

While it has often been edged out by the intellectual version, the "grassroots" type of Russian restlessness (rootlessness) has changed in precisely the same way. I am referring to those eccentric rustics of our recent literature, who derive from Turgenev's Kalinych and Leskov's "enchanted wanderer." Shukshin's "oddballs" (*chudiki*) were their much-loved recent incarnation.[9] One cannot describe them, in Herzen's words,[10] as "intelligent superfluities," rather, they are "naive," manifesting a kind of dislocation of the mind, maladjusted to the proficient existence of the majority, causing them to rummage for inconceivable and vanished essences: "So what's the purpose of the state?" "So why is the *troika*-Russia ruled by a dead soul?" "So why don't people reply to 'hello'?" Such sweet, sincere insanity, where the sentimental-humanist hope for "embrace, you millions" coexists with a holy fool's inversion of values and a desire to pinch as painfully as possible whoever happens to be nearby, for the sake of their spiritual good and useful edification.

And so this instructive oddball has somehow filtered out of our literature, having first been transformed into Yuz Aleshkovsky's sincere cynics, like sperm from a dying man, still inclined to multiply the social organism. In comparing, for example, the characters of Shukshin and Evgeny Popov (who, in his Siberian bluntness and a wildernesslike freshness of thought, had been proclaimed the former's young successor about fifteen years ago), one sees how a type once familiar to us is transfigured from an oddball into a screwball.[11] Once-appealing cleverness freezes on the flushed face of "such a guy" like the splattered grimace of a social cretin.

We have not yet fully appreciated or examined this powerful manifestation of the screwball in our literature of the eighties, which is comparable to the role of the oddball during the sixties. The latter takes leave of social reason, even while promising its future renewal. He represents an individual departure from overconstricted forms of social life—the hero of our sincere, confessional, exposé prose and poetry of the sixties and early seventies, with its officially approved or semi-approved nonconformism, its romantic prickling of the eyes from the smoke of the taiga and from hidden thoughts. The screwball is also meditative at times, to the point of an aching brain, and also departs from the norms of common sense; this is no longer an individual characteristic, however, but evidence of a collective being that has strayed from the path of reason and history. The oddball is an individual challenge to general common sense; the screwball is an image of societal madness. The screwball-vacationer will confide to you on a suburban train that in his basement he has the sack in which either Goebbels or Bukharin was hanged. The screwball-orator believes in an invisible source that radiates psychophysical waves of Zionism throughout the world, and demands international legal protection from such microwave interference in the minds of his compatriots. The screwball-people-lover takes an overaged idiot into his home for reeducation and then complains that his wife has had an abortion from the first love of his smitten charge.

There is no need to recount such ubiquitous plots: many of them may be found in prose works of the 1970s and eighties by Evgeny Popov, Victor Erofeev, and Viacheslav Pietsukh. In all of them, foolishness degenerates from a charming bit of cleverness to a joke of the Clever One (devil). The screwball is possessed by his own significance as a social being; this is an inanity from which the core of individual existence is removed. Neither superfluous people, nor enchanted wanderers remain in this world that has become extraneous to itself.

Conflicts of Styles

The current literary situation is often reduced to the opposition of two camps: the Right and the Left, the "grassroots" (*pochvenniki*) and the "Westernizers," or the "nativists" (*samobytniki*) and the "liberals." While this conflict has been heating up since the mid-1960s, it has recently reached the blinding intensity of a civil war. The polemic is so manifest as to require little commentary. The public positions of representatives of the two sides, for example, poets Vitaly Korotich and Stanislav Kuniaev, or novelists Grigory Baklanov and Iury Bondarev, are diametrically opposed, but become almost identical at the level of style. "Social concern," "duty to the people," "anguish for one's country," "the confession of guilt," "honest prose," "the truth of history," "the choice of a path"—such terms are used by feisty critics of the right as well as the left, and seem to be quite sufficient for understanding the work of the above-mentioned writers. They characterize a certain kind of moralizing literature, and within its context they are irreconcilably opposed.

Yet as early as the mid-seventies, a new generation began to emerge that was entirely indifferent to this struggle—or, to be more accurate, that has accepted its political, though hardly its aesthetic meaning. The "sixtyish" conception of literature as a social tribune or moral homily is utterly foreign to the new generation, which reached maturity during the eighties. It is not so much that this generation would remain haughtily above the fray, but, while close to the liberals in politics, they are nevertheless alienated from the aesthetics of "spiritual usefulness" and "lifelikeness." The "Village Writers" and "populists," with their naive experiments in mythologizing the age-old ways of the common people's life, are equally foreign to the new writers.

The generation of the eighties has splits of its own, which are barely perceptible to a broader reading public, because they are devoid of moral and political coloration. Two poles or extremes stand out, toward which, in one way or another, the writers of the "new wave" tend to gravitate. One of these is metarealism: an art of metaphysical revelations, striving for realities of the highest order, which begin to show through the thinning fabric of history. Or is this the maturity of time itself, which has come to the harvest of meanings in earnest, when God, as prophesied, would become everything in everything, no longer demanding separate prayer and seclusion in the temple?[12]

The other movement, or the other extreme of contemporary movements, is commonly called conceptualism. Here, linguistic signs do not strive for a fullness of meaning; on the contrary, they reveal the vacuousness of their essence, their freedom from the signified. Conceptualism, which emerged as an artistic movement in the West at the end of the 1960s, acquired a second homeland in the Soviet Russia of the seventies and eighties, where by this time ideological consciousness had decomposed into a rich collection of empty fictions and hollowed-out structures.

Represented by the works of Ilya Kabakov, Dmitry Prigov, Lev Rubinshtein, Timur Kibirov, Mikhail Sukhotin, and Arkady Bartov, conceptualism did not limit itself to playing with the signs of Soviet civilization—though these signs supplied it with examples of linguistic emptiness that began to spread to the languages of other eras and cultures. Thus, the prose writer Vladimir Sorokin creates a kind of cliché of the Russian psychological and realist novel of the nineteenth century—in a work of great size that is called just that: *Roman* (Novel)—which is also the protagonist's first name. Imagine them incarnated as a single artistic figure, "the nineteenth-century Russian writer": Turgenev, Goncharov, Leo Tolstoy and Chekhov together could have collaborated on this novel. "The nineteenth-century Russian novel" exists as a generalized reality, at least in the consciousness of readers and scholars, and this conceptualist writer undertook the task of reconstructing it as a single text. The creative synthesis is based on a preliminary, literary-critical analysis that identifies the common characteristics—the conceptual core—of many Russian novels.

What is the point of such an obviously derivative production of texts, based upon already-known linguistic models? This is in fact the point: Sorokin's novel is read like a work about language: language that exists by itself, independently of the reality it describes. The reader's consciousness glides over a number of signifiers: nature is described this way, a country estate that way, and here is the way to describe a young lady's face when she is in love. The effect is completely different from that of reading Tolstoy or Turgenev, where signs are more or less transparent and direct us to the signified, in order to evoke specific feelings, thoughts, motivations. Conceptualism separates signifiers from the signified and demonstrates the illusory quality of the latter.

Between conceptualism and metarealism there are many intermediate stages, many stylistic zones that may only be briefly outlined here. Thus, in poetry the "polystylistics" of Alexander Eremenko stands out, based on sharp linguistic splicing and the dissonances of the street, the forest, the laboratory; the social, the natural, and the technological. The seams and sutures between different aesthetic layers, between the highbrow and the colloquial, are themselves aestheticized. The extremes of metarealism and conceptualism are mediated in prose by a grotesquely fragmented manner of writing, which we find, for instance, in Victor Erofeev's novel *The Russian Beauty,* as well as in his short stories. For Erofeev, archetypes fished out from the depths of Russian history turn out, upon verification, to be divergent schemes in a field of ironic linguistic games, whereas the vulgar stereotypes of everyday Soviet life suddenly acquire depth and merge with projections of other epochs into an ample mythopoeic polyglossia.

The opposition or copresence of these stylistic extremes is observable not only in literature, but in painting, which leads to an internal dialogical (or even duel-like) tension between such artists as Ilya Kabakov and Mikhail Shvartsman in Russia, or Vitaly Komar, Alexander Melamid, and Mikhail Shemiakin in the Russian emigration. Despite all the intensity of arguments that reject conceptualism and metarealism, respectively, as a "cheap parody and a tongue stuck out at obsolete totalitarianism," and as a "vulgar attempt to create the imperishable through bypassing modernity"; despite the polarization of such reproaches, the relatedness of these two extremes of the new artistic consciousness is beyond doubt. One of them reveals the passing of the world's image, as well as all of its symbolic, "hierarchic" signifiers; the other seeks to reveal a new heaven and a new earth in the fullness of "hieratic" supersignifications.

Thus, there emerges a parallelogram of forces in contemporary literature. The opposition of liberal and nationalist positions forms one axis, where contemporary journalistic literature coexists with the artistry of a moral-historic pathos. But this opposition is in turn opposed to quite a different pairing between conceptualism and metarealism. The problematic of these two axial collisions, and the direction of their internal arguments turn out to be on such different planes that open conflict between them may not occur. The grassroots group automatically counts all metarealists and conceptualists as opponents, denouncing them precisely as liberal. Meanwhile, the liberals embrace neither of them, because of their lack of moral orientation or their failure to engage in current ideosocial battles. For their own part, while personally more committed to liberal values, the metarealists and conceptualists nonetheless see almost nothing in those values that could inspire them and that their work could serve.

The Cyclical Development of Literature

This entire game of mutual enmity—or simply misunderstanding—was not invented yesterday, of course: it is consistent with the laws and cycles of development of Russian literature and may be grasped only within their context. For all the uniqueness of the current stage, it can nonetheless be said that, "everything had been there in the olden days, everything will be repeated again, and sweet is only the moment of recognition" (Mandelshtam again). If we pause on this sweet moment of recognition, a kind of periodic table of the elements of Russian literature takes shape before us.

What did Russian literature begin with in the Modern Age, when it awoke from the Middle Ages? Before that, there was not any literature to speak of, and what there was merged with various serviceable types of writing (quotidian, didactic, scholarly, edifying, etc.). The new Russian literature begins with social and civil service, which in its first period, in the eighteenth century, is called classicism. Kantemir with his satires, Lomonosov with his odes, Fonvizin with his comedies, Radishchev with his revolutionary sermons—they are all in the service of the goals of the state, the good of the fatherland, the education of its worthy sons. Literature spreads out horizontally, addressing the consciousness of the reader-citizen, enlightening him with models of virtue and vice.

But then, as if reflecting some general law of creative development, Russian literature shifts from a social phase to a moral one. Individuality—its feelings and needs, its tears and tenderness—comes to the forefront. It was in this way that sentimentalism emerged, having undermined the dominance of social norms and criteria. Lomonosov gives way to Karamzin; the horizontal social plan narrows to a single point: the individual, who is entirely directed toward himself.

The next phase—the religious—is designated by a romantic tendency and associated with the name of Vasily Zhukovsky. Once again, the point extends into a line but is no longer directed toward the social plane; rather it is a vertical, metaphysical line. The individual discovers his kinship with the superindividual, the otherworldly, the absolute. Poetry takes on a myth-making function, offers revelations from above, the expression of the inexpressible, longing for the Ideal, creation of the Temple.

Finally, with the appearance of its own norm and power, art closes in on itself. The vertical contracts, though now it is not to a point, but to a circle: art exists not for the sake of the ascent to an external absolute. It is an absolute in itself, a language that speaks about the possibilities of language.

In Russian literature, this is the phenomenon of Pushkin and the school of "harmonious exactness" that he founded. At this point, art's other objectives—the service of society or morality—are done away with. In Pushkin's words, "Poetry is higher than morality, or it is something else altogether"; the artist is his own highest judge. According to Belinsky's accurate observation, the main thrust of Pushkin's work is its artistic quality: that which was once taken as a means—artistry—becomes an end in itself.

With Pushkin, the first cycle of the development of Russian literature is completed: having moved from the horizontal, through the single point and the vertical, it returns, in the circle, to itself, to literariness as such.

Then a new cycle begins, with the proclamation of those same ideas of social responsibility in heated polemics with the previous "schools," romantic as well as aesthetic. Belinsky ridiculed the epigones of romanticism, and Pisarev raised his hand even against Pushkin. The first phase of the new cycle, Gogol's "natural school," is to be seen as a "relentless exposure of the sores of social reality." Then there developed the physiological sketch, the denunciatory, or social critical, novel, "realism" and "nihilism," revolutionary-democratic criticism, homage to the criterion of practical good, and the reestablishment of Radishchev and Fonvizin's socially enlightening tendency in literature.

But the social function of art does not satisfy the greatest writers; already in the early work of Tolstoy and Dostoevsky the moral-psychological imperative begins to predominate: not types, but individuals, the "dialectic of the soul" and "the freshness of moral feeling" (Chernyshevsky on Tolstoy). These impulses serve to reconstitute the sentimental phase in the second cycle of literary development, marked by the obvious influence of Schiller on Dostoevsky and of Rousseau on Tolstoy. In fact, to the very end, all of Tolstoy's work remains fundamentally moralistic; its goal is to exert a direct emotional effect upon the reader, to "infect the reader with the writer's feelings" (as Tolstoy put it in his treatise *What is Art?*). And, in one way or another, the majority of Russian writers of the second half of the nineteenth century endeavored to come to terms with the same problem—the education of the soul, moral enlightenment, the awakening of conscience—from the revolutionary-populist moralism of Nekrasov and Nadson to the humanist-individual moralism of Chekhov, Garshin and Korolenko.

But already in Dostoevsky's work, Russian literature began to move into its next phase, the religious, which sees the world constructed along a vertical line, extending from heights to abysses. The religious function of literature was conclusively established by Vladimir Soloviev and his followers in

Russian symbolism,[13] which was directly inspired by the legacy of romanticism (as Blok was inspired by Zhukovsky). Language became allusive, a kind of initiation into the secrets of higher worlds. Art became theurgy, that is, the transformation of existence in God's image; and all artistic-philosophical thinking of the beginning of the century moved in this current, from Merezhkovsky to Berdiaev and Florensky, from Andrei Bely to Viacheslav Ivanov.

Yet this cycle was also destined to close with an aesthetic phase. The increased critical attacks on symbolism accused the latter of disembodying and mystifying art, of turning it into myth and cryptography, whereas the task should be to return it to a magical plasticity, to language as such. This problem was addressed in a variety of ways in postsymbolist movements: acmeism, futurism, and imagism all derived from the self-sufficient worth of the artistic vision. "Sublime clarity," "the self-sufficient word," "language art," "form as organism," "the image as an end in itself": all this brought literature along the new spiral, back to the work "as such." The formalist school of literary criticism also contributed to this trend, by conceiving of art as device.

Thus, having passed through the same four phases—the social, the moral, the religious, and the aesthetic—Russian literature ended its second cycle of development.

The third cycle corresponds to the Soviet era and coincides with its boundaries. Yet it seems that even if there had been no Bolshevism or October Revolution, literature would still have entered yet another cycle beginning with the horizontal, by posing social tasks and proclaiming a social mandate: proletarian culture, class loyalty, party loyalty, and the social face of the writer. After all, the cycles of the eighteenth and nineteenth centuries began in a similar way. Why should the twentieth century be an exception? While there would not have been killings of disobedient writers, there would still have been murderous condemnations of works diverging from the horizontal or lapsing into the previous phases of development, into a circle or a vertical. It is characteristic that the first phase of a new cycle is merciless with respect to the latter two phases of the previous cycle (the religious and the aesthetic)—summarily lumping them together as "decadence"—while adopting the first two (the social and the moral) and recovering them as part of its "classical heritage." Gogol and Tolstoy are revered, while Vladimir Soloviev and Nikolai Gumilev are devalorized or silenced. The social phase is lengthy: from the mid-twenties through the mid-fifties, and it is quite natural that, like the initial phase of the first cycle, one critic

(Andrei Siniavsky) called it "socialist *classicism.*" It is hardly necessary to list the greats of this period: beginning with Gorky and Mayakovsky, they were listed in all the textbooks—and quite deservedly so—as the "classics of Soviet literature."

But then, from the mid-1950s, from the period of the post-Stalin thaw, warming the soul and softening the heart, the second phase began, and it would be difficult to find a better name for it than "socialist sentimental-ism." Once again rigid classical canons come under critique; "sociologism" begins to seem "vulgar" and is rejected in favor of moral approaches based on the individual "soul" and "conscience." The unique human individual is the center of attention. "There are no uninteresting people in this world": this was Evgeny Evtushenko's credo, one of the founders of this new senti-mentalism. This credo could only be compared to Karamzin's immortal: "peasant women also know how to love." Once again we find images of "little people": tailors and stockingmakers, instead of generals and warriors. The principal demand made of literature is sincerity, arousal of feeling, confession. The principal direction—that of "moral searchings"—continued almost through the mid-eighties, already without hope of any findings. Voz-nesensky, Okudzhava, Aksyonov, Andrei Bitov, Iury Kazakov, Iury Tri-fonov—all of them were formed by this principal direction, regardless of the paths they were to choose later. "Variety-hall poetry," "confessional prose," "urban prose," "the urban romance"—these were the signposts and mile-stones of the "sentimental education" of our literature in the fifties and sixties. And it was here that a second, mature period of the same movement came to replace youthful reverie: Solzhenitsyn's stern sermons on moral cleansing: "to live not by lies." Also there were Tvardovsky, *Novyi mir,* the poetics of bitter truth and the tortured conscience.

But literature moves on and, following some unknown law, once again makes the transition from a moral stage to a religious one, constructing a vertical metaphysical line over the single point of the moral individual. Chronologically, perhaps the end of the "Prague spring" and of *Novyi mir* marked this transition most clearly. Above all, this was telling in the case of Solzhenitsyn himself, in his personal transition from "moral socialism" to Christianity. Morality was exhausted as a sovereign force, a humanist im-pulse, and a "conscience without God."

Several periods may be distinguished in this metaphysical phase of our literature. The earliest was the phase of "quiet poetry" and "rural prose," with their initial sense of resignation, the abdication of the "I," the embracing of age-old ways of life. But this religiosity is still of a naive, archaic, almost pagan model, with its cult of the earth, of nature, and of national roots. In its Orthodox version, it tends toward ritualization, and sacralization of the folk traditions of everyday life. Then came the turn to mythologism, no longer so morally bound and sermonizing, freely playing through the abysses and cliffs of the spirit, with the exoticism of Eastern religions and other esoterica: reincarnation, spells, demonic delusions, descent into the wells of times and spaces. Iury Kuznetsov emerged in poetry, while in prose it was Anatoly Kim and Iury Mamleev, with their "fantastic realism." Chingiz Aitmatov traversed the same path from the moral tone of his early works to the metaphysical overload of his later ones.

Finally, the third and culturally the most highly developed layer of this neoromantic movement comprises what we have already described as meta-realism: the poetry and prose of Olga Sedakova, Victor Krivulin, Ivan Zhdanov, Elena Shwarts—and also, in a different way, of Tatiana Tolstaia and Mikhail Kuraev. In their work there is less of the color and drunkenness of myth, and more a sobering and intense peering into the transparent outlines of things, the ascent up the staircases of cultural parallels, entering into aborted embryos of cultures, their eternal archetypes. The conflict between reality and superreality becomes ironically acute, as in Tolstaia, or washed in gnostic tones, as in Zhdanov; in both cases, however, analogies with the two previous "vertical" epochs in Russian literature suggest themselves.

Further on, as experience would suggest, literature is "rounded off," as it enters the last phase: the aesthetic, where it becomes an encyclopedia of the possibilities of literature, a collection of signs and a crossing of languages. The epoch of conceptualism arrives, when the mystical winds from the seventies begin to be perceived as the rotten fogs of the stagnation era, as the bequeathed "imperishables" of decayed and languishing souls. The word "vulgar" now clings to the preceding phases: if the metaphysicians deemed vulgar the *moralism* of the "sixties generation," who in their turn had condemned "vulgar sociologism," then the conceptualists find vulgar any kind of *mythologism* or metaphysical constructions. Language is free from the sin of content and must continue to purify itself, as it enters the zone of silence.

A striking feature of the new aestheticism is, in fact, its anti-aestheticism, which, in a sense, finds a parallel phase in the experiments of the futurists. The difference is that the futurists put great emphasis on the "trans-sense," or nonrational, sound of words, their majestic ugliness, while conceptualism tends toward humble squalor. Whereas Kruchenykh youthfully thundered the nonsense words "dyr bul shchil ubeshchur," Vsevolod Nekrasov's verse becomes senile, muttering: "that is, thus is it / this is what it is."[14] Language is ashamed of its chattiness and seeks to hide deeper inside the oral cavity, even at the cost of stuttering and lisping.[15] Language has come up with so many monstrosities in the twentieth century, it has told so many deadly lies, that now it wants to forget itself and go to sleep, like speech as one dozes off.

The recent aesthetic phase cannot be reduced to conceptualism alone, which is but its "lower" stratum, while a "higher" one exists as well: not anti-, but indeed aesthetic. Alongside futurism there was acmeism. Likewise, the concluding phase of the current cycle includes prose and poetry that appear to be purely phenomenal, cleansed not only of social, moral, and religious tasks, but also of conceptual minus-contents. Sensitivity is elevated to an attribute of the artist's supreme virtue: vision, hearing, touch—that is, all that would return aesthetics to itself, as a discipline of *sensitivity* (in the literal sense of the word "aesthetics"). In the work of Joseph Brodsky, one can sense a transition from the metarealism of his early collections to the phenomenalism of his later ones—not even so much a transition in and of itself as a retention and dynamic parity of the two different components. It is as if language does away with metaphysical aims through its own logic and finely honed syntax, though this is restored precisely because of the transparency of the syntax, which cannot but philosophize about the object in space—with noun cases and verb endings. In his best verses, Brodsky's world is ideally surface-based: it is depth turned inside out, in such a way that not a single grain of matter, not a single step upward or outward separates metaphysics from physics and physiology.

This phenomenalism, a poetics of the pure *presence*[16] of the object on the iris of the eye and on the tips of the fingers, is developed in the prose of Sasha Sokolov and Sergei Iurenen, in the poetry of Aleksei Parshchikov and Ilya Kutik. True, for the latter two, the logic of sensitivity, the "figure of intuition" and the "pentathalon of the senses" (the titles of Parshchikov's and Kutik's collections) become apparent not so much in the forms of metaphysics as in those of science, technology, or sport, as thought concretely applied, in terms of the devices for mastering the object and mapping out space. Generally, the transformation of the word into a term-metaphor is characteristic of phenomenalism, its appeal consisting of its dry visual precision, blocked off from both the metarealist "overflow" of meanings and from the conceptual "ebb tide." It is as if phenomenalism is deployed in a middle zone between myth and parody, between metaphysical seriousness and linguistic mischief, upon a surface that lies between the depth of the object and the comic inversion of this depth.

I think that in the literature of the émigré community this aesthetic middle is more fully represented than at home, where it is pushed aside by the extremes of metarealism and conceptualism, mystical enthusiasm, and quasi-nihilist grotesque. In general, emigration itself—whether external or internal—is conducive to the presentation of objects as phenomena, whose ulterior, substantive nature is concealed and covered in haze, like the motherland that has been left behind. It was Nabokov—today perceived in Russia as the freshest news and the principal writer of his time—who emerged as the precursor of this amazingly deep, surface writing. And on the whole, in being spatially removed, the emigration has been remarkably successful in lagging behind in the phases of time. It seems as if for seventy years, from Ivan Bunin to Sasha Sokolov, it has been preparing for the concluding, aesthetic phase—for merging with the principal course of the current, not just anywhere, but precisely at the mouth, right before it falls into the next and still unknown cycle.

It is possible, however, to surmise that the fourth cycle will also begin with a phase that will be strikingly social, whose anticipation took shape within the depths of glasnost, although they could just as well have come into being without it, without any jolts from the outside. Having exhausted the circuitous and self-sufficient aesthetic model, literature again finds itself at the mercy of the horizontal. Such is its inevitable destiny. What is to be done? There is nothing to be done.

Thus, the rectangle of forces considered in the preceding section is now revealed as the predetermined coexistence and rivalry of different phases of the development of Russian literature: the moral-humanist, the national-pagan, the religious-metaphysical, and the aesthetic-conceptual. In order that all of this not be confused in the reader's mind, we may introduce the promised table of the cyclical development of Russian literature, insisting upon its approximateness. The columns are drawn in a highly provisional manner; on more careful examination, they would turn into painting, where each individual phenomenon would be a spot of color, a brushstroke across all straight lines.

The most significant thing to note is the way in which the regular progression of the four phases in the historical movement of literature (horizontally) leads to steady repetition and correspondence through all three cycles

Table 1　Periodic Table of the New Russian Literature (The Cycles and Phases of Development)

	Phases	
	Social (the horizontal)	Moral (the single point)
Cycle 1 1730–1840	Classicism. The honor of nobility. Civic valor. Service to the homeland. Obligation toward society.	Sentimentalism. The distinct individual. The inner world. Sincerity, earnestness. Edification. Moral usefulness.
Cycle 2 1840–1920	Critical realism. The natural school. The physiological sketch. The denunciatory tendency. Social usefulness. Revolutionary democracy.	The new sentimentalism. Psychologism. Self-analysis. The "dialectic of the soul" and the "freshness of moral sensibility." Conscience. Guilt. Repentance. Denunciation of falsehood and vulgarity.
Cycle 3 1920–90	Proletkult. The music of the Revolution. The social order. The pen as a bayonet. Popular loyalty, class loyalty, party loyalty. Socialist realism. The hero as a fighter and a creator. Upbringing of workers in the spirit of socialism.	Socialist sentimentalism. Sincerity. Confessional prose. The poetry of the bared "I." The freshness of feelings. Self-expression. "We aren't screws." Moral searching. "To live not by lies." Conscience. Guilt. Repentance.
Cycle 4 1990–?	The new sociality. Metapolitics: the play with the signs of various politics. The synthesis of politics, literature, and theater.	?

Religious (the vertical)	Aesthetic (the circle)
Romanticism. The superindividual, the beyond, the inexpressable. "There," "in that direction." The pining for the heavens.	The pathos of the artistic. Harmonious exactness. "Poetry above morality." "We are born for inspiration."
Fantastic realism. Symbolism. Art as theurgy. Production of myth. The world's soul. Signs of ascent. The mysteries of other worlds.	Acmeism. Futurism. Imaginism. Sublime clarity. The self-spun word. Image-creation. The creation of a new language. Art as a device.
Neo-romanticism. (1) "Village prose" and "quiet" poetry. Humbleness. The grassroots. The people. The national roots. The fathers' faith. (2) Mythologism. Fantastic realism. The parable. Reincarnation. Werewolves. Doubles. (3) Metarealism. Sobering. Contemplation. The religious content of culture.	(1) Phenomenalism. The metaphysics and plasticity of language. The logic of sensitivity. Things as they are. Surface = depth. Terms = metaphors. (2) Conceptualism. The play with empty language. Signifiers over and above the signified. Schemas and skeletons of culture. The concept as a work of art. (3) The rear guard. Zero-degree writing. The dust and garbage of culture. Decentering. Entropy. Language as it is.
?	?

(vertically). A "sweet moment" of recognition is afforded in the vertical columns, where Lomonosov is somehow revealed in Mayakovsky; Zhukovsky in Blok, and Karamzin, perhaps, in Evtushenko.

The Arrière-garde

It is possible to anticipate the beginning of a new cycle, and in it, the beginning phase of a social and even a (multi)party literature. It seems, however, that this would be a different kind of sociality, intermixed with play and carnival, one that would recognize the art of politics—and, therefore, politics as a kind of art. This metapolitics, which freely plays with the signs of different political positions (left, right, centrist . . .), has already made itself manifest in the activity of the new politicians; thus, significantly, it may be seen as literary-artistic. The politicians use words in ways that cannot be taken literally, but more often than not—in an opposite, dislocated, or figurative sense—as the interplay of mutually exclusive viewpoints. It may be objected that Brezhnev's and Stalin's speeches could not be trusted either, but a lie that renounces reality is hardly the same thing as play that produces this reality. Today reality is so well known to everyone that there is no point in efforts to conceal it. The politicians' speeches contain not so much lies as the free play of signifiers and signifieds, as was first clearly suggested in Gorbachev's utterances. For example, a resolute protest against the existence of the post of the president may in fact signify the establishment of that post three months later and its occupation by precisely the figure who protested against it. A refusal to abolish the party monopoly could signify the readiness of the decision to renounce this monopoly. Words and actions do not correspond to one another, but rather enter into a free dialogue, which may be seen as a symptom of the synthesis of different arts (politics-literature-theater).

Now one begins to understand some literary critics' laments about the disappearance of the literary process in the recent period: new works seem to appear, but they do not constitute a process, an independent dynamic. Above all, what sort of literary process can there be with the simultaneous entrance into literature of the four Evangelists, Peter Chaadaev, Vasily Rozanov, James Joyce, Alexander Solzhenitsyn, and the thirty-year-old neoconceptualists? Instead of a process in the conventional sense (that is, as a linear succession of events), we are faced with a space of some kind that has many entrances and exits: Nabokov arrives, Fadeev departs; someone who had first come in through one entrance, now enters through another—as, for example, Gorky or Tvardovsky. Everything that happened at different times in the past, is now taking place at the same time: it is difficult to extract one thread of wax from this buzzing multicelled hive.

Moreover, the literary process departs from literature into nonliterature: into politics, philosophy, religion, culture in general. Previously literature, like a shared bathroom or a communal apartment, combined all missions, all goals; it was the sacred vocation of all types of projects. Now, having caught the scent of freedom, all of these aims leave the fray of literature to occupy their own living spaces and divided spheres of influence. What then, is left for a literature that is no longer either politics, religion, or philosophy? It is left with language, a kind of minimum and final bastion where it stipulates the terms of its capitulation.

Thus emerges the most contemporary literary phenomenon of recent times: It may be designated "the arrière-garde." Whether consciously or not, almost all of the emerging young literature has to do with this arrière-garde. It may be conceded to those who like classifications (including this author) that the arrière-garde is the last variation of the last cycle of our literary development. Having passed through the strata of phenomenalism and conceptualism, the aesthetic phase now exits into the rear guard of all art, where it is sustained by the barest minimum before it must break down and give way to the cruder and fresher forces of a new socialization.

What is it that constitutes the rear guard as a kind of last outlook? Contemporary aesthetics is equally weary of both "realistically" corresponding to reality and "avant-gardely" anticipating it. Reality turns out to be somewhere ahead, rapidly changing according to its own historical laws, while literature brings up the rear, noting and sweeping up everything along the way—though already as historical rubbish, as the disintegrating layers of reality. Having begun with the avant-garde, the art of this century ends with the arrière-garde. The avant-garde vigorously promoted new forms, technical devices, strictly organizing material into specifically designated constructions, doing away with the past out of love for the future: this is the way it had to be when the young century was lunging forward in predatory leaps. Now, on the verge of its last gasp, this century values an art of amorphousness—not of exacting experimentation, but of an all-encompassing and accepting bottom, the last gurgling crater into which the overdone excrements of the earlier majestic forms and grandiose ideas are to fall.

Garbage and excrement: this is the overarching metaphor in the art of the end. "No, but is this really life? This isn't life, it's fecal waters, a whirlpool of slops, a collapse of the heart. The world is plunged into darkness and is renounced by God" (from Venedikt Erofeev's *Vasily Rozanov through the Eyes of an Eccentric*). In the so-called parallel (arrière-garde) cinema, shots of people smearing themselves and each other with feces constantly flash by: a parody of the gesture with which at the beginning of the century people anointed each other for the kingdom, in the holy war of utopias and ideas. Forms that have become overripe and rotten in reality, and henceforth rejected by it, constitute the fertile, "manured" layer of the contemporary arrière-garde. Here one may add so-called necrorealism: a whole movement in literature and film, concerned with the depiction of corpses. The final limit and the beyond, the eschatology of matter and consciousness, the metaphysics of garbage—this is what takes center stage in art. And this is what defines not only the choice of theme, but also the construction of style, which is maximally weakened, flabby, boneless. In the eschatological perspective, it is more honorable—and aesthetically more productive—not to be the first, but rather the last, not to proclaim, but rather to stutter, not to lead, but rather to trail along. The one who is to be last will take up the place of Truth, the place of the End.

The prose of the arrière-garde does not yield to genre definitions. It is simply prose, a flow of writing: here one could enter twice or three times, without recognizing anything, as if it begins all over again with each sentence. We read Valeria Narbikova's *The Balance of Light of Daytime and Nighttime Stars* and *The Appearance of Us,* Igor Gerb's *The Sacrifice of a Horse,* Ruslan Marsovich's *The Prism-Kino.* Not only does the plot disappear in these works—as a sign of history that has melted away—but so does the skeleton of a coherent whole, which before was called composition and was drawn with graphic sharpness in conceptualism. An arrière-garde work may begin and end at any point and goes on at equal length in all directions, a continuum of weightlessness. Aesthetic reason, which Kant at one time defined as "a form of purposiveness in the absence of a purpose," is diluted in the arrière-garde into a new definition: "the absence of purposiveness as a form of the image." It is quite difficult to adduce examples of the new prose, because the selection of citations would already presuppose a purposiveness; it is necessary to go through many pages, in order to perceive its nonpurposiveness. Here is a description of a suicide, from the work of Ruslan Marsovich:

> When it grows dark, the bath is filled for Marat, for a brother, for an inlaw [*dlia Marata, dlia brata, dlia svata*]. When you array yourself in red and gloomily play the violin of the arm, chlorinated, tepid water would

carry you from pool to pool, from the river into the sea. "The sea awaits, but we are not there at all." It's frightening when the cups are alike, their rims quivering—one doesn't want to drink. If it is possible, despair crushes the glass of the cup in your hand—and no more is to be done for the sake of immortality.

The derealization of the flesh corresponds to the desemanticization of the word. When speech manages not to say anything, words are freed from the captivity of meaning. The arrière-garde is left with the simplest path of association by contiguity, metonymy: where there is a bath, there is also chlorinated water, where there is a pool, there is the sea as well. Where there is water, there is a cup, or glass. Where there is glass, there is a splinter, pain—and that means a chance for immortality. The goal of the text is to deconstruct language, to place the word in such a context that the overall structure must be washed away by other words, getting rid of all meanings: figurative, metaphorical, symbolic, or even simply denotative.

And the object's name comes off like last year's snow off the object, goes into the ground, falls into the Black Sea—that's why there are so many languages, that's why! to give a name to the object in a hundred, a thousand languages, so that names (languages) would mutually exclude one another and the object would again remain without a name. (From Narbikova's *The Appearance of Us*)

After ideological overexploitation, the semantic skeleton of the word—the "concept"—would still remain, though this too is soon transformed into sepulchral dust and desemanticized once and for all. The movement from conceptualism to the arrière-garde is a retreat to the rear of literature, to its graves and smoldering ruins: handfuls of gray dust instead of decked-out skeletons. The hard, bony state of death is replaced by a pulverization of posthumousness.

In the prose of Ruslan Marsovich (or at any rate, in the version that has fallen into my hands), the pages were not numbered, and this oversight may have betrayed the author's secret plan: to abandon all schemes and give the reader a freshly shuffled deck of cards, so that no one could suspect him of being a cardsharp. From the point of view of arrière-garde stylistics, a numbered page is the same as a marked card: one knows in advance where it is to be slipped in. And all previous literature, where pages would be dispensed to the reader in accordance with a preconceived plan, was in fact this kind of a fraud. Life was dealt out by an experienced hand, as "plot" or "composition," so that the author could beat the reader and instill a hierarchy of values, his own "new order."

It is precisely such a design—which, like an iron hand, would drive the reader toward the happiness of true understanding, the happiness of the great idea—that the literature of the arrière-garde fears most of all. Even belonging to a definite genre or a set order of pages could be perceived as guard towers of an aesthetic gulag, where the prisoners are distributed by zones and must strut about with numbers on their backs. Smashed into hundreds of dully glimmering prisms, the specter of postcommunism wanders over the most recent prose: the backbone of history—the plot—has been broken up into a multitude of vertebrae, as in Mandelshtam's poem "The Century." The century is ending. In place of a hard-pawed and relentless predator there are tender bugs that flash in different directions, with disheveled, light bits of the fluff of meaning in every phrase.

Simultaneously with the death of "scientific" and "state" communism, there is also its rebirth as a mystical heresy, as a kind of meltdown of bodies and souls in a millenial kingdom of erased borders and unconfirmed possessions. What was once a discipline of force, is only a Utopia of confluence, of the least possible effort of the will, that remains in the collapsing structures of society and consciousness. In this sense the arrière-garde preserves the last remnant of communism as an entropic thirst for the dissolution of all in all—a cloud of dust that has risen above the enfeebled earth.

In the contemporary artistic consciousness, as in society itself, the decentering and elimination of large structural units—of genre, plot, and ideas—has been accomplished at an accelerated pace. The peculiarity of this "literature without qualities" may be discerned from a comparison with both centered and eccentric literature. The centered prose of our time, above all that of Solzhenitsyn (but also Grossman, Vladimov, and others), has a definite voice and position of the author—who, like a demiurge, would create it with the slashing sword of the Word. Almost all words are autologic, used in their straight and straightened meanings, without any substitutions, disguises, clandestine displacements. "To live not by lies." "One word of truth will outweigh the whole world."

Eccentric prose developed in internal polemic with centered prose, seeming to elude the power of the center constantly, while freely playing with it—as in the works of Andrei Siniavsky, Vassily Aksyonov, Yuz Aleshkovsky, Venedikt Erofeev, Victor Erofeev. Like a little ball, meaning is tossed from word to word before the breathless reader who, in raptures, tries to catch it. The second type of prose is not burdened by straightforward meanings;

rather, it is lightened by figurative ones. Not autology, but metaphor. If the first type of prose says what it wants to say, the second type wants to say something that it does not say. It does not stare, but winks, exchanges glances. The first is seriousness itself and the love of truth; the second, play, spectacle, carnival.

Yet by the end of the eighties, a third type of prose had emerged and began to acquire currency, no longer eccentric, but fully decentered: the prose of the arrière-garde. While it does not yet have catchy names, Sasha Sokolov could be considered its mentor. If the eccentric constantly plays with the concealed and effaced center ("I say one thing and something else comes out"), decentered prose is completely devoid of such a structuring space, where even a minus-position, an anticonception could be reinforced. A net of distinctions is cast over the world, one that has no semantic knot that would allow it to be either tied or undone. There are no stubborn repulsions or passionate attractions between words. There is no subordination, hier- archy, directive; even the culture of comradely mutual help is lost. One could place periods not only between sentences, but indeed between words, so indifferent are they to one another. "When. It grows dark. The bath. Is filled. For Marat. For a brother. For an in-law." Metonymy keeps objects in a holding pattern, making no claim to the place of the center. You make your way through back alleys and back streets, knowing in advance that there is no center in the city of the text, that it consists entirely of outskirts. "I say something, and nothing is coming out."

The literature of the arrière-garde has a reliable remedy against being infatuated by the idea, against the totalization of any style or outlook: it is loaded boredom, which selects the most secondary of words and prolifer- ates a multitude of secondary meanings. This is an absentminded prose, devoid of either the seriousness of the first or the playfulness of the second, calling for nothing, referring to nothing: not even delusions or colorful voids. It eliminates first meanings without creating second ones, as it abides in the zero-degree zone of writing.

> One could run to the store, there is champagne there, but without medals—then beer is better, but is there beer with medals? Of course, the host has the name that his mother gave him; why do they give names to the taxi driver and the ticket inspector, or to the host whom we visited—in order to better remember them? then we won't name the bus driver who drove us, or the host, so as to better forget them. (From Narbikova's *The Appearance of Us*)

This prose takes away names rather than appropriating them, so that being is left with only a vanishing purposiveness: "so as to better forget."

Arrière-garde style is usually quite sound without particular authorial effort. There are no inarticulate snags, clumsinesses, poorly selected words, just as there are no rules for selecting correct words. Conceptualism was minus-, but not yet zero-degree writing; behind it one could divine a violated norm: this is why it was perceived as deliberate inarticulateness, a scoff at correct, literary language. If the avant-garde was striving to explode the system of rules, the arrière-garde gets rid of them by a less energetic means: by elevating every construction into a rule. Therefore, the arrière-garde succeeds at everything, and does not make mistakes, as the rules of the language itself are unerring as concerns orthography, morphology, syntax.

Literature begs language for refuge, trying to say no more than language itself—when the one who is speaking it is silent—and therefore it becomes desolately great and free. It is difficult to distinguish such literature from language itself, which is capable of expressing everything and therefore never says anything by itself. The arrière-garde is the speech of the great mute—language—in the full extent of its muteness. This silence is the best and most profound that may be heard in the arrière-garde: no longer separated from words, as the inexpressable, but rather dissolved in them as the inexpressive. Emptiness is no longer beyond words, but within them.

Our "Postfuture" and Western Postmodernism

And the last question, which is impossible to avoid: How is this "post-future" of contemporary Russian literature to be related to what in the West is commonly called "postmodernism"?

It would seem that we have fallen hopelessly behind in the development of Western literature, which during the twentieth century has passed logically through all the stages of modernism. What kind of postmodernism can there be for us if modernism was grasped only in its early beginnings, during the brief prerevolutionary segment of the twentieth century?

While we are bad at living in harmony with contemporaneity, we are not at all backward when the movement of time is arrested, when it becomes timeless, a pretemporality or a post-temporality. That which existed under the name "Soviet Literature," particularly from the 1930s through the 1950s, was clearly cut off from twentieth-century contemporaneity. The poet functioned more like an *aedes* or a rhapsode of prehistoric times who sang not of himself, but of what was on the lips and consciousness of everyone. Extrapersonal structures clearly formed the content and style; they thought and spoke through the writer. No modernist break with tradition—no privatization of style and the decomposition of the "great social canon," no fencing-off of individual plots in the collective farm of the all-national language and socialized moral property—could be possible.

As the time of modernism passed, it was discovered with amazement that, at key points, the system of "socialist exploitation of the spirit" coincides with the postmodern and postindividualist view of the world. It only remained to realize that this "inborn" socialism (that everyone was born with) was not a historical misfortune or captivity of the free personality, but rather a new posthistorical habitat, where we are rid of the captivity of our own personality. This process of rapid transition from a premodern consciousness to a postmodern one—based on the same material of "developed socialism"—occurred in our country mainly during the seventies, during the time of timelessness. And in the eighties, the basic premises of artistic consciousness were already completely postmodern, perhaps even more radically and consistently than in the West.

Is it not the case, for example, that "simulacra"—that is, maximally lifelike reproductions that have no original—began to be created by our culture much earlier and in greater quantities than in the West? What, for example, is one to make of the figure of Brezhnev, who personified the "businesslike, constructive approach" and the "progressive development of mature socialism"? In contrast to the figure of Stalin, ominously modernist and Kafkaesque, Brezhnev is a typical simulacrum: a postmodern surface object, even a kind of hyperreal object, behind which stands no reality. Long before Western video technology began to produce an overabundance of authentic images of an absent reality, this problem was already being solved by our ideology, press, and statistics, which would calculate crops that would never be harvested to the hundredths of a percentage point.

To be sure, it takes a certain technique of consciousness in order to perceive these likenesses not as lies that deviate from reality, but as the only reality available to us—the ideological (in our country) or videological (in the West) way of life. But already in the seventies, and even more so in the eighties, we had become almost incapable of reacting to objects of the Brezhnev or Chernenko type as *lies;* instead, they smoothed over our cheerless existence. They were parodies, not of some other object, but of themselves.

The socialist epoch also managed to carry out the work of deconstruction, which, in analyzing any meaningful text, arrives at a demonstration of its meaninglessness, so that neither the reader nor the writer is able to explain what a given word, an expression, an entire text means concretely: they mean so much that they contradict themselves, abolish their own signification. The vortex of words carries with it an empty funnel of meaning. Myriads of deliberately deconstructed texts (not in subsequent analysis, but in the very process of creation)—that is, ones that would have an outward visibility of meaning—prove devoid of it upon any attempt at definition.

Along with deconstruction, the socialist enterprise already witnessed the paradigmatic construction of texts that predominates at the expense of the syntagmatic, the linear-progressive. In this regard, texts constitute not so much a narrative structure as a list: a catalog, an inventory of possible opinions, facts, or desires. Once again this was the way in which socialist thinking operated, where all the diverse elements appeared as variations of an originating thesis, and all facts as evidence and confirmation of an earlier-discovered historical law. It is sufficient to compare the hurried stylistics of Lenin, still part of the linear motion of history, with the slowed-down stylistics of Stalin, who had already departed into the space of the completed social structure. The paradigmatic series made it possible to decline a given ideological position through all of its cases: in the "dialectical" and the "historical" particularities of the moment, against rightists, leftists, and centrists. On the whole, the speeches of the subsequent Soviet ideologues, such as Brezhnev and Andropov, seem to follow a paradigm adopted once and for all: the structural framing of a "paradise" attained: a paradisaic timelessness.

Finally, there is alienation, endured and decried by all the writers of the modernist epoch. Postmodernism no longer feels this as an oppression and a curse, because the ideal "subject" or "individual," from whom the surrounding world was presumably alienated, has turned out to be a mythical construction. The postmodern environment is so flattened out, culturally variegated, and uniform (one does not contradict the other), that alienation in fact ceases to be felt as pain and rupture. Alienation has been assimilated to such a degree that the mark of difference between what is one's own and what is the other's vanishes; the mature personality is constructed of superpersonal and extrapersonal components. But that is precisely the way in which the environment of social uniformity was conceived and experienced in our country, until the dissident-modernists declared it alien, depersonalized, threatening. The artistic consciousness of the eighties has gotten rid of this individualist prejudice: today not a single lyrical hero would rant against social oppression and degradation, as in the verse of our "sixties generation" poets, because the lyrical hero himself has in fact disappeared. Soviet postmodernism is devoid of the tragic anguish and the absurdist wail, characteristic of the modern (and especially of existentialism as its last and most extreme variety). The postmodern is optimistic, at least insofar as everything of one's own is already alienated, precisely to the extent that all that is alien is made one's own.

It would be possible to go on listing symptoms of Western postmodernism that are precisely confirmed by the experience of Russian literature. For this reason, it is impossible to concur with those scholars (Soviet as well as those abroad) who limit postmodernism to the field of activity of "late capitalism," "multinational monopolies," "computer civilization," "the schizophrenia of postindustrial society," etc. Postmodernism is a phenomenon of a much broader scale that has emerged both on the basis of total technologies and total ideologies. The triumph of self-valorizing ideas, which both imitate and abolish reality, has been no less conducive to the postmodern way of thinking than the predominance of video communications, which also create a world of arrested time, rolled up in itself.

The difference is that Russian-Soviet civilization is logocentric, while Western civilization privileges the silent values of gold and representation. But words are just as capable of impenetrably coating reality and creating an unbroken chain of signifiers, devoid of any signified, as are television representations. That is why in our country ideology naturally yielded its function to nothing other than glasnost, which brought the art of talking reality away and coating it in a shroud of words to the greatest degree of perfection.

Following the logic of glasnost (which literally means "voiceness"), there seemed to remain but one path for true literature: that of verbalized silence—or of the silenced word. To blurt out secrets so as not to divulge mysteries. To conceal the meaning of the word at the moment of its utterance. To preserve literature at the bottom of language, in its boundless silence. Such is the current poetics of the effacement of poetry. Such is our postfuture— perhaps the most radical of all existing variants of postmodernism.

PART II IDEOLOGY

CHAPTER 4 · Relativistic Patterns in Totalitarian Thinking: The Linguistic Games of Soviet Ideology

Socrates: Then it is not for every man, Hermogenes, to give names, but for him who may be called the name-maker; and he, it appears, is the law-giver, who is of all the artisans among men the rarest.—Plato, *Cratylus*

The spontaneously evolved speech has been turned into a national language. As a matter of course, the individuals at some time will take completely under their control this product of the species as well.—Karl Marx and Frederick Engels, *The German Ideology*

"When I use a word," Humpty Dumpty said, in rather a scornful tone, "it means just what I choose it to mean—neither more nor less."
"The question is," said Alice, "whether you can make words mean so many different things."
"The question is," said Humpty Dumpty, "which is to be master—that's all."—Lewis Carroll, *Through the Looking Glass*

Mastery of language exists only as mastery of its worst and most inadequate possibilities.—Martin Walser

Introduction

The crucial issue of the survival of ideology in our postmodern era brings into focus the concept of relativity. The defining feature of postmodern thought is the absence of any central patterns that might claim objective truth or absolute value. The fundamental quality of ideology, on the other hand, is its absolute commitment to a pattern of ideas that is strictly opposed to all others. Can it then be possible for ideological thinking to survive the postmodern kingdom of playful relativity, preserving all necessary ideological definitions of mandatory and absolutist modes of thinking?

This question was recently raised by Bernard Susser in *The Grammar of Modern Ideology:* "The question was, how do sophisticated ideological thinkers justify the certainties they claim about past and future, man and society, in the face of the relativist skepticism that is the common coin of modern intellectual consciousness. Posed in this way, the problem appeared singularly intriguing, for ideology was the unique exception to the modernist rule; no other discipline or mode of discourse made such strident truth claims or clung to its certainties in so uncompromising (and nonmodernist) a fashion."[1]

One could hardly disagree with such a formulation, with the exception of one term: modernism. It seems more appropriate to identify "relativist skepticism" with postmodernism than with modernism because the latter is known exactly for its "strident claims to truth," as in the philosophy of Marx and Nietzsche or futurist and surrealist art. Unfortunately, the answer given by Susser is not persuasive. "Ideology claims certainty because its social function is to do so. . . . An ideology that was nonchalant or equivocal about the activities it enjoyed or prohibited would be no ideology at all. . . . Ideology and modernism were to each other as an immovable object to an irresistible force" (3–4). Susser assumes that ideology follows a standard of certainty while the modern age follows a standard of relativism; their modes of thinking remain completely alien to each other. As Kipling said, "East is East, and West is West, and never the twain shall meet." Thus, the question of how Eastern ideology can survive in the epoch of Western relativity loses its intriguing appeal.

My answer, although preliminary and partial, is quite different. Far from being antithetical to postmodernism, ideology supplies a unique forum for the postmodern interplay of all conceivable ideas. Paradoxically, Soviet Marxism, the philosophy least expected to be involved in postmodern debate, helps us to provide an explanation. The ideology of Soviet Marxism has always enjoyed the reputation of being one of the most conservative and antimodern belief systems of the twentieth century. Totalitarianism was assumed to exclude the sort of relativism that flourished in Western culture and laid the basis for the transition to postmodernity. However, glasnost and perestroika have shed new light on this ideological system which, if regarded in the process of its formation, reveals a stunning example of relativism inscribed into totalitarian thinking. Totalitarianism itself may thus be viewed as a specific postmodern model that came to replace the modernist ideological stance elaborated in earlier Marxism. The difference between classical Marxism, which is recognized as a breakthrough in philosophical modernism, and Soviet Marxism in its Stalinist and especially Brezhnevian versions, can be described precisely in terms of the relationship between modernism and postmodernism. The latter largely absorbed and assimilated the former, eventually overcoming the original Marxist system of historical certainties and utopian beliefs.

The following discussion will attempt to answer a series of interrelated questions: What are the principal patterns of ideological thinking in general and of Soviet Marxism in particular? Is the so-called scholastic system of Soviet ideology alien to the mainstream of Occidental thinking, or does it reproduce and perhaps even precede some of the most striking intellectual developments of the West? How were relativistic patterns introduced into the structure of totalitarian ideology, transforming it into a variant of postmodern thinking?

Ideology is perhaps more strongly connected with language than is any other kind of social activity. Language is the main vehicle of communication, and the mission of ideology is to rule the process of communication and organize people into communities governed by specific ideas. Karl Marx himself noted that "ideas do not exist in separation from language."[2] Marxist ideology, especially in its Soviet manifestation, confirms the force of this union of language and ideas.

Language is the most honest witness of ideological contradictions, which in Soviet Marxism were painstakingly concealed from popular consciousness in order to mold more successfully the collective subconscious. Ideological language became the decisive tool for the Soviet regime's systematic construction of such "ideal" phenomena as the "Soviet man" and "Soviet mentality." Yet, despite its crucial influence on society, ideological language—or ideolanguage—has not been properly investigated in the Soviet Union as a single, comprehensive phenomenon. Until now, only individual aspects of Soviet Marxist ideolanguage have come under consideration: in the 1920s, ideolanguage was investigated as "the language of revolution," in the 1930s, as "social dialect" or "class language," and in the 1960s and 1970s, as journalistic, or publicistic, style. But the essential overall patterns of ideological language have thus far been neglected, and the analytical framework reduced to one historical epoch, one social stratum, or one functional style.

In fact, the "language of the revolution" is only one stage in the development of Soviet Marxist ideolanguage, "proletarian dialect" only one of its sources, and journalism only one of its thematic realms. Ideolanguage goes beyond these particular aspects; it is something constant and universal, possessed of its own logic, imagery and archetypes rooted in human consciousness. I propose the term "ideolinguistics" for this field of analysis, a field as important for understanding the nature of language and the development of society today as were sociolinguistics and psycholinguistics in the 1960s and 1970s.[3]

Most of the author's observations in this paper will be based on ideological practices of the pre-Gorbachev era in Soviet Marxism. As the following discussion will make clear, however, perestroika and glasnost did not abolish the fundamental patterns of Soviet ideological thought. Instead, these policies have laid bare the hidden foundations of Soviet ideocracy and made possible the deconstruction of its Babylonian sign system. A unique opportunity exists for linguistic and epistemological analysis of the most long-standing totalitarian ideology of modern times.[4]

Words as Ideologemes

What is ideology? Although definitions vary enormously, most define ideological discourse as a combination of theoretical knowledge and practical evaluation, as the following four independent sources demonstrate (emphasis throughout is mine):

> Raymond Aron: "Political ideologies always combine, more or less felicitously, *factual* propositions and *value* judgments. They express an *outlook* on the world and a *will* oriented towards the future."[5]

> Daniel Bell: "Ideology is the conversion of *ideas* into social levers. . . . What gives ideology its force is its *passion.* Abstract philosophical inquiry has always sought to eliminate passion, and the person, to rationalize all ideas. For the ideologue, *truth* arises in *action,* and *meaning* is given to experience by the '*transforming* moment.' "[6]

> *Encyclopaedia Britannica:* "An ideology is a form of social or political philosophy in which *practical* elements are as prominent as *theoretical* ones; it is a system of ideas that aspires both to *explain* the world and to *change* it."[7]

> *Great Soviet Encyclopaedia:* "Ideology is a system of views and ideas within whose framework people *perceive* and *evaluate* both their relations to reality and to each other."[8]

It is essential that an idea taken as a unit of ideology include not only a perception, but also an evaluation of reality. This combination of perception and evaluation differentiates an idea as a unit of ideology from a concept as a unit of scientific thinking (in Russian, this is the difference between *ideia* and *poniatie*). For example, matter is a scientific concept that can be based on physical observation. When we endow this scientific concept with an evaluative meaning implying that matter is the primary element of the universe preceding all spiritual phenomena, then we have materialism, an ideological construction. The idea of materialism includes the objective concept of matter plus a value judgment about this concept. An idea, as distinct from a concept, contains an element of active goal-setting; it is possible to fight for an idea, to be faithful to it, to sacrifice oneself for its sake. It is impossible, however, in all these instances to substitute the concept for the idea. One does not fight for matter, but for materialism, as do the literary heroes of Turgenev and Chernyshevsky.

An idea in an ideological system is not, however, simply an issue of personal taste, an emotional or subjective attitude toward something. Phrases such as "delicious ice cream" or "beautiful hair" are evaluative, but not ideological. These phrases express a personal preference for individual items and do not contain any broader, generalized concepts that are essential to ideological thinking. It is the interaction of the conceptual and evaluative meanings in the semantic structure of language that allows for its ideological use.

There are three classes of lexical units, varying between the extremes of "factual propositions" and "value judgments," to use Aron's terms. The first class contains those words whose significance is purely factual and does not presuppose an attitude on the part of the speaker toward the designated phenomena. The words "house," "forest," "table," "weather," and the verbs "to walk" and "to look," are examples of descriptive, not evaluative, meanings. The second class includes words whose meaning is evaluative, but not directed toward a particular fact or object. These may be such words as "good," "bad," "useful," "harmful," "delicious," "beautiful," "charm," "horror," etc. Only a specific context can indicate what fact is evaluated by words in this group. It is the third class that is the most ideologically significant. Words in this class indicate a definite fact and simultaneously evaluate this fact. The descriptive and evaluative meanings are strongly linked in these words. For example, the word "peacefulness" (*miroliubie*) has a positive connotation, while the words "conciliatoriness" or "appeasement" (*primirenchestvo, umirotvorenie*) have a negative one. All three words describe the same act—striving for peace—and at the same time endow it with either a positive or negative evaluative meaning.

In many cases, it is difficult to find the appropriate English-language equivalents for Soviet terms. Often this is because Soviet ideological language actually has an entirely different aim than a "normal" language. Instead of placing the emphasis on an exchange of information, it attempts to control and restrict the thinking of the speaker and listener. For example, the Soviet ideological words *oshel'movat'* and *zakleimit'* have the same meaning: "to denounce," "to disgrace." However, the first of these words, *oshel'movat'*, has a negative connotation: to disgrace unfairly in a contemptible manner. The second word, *zakleimit'*, expresses a positive attitude toward this action: the speaker agrees that someone was disgraced justifiably. We might read in Soviet newspapers: "Pinochet's junta is denouncing (*shel'muet*) all the honest freedom-fighters in Chile, especially communists." Or we might read: "The honest people of the entire world are denouncing (*kleimiat*) Pinochet for his bloody crimes against the communists." In American English, one can find numerous equivalent words that have a negative connotation: "to defame," "to brand," "to stigmatize"; however, English seems to lack a single word that would convey a speaker's approval of such dishonor.

In Soviet dictionaries, definitions of these and similar words usually combine descriptive and evaluative components. The latter may be written in various ways, either in the form of a stylistic note ("contemptible," "disapproving," "lofty," "deferential"), or by including evaluative words in the definition itself ("bad," "false," "alleged," "truthful," "progressive," "criminal," "reactionary," etc.).

Let us compare two definitions in Ozhegov's well-known dictionary of the modern Russian language:

> accomplice (*posobnik*) [disapprov.]: a helper in evil, criminal, activities.
>
> comrade-in-arms (*spodvizhnik*) [lofty]: a person who participates as someone's helper in an activity in someone's field of endeavor.

While these words possess an identical factual meaning, they express opposite attitudes on the part of the speaker regarding a person who might be neutrally indicated as a helper. Kalinin or Dzerzhinsky, for example, would be called "Lenin's comrades-in-arms" in the Soviet press, whereas Goering or Goebbels would only be identified as Hitler's "accomplices." "Helper" is

the neutral factual component to which either positive or negative evaluative components are added.

To sum up, three types of words can be identified:

1. "Descriptive" words, which acquire their evaluative meaning only in
a broader context: a criminal *agreement.*
2. "Evaluative" words, which acquire their factual meaning when combined with a descriptive word: a *criminal* agreement.
3. "Descriptive-evaluative" words whose lexical meaning combines the
two components. A "criminal agreement," for example, is compressed
into "collusion" (Russian, *sgovor*). A typical sentence would read: "Imperialist powers entered into collusion against the Palestinian people
in order to rob them of their right to statehood." Here the denotative
meaning "an agreement" and evaluative meaning "criminal" are united
to make up a single ideological meaning of "collusion."

Words that combine descriptive and evaluative meaning in such an inseparable way that they make one whole lexical meaning, I shall call "ideologemes." Words of the first and second categories, such as "house," "agreement," "good," "bad," are not ideologemes. Their meanings are dependent
on context and connections with other words. As for ideologemes, their
contextual potential is included in their meaning, which is stable and presupposes a definite attitude of the speaker to the signified object. Ideologemes are not only nominative, but communicative units of speech; that is,
they not only name the facts (objects, actions, or qualities), but communicate
some message (an opinion, an idea) of how one should treat these facts.

Let us look at some examples from Soviet language usage. *Ob"ektivnost'*
means "objectivity" in a positive sense, while *ob"ektivizm* implies that a
scientist or a scholar is loyal to so-called minor facts at the expense of the
Party line and "historic tendencies." The adjective *opytnyi* means an experienced person who can work productively, while *materyi* means an enemy
who has great experience in criminal actions. *Splochenie* is the solidarity
and unity of all Soviet allies and compatriots, while *blokirovanie* refers
to the united activities of all anti-Soviet forces. For example: "The celebration of May 1 is a call for solidarity (*splochenie*) among all the working
people in the world." "All forces of neo-colonialism are now forming a bloc
(*blokiruiutsia*) against Libya's independence." All these words serve as ve-
hicles of communication, naming the object and establishing an attitude
toward it.

Ideologemes, being the elementary particles of ideological thinking, are not simply words, but concealed judgments that take the form of words. Usually a judgment is developed in an entire sentence, where it is divided into a subject and predicate. This kind of judgment is open to discussion because the link between subject and predicate is explicitly relative. For example, the typical Soviet ideological judgment that "Vladimir Ilyich Ulyanov is the greatest man in human history" is debatable. We can combine the subject of this sentence with another predicate such as "the greatest criminal" or combine the predicate "is the greatest man" with another subject such as Shakespeare or George Washington. But in Soviet Marxist ideolanguage, "Lenin" is *already* an ideologeme that refers both to a concrete man, Vladimir Ilyich Ulyanov, and to an abstract evaluative concept, the "greatest man in human history."[9] The factual meaning of the ideologeme usually serves as the subject of the judgment, the evaluative meaning, as the predicate. Thus, "Lenin" is a condensed judgment where the subject and predicate are combined in one word.

In the same way, the ideologemes *pochin* and *samoupravstvo* both have as their subject "initiative," while their predicates are opposites: "is useful and must be supported," versus "is harmful and must be rejected." Let us compare two kinds of judgments: explicit and implicit. "The initiative turned out to be inappropriate (We may ask: For what reason?) and resulted in much damage (What sort of damage?)" This is an example of an explicit judgment in which a vacant place remains (shown in parentheses) for the substantiation or refutation of the argument. On the other hand, however, "Adventurism!" (*avantiurizm!*) or "arbitrariness!" (*samoupravstvo!*) are examples of implicit judgments in which the subject, "initiative," is closely intertwined with the predicate, "is inappropriate and must be defeated." An ideologeme is nothing other than an idea that is hidden in one word (or, sometimes, in one indivisible phrase or idiom). In this way it can be inserted into the listener's consciousness without the possibility of argumentation or objection. One cannot quarrel with a single word.

Thus, such typical judgments as "this *pochin* (good initiative) should be supported" or "this *samoupravstvo* (bad initiative) must be condemned" are mere tautologies: the meaning of the word *pochin* already implies that it is necessary, and therefore must be supported. Many Soviet ideological texts are lengthy repetitions of those judgments that are contained in single ideologemes. For example: "All Soviet people unanimously approve and support the courageous initiative (*pochin*) of the workers of the Dnepropetrovskii metallurgy plant that took on the obligation to produce an additional 25,000 tons of steel by the anniversary of the October Revolution." The ideological meaning of this entire sentence is equivalent to that of a single word: *pochin*.

It is not sufficient, however, only to identify ideologemes as a special category of language units. We must also analyze and systematize relationships between ideologemes in order to discover a model that gives rise to varied ideological uses of language. For the remainder of this paper, I shall use the linguistic terms "denotation" and "connotation" to designate the two components of an ideologeme: its factual and evaluative aspects.

Relationships between Ideologemes

The connections between ideologemes are determined by the same relationships of similarity and opposition, synonymy and antonymy that are characteristic of lexical systems in all languages. However, ideologemes have double denotative and connotative (factual and evaluative) significance. Hence, all relationships between them are doubled. Instead of antonymy and synonymy, four relationships exist between ideologemes: (1) full antonymy; (2) denotative synonymy combined with connotative antonymy; (3) denotative antonymy combined with connotative synonymy; and (4) full synonymy.

Full Antonymy

Full antonymy is the opposition of both the denotative and connotative meanings. I shall call this relationship "contrative," and the words that are connected with this relationship, "contratives." The following word pairs could be classified as contratives:

internationalism–nationalism (or chauvinism)
peacefulness–aggressiveness
collectivism–individualism
freedom–slavery (or oppression)
perestroika–stagnation
solidarity–division

internatsionalizm–natsionalizm (or *shovinizm*)
miroliubie–agressivnost'
kollektivizm–individualizm
svoboda–rabstvo, gnet
perestroika–zastoi
splochenie–raskol[10]

These ideologemes are opposed not only on the denotative plane but on the connotative as well. "Collectivism" means the presence of communal awareness among people or the striving toward this awareness; the word carries a positive connotation in Soviet ideolanguage. "Individualism" means the absence of such communal thinking or the striving to abandon it; the word has an extremely negative connotation. All words on the left-hand side of each column above have a positive connotation, while all words on the right-hand side are completely negative. Contrative oppositions are characteristic of the earliest stage of development of Marxist ideology, as in the classical oppositions of socialism to capitalism, or labor to exploitation, or of the working class to the bourgeoisie.

I shall continue to place words with positive connotations on the left and those with negative connotations on the right in each pair. This will not only be easier for the reader's perception (one must perceive something before one can perceive its negative), but corresponds to the Soviet ideological dichotomy of left and right, where the left is usually associated with good and the right with bad.

Synonymy of Denotative Meanings, Antonymy of Connotative Meanings

These ideologemes indicate identical or similar phenomena, but give them opposite evaluations. I shall call this relationship *conversive*.[11] Conversives are as follows:

> internationalism–cosmopolitanism
> peacefulness–appeasement, conciliatoriness
> freedom–license (or laxity)
> initiative–arbitrariness
> traditional–backward

> *internatsionalizm–kosmopolitizm*
> *miroliubie–umirotvorenie*, or *primirenchestvo*
> *svoboda–raspushchennost'*
> *pochin–proizvol, samoupravstvo*
> *traditsionnyi–otstalyi*

The words "peacefulness" and "appeasement" have the same denotative meaning—a striving to establish peace—but have entirely different connotative meanings that indicate the speaker's attitude concerning this striving toward peace. "The entire world had the opportunity to recognize and appreciate the *peacefulness* of the Soviet people during the postwar period," but "Communists will never *appease* the imperialists by accepting their involvement in the internal affairs of developing countries."

From the linguistic point of view, the conversive relationship is especially interesting, as connotative meanings become the only factor that differentiate words with a common denotative meaning. This is typical of Soviet ideolanguage:

rally–mob scene
soldier–mercenary (or martinet)
comrade-in-arms–accomplice
efficiency–careerism, utilitarianism

sobranie–sborishche
soldat–naiomnik (or *voin–voiaka*)
spodvizhnik–prispeshnik (or *soratnik–soobshchnik*)
delovitost'–deliachestvo

Entire ideological expressions may sometimes maintain parallel denotative structures, but diverge at the connotative level. "The experienced politician concluded an agreement with the leaders of rebel detachments" (Opytnyi politik zakliuchil dogovor s rukovoditeliami partizanskikh otriadov) can thus be conversed into "The unscrupulous politico made a deal with the ringleaders of bandit gangs" (Materyi politikan vstupil v sgovor s glavariami banditskikh shaek). The law of ideological agreement does not allow elements of these two statements to change places. One could not say "the ringleaders of the partisan detachment" (glavari partizanskogo otriada) because the word "ringleaders" has a negative connotation that does not agree ideologically with the rest of the sentence. This necessity for expressive concord was aptly exemplified in the thirties by the Soviet educator Makarenko, who commented, "Try to slip the phrase 'the collective of Krupp factories' past any Soviet audience. Even a Soviet citizen unschooled in sociology will find the juxtaposition of the words 'collective' and 'Krupp' absurd. . . . A collective is a social organism within a healthy society. Such an organism cannot be imagined in the setting of bourgeois chaos."[12] Thus, Soviet ideological stylistics does not permit the combination of two words with opposite connotations in one phrase.

Evaluative conversion, changing the connotative meaning while retaining the denotative meaning, is routine practice in Soviet ideology.[13] Soviet journalists have often used information from Western sources, translating it word for word, but selecting terms that possess opposite connotative meanings. Experienced Soviet readers, however, perform an almost instinctive ideological conversion that allows them to decipher the original Western text and draw precisely the opposite conclusions than those stated by the journalist. This mental transformation following conversive patterns occurs when, for example, a Soviet citizen reads information about the rebels in Afghanistan or the contras in Nicaragua in Soviet newspapers: "bandit gangs" are deciphered as "rebel detachments."

The celebrated Marxist formula "goods–money–goods," which designates the circulation of capital in bourgeois society, turns out to be appropriate for the circulation of ideas in socialist society. An example would be "soldier–martinet–soldier" (*voin–voiaka–voin,* or *soldat–soldafon–soldat*). The first conversion "soldier–martinet" occurs in the mind of a Soviet journalist when he transforms information about American troops into Soviet ideolanguage. The second conversion "martinet–soldier" occurs in the mind of the Soviet reader when he processes information from a Soviet newspaper that has already converted the original American report. Soviet political language is thus subjected to a system of double conversion. One can conclude that the law governing the circulation of goods and ideas follows the same pattern; for the typical Soviet mentality, objective facts ("goods") are exchanged for ideological words ("money").[14]

Antonymy of Denotative Meanings, Synonymy
of Connotative Meanings

This type of relationship is the opposite of a conversive relationship and can be called *correlative.* Correlatives are ideologemes with opposing denotations, but identical connotations:

> internationalism–patriotism
> peacefulness–steadfastness, irreconcilability
> class struggle–classless society
> materialism–spirituality
> innovation–tradition
> vigilance–trust

> *internatsionalizm–patriotizm*
> *miroliubie–neprimirimost'*
> *klassovaia bor'ba–besklassovoe obshchestvo*
> *materializm–dukhovnost', ideinost'*
> *novatorstvo–traditsiia*
> *bditel'nost'–doverie*

The above are correlatives with opposing denotations, but equally positive connotations. In Soviet ideolanguage, "internationalism" and "patriotism" mean "equal love for all nations" and "exclusive love for one's own nation," respectively. Both have highly positive connotations. Below are correlatives that have equally negative connotations:

subjectivism–objectivism
hard-headed–soft
to whitewash–to blacken

sub"ektivizm–ob"ektivizm
tverdolobyi–miagkotelyi
obeliat'–ocherniat'

Frequently, correlatives serve as homogeneous components of a sentence. For example: "We must enhance the *internationalist* and *patriotic* upbringing of the younger generation." Or: "Both *innovation* and *tradition* constitute a firm foundation of artistic creativity." And finally, "The struggle against *subjectivism* and *objectivism* in the humanities is a pressing problem for Soviet scholars." At other times, correlatives coalesce in a way that creates oxymoronic expressions that often become popular idioms of Soviet ideology: "the fight for peace," "solidarity in class struggle," "ideological commitment to materialism," or an "optimistic tragedy."[15] Correlatives and their oxymoronic epiphenomena are usually explained by the dialectical essence of Marxist thinking, which strives to combine opposites such as "national" and "international," or "objective" and "subjective."

Two correlatives have become very popular in the years since perestroika was launched in 1985: "the plan" and "the free market." For seventy years, the first term was considered sufficient to explain the advantages of the Soviet regulated economy. The second term previously denoted the evils of bourgeois economic anarchy, but now it is appreciated as a means of re-animating the dormant Soviet economy. Today, these two positive ideologemes are correlatives in one incredibly oxymoronic expression: "the planned, or regulated, free market."

Full Synonymy

Full synonymy is the identity (or close similarity) of both denotative and connotative meanings. For example, such ideologemes as "discipline–organization–consciousness" (*distsiplina–organizovannost'–soznatel'nost'*) all have the same denotative meaning and positive connotation in Soviet language. These words can be called *substitutives* because, as a general rule, they can be substituted for one another in the same context.[16] "It is consciousness first of all that communist commissars tried to raise in the ranks of Red Army soldiers during the Civil War." Here "consciousness" can be replaced by "discipline" or "good organization." Substitutes like "anarchy–lack of control–license–permissiveness" (*anarkhiia–stikhiinost'–raspushchennost'–vsedozvolennost'*) are used to dismiss both bourgeois morals and the bourgeois system of production.

As the substitutive relationship has no oppositional elements, it is not included in the main model of ideological thinking (see the next section). The substitutive relationship is, however, essential for bringing the ideological model to life in lexical variations of Soviet ideolanguage and thus will be treated extensively below in the section "Ideological Functions, Lexical Groups, and Philosophical Oppositions."

The Structure of Tetrads

Three relationships between ideologemes—contrative, conversive, and correlative—make up the entire structure of Soviet Marxist ideolanguage. The basic model is composed of four elements (a tetrad), each of which interacts with the others in three separate ways, and can be presented as a diagram. For the sake of clarity, horizontal lines in the diagram are used to indicate contrative relationships; vertical lines, correlative relationships, and diagonal lines, conversive relationships. The meaning of each element in this structure is determined by its relationships with the other elements; it is the relationships that give the structure its integrity.[17]

In Figure 1 the ideologeme "internationalism" participates in all three possible relationships with the other ideologemes. It makes a contrative pair with "nationalism," a conversive pair with "cosmopolitanism," and a correlative pair with "patriotism." In other words, "internationalism" has opposing denotative and connotative meanings in relation to "nationalism," the same denotative and opposite connotative meaning in relation to "cosmopolitanism," and the same connotative and opposite denotative meaning in relation to "patriotism." Moreover, we can see that not only is "internationalism" linked by three relationships with the other words, but each of the four words participates in all possible relationships with one another. Thus "patriotism" makes a contrative pair with "cosmopolitanism," a conversive pair with "nationalism," and a correlative pair with "internationalism."

(+) internationalism   (-) nationalism

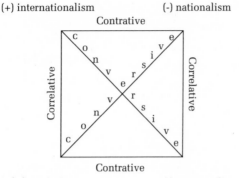

Figure 1   (+) patriotism   (-) cosmopolitanism

One can trace the same underlying structure of relationships between other Soviet ideological words, bearing in mind that it is sometimes difficult to find the same relationships between synonyms and antonyms in the English language, or in any other language not so deeply permeated by ideology. In the tetrad below, "peacefulness" makes a contrative pair with "aggressiveness," a conversive pair with "appeasement," and a correlative pair with "uncompromisingness."

    peacefulness–aggressiveness
    uncompromisingness–appeasement

    miroliubie–agressivnost'
    neprimirimost'–primirenchestvo

The same structure can be seen in the following tetrads:

    innovativeness–backwardness
    traditionalism–avant-gardism

    steadfastness–spinelessness
    flexibility–hard-headedness

    generosity–miserliness
    thriftiness–wastefulness

    realism–dogmatism
    loyalty to principles–unscrupulousness

    vigilance–gullibility
    trust–suspiciousness

    efficiency–inefficiency
    selflessness–careerism, utilitarianism

acceleration–stagnation
stability–instability

strictness–permissiveness
tolerance–captiousness

freedom–repression
discipline–anarchy

materialism–idealism
spirituality–lack of spirituality

novatorstvo–otstalost'
traditsionnost'–avangardizm

tverdost'–beskhrebetnost'
gibkost'–tverdolobost'

shchedrost'–skarednost'
berezhlivost'–rastochitel'stvo

realizm–dogmatizm
printsipial'nost'–besprintsipnost'

bditel'nost'–rotozeistvo
doverie–podozritel'nost'

delovitost'–beskhoziaistvennost'
beskorystie–deliachestvo

uskorenie–zastoi
stabil'nost'–destabilizatsiia

trebovatel'nost'–popustitel'stvo
dobrozhelatel'nost'–pridirchivost'[18]

svoboda–podavlenie
distsiplina–anarkhiia

materializm–idealizm
dukhovnost'–bezdukhovnost'

A binary system can be used to analyze the tetrad as a semantic structure, with the first number of each pair identifying an ideologeme's connotative meaning, the second, its denotative meaning. In the first position of each set of numbers, let's use the number 1 to designate a positive connotative meaning, 0 to designate a negative connotative meaning. In the second position, we will use the number 1 to designate the presence of a denotative meaning, 0 to designate the absence of this denotative meaning. All four ideologemes can then be coded using four possible combinations of the digits 1 and 0.

For example, the word "peacefulness," which has both positive denotative and connotative meanings, would be designated 11. The first 1 indicates a positive connotation and the second, a positive denotative meaning ("the striving for peace"). "Aggressiveness" would be marked 00 because it has a negative connotative meaning and denotes the absence of peacefulness. "Uncompromisingness" would be marked 10 because it has a positive connotation, but denotes the absence of peacefulness. "Appeasement" would be marked 01 because it has a negative connotation, although it denotes a "striving for peace."

All the tetrads listed above will have the same structure of binary pairs, which may be diagrammed schematically as follows:

11   00
10   01

If the first and second numbers of each pair are different, the relationship between the ideologemes is contrative (11−00 or 10−01). If they differ only in the first digits (connotations), the relationship is conversive (11−01 or 10−00). If they differ only in the second digits (denotations), the relationship is correlative (11−10 or 00−01).

We can now see how this structure generates interdependent ideologemes. Let us designate the original meaning of an idea or concept as an *archetheme*. The ideological mind reworks the original meaning, or archetheme, of the idea into four components, first dividing it into two opposite denotative meanings and then multiplying the two denotations so that each has two connotative meanings. Take, for example, the archetheme "pace of development." Its ideological transformation would result in four ideologemes. A denotative split of the archetheme produces two opposing concepts: rapid development and a lack of development. Both of these concepts are then split into two connotative units: positive and negative attitudes to rapid development (acceleration−instability) and positive and negative attitudes to a lack of development (stability−stagnation).

Similarly, the ideological transformation of the archetheme "expenditure," would result in four ideologemes: positive and negative attitudes toward substantial expenditures (generosity and wastefulness) and positive and negative attitudes toward savings (thriftiness and miserliness). Under the archetheme "attitude toward nations," an equal feeling toward all the other nations is ideologically approved (internationalism) and disapproved (cosmopolitanism), just as an exclusive love for one's own nation is both approved (patriotism) and disapproved (nationalism or chauvinism).

The structure of tetrads is a pairing of dualities. Thus tetrads are as simple and persuasive as $2 \times 2 = 4$. Herein lies the enormous power of the ideological mode of thinking.

Ideology as Hidden Dialogue

The tetradic structure described above has been present in the linguistic practice of mankind since ancient times. Thucydides' *History of the Peloponnesian War* offers a vivid example of the ideological use of language, observing changes in word usage during periods of social upheaval:

> Words had to change their ordinary meaning and to take that which was now given them. Reckless audacity came to be considered the courage of a loyal ally; prudent hesitation, specious cowardice; moderation was held to be a cloak for unmanliness; ability to see all sides of a question, ineptness to act on any. Frantic violence became the attribute of manliness; cautious plotting, a justifiable means of self-defense. The advocate of extreme measures was always trustworthy; his opponent a man to be suspected.[19]

Two sets of ideological evaluations belonging to various social groups, political parties, or subjects of speech are presented in this passage. What one group considers to be a positive display of "courage," the other characterizes negatively as "recklessness." By the same token, the deliberate and careful behavior of one camp is perceived from within as "prudence," but may be reproached from without (by the opposing camp) as hidden "cowardice." The essence of this ideological controversy can be conveyed by using the following tetrad:

courage–cowardice
prudence–recklessness

As indicated earlier, the very usage of an ideological word frees the speaker from the necessity of logical proof. The judgment that prudence is better than recklessness, or that courage is better than cowardice, is contained in the words themselves, in their stable connotative meanings rooted in the lexical system of language.

We can observe further that the tetrad is not just an abstract, logical scheme, but composed of dyads that belong to opposing sides. One side can be characterized as radical; it uses the first line of the tetrad to exhort citizens to courageous action and condemn cowardice. The other side is conservative; it uses the second dyad to encourage citizens to exercise prudence and resist recklessness. The tetrad cited above actually represents the intersection of two dyads, each of which can be used separately by opposing sides in a political struggle.

The structure of opposing dyads helps us to understand how tetrads serve to unify opposing ideological attitudes. For example, the dyad "internationalism–nationalism" may be regarded as leftist; it is the very essence of early Marxist ideology. Another dyad, "patriotism–cosmopolitanism," arose much later, after World War II, when Stalin tried to introduce extremely rightist principles into the Soviet worldview. However, Stalin did not eliminate the first dyad (the traditional Marxist approach); rather, he combined the two. The combination of leftist and rightist concepts is typical of totalitarian ideology, which must be simultaneously "left" and "right," radical and conservative at the same time. Totalitarian politics uses leftist slogans to defeat the right, rightist slogans to defeat the left.

In recent Soviet political language, specifically that of the late 1980s, two separate dyads have been used by opposing parties: one advocates change and reform, challenging stagnation; the other defends the value of stability, claiming radical reform will completely destabilize society. These dyads can be contrasted as the political views of two Soviet politicians:

Yeltsin's dyad: reform–stagnation
Ligachev's dyad: stability–instability

For Gorbachev and his followers, the above dyads together constitute a tetrad. This tetrad was used extensively in all of Gorbachev's speeches as president of the USSR and as general secretary of the Communist Party, the first being more radical, the second, more conservative:

Gorbachev's tetrad: reform–stagnation
                    stability–instability

In denouncing the political position of former Communist Party Politburo member Egor Ligachev, Gorbachev used the first dyad; in his attacks on Yeltsin, the second.[20] Gorbachev's speeches were generally constructed to achieve a balance between these two dyads while using the expressive force of all elements in the tetrad. Condemning stagnation, Gorbachev praised stability; proclaiming faithfulness to socialist ideals, he tried to establish a free market.

Gorbachev is famous for confounding Western observers with his political swings to the left and right. The key to the riddle of his political behavior may lie in the tetradic model, which imposes ideological constraints upon political leaders. Usually, a Soviet political leader adopts two positive positions in a tetrad and uses them to oppose leftist and rightist political rivals. Examples of such tetrads would be:

Stalin (right)–Trotsky (left)
Stalin (left)–Bukharin (right)

Gorbachev (right)–Yeltsin (left)
Gorbachev (left)–Ligachev (right)[21]

In the same manner, Lenin first struggled against "patriots" who called for the defense of Russia ("the fatherland") during World War I, then against "internationalists" who suffered from "the infantile sickness of leftism" in attempting to ignite a world revolution.

As a language structure, the tetrad can be actualized in three different modes of speech: expressive, analytical, and totalitarian. In the *expressive* mode, the tetrad is actualized in separate dyads, each of which represents the position of a specific political group. A speaker using this mode can be identified as a convinced follower of particular ideological tenets. Thus, radicals would use only the dyad "courage–cowardice," conservatives, only "prudence–recklessness." The second mode is *analytical.* Here the tetrad is examined as a whole in theoretical terms; the speaker tries to describe how the mechanism of the tetrad functions from a bystander's point of view. The previously cited passage from Thucydides is an illustration of the analytical mode.

The totalitarian mode of speech is distinguished from the other two in that it is not dominated by political emotionalism, as is the expressive mode, nor is it purely theoretical, as is the analytical mode. The totalitarian type of speech *uses the emotions rationally.* The speaker embraces the entire tetrad in his practical vocabulary, but does not use it immediately in its entirety, only in dyadic fragments. The same speaker uses both dyads, "courage–cowardice" and "prudence–recklessness," in turn, defeating moderate ("cowardly") adversaries in one case, and leftist radicals (former "courageous" allies) in another. One subject of speech adopts the role of two opposing subjects and uses both dyads contained in the tetrad.[22] In this way, the totalitarian subject (speaker) acquires a practical advantage against opponents on either end of the political spectrum, using the strength of each side–the evaluative force of its words–to gain a victory over the other.

Niccolò Machiavelli brilliantly formulated the strategy of this kind of political maneuvering: "you assist at the destruction of one by the aid of another who, if he had been wise, would have saved him; and conquering, as it is impossible that he shouldn't with your assistance, he remains at your discretion."[23] We can see how Lenin followed Machiavelli's advice: after the February revolution of 1917, Lenin appropriated the slogans of the Socialist Revolutionaries and exhorted the peasants to seize the landowners' property; then, having seized power in October 1917, he promptly removed the Socialist Revolutionaries and destroyed them.

Having at its disposal the set of all four ideologemes for two opposing forces, A and B, the totalitarian speaker is capable of seizing complete control over them. In a situation that requires the strengthening of position A and a corresponding weakening of position B, the ideologemes "$+a$" and "$-b$" are used ("internationalists" versus "Great Russian chauvinists"). However, if A acquires too much popularity and threatens to dominate the political scene, the speaker changes the names and uses the other contrative dyad, "$+b$" and "$-a$" ("Russian patriots" versus "rootless cosmopolitans"). In Machiavelli's words, the Prince "sets up an arbiter, who should be one who could beat down the great and favour the lesser" (27). In a totalitarian state, ideological language itself becomes such an arbiter.

The tetrad provides a speaker with the optimal speech strategy in conflict situations. Applying lexical evaluations against two opposing sides with the aim of weakening both of them, the speaker achieves total advantage. The totalitarian speaker who controls the tetrad does not so much participate in conflicts as he uses them, playing upon their contradictions. The tetrad itself generally remains hidden in separate acts of speech; if it were openly used in its entirety the force of its practical application would be reduced.

Lenin and the Logic of Ideology

Let us now turn to a more extensive examination of the use of tetrads in Lenin's public statements on war, peace, and the nationalities question. An analysis of these statements will reveal the logic upon which Soviet Marxist ideolanguage is built.

In an article written in 1916, entitled "The Military Program of the Proletarian Revolution," Lenin proclaimed, "Disarmament is the ideal of socialism. In socialist society, there will be no war; consequently, disarmament will be realized."[24] However, in another article written several days earlier, "On the Slogan of 'Disarmament,'" Lenin proclaimed with equal fervor, "Having triumphed in one country, socialism will in no event exclude war in general; on the contrary, it will presuppose war" (30:133). Lenin unambiguously declared that an object is white, but that this does not exclude the possibility of its also being black. This logic presupposes that the very word "war" has two distinct ideological meanings. The phrase "there will be no war," means that war is aggression, imperialist banditry, provocation, blackmail, an arrogant challenge; in short, war is a crime against all humanity. The phrase "socialism will presuppose war" indicates that war is a sacred duty that is part of the class struggle, a fatal blow struck against reactionary forces and dedicated to the elimination of class enemies.

Lenin openly confirmed this ambiguity of the word "war": "We are not pacifists. We are opponents of *imperialistic wars* . . . , but we have always considered it an absurdity that the revolutionary proletariat would renounce *revolutionary wars* which may turn out to be necessary to the interests of socialism" (31:91; emphasis mine). Here we encounter the concept of ideological *homonymy:* the two words, "war" and "war," have little in common. One is defined as "revolutionary" and has a positive connotation, the other is defined as "imperialistic" and has a negative connotation.

This duality can also be found in the ideological homonyms "peace" and "peace." In opposition to revolutionary war, "peace" is classified as "appeasement, heinous opportunism, rotten pacifism, apostasy, a betrayal of the proletariat's class interests." However, in opposition to imperialist war, "peace" signifies "an expression of the people's will, a striving toward friendship and cooperation with all nations, an indication of our long-standing peacefulness and of our higher ideals." In Lenin's words, this kind of peace is "[t]he end of wars, peace between nations, the cessation of robbery and violence, this is indeed our ideal" (26:34).

In all of Lenin's statements, the use of a tetrad can be detected, even though the tetrad itself remains hidden:

good peace–bad war   peacefulness–imperialistic war
good war–bad peace .   revolutionary war–pacifism

Lenin's views on the nationality question also reveal hidden tetrads: "The proletariat is creating the possibility for the full elimination of nationalistic oppression . . . right up to the definition of state boundaries, according to the 'sympathies' of the population, including full freedom for secession" (30:21–22). "We desire free unification, and therefore we are obliged to acknowledge free secession" (34:379). Lenin's dialectic would not be complete, however, if it did not include conflicting assertions. "The interests of socialism are more important than the right of nations for self-determination" (35:251). "Self-determination is not absolute, but a small particle of the common democratic (now, common socialist) world movement. It is possible that in specific, isolated cases this particle will contradict the whole; then it will be necessary to overthrow it," (30:39). In one article, "The Results of the Discussion on Self-Determination" (1916),[25] Lenin does not simply change his point of view, he simultaneously supports two conflicting opinions. Further evidence for this conclusion can be found in the so-called dialectical proclamations of Lenin, where two blatantly conflicting points of view are juxtaposed, as the following two statements on self-determination make clear: "The unconditional acknowledgment of the struggle for freedom and self-determination by no means obligates us to support any requirement of national self-determination" (7:233). "It is impermissible to mix the issue of the right of nations for free self-determination with the issue of expediency of the secession of this or of any other nation at this or any other moment" (31:440).

All these statements on nationality issues contain a hidden tetrad: a nation may assert its right to self-determination either as a result of "socialist achievement" or of "bourgeois nationalism" (which is contrary to the "socialist unity of nations"). On the other hand, nations may be united either by the force of "socialist internationalism" or "imperialist oppression" and "great power chauvinism." The tetrad can be diagrammed in two variants:

>secession of nations–national oppression
>unity of nations–national separation

or

>right to self-determination–great-power chauvinism
>socialist internationalism–bourgeois nationalism

>otdelenie natsii–natsional'nyignet
>edinstvo natsii–natsional'nyi separatizm

or

>pravo na samoopredelenie–velikoderzhavnyi shovinizm
>sotsialisticheskii internatsionalizm–burzhuaznyi natsionalizm

In this game of ideologemes there is a certain logic. Marxist-Leninists usually call this logic "dialectics," but it has nothing to do with the Hegelian conception that uses a triadic construction. In classical German philosophy, the thesis and antithesis conflict with each other but ultimately form a synthesis. No such synthesis occurs in Soviet Marxist ideological thinking, which could be called *tetralectical,* as opposed to dialectical. In Soviet ideology, the two halves of the tetrad change places—the positive becomes negative and the negative becomes positive—but no qualitative change occurs that might result in synthesis. The failure to achieve synthesis does not mean, however, that tetralectical thinking is inferior to dialectical thinking. On the contrary, in a practical political sense tetralectical thinking may well be superior to its dialectical predecessor.

The structure of ideo-logic merits special research beyond the scope of this chapter. I believe that the tetrad as an ideological model includes essential components of other logics, uniting them in an ideally constructed whole. A comparison of the structure of Soviet Marxist ideo-logic with the structures of formal, dialectic, and relativist logics would be especially illuminating. The cursory comparison that follows indicates the principal directions additional research could explore.

The central component of formal logic is the principle of contradiction: A is not non-A, which is expressed in the contrative relationship of ideologemes in the tetrad. For example, "Freedom" is contrary to "slavery" and "discipline" is contrary to "anarchy." The central component of dialectical logic is the principle of the unity of contradictions: A is non-A. This relationship is revealed in the correlative relationship of ideologemes, where contradictions display their own unity. In spite of being opposites, "freedom" and "discipline" are both equally approved, while "slavery" and "anarchy" are both rejected. Finally, relativist logic holds that the qualities of an object are dependent on the position of the observer, corresponding to the conversive relationship of ideologemes. The same object displays different qualities and is characterized by opposing ideologemes depending on the speaker's convictions. What is regarded as "freedom" from a democratic point of view may be assessed as "anarchy" from an authoritarian point of view. Similarly, "discipline" may be perceived negatively as "compulsion" or "compulsion" may be perceived positively as "discipline."

Thus, opposites are arranged in the tetrad in such a way that they:

1. are opposed to each other: A is not non-A (contratives);
2. are unified and equated: A is non-A (correlatives);
3. are transformed into each other: $A \leftrightarrow$ non-A (conversives).

These relationships correspond to the three operations carried out in the domain of different logics. Each operation appears to be illegal in the system of the other logic. For example, formal logic does not allow the dialectical union of opposites. Tetralectics, however, legalizes all three logical opera-

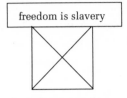

Figure 2   discipline—anarchy

tions because they form the three relationships inside the tetrad. What seems to be an unsolvable contradiction in the framework of one logic is transferred through the tetrad into another system where the contradiction is easily resolved. Tetrads allow "the use of logic against logic," as Orwell's Newspeak demonstrated.

Thus, "freedom" as proclaimed by Marx–Engels–Lenin is strictly opposed to the "compulsion" and "slavery" practiced in "antagonistic" class societies. "Freedom" can correspond with this same "compulsion," however, when regarded as the "iron discipline" or "revolutionary violence" found in communist societies. One can read in Lenin that no freedom is possible without violence against the exploiting classes. On the other hand, "freedom" in capitalist societies can easily be equated with "anarchy" or "license" (i.e., transformed into its negative counterpart) and consequently considered to promote "violence" or "slavery."

The celebrated Orwellian slogans, "Freedom is Slavery" and "War is Peace," which symbolize the totalitarian ideology in his novel *1984,* are, of course, artistic hyperboles. Any follower of "scientific" communism would object, "Our ideology is striving for freedom and helps humanity to overcome slavery." However, in essence Orwell was right. Although "freedom" and "slavery" are contratives, they are mediated by correlative and conversive relationships that actually make them equivalents. "Freedom" demands, as a correlative, "revolutionary discipline," which in totalitarian language is nothing but a substitutive for "revolutionary violence." This latter expression is in turn nothing but a positive conversive of "oppression" or even "slavery" (see Fig. 2). All components of the tetrad are transcoded and transformed into one another along the vertical and diagonal lines according to the principles of dialectical and relativist logics. Thus, two formally contrary and incompatible ideologemes, freedom and slavery, become interchangeable. Orwell's slogans directly juxtapose the initial and final links of this logical chain, omitting the intermediate links. "Freedom is Slavery" is not simply an extravagant formula; the paradox of the slogan reveals how ideo-logic works through a tetradic structure, ending by equating ideas that are proclaimed to be exact opposites.

The ability to equate opposites explains why it is so difficult to fight Soviet Marxist ideology by logical means: ideology is invulnerable to logical critique because it is free to use the components of various logics in response. If one attempts to prove that this ideology actually justifies aggression, the ideology answers that its final goal is worldwide peace, but that peace cannot be achieved without a decisive struggle and this struggle may require military means. Therefore, so-called pacifists, who deny the need for a decisive struggle against "imperialism" or "capitalism," encourage an oppressive government to be more aggressive. The structure of the *defensive* argument is always the same: to convert a negative, accusatory term (aggression) into a positive one (struggle) and correlate it with another positive term (peace). The structure of the *offensive* argument is also derived from the tetrad: to convert a positive term (peacefulness) into negative one (pacifism, appeasement) and correlate it with another negative term (aggression, militarism). Thus the opponent may be categorized simultaneously as a pacifist and warmonger.

Tetradic thinking surpasses the binary system of formal logic and the trinary system of dialectical logic in the quantity of its functions as well as the relationships possible among its elements. At the same time, tetradic logic can be distinguished from the amorphous structures of relativist logic, which have an indefinite quantity of elements. The diversity of relationships within the tetrad and their integrity as a unit make the tetrad an effective means of subordinating the interpretation of reality to the will of one person or organization.

The Nature of Ideology and the Evolution of Soviet Marxism

Ideology is a powerful instrument for working with the fundamental oppositions that have determined the evolution of philosophical thought throughout the ages. While ideology and philosophy both deal with the same basic concepts—ideas and matter, freedom and necessity, unity and diversity—they do so in very different ways.

For instance, the relationship between reality and ideas, or the material and the ideal, is a basic question of philosophy, the starting point for many of its divergent theories. Some philosophers proceed on the assumption that matter (or being, or reality) is primary; others give the priority to idea, spirit, or consciousness. Another group considers that both material and spiritual principles are combined in dualistic structures. Yet another group believes that it is impossible to establish any universal principle from which all existing phenomena can be deduced. The problem of the real and the ideal, as solved by philosophers, gives birth to such schools as materialism, idealism, dualism, agnosticism, etc. In spite of their disagreements, all philosophies try to reveal the truth as it exists in the nature of things; it is this common goal that makes all different "schools" branches of philosophical thought.

Ideology, on the other hand, is not interested in understanding the world; rather, it seeks to change it by organizing ideas to gain the greatest number of followers. Marx himself unconsciously formulated the difference between philosophy and ideology in his famous thesis: "the philosophers have only *interpreted* the world in various ways; the point is to *change* it."[26] Soviet Marxist ideology interprets the problem of the real and the ideal in non-philosophic terms by using "double dialectics," or tetralectics. The "ideal" and the "material" are conceived not as constituent parts of the universe, but as flexible components within the framework of changing historical conditions. Either component can acquire "primary" meaning in this framework; in some circumstances, "material" interests dominate, in others, "spiritual" elements have the upper hand. Economic forms of class struggle are combined with ideological forms; the "ideological superstructure" becomes of equal or even greater importance than the "material basis" from which it springs. Hence, Lenin's theory of the "decisive link" (*teoriia reshaiushchego zvena*), which changes depending on the situation. Grasping this link enables Marxist-Leninists to control the whole chain, master the situation, and gain victory over opponents.

If Marxist philosophy firmly holds that matter is primary and that consciousness is secondary, then Marxist ideology solves this basic question in accordance with concrete political goals, which often dictate that consciousness be given priority over matter. In most cases Soviet ideology, as opposed to Marxist philosophy, proclaims that ideas ("progressive," "revolutionary," "socialist," "communist," etc.) are the moving force of current historical transformations. Ideology thus appeals to the Soviet people's high level of consciousness, rather than their low level of material life, which remains as poor as ever.[27]

Like any binary opposition, "materialism" versus "idealism" is only the starting point for further ideological formulations created by the complicated permutation of the original binary pair. Accordingly, ideologemes are established that give tactical political advantage to both principles: good materialism versus bad idealism, and good *ideinost'* (commitment to ideas) versus bad *bezydeinost'* (indifference to ideas). Both "good" principles can then be combined, forming the oxymoronic idiom *materialisticheskaia ideinost* (commitment to the ideas of materialism). In the same manner, combining both "bad" principles creates the postulate that *bezydeinost'* (or, absence of ideas) may bring an "unstable" person to the swamp of idealism. In Soviet Marxist ideology, "material" and "ideal" principles can be used separately, simultaneously, or sequentially to give a political actor tactical flexibility in a changing situation.

In its early stages, Soviet Marxist ideology as a rule used only contratives in strong opposition to one another: "labor" versus "capital," the "proletariat" versus the "bourgeoisie," "internationalism" versus "nationalism," "collectivism" versus "individualism," and so on. However, as the ideology matured, it introduced new oppositions that transformed the initial dyads into complete tetradic structures. Thus, to the contrative dyad "materialism–idealism," the opposing contrative dyad "commitment to ideas–indifference to ideas" (or, spirituality–nonspirituality), was added. To the dyad "internationalism–nationalism," was added the complementary dyad "patriotism–cosmopolitanism." Thus, Soviet Marxism argued that internationalism was the goal of the proletarian movement—its highest achievement—and condemned narrow-minded, "bourgeois" nationalism and chauvinism. At the same time, however, the ideology ardently praised patriotism and demanded that citizens love the "socialist fatherland" more than their own fathers, while ridiculing both "bourgeois" cosmopolitanism and "Ivans" who did not remember their origin and kin. The question arises, should one regard Soviet ideology as "internationalist" or "chauvinist"?

Conditionally speaking, we can distinguish two types of ideologies: fighting ideology and governing ideology, or the ideology of opposition and the ideology of domination. The first is dyadic—no matter how radical or conservative in essence—because it is opposed to another ideology. The second is tetradic; it combines elements of opposing ideologies to maintain its power over the whole society and the various political factions of the ruling group. Marxist ideology originally had a leftist orientation, but as it was transformed into Soviet governing ideology it incorporated many conservative elements (such as civil obedience and patriotic duty) without abandoning its radical roots. On its path to maturity, Soviet Marxist ideology moved from the dyad to the tetrad as traditional Marxist dyads were complemented by new Leninist, Stalinist, and Brezhnevist dyads over the course of Soviet history.

It is during this process of transition from dyadic to tetradic structure that ideology meets its severest test: the challenge of the so-called deviations. Each deviation singles out one particular relationship from the tetradic whole and tries to absolutize it as the only truth. In Soviet Marxist ideology, the "left" deviation of the twenties associated with Trotsky singled out the contrative dyad "internationalism–nationalism," ignoring the correlative and contrative dyads "proletarian internationalism–socialist patriotism" and "socialist patriotism–bourgeois cosmopolitanism," respectively. The "left" also chose to exaggerate the importance of the "class struggle" at the expense of "peaceful coexistence." The "right" deviation associated with Bukharin emphasized an opposing set of dyads, advocating the "peaceful incorporation of kulaks in socialism" in place of the "class struggle against kulaks."

Though Stalin had already defeated his main political opponents, Trotsky and Bukharin, by 1930, the idea of "ideological struggle" took especially fierce forms in the late twenties and thirties. These "deviations" were not, for the most part, real forces, but inventions of the ruling ideology, which was rapidly passing from the "dyadic" to the "tetradic" stage precisely at this time. During the 1920s and 1930s, Soviet Marxist ideology needed to portray right and left deviations as one-sided ideological structures in order to distinguish the new, governing ideology from the old, "naive" fighting ideology.

If the Party constantly battled against deviations of both the left and the right, what was its true political identity? The answer is obvious: since it corrected the leftist deviation from the right and corrected the rightist deviation from the left, it was simultaneously a right-wing and a left-wing party. As the great Russian writer Andrei Platonov noted, the Party line did not admit the slightest creeping toward either the right or the left from the sharpness of the correct line. Indeed, the Party line was as sharp as a razor, one could not stand on it without being bloodied. Only Stalin managed to stand on it firmly with both feet.

Stalin's public statements illustrate the pendulum effect of Party politics. On 21 January 1930, Stalin published the seminal article "Concerning the Policy of Eliminating the Kulaks as a Class." In this article he insisted:

In order to oust the kulaks as a class, the resistance of this class must be *smashed* in open battle and it must be *deprived* of the productive sources of its existence and development (free use of land, instruments of production, land-renting, right to hire labor, etc.). That is a *turn* toward eliminating the Kulaks as a class. . . . Without it, talk about ousting the kulaks as a class is empty prattle, acceptable and profitable only to the Right deviators. Without it, no substantial, let alone complete, collectivization of the countryside is conceivable.[28]

Here, Stalin justified a turn to the left, or as he described it, "a *turn* away from the old policy of *restricting* (and ousting) the capitalist elements in the countryside toward the new policy of *eliminating* the kulaks as a class." Playing with the words "restricting" and "eliminating," Stalin found in the difference of their meanings an illusory possibility for the existence of a right deviation, which allegedly tried to represent the new policy of collectivization as a continuation of the old, meeker policy of restricting the kulaks. By stressing the need "to eliminate the kulaks as a class," Stalin attacked those "Right deviationists" who were not willing to support such a radical turn to the left.

On 2 March 1930, however, just forty days after the publication of the article cited above, Stalin published another, even more important work, "Dizzy With Success." In this article, he excoriated the "Left deviation" with the same characteristic vigor:

Collective farms must not be established by force. That would be foolish and reactionary . . .

We know that in a number of areas of Turkestan there have already been attempts to 'overtake and outstrip' the advanced areas of the USSR by threatening to use armed force, by threatening that peasants who are not yet ready to join the collective farms will be deprived of irrigation water and manufactured goods.

What can there be in common between this Sergeant Prishibeev 'policy' and the Party's policy of relying on the voluntary principle? . . . Who benefits by these distortions, this bureaucratic decreeing of the collective-farm movement, these unworthy threats against the peasants? Nobody, except our enemies! . . .

Is it not clear that the authors of these distortions, who imagine themselves to be 'Lefts,' are in reality bringing grist to the mill of Right opportunism?" (12:199, 201)

Stalin's second article clearly indicates a sharp turn to the right: the *leftists* are now accused of violating the sacred "voluntary" principles of collectivization.

In essence, both articles constitute a single political maneuver on Stalin's part: the destruction of all rivals on both the left and the right. It is impossible to ascertain his own "true position" vis-à-vis these "deviations." On the one hand, Stalin claims that the resistance of kulaks must be smashed in open battle (*nado slomit' v otkrytom boiu soprotivlenie etogo klassa*). On the other hand, Stalin insists that collective farms must not be established by force (*nel'zia nasazhdat' kolkhozy siloi*). How can these two opposing statements, "*nado*" and "*nel'zia*" ("must" and "must not"), be reconciled? How can one demand that "noncollectivized" peasants be "deprived of the productive sources of their existence and development" (*lishit' proizvodstvennyx istochnikov sushchestvovaniia*), if the threat "to deprive them of irrigation water and manufactured goods" (*ugrozy lishit' polivnoi vody i promtovarov*) is condemned as a severe political mistake? No rational position exists in between these two approaches to collectivization, yet both are branded as "deviations."

One would suppose that, given this "struggle on two fronts," Stalin identified himself as "centrist." Interestingly enough, however, he did not forget to also fight centrism as a "rotten compromise" between right and left deviations. In a 1931 article, "On Some Questions of the History of Bolshevism," he wrote:

> Underestimation of centrism is, as a matter of fact, a refusal to engage in all-out struggle against opportunism. . . . Everyone knows that Leninism was born, grew up, and got stronger in the merciless struggle against opportunism of every stripe, including centrism in the West (Kautsky) and in our country (Trotsky and others). Even direct enemies of Bolshevism cannot deny it. This is an axiom.[29]

It is instructive to trace the logic of Stalin's successive political maneuvers of 1930–31. First, he identified himself with the left against the right, then he swung right in order to fight the left, and finally, he attacked the center itself. We can find here two overlapping tetradic structures. In the first tetrad the "centrist" position is praised as the so-called party line and is opposed to "perilous deviations"; at the same time, sharp political demarcation and "the struggle on both fronts" is opposed to "rotten centrism" and "unprincipled compromise."

+center	−extremes
General Party line	Right and Left deviations
+extremes	−center
Demarcation, a fight on two fronts	Centrism, compromise

The second tetrad concerns the "extremes" themselves. On the one hand, the officially approved leftist slogan calling for the elimination of the kulaks as a class, is opposed to the distinctly rightist call for "ousting" (or "restricting") the kulaks and to the call of the "far right" for the peaceful incorporation of kulaks into socialist society. On the other hand, the rightist principle of voluntary collectivization is distinctly positive when opposed to the "inadmissable" leftist threat to use the Army and conduct a "Sergeant Prishibeev" policy.

+left	−right
("smash," "battle," "elimination")	("opportunism," "half-measures")
+right	−left
("the voluntary principle,"	("threat," "force," "bureaucratic
"contact with the masses")	decrees")

Here we see how tetrads overlap and proliferate in ideological thinking. In the first tetrad, "extremes" are opposed to the "center"; in the second tetrad, the "left" extreme is opposed to the "right" extreme. Tetralectics constantly works through different conceptual levels, further dissecting those concepts that have already been split into binary oppositions on a more abstract level. The "center" can be both positive and negative in contrast to "extremes," whose evaluation also changes depending on the situation:

$$+center \qquad\qquad -extreme$$
$$-right \qquad -left$$
$$+extreme \qquad\qquad -center$$
$$+left \qquad +right$$

One secret of Stalin's influence was his lack of specific political positions; hence, his brilliant mastery of tetralectics. Trotsky and Bukharin had definite positions that made them easy to attack. They were naive from the point of view of totalitarian thinking: in spite of their other tactical skills, both tried to adhere to certain stable principles. While Stalin understood the undefined X variable in Soviet Marxist political algebra, Trotsky and Bukharin used a more "classic Marxist" political arithmetic in which all expressions were constants. Alexander Herzen's famous definition of dialectics as the "algebra of revolution" was perhaps a prophetic vision of Stalin's manipulation of the X factor.

Karl Marx first described this concept of political mathematics in 1881: "What should be done spontaneously in any specific moment in the future of course depends completely on the given historical conditions in which one will have to act. We cannot solve an equation which does not include the elements of its solution among its data."[30] Marx believed that the information necessary to pin down the unknown variable, the X of the equation, would become available at the appropriate moment. Stalin, however, found it advantageous to keep the value of X undefined, a variable that could not be reduced to any specific meaning.

In varying historical conditions X could mean: to attack the left from the right, to assault the right from the left, or to trample the centrists on their own middle ground. In each case, it is the absence of position that struggles and prevails. The introduction of variables, or blank chits, into the ideological scrabble game increases the stakes, as all positions of one's rivals and opponents can then be utilized. In his fight against rightists, Stalin was more "left" than Trotsky himself, while in his fight against leftists, Stalin was no less "right" than Bukharin. Stalin used his enemies' own ideas against them, in the same flexible manner that Lenin used "extreme leftist" slogans of the Socialist Revolutionaries in 1917–18 and "definitely rightist" bourgeois slogans in 1921–22 (NEP).

A recent example of tetradic left-right discourse elaborating the opposition of liberty and organization may be found in Mikhail Gorbachev's Report on the First Congress of the People's Deputies of the USSR (30 May 1989).[31]

Here is a fragment of his speech where I have emphasized the key concepts constituting the tetrad and marked them with corresponding "+" and "–" signs:

Our Congress can not depart from the issue which is the source of increasing anxiety in the society. I have in mind the current state of *discipline and order* (+A). To speak frankly, this state does not satisfy us and demands decisive improvements. We have suffered large losses, both economic and moral, because of *poor discipline* (−B) and bad implementation of official duties, primarily in the sphere of labor.

This has extremely negative consequences for all of society; *irresponsibility and disorder* cause *disorganization* (−B) in the daily lives of people, add unnecessary stress, drive people crazy, and evoke dissatisfaction. In spite of all this, for some reason it became shameful to demand *discipline and order* (+A). Some people identify such timid attempts as the undermining of *democracy* (+B), the intention to revive the *command system, and the slave psychology* (−A) in people.

Certainly for some people, this talk about discipline is nothing but nostalgia for the old times. Indeed, comrades, this is true for some people. One speaks about discipline while thinking about the '*iron hand*' (−A) and a return to the *old order* (−A): "it is said, just do it without any discussion." Probably such nostalgia has a place.

However, comrades, today the main point is different. From our own experience, each of us feels where *poor discipline* (−B) leads and thus we must take a firm position at this Congress: without *discipline* (+A), without *order* (+A), the cause of *perestroika* (+B) will not move ahead. [*applause*]

Democratization (+B) needs an increase in *discipline* (+A) proceeding from the growth of people's social activity. To all *disorder* (−B), we must oppose the criteria of high responsibility for all entrusted tasks. We shouldn't be ashamed to increase our requirements for *discipline and order* (+A).

Definitely the main point of this passage is the call for improved discipline. However, this idea is formulated in the typical tetradic mode. The first ideological argument is expressed with a contrative opposition: discipline must be decisively supported against disorder and irresponsibility (+A against −B).

Then the conversive relationships in the tetrad are clearly introduced: discipline may be identified with such negative phenomena as the "iron hand," nostalgia for the command system, and a slave mentality (+A mistaken for −A). These relapses may be opposed to democracy under the pretext of strengthening discipline.

Gorbachev proceeds to confirm his commitment to democracy and distaste for the command system (+B against −A). Taking a conversive path, he reverses the pattern of the first dyad consisting of discipline and disorder (+A and −B) and creates an opposite dyad of democracy and the "iron hand" (+B and −A).

Then he elegantly completes the circle by emphasizing the correlative relationship of the two positive terms, democracy and discipline (+B and +A). "Democratization needs the improvement of discipline." This juxtaposition of two ideologemes, opposite in their denotative meanings, typically constitutes the most rhetorical and ultimately dialectical component of Soviet ideological discourse.

These (ideo)logical operations may be presented in the following scheme:

1. The main point, or initial *contrative* dyad:

   discipline–disorder $(+A/-B)$

2. Reservations involving the *conversive* elements: opponents identify discipline with an "iron hand" and democracy with "disorder," which must be distinguished as conversives:

   discipline–"iron hand" $(+A/-A)$
   democracy–disorder $(+B/-B)$

3. The parallel argument, complementing the initial *contrative* dyad with yet another contrative dyad:

   democracy–"iron hand" $(+B/-A)$

4. The conclusion, juxtaposing *correlative* elements:

   discipline–democracy $(+A/+B)$

Thus the full range of relationships in the tetrad is coherently introduced in Gorbachev's speech:

   discipline–disorder $(+A/-B)$
   democracy–"iron hand" $(+B/-A)$

Having defeated both the right and the left, Soviet Marxist ideology could assert itself as a qualitatively new, "left-right" ideology. No political deviation could create a constructive alternative to this totalitarian ideology, because all deviations—so plentiful in the history of Soviet Marxism—had no choice but to speak the native language of the single, "correct" ideology. They suffered from a severe "speech impediment": as small, individual parts of the total ideological structure, they posed no threat to the ideology's overall existence. In fact, the one-sidedness of deviations only served to demonstrate the advantages and correctness of the ruling left-right ideology.

Ideological Functions, Lexical Groups, and Philosophical Oppositions

Now that we have elucidated the inner principle of tetradic thinking, we can further develop the model by describing how it works through the lexical diversity of ideolanguage. The reader may already have noticed that I have consistently placed certain words in the same position in tetrad diagrams. Words such as "internationalism," "collectivism," and "peaceful-ness" have been placed in the first position on the first line, for example, and words like "nationalism," "individualism," and "aggressiveness" in the second position on the first line, and so on. In fact, each position in the tetrad is occupied not by a concrete word, but by a generalized ideological meaning that can be realized by a multiplicity of words. This section will attempt to demonstrate that, just as each position in the tetrad represents a generalized meaning, tetrads themselves incorporate generalized semantic functions that correspond to the fundamental oppositions of philosophy.

The Opposition of "Unity and Differentiation".

Let us compare several similar tetrads:

> peacefulness–aggressiveness
> uncompromisingness–appeasement
>
> cooperation–confrontation
> fighting spirit–compromise
>
> collectivism–individualism
> concern for the individual–depersonalization
>
> classlessness–class antagonism
> class struggle–non-class approach
>
> *miroliubie–agressivnost'*
> *neprimirimost'–primirenchestvo*
>
> *sotrudnichestvo–konfrontatsiia*
> *boevitost'–soglashatel'stvo*
>
> *kollektivizm–individualizm*
> *individual'nyi podkhod–obezlichka*
>
> *besklassovoe obshchestvo–klassovyi antagonizm*
> *klassovaia bor'ba–vneklassovyi podkhod*

In spite of their lexical differences, it is obvious that all these tetrads modify one set of semantic functions:

> positive unity–negative differentiation
> positive differentiation–negative unification

Depicted schematically, these functions are:

> +un　　−dif
> +dif　　−un[32]

Each function represents an entire group of words that are connected by a *substitutive* relationship. This fourth type of relationship between ideologemes, which was not incorporated in the tetradic model (see above), plays an enormous role in the lexical realization of the tetrad. Let us examine a list of substitutives for the four ideological functions diagramed above:

+un		−dif	
peace	*mir*	hostility	*vrazhda*
unity	*edinstvo*	split	*raskol*
solidarity	*splochenie*	antagonism	*antagonizm*
cooperation	*sotrudnichestvo*	confrontation	*konfrontatsiia*
equality	*ravenstvo*	inequality	*neravenstvo*
brotherhood	*bratstvo*	(bourgeois) competition	*konkurentsiia*
classlessness	*besklassovost'*	antagonism	*antagonizm*
peacefulness	*miroliubie*	militarism	*militarizm*
collectivism	*kollektivizm*	individualism	*individualizm*
internationalism	*internatsionalizm*	nationalism	*natsionalizm*
friendship of nations	*druzhba narodov*	chauvinism	*shovinizm*

+dif		−un	
struggle	*bor'ba*	appeasement	*umirotvorenie*
uncompromisingness	*neprimirimost'*	compromise	*primirenchestvo*
steadfastness	*nepokolebimost'*	all-forgiveness	*vseproshchenie*
fighting spirit	*boevitost'*	capitulation	*kapituliatsiia*
class consciousness	*klassovoe soznanie*	nonclass approach	*vneklassovyi podkhod*
demarcation	*razmezhevanie*	forming a bloc	*blokirovanie*
concern for the individual	*individual'nyi podkhod*	depersonalization	*obezlichka*
(socialist) competition	*sorevnovanie*	wage-leveling	*uravnilovka*

This list is by no means complete, but suffices to demonstrate how tetralectics works with the aid of substitutive ideologemes. The traditional philosophical opposites of "unity" and "differentiation" are split into four ideological functions, which in turn are split into a multiplicity of concrete words that give a positive and negative evaluation to both "unity" and "differentiation." Thus abstract philosophical concepts are integrated into and dispersed throughout the lexical variety of language.

It is apparent from the above list that substitutives are not true synonyms in the usual linguistic sense. The principle of their unification lies in the pragmatic, not semantic, realm of linguistic analysis. Substitutives such as "struggle," "demarcation," "class consciousness," "fighting spirit," etc., express a particular evaluative judgment (here, positive) about a general phenomenon (in this case, differentiation). While they are unified, or classified, by their functional meaning (+dif, −un, etc.), the substitutives differ according to the specific subject area of their referential meaning. For instance, in Soviet ideolanguage the word "struggle" signifies the opposition of "our people" to "their people." The word "demarcation" signifies the opposition between "our people" and "our people," with the latter destined to become "their people." Two words for "competition" exist in Soviet ideolanguage: *konkurentsiia,* or bourgeois competition, is used to show how "their" people compete against each other; *sorevnovanie* is used to show "healthy competition" between "our" people.

Each substitutive ideologeme may be signified by utilizing a combination of its ideological function (+un, −dif, etc.) and a descriptive marker (placed in brackets) identifying the subject area to which the function applies. When, for instance, the function +dif is accompanied by different markers, it is lexically transformed into a variety of words, depending on the subject area. Let us examine the following three examples:

Subject Area: "us" versus "them"
+dif [us–them] is transformed into the word "struggle"
−dif [us–them] is transformed into the word "confrontation"
+dif [us–us] is transformed into "socialist competition"
−dif [them–them] is transformed into "bourgeois competition"

Subject Area: the "nation" or national feeling
+un [national] becomes "internationalism"
−un [national] becomes "cosmopolitanism"
+dif [national] becomes "patriotism"
−dif [national] becomes "chauvinism"

Subject Area: "society" or social identification
+un [social] becomes "collectivism"
−un [social] becomes "depersonalization"
+dif [social] becomes "concern for the individual"
−dif [social] becomes "individualism"

These groups of symbolic constructions clearly demonstrate that Soviet Marxist ideological language is by its very nature artificial; it would be possible to outline its structure using abstract formulas. With specific formulas of functions and markers, a computer would be capable of composing Soviet ideological texts.

The "Real–Ideal" Opposition

A second important philosophical concept incorporated into ideological thinking is opposition of "the real" and "the ideal." Ideological thinking divides these opposing concepts into four broad functions, each of which is represented by its own group of ideologemes:

+real		−ideal	
realism	*realizm*	idealism	*idealizm*
materialism	*materializm*	spiritualism	*spiritualizm*
objectivity	*ob"ektivnost'*	subjectivism	*sub"ektivizm*
atheism	*ateizm*	religion	*religiia*
truthfulness	*pravdivost'*	myth-making	*mifotvorchestvo*
scientific method	*nauchnost'*	obscurantism	*mrakobesie*
sober-mindedness	*zdravomyslie*	fanaticism	*fanatizm*
historicism	*istorizm*	dogmatism	*dogmatizm*

+ideal		−real	
commitment to ideas	*ideinost'*	indifference to ideas	*bezydeinost'*
spirituality	*dukhovnost'*	lack of spirituality	*bezdukhovnost'*
having ideals	*ideal'nost'*	devoid of ideals	*bezydeal'nost'*
adherence to principle	*printsipial'nost'*	nonadherence to principle	*besprintsipnost'*
heroic spirit	*geroika*	Philistinism	*meshchanstvo*
romantic appeal	*romantika*	naturalism	*naturalizm*
enthusiasm	*entuziazm*	empiricism	*empirizm*[33]
inspiration	*vdokhnovenie*	positivism	*pozitivizm*
winged inspiration	*okrylionnost'*	shackled inspiration	*beskrylost'*

All of the above substitutives may be distributed among varying referential subject areas. For example, the words "materialism," "realism," "atheism," and "historicism" give a positive evaluative meaning to the material principle ("the real"), which is viewed as superior to "the ideal." However, these ideologemes are utilized in different areas of social consciousness: "materialism" in philosophy, "realism" in literature and art, "atheism" in religious matters, and "historicism" in the area of the social sciences:

+real [philosophy]   =   materialism
+real [literature]   =   realism
+real [religion]   =   atheism
+real [humanities]   =   historicism

Not only single words, but many phrases and idioms are capable of executing the same ideological function. The following are standard expressions of Soviet literary criticism:

+ real function

the truth of life	*pravda zhizni*
a close connection with reality	*tesnaia sviaz' s deistvitel'nost'iu*
the genuineness of experience	*podlinnost' perezhitogo*
an emphasis on the facts	*opora na fakty*

− real function

dragged down by facts	*plestis' v khvoste u faktov*
description without feeling	*beskrylaia opisatel'nost'*
to be a prisoner of one's own sensations	*ostavat'sia v plenu sobstvennykh oshchushchenii*

+ ideal function

flight of the imagination	*polet voobrazheniia*
to create a new, spiritualized reality	*sozdavat' novuiu, odukhotvorennuiu real'nost'*
to soar to higher generalizations	*voskhodit' k vysshim obobshcheniiam*
artistic transformation of the facts	*khudozhestvennoe preobrazhenie faktov*

− ideal function

romantic delirium	*romanticheskie bredni*
a struggle against common sense	*bor'ba so zdravym smyslom*
arbitrary subjectivity and contempt for the facts	*sub"ektivnyi proizvol i prezrenie k faktam*
idle daydreaming	*prazdnye grezy*

Because ideological functions are stable and embrace a variety of single and multiple-word units, it would be instructive to trace the history of at least one of these functions through different ages and cultures. Although expressions may change, the functions remain the same. Entire texts of literary and political works may principally express one or another ideological function; for example, practically all works of the famous Russian literary critic Pisarev embody the "−ideal" function, which represents a nihilistic worldview.

The "Liberty–Organization" Opposition

Now we will consider the tetrad of ideological functions dealing with "liberty" and "organization" ("lib" and "org"). We must emphasize that in the Soviet ideological mentality, "organization" indicates that "liberty" is limited by "necessity," "order," and "discipline."

+lib		−org	
liberty	*svoboda*	oppression	*gnet*
freedom	*svoboda, volia*	slavery	*rabstvo*
love of freedom	*svobodoliubie*	repression	*podavlenie*
free-thinking	*vol'nomyslie*	authoritarianism	*avtoritarnost'*
emancipation	*raskreposhchenie*	enslavement	*zakreposhchenie*
rebelliousness	*buntarstvo*	submissiveness	*pokornost'*
independence	*nezavisimost'*	dependence	*podnevol'nost'*
insurgency	*miatezh(nost')*	subjugation	*poraboshchenie*
democracy	*demokratiia*	totalitarianism	*totalitarizm*
activism	*aktivizm*	fatalism	*fatalizm*
self-government	*samoupravlenie*	tyranny	*tiraniia*
initiative	*pochin*	coercion	*prinuzhdenie*

+org		−lib	
order	*poriadok*	anarchy	*anarkhiia*
discipline	*distsiplina*	license	*raspushchennost'*
proceeding according to plan	*planovost'*	spontaneity	*stikhiinost'*
centralism	*tsentralizm*	provincialism	*mestnichestvo*
necessity	*neobkhodimost'*	arbitrariness	*proizvol, samoupravstvo*
organization	*organizatsiia*	chaos	*khaos*
determinism	*determinizm*	voluntarism	*voliuntarizm*
responsibility	*otvetstvennost'*	connivance	*popustitel'stvo*
vigilance	*bditel'nost'*	carelessness	*bespechnost'*
lawfulness	*zakonnost'*	lawlessness	*bezzakonie*

The "Property" Opposition

The fourth functional tetrad is based on oppositions that involve the concept of property, such as "to give–to take," "to share–to acquire," "to donate–to become rich." Here the attitude toward the ownership of material goods (generosity–stinginess), as well as the corresponding attitude toward one's own life (bravery–cowardice), should be borne in mind. I derive the names of the four ideological functions from the Latin words *donare* (to grant, to refuse) and *habere* (to possess, to keep).

+don		–hab	
generosity	*shchedrost'*	stinginess	*skupost'*
bravery	*khrabrost'*	cowardice	*trusost'*
selflessness	*samootverzhennost'*	selfishness	*svoekorystie*
altruism	*al'truizm*	egoism	*egoizm*
philanthropy	*zhertvennost'*	exploitation	*ekspluatatsiia*
magnanimity	*velikodushie*	acquisitiveness	*stiazhatel'stvo*[34]
selflessness	*beskorystie*	hoarding	*nakopitel'stvo*
heroic asceticism	*podvizhnichestvo*	utilitarianism, careerism	*deliachestvo*

+hab		–don	
thriftiness	*berezhlivost'*	wastefulness	*rastochitel'nost'*
enterprisingness	*predpriimchivost'*	mismanagement	*beskhoziaistvennost'*
efficiency	*delovitost'*	negligence	*khalatnost'*
zealousness	*rachitel'nost'*	laziness	*lenost'*
practicality	*praktichnost'*	impracticality	*nepraktichnost'*
effectiveness	*effektivnost'*	ineffectiveness	*neeffektivnost'*
prudence	*predusmotritel'nost'*	recklessness	*bezrassudstvo*
		slipshodness	*razgil'diaistvo*

The "Time" Opposition

Finally, the fifth functional tetrad consists of evaluations connected with the passage of time. Here the general oppositions of new and old, development and succession, of *nov*elty and *trad*ition, are ideologically transformed:

+nov		–trad	
the new	*novoe*	the old	*staroe*
innovation	*novatorstvo*	conservatism	*konservatizm*
revolution(ary)	*revoliutsiia*	reaction(ary)	*reaktsiia*

progress	*progress*	regression	*regress*
development	*razvitie*	backwardness	*otstalost'*
renewal	*obnovlenie*	staleness	*kosnost'*
perestroika	*perestroika*	stagnation	*zastoi*
acceleration	*uskorenie*	retardation	*otstavanie*
shock-worker	*udarnik, peredovik*	laggard	*otstaiushchii*
creative spirit	*tvorcheskii dukh*	dogmatism	*dogmatizm*
topical	*aktual'nyi, nasushchnyi*	outdated	*ustarelyi*
striving toward the future	*ustremlennost' v budushchee*	remnants of the past	*perezhitki proshlogo*

+trad   −nov

tradition	*traditsiia*	breaking with tradition	*razryv s traditsiei*
continuity	*preemstvennost'*	revisionism	*revizionizm*
stability	*stabil'nost'*	subversive activities	*podryvnaia deiatel'nost'*
the classics	*klassika*	avant-gardism	*avangardizm*
tried and true	*ispytannyi*	newly fashionable	*novomodnyi*
veteran	*veteran*	upstart	*vyskochka*
Marxist testament	*zavety marksizma*	revision of Marxism	*reviziia marksizma*

The Classification of Ideologemes

A tentative examination of Soviet ideolanguage reveals that the overwhelming majority of ideologemes belong to one of the five lexical subsystems listed above. Ideologemes can thus be arranged according to the twenty ideological functions contained within the tetrads of these five groups:

1. +un   −dif   +dif   −un
2. +real   −ideal   +ideal   −real
3. +lib   −org   +org   −lib
4. +don   −hab   +hab   −don
5. +nov   −trad   +trad   −nov

At this time, we can only conjecture as to why these five specific subsystems encompass so many ideological concepts. The oppositions of "unity–differentiation," "the real–the ideal," "freedom–necessity," "giving–acquisition," "development–continuity" are those most deeply rooted in the structure of the human intellect, to which the long history of philosophy attests. We can find expressions of these basic oppositions in the paradoxes of Heraclitus, in Zenon's "aporia," in the Kantian antinomies of reason, and in the Hegelian principles of the dialectic.

It is significant that three of the oppositions discussed in this section approximate three of the Kantian antinomies, those that concern the relationship between "unity and divisibility of composed substance," "freedom and causality," and the "finiteness and infinity" of time. A purely theoretical solution of the problem posed by the two opposing components of an antinomy is extremely difficult, perhaps impossible, to reach. For this reason, human thinking is inclined to subdivide these irreconcilable concepts further, giving each one a set of two opposing evaluations—overcoming the tension of the dual structure by establishing a tetradic framework. The predilection of human beings to do away with logical paradoxes may explain the attraction and power of ideology in society.

A paradox is divided into two opposite, yet individually self-evident, even trivial statements that together constitute the basis for ideological thinking. Instead of one intractable antinomy of freedom and causality, two indisputable judgments emerge: that freedom is superior to slavery (complete causality) and that organization is superior to anarchy (complete freedom). In this manner, ideology suggests nothing other than the solution to the sharpest contradictions of the human mind. The theoretical insolubility of antinomies leads one to believe that only in a specific historical situation can the priority of one particular element of the antinomy be established. Since the thesis and antithesis (freedom and causality, or matter and ideas) are equally valid, their relationship is removed from the sphere of objective truth to the sphere of pragmatic evaluation. The practical determination of this relationship is the core of ideological thinking, which endows each concept with a relative value.

Hegel and Marx both suggested ways of treating these radical antinomies. Hegel tried to solve such a contradiction through the self-development of an absolute idea, which divides itself into thesis and antithesis in order to promote a final synthesis. For Marx, the highest principle is not the ideal absolute, but the historical subject (class, party, or group), which uses both thesis and antithesis to raise itself above their one-sidedness to the status of a historical totality. The Hegelian absolute is located beyond history and thus displays a dialectical triad, as the struggle between thesis and antithesis results in synthesis. Ideology is immersed in the dynamics of the historical process itself; thus, instead of reconciling thesis and antithesis, it constantly rejects one-sided elements, only to use their energy to ascend to higher and higher levels of totality.

Since this totality is intrahistorical (i.e., "within" history), it cannot be resolved in a synthesis of all elements, but exists only in the process of its own self-construction and self-destruction. The totality appears not as a comprehensive synthesis where all oppositions are reconciled, but as an incessantly fluctuating system that moves from left to right and back again. The opposites themselves double, alternately approved and condemned, included and excluded, from the totality. Thus Marxist ideology, as distinct from Hegelian idealism, is best described in tetradic, not triadic, terms. While the triadic model accounts for the birth of a new idea and thus is progressive, the tetradic model is circular and envelops opposing ideas without producing anything substantially new.

Marxist ideology fulfilled the need to explain certain peculiarities of Russian history—peculiarities that display a huge diversity of, as well as alternation between, opposing tendencies. Russian history appears to revolve around a stable axis instead of advancing in a particular direction. Revolution and reaction, conservatism and radicalism, monarchy and democracy, authority and the people, leader and the masses, freedom and unity, material and spiritual, idealism and realism—all these theses and antitheses never reach a synthesis in Russia. Rather, they continually succeed one another.[35] Constantly evolving tetradic models suggest a logical expression of this cyclical historical process.

It is therefore natural that the largest groups of ideologically charged words in Soviet ideolanguage can be classified according to the fundamental oppositions of philosophy. All possible methods of solving these basic oppositions are present in the ideolanguage itself, embodied in its system of lexically fixed evaluations.

Ideological Syntax: Forms of Address

Although syntax seems to be an ideologically neutral dimension of language, in this section I shall try to demonstrate that the tetradic patterns of totalitarian discourse can be found not only in the lexical realm, but even in such a grammatical sphere as forms of address. These forms usually appear in oral communication in Soviet ideolanguage, but occasionally permeate the written language as well. I am not referring here to forms used to address a mass audience in oratorical speech, but to those used between individuals.

The Russian language has two typical forms of address, formal and informal. The formal combines the second-person-plural pronoun with an individual's first name and patronymic: "*Vy*, Aleksei Nikolaevich (You, Aleksei
Nikolaevich)." The familiar form of address combines the second-person-
singular pronoun with only the forename, often shortened to become a diminutive (in the same way Americans might change "Stephen" to "Steve"):
"*Ty*, Aliosha (Thou, Aliosha)."[36]

Ideological language, however, most often combines the familiar pronoun
with the formal name and patronymic: "*Ty*, Aleksei Nikolaevich." This form
of address is the norm between members of the Communist Party, even in
the Politburo. Such a combination reflects the twofold nature of ideological
language: in addressing an ideological brother it is impossible to use the *vy*
form, but since this "brother" is not a blood relation, it is necessary to retain
some element of formality when addressing him. The element of formality
was strengthened when ideological language became the official language
of Soviet society. Thus, ideological language is simultaneously brotherly
and official, a combination of familiarity and formality.

Members of the Communist Youth League (Komsomol) adapt this ideological form of address to correspond to their (younger) age; they drop the
patronymic and employ the *ty* form with the formal forename: "*Ty*, Aleksei."
In principle, "Aleksei" sounds as formal as "Aleksei Nikolaevich," perhaps
even drier. In colloquial speech, the formal first name is used very seldom,
especially between young people of the same age, who normally address
one another with shortened, or diminutive, forms of their first names: Aliosha, Misha, Lena, and so on. In the famous novel of Nikolai Ostrovsky,
How the Steel Was Tempered (1932–34), the central character—Komsomol
leader Pavel Korchagin—is usually addressed in the typical Komsomol
manner, "*Ty*, Pavel," although older people and intimate friends sometimes
call him the informal "Pavka."

It is significant that within intelligentsia circles, the most common form
of address between young people first meeting or not closely acquainted is
the polite, plural pronoun with a shortened first name: "*Vy*, Aliosha." This
form of address is the diametric opposite of that encountered in ideological
language ("*Ty*, Aleksei Nikolaevich"). It is possible to conclude that both the
choice of the form of an individual's name and the choice of pronoun have
their own significance. The choice of name is largely a question of the level
of officialdom: Komsomol or Party dealings are decidedly formal, whereas
dealings between members of the intelligentsia are purposefully informal.
On the other hand, the use of a particular pronoun indicates the relationship

between the two people. By using the polite pronoun, a person shows respect for his interlocutor as an individual and indicates that he seeks neither to belittle nor intrude into the life of his conversation partner. By addressing a man as "*ty* + full name,"[37] ideological language elevates officialdom at the expense of personal dignity and private freedom. The language of the intelligentsia combines precisely the opposite components: informality and politeness.

In terms of ideological evaluation, forms of address constitute a tetradic structure. They have two sets of oppositions: official–informal and positive–negative. From an ideological point of view, official forms of address in ideological language have both positive (full-name) and negative (*vy*) modes of expression. Informal address also has ideologically charged positive (*ty*) and negative (short-name) forms of address. The schematic of this tetrad could be drawn as follows:

+familiar	−formal
+formal	−familiar

or

+	−
Singular pronoun	Plural pronoun
(*Ty*)	(*Vy*)
Full name	Short name
(Aleksei Nikolaevich)	(Aliosha)

All previously described relationships between ideologemes can be observed in the pairings of the forms of "you" with variants of a person's name. "*Ty–vy*," as well as "Aleksei Nikolaevich–Aliosha," constitute contrative pairs; they have opposite denotative (official–informal) and connotative meanings (ideologically acceptable–ideologically unacceptable). "*Ty–*Aliosha" is an example of a conversive pair; both elements have an informal meaning, even if one (*ty*) has a positive ideological connotation and the other does not. The same goes for the other conversive pair, "*Vy* (ideologically negative)–Aleksei Nikolaevich (ideologically positive)." It is noteworthy that these two conversive combinations are the forms of address typical in nonideological usage; the concepts of officialdom and politeness naturally coincide in ordinary language. In nonideological language, either an individual's full name is used with the plural pronoun, or his or her diminutive is used with the singular pronoun.

Finally, "*Ty*–Aleksei Nikolaevich" constitutes a correlative pair: both the informal and official components have a positive connotative meaning. It is only ideological language that uniquely combines officialdom with familiarity. As seen earlier, correlatives are usually juxtaposed in ideological speech as grammatically homogeneous units. The juxtaposition of informal and official components in "*Ty*–Aleksei Nikolaevich" is an example of the same kind of correlative combination as "the strengthening of international and patriotic upbringing" or "commitment to materialistic ideas" (*materialisticheskaia ideinost'*).

Each of these oxymoronic expressions is a result of a modification of orthodox Marxism by totalitarian ideology. For example, the original Marxist conception of international proletarian solidarity had to accept the incorporation of patriotic sentiment for the sake of protecting the Soviet state. Likewise, the original orthodox conception of materialism was supplemented by Lenin's conception of "Party spirit" (*partiinost'*) and ideological commitment (*ideinost'*). Finally, pre-Revolutionary feelings of proletarian brotherhood called for the use of *ty,* but this class, having attained power, could not but adopt the traditional forms of address of the state bureaucracy. Thus, the forms of address used in Soviet ideolanguage demonstrate again the oxymoronic nature of totalitarian thinking originating in Soviet Marxism's dual "governing–revolutionary" structure.

The Self-Evaluation of Ideology:
The Metatetrad

The rules of ideological syntax are determined by the relationships between ideologemes. These ideologemes, however, not only evaluate reality, they evaluate one another as well. The system of metaideologemes—the metatetrad—is so vital to the operation of ideological language that it merits special discussion as a lexical subsystem apart from those lexical groups classified earlier.

The metatetrad is the premise for the existence of all other lexical subsystems; it is this "supertetrad" that extends ideolanguage beyond the simplistic level demonstrated above and allows it to counter all criticisms. For example, the ideologemes "to blacken," "to smear" (*ocherniat'*) or "to whitewash" (*obeliat'*) impart a negative evaluation to words that already have been used ideologically. Let us take another look at the situation described by Thucydides: *A* characterizes his own inclination to risky activities as "bravery," while his opponent *B* characterizes *A*'s inclination as "recklessness." The positive and negative evaluations contained in these words may then be reevaluated and reflected by each opponent. From *A*'s point of view,

B is "blackening" his bravery, but from *B*'s point of view, *A* is "whitewashing" his recklessness; one evaluation becomes grounds for further evaluative judgments and the alteration of defensive and offensive arguments. *A* uses *B*'s negative evaluation of his reckless behavior as grounds to condemn *B*'s "blackening" of *A*'s acts. *B*, on the other hand, uses the positive term that *A* used to describe his own actions (bravery) as the basis for condemning *A* (whitewashing).

Verbs like "to blacken," "to whitewash," "to falsify," and "to discredit" are elements of an ideological metalanguage that describes (or evaluates) ideologemes themselves. In this discussion, I shall differentiate between primary ideologemes and the "metaideologemes" that describe them. In analyzing the structure of metaideologemes, we will use the same plus and minus (+ and −) scheme we used for primary ideologemes. The first "+" or "−" will describe the connotative meaning of the metaideologeme, the second "+" or "−" will describe its denotative meaning. As distinct from primary ideologemes, which denote specific objects or concepts ("+freedom" or "−unity"), metaideologemes are evaluations of evaluations; thus their denotative meanings are indicated not by concrete words, but by a "+" or "−." For example, the metaideologeme "to blacken" may be designated as "− −" because it gives a negative evaluation of something positive, and is thus itself negative (a person who *blackens* another person is reprehensible). The metaideologeme "to whitewash" may be designated as "− +" because it gives a positive evaluation of something negative, and so must be evaluated negatively itself.

A mutual interdependence between ideologemes of the two levels is regulated by the following rules. If a primary ideologeme is positive, then a metaideologeme can give it either a positive evaluation and evoke a positive attitude in the speaker (+ +), or a negative evaluation and evoke a negative attitude (− −). Such positive ideologemes as "peace," "freedom," "equality," and "progress," may be referred to by metaideologemes of the "+ +" type: "to proclaim" (*provozglashat'*), "to praise" (*vospevat'*), "to glorify" (*slavit', proslavliat'*). For example, "Marx and Engels *proclaimed* (+ +) full emancipation not only for the working class, but for all mankind." However, the same positive ideologemes can also be invoked by metaideologemes of the "− −" type: "to blacken" (*ocherniat'*), "to find fault with" (*okhaivat'*), "to defame" (*shel'movat'*), "to slander" (*klevetat'*), "to trample upon" (*popirat'*). For instance, "our nation's enemies are *slandering* (− −) the freedom the Soviet people won through fierce battles of the Great Patriotic War." These metaideologemes contain a negative evaluation of some positive object, thereby also giving a negative characterization of the speaker who "slandered" or "defamed" the positive value.

Negative primary ideologemes like "aggression," "violence," "confrontation," "exploitation," and "lawlessness" can be referred to as "+ –" or "– +" metaideologemes. Metaideologemes of the "+ –" type, for example, "to unmask" (*razoblachat'*), "to stigmatize" (*kleimit'*), "to condemn" (*osuzhdat'*), "to denounce" (*oblichat'*), express a negative attitude toward negative objects and therefore are themselves positive. "One of the primary goals of Soviet political education is to *unmask* (+ –) the subversive intentions of imperialist circles against the legitimate socialist governments of Eastern Europe." The same negative primary ideologemes can be referred to by metaideologemes of the "– +" type—to relish" (*smakovat'*), "to whitewash" (*obeliat'*), "to cultivate" (*kul'tivirovat'; nasazhdat'*), "to extol" (*prevoznosit'*), "to proclaim" (*proklamirovat'*)—which express an actively positive attitude toward negative phenomena and therefore have negative meanings. "The mass culture of the West *relishes* (– +) violence and permissiveness."

The aforementioned rules of ideological syntax allow us to predict the most probable word combinations. In Soviet usage, certain ideologemes may be used only with specific metaideologemes. We can "strengthen" (+ +) or "trample upon" (– –) lawfulness (+org [organization]): *ukrepliat'* or *popirat' zakonnost'*. We can "condemn" (+ –) or "cultivate" (– +) lawlessness (–lib [liberty]): *osuzhdat'* or *nasazhdat' bezzakonie*. But it is impossible for ideology to use the following combinations: "to trample upon lawlessness" (*popirat' bezzakonie*) or "to cultivate lawfulness" (*nasazhdat' zakonnost'*). If the verbs "to falsify" (*fal'sifitsirovat'*), "to discredit" (*diskreditirovat'*), or "to torpedo" (*torpedirovat'*)—that is, negative metaideologemes—are encountered in an ideological text, then the object of these verbs will invariably be a word with a positive connotation: "a constructive suggestion" or "a peaceful initiative." On the other hand, positive metaideologemes, such as "to condemn," "to restrain," and "to unmask" necessarily refer to negative objects: "criminal actions," "the arms race," etc.

We can now create a diagram depicting the possible combinations for two levels of ideologemes:

Level 1: Primary Ideologemes	Level 2: Metaideologemes
+(peace)	+ +(proclaim)
+(peace)	– –(discredit)
–(aggression)	+ –(condemn)
–(aggression)	– +(cultivate)

If the relationship of ideologemes in a tetradic structure is as simple as 2 × 2 = 4, then the relationship between metaideologemes and primary ideologemes in linear text further mirrors the rules of multiplication: multiplying two identical signs produces a positive result and multiplying a positive sign by a negative sign produces a negative result. The tetradic structure of metaideologemes reproduces exactly the ideological functions represented in level 1. Thus metaideologemes carry out four functions that in turn constitute a metatetrad:

+pro   −contr
+contr   −pro

The essence of ideological thinking is expressed in an even purer and more abstract form by this metatetrad than by primary ideologemes. On level 1, ideologemes are connected with real phenomena: specific and informative concepts such as "freedom" or "necessity," "innovation" or "tradition." On level 2, ideological language abandons this diversity of ideas because it does not describe phenomena, but the ideologemes themselves. The denotative meanings of metaideologemes reflect the connotative meanings of primary ideologemes; the metaideologeme is an "evaluation of evaluations." The double evaluation results in a combination of all "+'s" and "−'s," which we see in the structure of the metatetrad.

++   − −
+−   − +

The following list summarizes the substitutives that carry out the four functions of the metatetrad.

	+pro		−contr
to praise	vospevat'	to find fault with	okhaivat'
to glorify	proslavliat'	to defame	shel'movat'
to proclaim	provozglashat'	to encroach	posiagat'
to exalt	vozvelichivat'	to discredit	diskreditirovat'
to augment	priumnozhat'	to undermine	podryvat'
to elevate	vozvyshat'	to debase	unizhat'
to ennoble	oblagorozhivat'	to disgrace	porochit'
to beautify	krasit' or ukrashat'	to blacken	ocherniat'

	+contr		−pro
to unmask	razoblachat'	to whitewash	obeliat'
to brand	kleimit'	to extol	prevoznosit'

to condemn	*osuzhdat'*	to relish	*smakovat'*
to sweep away	*otmetat'*	to implant, to cultivate	*nasazhdat'*
to nail down	*prigvozhdat'*	to provoke	*provotsirovat'*
to denounce	*oblichat'*	to cultivate	*kul'tivirovat'*
to debunk	*razvenchivat'*	to proclaim	*proklamirovat'*[38]

It is important to note that metaideological functions are not always expressed by verbs, they can also take the form of interjections, nouns, and adjectives, as seen below:

Interjections:	"long live!"	*da zdravstvuet!*	(+pro)
	"hurrah!"	*ura!*	(+pro)
	"hands off!"	*ruki proch!*	(+contr)
	"down with!"	*doloi!*	(+contr)
Nouns:	"proclaimer"	*provozvestnik*	(+pro)
	"comrade in arms"	*spodvizhnik*	(+pro)
	"apologist"	*apologet*	(−pro)
	"adherent"	*adept*	(−pro)
Adjectives:	"respectable"	*respektabel'nyi*	(−pro)
	"fashionable"	*feshenebel'nyi*	(−pro)

In spite of their apparent semantic simplicity, the adjectives "respectable" and "fashionable" serve as metaideologemes in Soviet ideolanguage: they ironically endorse and praise negative phenomena ("a respectable bourgeois," "a fashionable resort for American moneybags [*tolstosumov*]") and thus have a negative connotation.

The metatetrad "++   −−   +−   −+" is in its own way a structural nucleus of Soviet ideological language; a nucleus capable of division and reproduction at higher and higher levels of self-consciousness. This ability of the basic structure to reproduce itself confirms that ideological thinking is not confined to one level; rather, it is capable of working on any level of consciousness. Ideological thinking can counter criticism by moving to a higher level of abstraction and encompassing the negative evaluations directed against it by subjugating them to its own logic. Critics of Soviet Marxist ideology can label it "scholastic," "dogmatic," "authoritarian," "nationalistic," "imperialistic," or "aggressive," but these evaluations do not undermine it; they simply become prisoners of the ideology's own logic and are assigned a place within the tetradic model. Metaideologemes can be counteracted by meta-metaideologemes, as any negative description of ideology can be incorporated into its multileveled system of evaluative signs. The breadth of this pattern allows ideology to further extend its totalitarian activity by means of self-reflection and self-reproduction. Any type of criticism only serves to raise the tetradic model to a higher level of generalization, allowing it to proliferate in much the same way as cells reproduce themselves within an organism.

Soviet Marxism in a Postmodern Perspective

Soviet Marxism is an enigmatic, hybrid phenomenon in the history of human consciousness. Like postmodern pastiche, it combines within itself very different ideological doctrines, including, among others:

- —Marxist teachings on class struggle and communist revolution
- —Teachings of the French Enlightenment directed against the church and clergy
- —Slavophile ideas of the spiritual preeminence of the Russian nation, destined to resolve all Western European controversies and unite the whole world
- —Ideas of revolutionary democrats and Populists (Nikolai Chernyshevsky, Nikolai Dobroliubov, Peter Tkachev, and others) who proclaimed the Russian peasant commune, as the germ of future social structures under socialism
- —Nikolai Fedorov's ideas about armies of labor overcoming the laws of nature, resurrecting the dead, and exploring and populating cosmic space
- —Tolstoy's idea of simplification, calling the intelligentsia to return to the way of life of simple working people
- —Mythological beliefs about the coming of a golden age and immortal heroes whose blood and suffering will become a foundation for the happiness of future generations.

Viewed from this broad perspective, Soviet Marxism escapes all specific definitions and appears to be an aggregate of widely varying ideas that chiefly serve the pursuit of maximal power. An ideology is usually perceived as a set of integrated ideas that give a very specific, coherent picture of the world. This postulate of inner consistency and self-sufficiency does not apply, however, to totalitarian ideology. The fact that Soviet Marxism incorporated ideas from so many different sources was indispensable to its power and survival. Just as the Bolsheviks proclaimed a party of a completely "new type," Soviet ideology was rightly celebrated as an ideology of a "new type" and contrasted to all previous ideologies.

Traditional logic can be applied only to "specific" or "partial" ideologies that are not self-contradictory and express the outlook of some concrete individual or collective. Classical Marxism, the French Enlightenment, American abolitionism, Russian Slavophilism, Russian nihilism, and Tolstoyism are examples of particular ideologies whose messages are pure to the point of sterility. Each elaborates a very stable hierarchy of values that never contradict one another. This generation of "specific ideologies," so characteristic of the eighteenth and nineteenth centuries, was succeeded in the twentieth century by a new generation of ideological "thinking-machines," produced in much the same way as technology creates newer, improved generations of computers. This new mode of ideological thinking has accurately been called "total," or "totalitarian." Total ideologies, as distinct from specific ideologies, are not limited to a single set of ideas and therefore are not bound to proclaim the same stable views. The history of totalitarian ideologies is a series of betrayals: ideology betrays its own prerequisites and its own assertions of yesterday. Totalitarian ideologies must betray and be betrayed in order to maintain their all-encompassing grip on society. Ironically, "total" ideologies often complain that they are betrayed by followers who deviate from the purity and cohesiveness of the "orthodox" line (which coincides with the will of the absolute leader).

Most previous theories of ideology, including those elaborated in the Marxist tradition, proceed from the idea that specific ideologies are forms of false consciousness. Such theories describe ideology as "a process accomplished by the so-called thinker consciously indeed but with a false consciousness. The real motives impelling him remain unknown to him, otherwise it would not be an ideological process at all. Hence he imagines false or apparent motives."[39] Of course, every specific ideology does give priority to certain ideas, the worth of which can be disputed as subjective bias or a deviation from reality. Thus, Slavs are said to have their advantages over Western European nations, but the English and French also have certain undisputed advantages over Slavs; this line of reasoning reveals the limitations and subjectivity of the doctrine of Slavophilism.

However, the definition of ideology as false consciousness cannot be applied to totalitarian ideologies, which reconcile and incorporate very different, even opposing, ideas. Totalitarian ideologies embrace all aspects of contending ideas, encircling and assimilating the whole of reality until reality becomes indistinguishable from the ideology that transforms it. "Five-year plans" or "communist *subbotniks*" (voluntary unpaid labor on Saturdays) are ideological conceptions and, at the same time, indispensable aspects of Soviet reality. As Herbert Marcuse remarked in his discussion of Soviet Marxism, "ideology thus becomes a decisive part of reality even if it [is] used only as an instrument of domination and propaganda."[40] The difference between false and real images loses all relevance because ideology itself becomes a comprehensive way of life. *In a totalitarian society, ideology cannot but be a faithful reflection of reality because reality itself is a faithful reflection of ideology.* Internationalist ideology cannot but be truthful in a society where all national traditions are broken or neglected, just as patriotic ideology cannot but be truthful in a society separated from the entire world by an "iron curtain."

Soviet Marxist ideology is totalitarian because it erases the difference between idea and reality, as well as that between opposing conceptions. Ideas become indistinguishable not only from reality, but from each other. "Internationalism," "materialism," "communism," "socialism," "Marxism," "Leninism," "five-year plans," "collective farms," and "space exploration" merge into one concept and become signs of the same monolithic signified. This signified may be rendered equally as "truth," "strength," "greatness," "victory," or simply, "hurrah!" Even opposing ideas lose their distinction. Ask an average Soviet citizen to explain the difference between internationalism and patriotism, and he will find it difficult to answer. For the majority of Soviet people, these conflicting concepts have been transformed into one "ideologically correct" expression. Soviet ideology has assimilated so many words that all words come to constitute a single language unit, signifying nothing but the ideology itself. "Spirituality," "freedom," "discipline," "tradition," "innovation" all refer to a single penultimate concept: "the triumphant and all-powerful ideology." Whereas specific ideologies developed their own particular systems of signs for interpreting reality, totalitarian ideology is itself the only reality, the supersignified, to which all ideological signs and interpretations refer.

There is reason to believe that Soviet Marxism, which survived for seventy years as the dominant ideology of the Soviet Union, accommodating itself to enormous historical change in the process, has become de-ideologized in direct proportion to its expansion. This ideology exceeded and absorbed all other systems until it approached the limits of ideological imagination. Over the course of seven decades, Soviet Marxism lost its specificity as a particular ideology and became instead an all-encompassing system of ideological signs that can acquire any significance desired. The era of glasnost and perestroika has not changed the "multi-ideological" essence of Soviet mentality. Rather, it has brought the ideology even beyond the limits of totalitarianism and transformed it into a new type of ideological consciousness, one that might be called postcommunist, or universal.

Under perestroika, practically all meanings and all words became ideologically charged, yet at the same time, they ceased to express any particular ideological values. For example, the classic Marxist opposition of "private property" versus "public property" long identified the basic difference between capitalism and socialism. Today, however, following the process of ideological maturation discussed above, the original dyad "private property–public property" has been submerged into a tetradic structure and its meaning completely obfuscated. By adding the dyad "citizen's property–state property" (the first, a creation of perestroika, the second, blamed for inefficiencies of the Soviet economy), the "universal" ideology creates a tetradic structure that enables it to be "socialist" and "capitalist" at the same time:

+	−
public property	private property
citizen's property	state property
obshchestvennaia sobstvennost'	chastnaia sobstvennost'
sobstvennost' grazhdan	gosudarstvennaia sobstvennost'

Obviously, "citizen's property" is nothing but a positive evaluation of what was previously condemned as "private property," and "state property" is a denunciation of what was previously extolled as "public property." To introduce private property into economic reality proved easier than to rehabilitate this very expression and endow it with a positive meaning. Ideology must retain its sacred and accursed words regardless of what economic development occurs. Deprived of any particular system of opinions, Soviet ideology continued to manipulate different ideologies, even combining capitalist and communist ideas. As a result, ideology becomes simply a habit of thinking, a manner of expression, the prism through which all views and expressions are refracted without depending on particular views and ideas—a sort of universal network that may be compared to the advertising networks of Western nations.

If, as Marshall McLuhan put it, "the media is the message," then ideology is the message of all modern Soviet media. What sort of ideology? It does not matter. In the late Soviet Union, ideology exists unto itself, a form of discourse independent of any specific content, be it scientific, religious, aesthetic, or something else. Practically no one in the Soviet Union would have interpreted a statement regarding a specific element, say a religious or artistic pronouncement, at face value. Such statements are perceived above all as ideological pronouncements for which religion or literature simply provide a convenient vehicle.

Over the course of seventy years of Marxist rule, even economics has turned out to be a matter of pure ideology. No specific economic cause, law, or regularity can be definitively identified as the reason for the regime's periodic transitions from one economic policy to another—from the amalgamation of all kolkhozes to their disintegration, from the requisitioning of farm produce to taxes in kind, from intensified cultivation of potatoes to urgent cultivation of corn. All these changes in economic policy were the result of the interplay of different ideas, not economic realities.

Marx and Engels used to say that in precommunist social formations, there was no such thing as a history of ideas because ideas in those societies served only as false miraculous reflections of economic history. Following this logic, we must conclude that after a socialist revolution, there is no *other* history than that of ideas; economic history only serves as its "miraculous reflection." The entire hierarchy is reversed: ideology becomes the base and economics the superstructure. Under Soviet socialism, the life of ideas was self-sufficient and self-propelling, and economic issues arose out of their ideological foundations. Supposedly, the genuine significance of a "socialist" revolution is not just its reversal of the power of the lower and upper classes in a society, but the reversal of the society's base and superstructure as well. It is hardly surprising, then, that Soviet Marxist ideology has become the underlying force of all economic, political, and aesthetic movements in the USSR, relating to each of them as a whole relates to its parts. Engels and Lenin were clever to admit that in different countries and under different circumstances, ideology might take the place of economics as the basic structure of the whole society. This was precisely the case in communist countries: economics and ideology changed roles so that ideas, not economics, determined material life and produced the "real."

In Western society, postmodernism is often regarded as a continuation of the logic of "late capitalism," a condition in which all ideas and styles acquire the form of commodities, becoming "manageable" and "exchangeable." In the Soviet Union, a postmodern relativity of ideas arose from its own ideological, not economic, base, as an extension of the logic of "late communism," a condition in which all elements of reality acquire the form of ideas and all ideas become "acceptable," "manageable" and "exchange-able." All those concepts previously alien to the essence of communist ideology, such as "private property" and the "free market," freely entered this ideological space, stretching it beyond its limits—allowing the ideology to embrace its own opposite. This is a process of de-ideologization, but not in the sense of Daniel Bell's understanding of the phenomenon in his fa-mous *The End of Ideology*. In the Soviet Union, de-ideologization means the end of the "particular" ideology that originally had a definite class charac-ter, social ideals, and aimed to inspire the proletariat to launch a socialist revolution and construct communism. The current de-ideologization of Marxism in the USSR is a process of the universalization of ideological thinking as such, its final move from the realm of militant modernism to a more playful, relaxed, postmodern mentality.

Late capitalism and late communism are polar opposites in terms of eco-nomic structure and efficiency, but economics alone does not determine culture as a whole. The fundamental underlying patterns of cultural post-modernism in the East are not economic, they are ideological. Communism has proved to be a more radical challenge to capitalism than was originally thought: not only did it change the mode of production, it changed the relationship of base and superstructure in society.[41] A comparison of cap-italist economics and communist ideology is imperative for elucidating the postmodern traits common to both societies. Such a "cross"-examination would be more interesting than a parallel comparison; if one compares communist and bourgeois ideologies, or socialist and capitalist economics, little can be found beyond commonplace oppositions. It is far more rele-vant—even from a Marxist-Leninist perspective—to examine the common ground between communist ideology and capitalist economics, as the two perform identical functional roles in their respective social structures.

The famous formula of a capitalist economy that Marx suggested in *Das Kapital* is "goods–money–goods" or "money–goods–money." The same formula can be applied in modified form to the ideology of Soviet Marxism: "reality–idea–reality," or "idea–reality–idea." Facts came to be exchanged for ideas in communist society in much the same way as goods are ex-changed for money in capitalist societies. Ideas, as a sort of currency, ac-quired an abstract form of "ideological capital." They do not constitute material wealth, but the "correctness" of communist ideology. This "cor-rectness," or absolute truth, compensates people for their labor ("heroic deeds and sacrifices"), and also recoups the cost of so-called particular mistakes resulting from Party policy.

What happens in the late stage of communist development? Why does it move toward a "postmodern condition" along the same path followed by "late capitalist" societies? Totalitarianism was a superlative machine for accumulating and exploiting all sorts of ideas. However, this machine spawned a phenomenon bigger than itself. Just as capital eventually outgrows the capitalist "machine" and becomes a self-sufficient entity, Soviet ideological capital outgrew the "machine" of a particular personality or system of ideas and became an omnipresent mentality, appropriating any fact to serve any idea. Marxist ideology, the most powerful of all modern ideologies, lost its identity and became only one possible interpretation of reality (in the former Soviet Union, it would be the least probable one!). The expansion of Marxist ideology overcame Marxism as a form of modernism and created postmodern conditions in the USSR.

The overarching expansion of Soviet ideology occurred in the Brezhnev era, when the difference between facts and ideas was virtually erased. Ideology was gradually transformed from a system of ideas into an all-encompassing ideological environment that retained all possible alternative philosophical systems as latent components within itself. Existentialism and structuralism, Russophilism and Westernism, technocratic and ecological movements, religious and neo-pagan outlooks—everything was compressed into the forms of Marxism, creating a sort of postmodern pastiche.

The Gorbachev era magnified the postmodern condition of Soviet society by encouraging the growth of tens, hundreds, even thousands of new ideological trends, each of which playfully used all the bywords of Soviet Marxist ideology for its own ends. Gorbachev himself was a highly ideological leader; in his domestic speeches one could find nothing but ideology. Don't ask him, however, what sort of ideology he proclaimed. It is simply "ideology," nothing more, usually following the routine tetradic patterns: "democrats" were criticized for endangering "stability" and "unity," while "conservatives" were criticized for threatening the ideals of "reconstruction" and "acceleration."

In the late USSR there emerged a continuous, complete ideological environment that was transpersonal, transcollective, transparty, and ultimately, transideological, because no particular ideological position remained consistent or comprehensive. Soviet ideology developed beyond any particular rational or irrational system; it was reality itself—chaotic, charming, exciting, disgusting, boring, physically threatening, maddening. No other reality existed except that of ideology: there was little food, but plenty of ideas about how to feed the country; there was no clean air, but an abundance of ideas on how to make it clean. Communist ideology succeeded in creating an "ideological personality" and, through the triumph of pan-ideology, abolished communism itself.

Thus, postcommunist ideology is universalist rather than totalitarian. Totalitarian ideology incorporates all available ideas and claims to be a unified and coherent system, sharply opposing left and right deviations. Universalist ideology tries to eliminate all oppositions and use the entire range of ideas as if they were complementary. The transformation of all oppositions into complementarities was Gorbachev's ideological strategy under perestroika and, although it undoubtedly brought him success, it could not prevent real rightists and leftists from fighting this ideology of compromise from both sides.

Perhaps the most striking postmodern trend found in universalist ideology is its ability to surmount historical differences and eliminate the dimension of time. Louis Althusser made the stunning pronouncement that "ideology *in general has no history* . . . or, what comes to the same thing, is eternal, i.e. omnipresent in its immutable form throughout history."[42] However, Althusser's famous definition of ideology as "the imaginary relationship of individuals to their real condition of existence" (162) seems too broad, too vague: it does not allow one to distinguish ideology from other realms of consciousness such as mythology, religion, art, dreams, utopia, etc. In my view, ideology is a very specific sphere of consciousness: the doubling and reversal of mental oppositions that cannot be reconciled in purely theoretical terms and therefore need to be permanently evaluated and reevaluated in order to create a hierarchy of values. It is this permanent play of evaluations that pushes mature ideology beyond history to converge with postmodernism in its rejection of any specific ideology and of historicity as such.

Specific ideologies with stable hierarchies of values and ideas develop histories arising out of the differences between them. Totalitarian ideologies, which transpose every idea into its diametric opposite, indeed tend to become one ideology, "omnipresent in its immutable form throughout history." Finally, universalist ideology is so total that it expands infinitely to incorporate all possibilities of ideological thought. Despite the variety of specific ideologies, it is hardly disputable that there exists only one ideological consciousness, as distinct from religious, mythological, scientific, or artistic forms of consciousness. The process of building totalitarian ideologies from specific ideologies makes the resulting amalgamation of ideas increasingly coincide with the entire spectrum of ideological consciousness as such. It is this process of enveloping multiple ideologies into one all-comprehensive, omnipresent ideological environment that makes possible the phenomenon of "de-ideologized ideology."[43]

The ideology of Soviet Marxism has been considered the most rigid and stagnant component of twentieth-century intellectual development. I have tried to argue that this rigidity is a form of the postmodern elimination of time and significance, one that works through a constant play of meanings and redistribution of evaluations. I believe there is no more relativistic system of ideology than this one: it constantly changed and expanded its set of ideas in order to maintain its power. In order to win the world, this ideology stood prepared to lose its identity.

Conclusion

I would like to finish this rather dry scholarly presentation with a somewhat lighter essay, originally composed prior to the coup d'état that ultimately removed Gorbachev from power and well before inflation reached its painful present level in formerly Soviet Russia.

Soviet money is very beautiful: it is green, blue, red, lilac, and decorated with fine multicolored lines and iridescent patterns. Soviet money is intended above all to satisfy the aesthetic needs of its proprietor. It is very pleasing to have beautiful money, and therefore not necessary to spend it. This money is much brighter and more attractive than the dull, dusty goods it can purchase in Soviet shops. In America, the flagship country of capitalism, the situation is quite the reverse. American bills are so dull that one wants to get rid of them as soon as possible, to exchange them for bright, eye-catching products displayed in store windows. Under communism, money is a series of pictures in the style of op art, artistic miniatures, distributed in billions of copies to satisfy the need of the citizen for pocket portraits of Lenin and sights of the Moscow Kremlin.

No society, however, can do without some kind of conventional currency that functions as the general equivalent of all values. What can be considered real money and used to acquire tangible goods in a socialist society? This question has yet to be answered. The "political economy of socialism" was never established, although a discipline under this title has long been studied in Soviet universities. This Soviet discipline assumes that "the basic economic law of socialism ensures the complete well-being and free all-round development of all members of society through continual growth and improvement of social production." This definition could explain, with equal success, the basic aesthetic law of socialism or the basic sexual law of socialism, because these, too, serve to satisfy the growing needs of society and provide its members complete well-being. The political economy of socialism was never created because under socialism, economics is only the superstructure, while ideology (capitalism's superstructure) has become the base.

For all that, what is the general equivalent of ideas, if money is the general equivalent of goods? Language is such an equivalent, attaching various ideological labels to phenomena. With the aid of language, people have the opportunity to enrich themselves and impoverish their enemies—ideologically. The ideological value of various words is in a permanent state of flux. The value of "internationalism," for example, once had the greatest exchange rate in Soviet society. Then it fell to the lowest rate, in the guise of "cosmopolitanism." The highest rates are now reserved for Russian nationalist bills: "motherland," "memory," "patriotism." These securities do not represent numbers, only words, but nevertheless are the currency used in Russia to buy power, work, life, and further satisfaction of all growing needs.

Words and money have much in common. Each may relate to such concepts as inflation, devaluation, speculation, and the rise and fall of the exchange rate. It appears that a flexible relationship exists between a sign and its significance, or a bill and its value. A proprietor can use the difference between a bill and its value to enrich himself; in the same way, an ideologist can use the difference between a sign and its significance to gain "surplus evaluation." The same phenomena can increase in value if signified as "ideological commitments," or become unprofitable if signified as "idealistic biases." Language is a system of rising and falling prices, a semantic stock exchange that allows a skilled player to accumulate enormous ideological capital. By attaching different labels to different facts, the ideologist appropriates the difference between their values. One can play the market to multiply one's own stocks or reduce the stocks of one's rivals.

When one hears that "the October Revolution has liberated the toiling people from capitalist oppression," or that "a fascist putsch has brought innumerable sufferings upon the toiling people," one cannot but agree. Why? Because the very words "revolution" and "putsch" already contain a final judgment; the first word is a commendation, the second a condemnation. A standard ideological device is to designate the same or similar phenomenon with opposite evaluative signs and extract ideological surplus value from the evaluative difference of their meanings. The difference between "revolutionaries" and "putschists" is purely emotional and evaluative, but all the more useful for that in accumulating ideological capital. "Putsch" is a negative value, a great loss, while "revolution" is a winning ticket, one that has brought Soviet power great benefits over a period of seventy years.

Capitalism rules the citizen with the help of a check (*chek* in Russian), while socialism rules with the help of the Cheka (the Soviet secret police). The difference is in the first letter of the two words: one is lower-case, the other, upper-case. Socialism adores capital letters, it lives off the profit derived from their verbal capital; thus the repeated use of words such as "Fatherland," "October," and the "Communist Party." The total significance of each of these words is superior to its direct meaning. The basic law of socialism is the surplus significance of all phenomena. These phenomena do not simply exist, they also represent highly valued historical laws and progressive tendencies.

Soviet money is indeed beautiful, but not because of its picturesque bills; these are nothing more than soft currency. Soviet money should be considered the most beautiful in the world because it is composed of bright, expressive words and not dry numbers. Of course, such money cannot help you acquire commodities, but can provide you with power. Imagine the whole world plastered with bills printed with the words of Soviet Marxist ideolanguage: "revolution," "reaction," "labor," "freedom," "honor," "glory," "spirituality," "heroism," "sacrifice," "the bright future." These words are the genuine units of Soviet hard currency. What can be acquired with such words cannot be measured. Quality, not quantity, is of primary significance. Soviet Marxist ideology has proven rich enough to appropriate the mighty forces of progress and youth, rich enough to acquire fiery souls filled with hatred for capitalism, striving for "the bright future." How miserable is capitalist money, which can only buy that which is for sale! But linguistic currency can buy things that never stand on store shelves—the world itself can be bought with such "beautiful money."

CHAPTER 5 · Labor of Lust: Erotic Metaphors of Soviet Civilization

There's a labor of lust and it's in our blood . . .—Osip Mandelshtam

1

Sometimes, a single metaphor cuts more deeply to the heart of a matter than do hundreds or thousands of monographs. Here in the Soviet Union, we have written endlessly about the socioeconomic nature of labor, about its previous exploitation and current freedom, and about its future transformation into a means of general human development. And yet we still labor badly, although no one can say that we don't labor much.

How we labored from the twenties to the fifties before becoming lazy in the sixties! Day and night, to bloody blisters and an early grave, we burned to work, as they used to say about zealous laborers. Even so, this didn't make us wealthy. What was it we poured our labors into then? What weighty forms and tangible wonders of civilization were produced? Perhaps all we got was a miracle of cosmic weightlessness—almost as if people hadn't burned themselves out in factory and field, laying the land to waste, and wearing out powerful machines. And now, there are shortages of everything: food, clothing, books. Worst of all, we have produced no understanding of how and why we got into this state.

Perhaps our endless labor is of a special type that saps strength and yet gives nothing in return; perhaps it is not really labor at all? If, for example, a little boy digs in a sandbox with his shovel, wouldn't we do better to define his activity with a metaphor like "shovel babble," rather than describe it with statistical measures of productivity or chemical analyses of the sand?

And then along comes a poet who whips off a single line. He connects a couple of previously unconnected words—"There's a labor of lust, and it's in our blood"[1]—and the political economy of socialism, a shapeless, beggarly science, constantly suffering from its inability to grasp its proper subject, attains its ideal explanation.

Mandelshtam was able to express our eternal relation to labor, quickly and easily, in a single phrase. *Homo Soveticus,* successor to *Homo Russicus,* labors long and willingly, but his love for labor somehow lacks foundation. His love is lustful, too quickly bestowed and insufficiently selective, rarely developing into a solid marital union. There is no firm lifelong bond with the object and product of labor. This love is general, public, and belongs to no one, which is why, in the feverish passion of labor, something hopeless and depraved suddenly washes up: you pour your seed together with everyone else's onto the same eggs ("Collective ownership of the means of production"). In this atmosphere, even a truly industrious person feels like a fornicator; and, if he continues to work under these conditions, then he does so in secret, keeping his pet project for himself, not for the common pot. He may still be employed at the engineering firm, but he locks away his favorite, unrealizable blueprint deep inside a desk drawer. Or better yet, he takes his own little drawer away from the collective desk, or withdraws his bit of land from the collective field and carries it into his house, his yard, where he can nurture it away from prying eyes.

At the root of the word "ownership" is the concept "one's own." And the first miracle is that ownership can be not "one's own" but no one's, collective: an oxymoron, equivalent to a white raven or black snow. We Soviets did not invent this most miraculous of miracles, but we have worked hard to make of all humankind a collective miracle-worker; in the meantime, as an example and a lesson to the world, we have shown what can be done with one remarkable nation. *Own*ership was removed from the sphere of "one's own" and became "*other*ship": the peasant community or the artel, the *mir* or the collective farm, the landowner or the party secretary, the pre-Revolutionary bailiff or the post-Revolutionary bureaucrat—all worked as one, making it impossible for anyone to work for himself. And thus it happened: a nation that had outgrown its innocent childhood did not accede to lawful wedlock, but became careless, undiscriminating, and took up dangerous habits. The love of a lifetime or of a passing moment, brilliant genes or those of an alcoholic were all thrown into the collective pot, where they congeal into a headcheese, like a welter of gross outputs: cubic meters, tons, calories; into a cartilaginous idiot-child with "the face of collective degeneracy." Diseases are the only systematic trait of such a system.

At times in our history, the only people who labored with pleasure were those who for some inexplicable, eccentric, almost sick reason had become addicted to work as to a drug: once having tasted, you can never get enough. How easy it is to mock these unreasoning workaholics, mired in their hopeless and unrewarding task, as if they had fallen head over heels for a prostitute and taken to writing her exalted poetry, while she continued sleeping with the whole neighborhood. Concern for the fruits of labor disappears in this case as well. All that matters is the bitter satisfaction and oblivion that labor itself provides. And as for what gets produced or who disposes of or uses it—who really cares? The prostitute gives your child up to an orphanage and you'll never know it, nor it you.

Thus, through unyielding obstinacy, we have arrived at an amazing paradox: for want of a clearly delineated purpose, gigantic quantities of labor produce the tiniest of results. If you flail the air until your arms ache in order to oxygenate the air then surely you are just flailing away. What could be the point of digging a canal from which the water evaporates before it reaches the fields you want to irrigate (as happened in Central Asia)? Or building dikes that prevent effluents from washing out to sea, thereby filling the city with dirt and silt, instead of preventing floods (as happened in Leningrad)?

Needless to say, the principle of disinterested labor has not been foreign to the abstract ratiocinations of other peoples as well. In the *Bhagavad-Gita,* Krishna instructs Arjuna to be true to his work, to give himself over to it unreservedly, but not to become dependent on its results. In Kant's *Critique of Practical Reason,* activity without concern for results, which finds reason and enjoyment in itself alone, is called play. Nevertheless, no matter how tempting the parallels, our labor-lust has little in common with the Hindu ethics of pure duty or Kant's aesthetic of self-motivated play. In those systems the individual is not dependent on the results, whereas in our system the results do not depend on the individual. There one is liberated from attachment to the product of one's labor, here one is tortuously attached to the process itself. There he achieves dispassion in work; here the work itself becomes an intoxicating passion.

In other words, when the individual controls his own property, he can dispense it or overcome it, in order to achieve self-transcendence and reach the heights of self-perfection. When nothing of one's own is available or even imaginable, then the process works backward, and the individual descends to the realm of self-abasement, experienced as an inability to control even oneself. The path from one's own thing leads to one's own soul, but from a thing not one's own, the path leads to someone else's soul, to the soul of a robot that slams its sledge or wedge into whatever object is placed before it. In Russia, we say that this kind of person works as if he has been "wound up" (*kak zavedennyi*).

Such labor is a convenient way of blinding oneself, satisfying a maniacal need to do something, to be occupied; it is a formula for self-depletion. The individual is not in control, but in thrall to the devil of labor who instructs him: "smash, slash, chop" or "fry, shred, season." The more physically debilitating the work, the easier it is to forget yourself in it, to chase away importunate thoughts of death, to kill exhausting blocks of time. Labor becomes a wonderful means of self-abnegation, the truest desire of a despairing soul. Through intercourse with an object our tormenting humanity is forgotten.

Too frequently in Soviet society, labor becomes a form of escape from the freedom that importunately leaves one alone with oneself, with one's conscience. For if you have a simple, tangible object, the kind that wants nothing but a firm hand, then away with self-consciousness: the world becomes as simple as seduction, the soul as simple as desire. One of Andrei Platonov's principal characters, the engineer Prushevsky, is "desirous of acting firmly, of concerning himself with current subjects and building any building at all for the use of others, just so as not to arouse his consciousness."[2] Lust is a means to escape an unsuccessful or impossible love: the soul can't stand the tension and surrenders to the tender mercy of a basic physical urge. To be useful, to be manly and courageous, to feel your being by the first available means—that is what we call a feat of labor: dive into any opening and stick your finger in the first dike you see.

Gorky's hero Nil, a worker in the play *Philistines,* considered by many to be the first politically conscious proletarian in Russian literature, says eagerly: "One should love an occupation in order to manage it well. You know I terribly love to forge. A red, formless, wicked, burning mass is before you. . . . To beat it with a hammer is delightful! It is alive and resilient. . . . And here, with strong blows, you make everything you need from it."[3] One need not be an experienced psychoanalyst to see this forging as an undisguised, yet unconscious, symbol of mechanical copulation.

For some reason, in Soviet culture we often combine the words "labor and creativity," "creativity and labor." What we do not seem to realize is that the urge to labor can sometimes arise from creative incapability, from a weakness of imagination, even a kind of impotence: an inability to love. Is it an accident that all totalitarian regimes praise labor as a primary virtue and proclaim that diligent workers are ideal citizens? Of course not. The laborer is safe. He works himself to death, never taking his eyes off the ground. When someone works hard, we say he "slaves away." Human beings became the slaves of sin and must slave away by the sweat of their brows on the face of the earth, but does this mean we should turn the curse of humankind into a virtue? If you look for the original meaning of the word "freedom," you will find that it did not mean "freed labor," but "freedom from labor." How often in the Soviet Union have we bitterly mocked the biblical references to heavenly birds or lilies of the field that "neither sow nor reap"—the image of a person redeemed from sin.

Technology gradually frees mankind from the curse of labor, bringing the work process closer to dream, fantasy, the doings of the soul. But labor-lust hates technology, as debauchery hates romance. It is too closely bound to the flesh, to all that is mortal and vicious in it. Better to harvest potatoes by hand for a week than to do it in an hour with a machine because people who bend down to the earth have a harder time forgetting they are slaves. It may be rational, of course, to prefer the machine, but the soul demands strain, blisters, friction over the surface of things, in order to calm the physical urge, the devilish itching that tortures so sweetly.

Russian literature offers a host of examples of labor-lust: Turgenev's Bazarov throws himself into "feverish work" after he fails with Odintsova; Nekrasov's Daria chops wood in a frenzy to forget the pain of her husband's death. Here we see none of Arjuna's stern concentration nor of Kant's self-motivated play. The goal is to strangle something within yourself: "I subdued myself, setting my heel / on the throat of my own song."[4] Some shoot themselves, like Treplev in Chekhov's *The Sea-Gull*. Others, like Uncle Vanya (in Chekhov's play of the same name), kill themselves through work. Sometimes a person who wants to shoot himself decides that this is not enough and kills himself through work instead, like Korchagin in Nikolai Ostrovsky's novel *How The Steel Was Tempered* (1932–34). And yet again, the reverse may happen: a person kills himself through work, but that still is not enough, so he shoots himself as well, like Mayakovsky.

In the case of Turgenev's and Nekrasov's characters, binges of lustful labor can be explained with reference to concrete psychological circumstances. But if we recall how Gorky's heroes perform their labor (in *My Universities* or *The Artamonov Business*) or Platonov's (in *The Foundation Pit* or *The Sea of Youth*), we begin to discern the ever-repeated basis of these situations in the life of the nation as a whole: they allow for an escape from stupefying emptiness through work that leads to stupefaction. There is a kind of gloomy ecstasy achieved in being swallowed up by this intoxicating and terrifying festival known as labor, as if people are heaping logs on a chronic fire that consumes their souls.

In *My Universities* Gorky depicts his autobiographical hero unloading a sinking barge in the rain:

> They worked as though playing, with the gay enthusiasm of children, with that intoxicating zest of labor, than which only a woman's embrace can be more sweet. . . . I, too, grabbed sacks, dragged, hurled, ran, grabbed again. And it seemed to me that I, and everything about me, had been caught up in some wild and furious dance. . . . I tasted that night of joy which I had never before experienced. My heart flamed in the wish that all of life might be spent in such semi-insane ecstasy of labor.[5]

Soviet writers often present labor as a temptation, as the promise of some thrilling physical enjoyment. This is quite understandable, since all other motives, such as expectation of deserved reward or effective result, are lacking. The only factor that can inspire such labor is enjoyment for its own sake. Labor is charged with eroticism precisely to the same extent that eroticism is presented in terms of labor. The most famous definition of love in Soviet literature belongs to Mayakovsky: "To love means this: to run / into the depths of a yard and, till the rook-black night, / chop wood with a shining axe, / giving full play to one's strength."[6]

In an attempt to reduce personal relationships to social functions, Soviet literature has always kept silent on the subject of sex. A family has been considered the primary cell of society, where good workers and citizens are fashioned, or as a factory producing the happy generations of the future. The only sexual motifs to be found in many Soviet classics are those implanted in scenes of labor.

In Boris Gorbatov's novel *Donbass,* the coal miner Victor Abrosimov descends into the mine in order to experience the piercing enjoyment of drilling:

> He got down on his knees before the wall of coal and switched on his hammer. A familiar tremor of joy rolled over his hands and then embraced all his body. . . . His dream came true and the body of coal lay before him submissively as the miner was free to let himself go. The solid wall of untouched black forest moved excitingly close to him, enticing and luring him. Suddenly Viktor Abrosimov felt his muscles fill with daring, previously unknown force, his heart was consumed with bold courage, and he believed that he would be able to do everything, to overcome everything, and to achieve everything this night.[7]

Soviet critic Brovman praises Gorbatov for "genuine achievement in depicting the miner's labor. . . . The reader spontaneously participates in Victor's labor, because it is presented in such a vivid, physically tangible manner."[8]

It is doubtful, however, that this fierce, furious labor, which proceeds from desire rather than from dry calculation, could result in anything but destruction. Where lustful labor prevails, many things are done haphazardly, and much is torn to pieces and quickly tossed away. He who lusts takes what he wants, kneading the flesh, grinding out products. Not worried about making sense or taking the measure of a thing, he cuts (or rather, chops it up) to fit his Procrustean bed. Does this not characterize all our industry? Our country is filled with hidden avatars of the Marquis de Sade, who amass heaps of corpses in their castles, fitted out with machines for the voluptuous torture of voiceless victims, like so many untouched veins of ore and metals, virgin mountains and virgin forests. One can guess at the extent of the torture: its traces remain on the faces of our cities and villages, in the broken patterns of our fields and forests, in the gullies and potholes on the body of our exhausted land. Whatever once stood has long since bent to the ground, and whatever lay flat has been raised on its haunches. Whatever had parts has become an unbroken whole, stored in endless morgues euphemistically called warehouses or landfills, but both of which contain, for all intents and purposes, the very same things.

2

Lust is practically indifferent to the qualities of the partner, so long as, in the words of Fedor Karamazov, it is of the right gender. Labor-lust is equally indifferent to its object: so long as you can get into it, work it over, and lose yourself in it. If labor activities are interchangeable, then equally interchangeable are the individuals who labor. "No one is irreplaceable" (*nezamenimykh net*) is a favorite Soviet phrase. It entered our language as if from brothel parlance, but what might initially have been a sexual joke has become a dark threat and a solemn curse.

A simple thing, an individual for example, can easily become an algebraic X. Remember the engineer Prushevsky in Platonov's *The Foundation Pit.* Since he does not have a beloved woman, he wants, again and again, to expend his unnecessary body for "someone else's good," so he gives himself up to the cold and lazy caress of equipment.

Now he wished to concern himself with objects and structures constantly, so as to have them in his mind and his empty heart in place of friendship and attachment to people. His study of the technology of a body in a state of rest, in relation to the future building, provided Prushevsky with an equanimity of clear thought comparable to physical enjoyment... External substance, requiring neither movement, nor life, nor disappearance, replaced for Prushevsky something forgotten and as essential as the person of a lost sweetheart.[9]

Indifference comparable to enjoyment, or enjoyment comparable to indifference; this is indeed a most exact formula for lust.

And of course it is not necessary that the object of labor substitute for a lover's body per se. Labor can substitute for anything, as long as the objects are substitutes and enjoyment of them can be combined with indifference to their specific substance. You can command a platoon, build a railroad, lead a propaganda sector, or write an autobiographical novel. You can "work" an epic poem or an advertisement. In Sholokhov's *Virgin Soil Upturned,* one of the characters, the communist Razmyotnov, refuses to weed the cabbage because in his opinion, this is not a man's job. Another communist, Makar Nagulnov, angrily reprimands Razmyotnov on behalf of the Party:

> "This is a man's job if the Party dispatches you to it. They'll tell me, for example, 'Go, Nagulnov, and cut the heads off of counter-revolutionaries,' and I will go with joy! They'll tell me, 'Go dig up the potatoes,' and without joy I'll go just the same! They'll say, 'Go milk the cows, become a milkmaid,' and I'll gnash my teeth, but go nevertheless! I'll pull the hopeless cow's teats from side to side, but I will milk that damned cow to the best of my ability! If I pull the animal down, I will pick her up again, but I will milk her until I have drained the last drop from her."[10]

Labor-lust turns out to be the expression of a kind of higher loyalty, to an idea or an ideal. You can corrupt a thing by exploiting it obscenely, but it is unthinkable to betray an idea. You can scatter children and old people to the four winds, and God knows you can strain a cow's udder, but you cannot stint when it comes to giving world revolution (in whose name all this is done) your ardent devotion. "Suddenly Nagulnov cried wildly, 'As for me . . . let them stand by the thousands—grandfathers, women and children— . . . and tell me they should be shot. . . . If it is necessary for revolution . . . I will mow them all down with my machine-gun!' "[11] One can give oneself promiscuously to any occupation, but during the most accidental of couplings, even in the event of rape, revolution's blue eyes must shine, call out, enrapture. Thus, in Platonov's novel *Chevengur,* the voluptuous revolutionary woman, represented by Rosa Luxemburg, leads Commissar Kopenkin through the Civil War, promising him a loving communist heaven in reward for all the bloodshed.

Lust can easily be linked to loyalty through the concept of mania. Don Juan is wholly devoted to women, and that is precisely why he deceives one after another. Labor-lust is loyally devoted to the *idea* of labor. Since "labor created humanity" and since "the future belongs to those who labor," we must labor wherever the party of "laboring people" sends us. And for us, therefore, labor is as glorious and honorable as the conquest of a woman in the eyes of a fornicator. From all possible types and potentials of labor, we abstracted the idea of labor in and of itself as the most sublime and necessary meaning in life. Ever afterward this all-encompassing principle has spiraled out of control and taken root in all the various concrete forms of labor; after briefly fertilizing each, it moves on.

Let me cite from memory a song one could hear on the radio almost every day during the 1960s and 1970s, a song that bored its way into our consciousness:

> Are we the ones to stand in place?
> Right is on our side in all our strivings.
> Our labor is our badge of honor, a badge of valor and glory.
> Whether toiling at the lathe or entering the mines,
> A sublime dream, as clear as sunshine, calls you ever on.
> We can't be blocked on land or sea.
> We don't fear ice or fog.
> We'll carry forth our flaming soul and our country's banner
> Through all the worlds and ages.

Here is the poetics of our Principle, its ardent imagination. Lathes and mines are not enough; we need whole worlds to keep the flames of our soul from going out.

An apparatchik, sent out on various missions, first to deal with agriculture, then with propaganda, then with transport, then with education and culture is a kind of idle *flâneur* who wanders the vice-filled streets from one office to another. Why even call him a *flâneur?* As a true apparatchik then, he is more like the owner of a harem: he can resolve all problems simultaneously without leaving his office, lounging behind his luxurious four-poster desk. He has no need to lower himself to the amusements of the street, since agriculture or education and culture come willingly to his chamber as soon as they are called. The order of their appearance is determined by a eunuch, his so-called secretary, who is in charge of catering to his whims and guarding the secrets of his nights.

One might imagine that these lapses—in the relationship of labor to property, to object, to type, and reward—were simply the overzealous invention of a host of former peasants more accustomed to shooting and noise than to rational thought. Look, brothers, it's just the price we had to pay for oversimplification, a falling away from our original program, a distortion, a twisting, or a perversion of the wise commandments of our founders. But when we read carefully, the most authoritative author of all emphasizes the centrality of these very principles, their general and obligatory character: "Communism, if we are to take the word in its strict definition, means unremunerated work for the good of society, without taking account of individual variations, erasing all memory of quotidian prejudices, erasing sluggishness, old habits, differences between separate kinds of work, differences in the size of salaries, etc."[12]

Is it possible to frame a more explicit definition? Lenin enumerates each of the characteristics of labor-lust: it doesn't matter who, with whom, or why. There is no need to take individual variations into account, or respect the differences between various kinds, expecting something in return. But it is also striking to note that some of these words are drawn from a wider cultural context—not from industrial vocabulary, but from that of marital or sexual life. And it is in this context that Mandelshtam's metaphor seems already to have been lurking just around the corner. Because once upon a time, you know, there were "prejudices" that tied a person to his or her one and only beloved. There was "sluggishness" that did not permit the substitution of one woman or kind of work for another. There was the "habit" of expecting a reward, hope for affection in return. Now, this whole familial gemütlichkeit, trapped in its individualistic prejudices, is supposed to give way to communal labor for the common good, without distinctions, habits, or memories.

Who simplified whom? Have the negligent, careless laborers simplified Lenin, or did Lenin simplify labor? And doesn't this brave new leap into the future equate human labor with something even worse than debauchery, since, after all, "reward" is individual and human, while only a mechanical arm (or phallus) works gratis? Remember the bear-hammerer, the model proletarian in *The Foundation Pit:* this is the only being who could satisfy Lenin's definition in the strictest sense. And even he might fail: he demanded food and vodka. Nevertheless, maybe he will be the first to achieve communist labor, striding directly from a hunting-gathering society to communism.

When a real professional takes up a trade, he takes it up with all his heart, as entering wedlock. Professionalism is a mysterious dedication, a tormenting but happy wedding ring, an unbreakable connection with the world of an object, the mystery of a human being and a transformation into "one flesh." Whatever the professional makes grows out of this vow of fidelity. His product carries the stamp of love, a sign that the object produced is the fruit of privation and a long process of mutual understanding.

Where has that kind of competence gone? In our country the word "competent" has been used appropriately only in the phrase "competent organs" (namely, the KGB), organs that did in fact possess a potent and all-encompassing power. Sporadic and spontaneous dilettantism spreads its nets in all other spheres, entrapping one area after another without methodology, attachments, or obligations. We raise neither seed corn nor children, but we busily squander the common funds of mankind. Our favorite hero, labor's love, is the jack-of-all-trades: he sews, he mows, and he plays the oboe. Our dream for society is to produce a Renaissance man who sews like a clothing factory, mows like a tractor, and plays like a symphonic band. Each hand works miracles: incredible dress designs, incredible harvests, incredible melodies—while in reality we had convicts in rags, starving millions, and an eerie silence in which a single hoarse voice could scarcely be heard.

It is easy to look down from on high and demand that people work more intensively and profoundly, yet in order to accomplish anything profound, there must be boundaries. But our country is so gigantic that your legs just carry you farther and farther, "breaking boundaries on all sides" (Aleksandr Blok).[13] Our fabled size—is this not just the sweep of lust, a lustful incorporation of space? What, after all, is our gigantic and insatiable desire for territory, but a lust for expansion? We have acquired region after region, kilometer after kilometer, without the strength to stop, to map out a border, to build a solid home of our own. The earth's plain itself, splayed out flat in all directions, is the model of our loose views on labor, for wanderlust is, of course, a kind of lust as well, for the roaming, rolling, unsettled life. Lust is a psychological nomadism; perhaps we developed it from the nomadic tribes and hordes who broke into and overran Ancient Rus in the thirteenth century. "And it's in our blood"—is this not the same blood that streamed into

Russia's veins during the Mongol invasion and was later poured out bound-
lessly and recklessly by bands of rebels and revolutionaries, rising from the
farthest reaches of the Volga, from the old enclave of the Golden Horde, to
redden the earth and deaden the mind?

Sometimes the leading detachment of an invading army is unable to get
out again and perishes, surrounded by the enemy. So are we unable to
escape our fabulous borders, which hold us firmly in their grasp, predeter-
mining the whole lustful, nomadic spirit of our historical existence. It is
immoral for a man to have ten wives, just as it is immoral for a people to
control a territory that would satisfy ten peoples' needs. We have more than
we need, and therefore work worse than we should.

And now, the final stage. Everything that we have absorbed and taken
over but that we failed to make our own is going to be sold off in secret out
from under us. This State, whose legs spread over Siberia and whose elbow
leans on the Caucusus (Lomonosov's proud image), is simply too gigantic
for the people who own it. So, having lusted over the land, in loveless labor,
the people have no choice but to become procurers of land through trade
and barter. Procuration is the final stage of lust. Free not only of moral
obligations but of physical passion as well, all that remains is an intimate
bond stripped of intimacy, as regular and regulated as the state of marriage,
but with the plus sign changed to minus.

Psychologically, this is understandable: lust eventually encounters an
uncontrollable alien force. This inevitably leads to the temptation to get rid
of that uncontrollable thing, but not, of course, without consideration of
one's self-interest. The thing that burned our lustful hands must be sold off
on the world market. Others won't hesitate to buy, although they know it is
stolen property. Lust in production leads to procuration in trade; instead of
finished goods, you sell natural resources. Why should we sell our work,
when we have goods just lying underfoot? And so we sell the guts of our
(formerly?) beloved homeland, and they are carted off to satisfy the desires
of distant and thriftier industries. Then we can lie down on it and sleep
until we die. Lacking the energy to live off our land, maybe we can simply
live at its expense.

3

So we see that Mandelshtam's metaphor has led us into the most hidden
corners and revealed the most embarrassing secrets of our relationship to
our land.

I can not help recalling that this piquant metaphor was prepared by social "science" many years before that same science was forced to eat its words. In all of the projects meant to save the world, from the earliest socialist teachings up to the most scientific communism, the collectivization of both property and women have always gone hand in hand. Socialism's detractors are wrong to insist that socialism mandates laziness or abstinence. Rather, it mandates work and sexual activity that give up control of their own fruits, allowing a government, in its infinite wisdom, to dispose of them as it sees fit. All must work for all, in the family and in the factory. Collective property as a means for the creation of "things" and for the re-creation of human beings already presupposes and sanctifies the ritual lust that is labor in the absence of the institution of private property, or the conjugal state in the absence of marriage or the family. Mandelshtam's metaphor is not his invention, but the truth of a realized utopia in which socialist production and communal marriage grow organically together.

The ideas of social property and common wives were initially connected in Marx and Engels's vision of the future. In the *Communist Manifesto* they do not conceal their radical view of increasing promiscuity as a trend toward social progress. Socialization of labor had already been attained inside the capitalist mode of production: the goal of socialist revolution was only to establish public ownership of that which had already developed in huge capitalist enterprises. In the same manner, these two believed that bourgeois society had already socialized the institution of marriage:

> Nothing is more ridiculous than the virtuous indignation of our bourgeois at the community of women which, they pretend, is to be openly and officially established by the Communists. The Communists have no need to introduce a community of women; it has existed almost from time immemorial.
>
> Our bourgeois, not content with having the wives and daughters of the proletarian at their disposal, not to mention common prostitutes, take the greatest pleasure in seducing each other's wives.
>
> Bourgeois marriage is in reality a system of wives in common and thus, at the most, what the Communists might possibly be reproached with is that they desire to introduce, in substitution for a hypocritically concealed, an openly legalized community of women.[14]

Russian socialists held very similar views. In his novel *What Is to Be Done?* which became a manifesto for all Russian revolutionaries, Chernyshevsky also connects these themes through the famous utopian dream of the protagonist, Vera Pavlovna. The crystal palace of the future, where all people will be equal in rights and duties, is not only a gigantic factory, but also a huge brothel. Men and women attend a daily feast, consummating their collective labor, and then with mutual desire, retire to specially designed rooms. And what is more, for Chernyshevsky labor is merely a means for the physical perfection and sexual enjoyment that constitutes the end of human existence.[15]

But why, then, was community of property introduced in the Soviet Union, but never the community of wives? Is it not because common ownership somehow absorbed all other activities, including those once intended for sexual realization? This hypothesis forces us to shift our discussion from Marxist to Freudian terms.

Marcuse remarks that "in psychoanalytic literature, the development of libidinal work relations is usually attributed to a 'general maternal attitude as the dominant trend of a culture,' "[16] in another striking, if unintended, allusion to Soviet society. The USSR rejected the father principle and established itself on the basis of pure maternity. Materialism and atheism are important components of this self-indulgent civilization that recognizes only one reality besides its own: Mother Earth. The feminine and specifically maternal basis of Russian civilization has been grasped by many Russian poets and philosophers. Aleksandr Blok addressed Russia as "O, my Rus, my wife" (*O Rus' moia, zhena moia*). Georgy Fedotov argued that "at every step in studying Russian popular religion one meets the constant longing for a great divine female power."[17] Nikolai Berdiaev believed that "the fundamental category in Russia is motherhood."[18] It was the extension of the mother cult in Russia that provided for the triumph of materialism after the Christian religion of the Heavenly Father was overthrown by the Bolshevik revolution.

We will attempt to explicate some of the historical premises of this vision. Russia's vast expanses of open plains have often been compared to a womb that must be defended from invasion. For many centuries, Russia was an agricultural society; hence the mythological images of the earth as divine mother. A peasant who plowed and fertilized his fields could metaphorically see himself as a man impregnating his wife. Ritual fertilization of the earth survived in Russia into the twentieth century, despite almost a millennium of Christian tradition. Finally, the very names *Rus'* and *Rossiia* are of feminine gender, lending themselves naturally to such phrases as "Mother Russia" and "Rus-Wife" (*Rossiia-matushka, Rus'-zhena*).

One can be certain that the mythological relics of femininity and maternity are still relevant to twentieth-century Russia, regardless of its obsession with political, social, economic, and technological issues. But, characteristically, even in the most comprehensive Western investigation of feminine themes in Russian culture,[19] Soviet ideology is not considered at all. Materialism, however, is an important outcome of worshiping Russia as mother, particularly as the Russian *materiia*, of feminine gender, is more strongly imbued with "maternal" associations than is the English "matter."

Lenin's *Materialism and Empirio-Criticism* (1908), defended materialist philosophy against what was termed "physical idealism," a philosophy that had been elaborated by western European scientists (Mach and Avenarius), and by their Russian followers (Bogdanov, Lunacharsky, and Bazarov) in the early decades of the twentieth century. The main thrust of Lenin's book is that matter is primary, and consciousness secondary. He denies the subjective and ideal qualities of knowledge, insisting that material objects are directly and naturally "copied," "reflected," and "photographed" in human consciousness.

I will not discuss the philosophical aspects of Lenin's work per se. Instead my question is, Did the Leninist doctrine of Soviet materialism arise spontaneously, or did it have roots in earlier Russian thought and in the national character? One often encounters the view that materialism was alien to Russian philosophy and was mechanically borrowed from western European thought. Russians allegedly are natural-born spiritualists and do not perceive matter as a specific, separate reality; they supposedly lack western European sobriety and the habit of relying on objective laws that operate beyond one's subjective will or wishes. Russians are a mystical people, for whom rational knowledge of the objective world is alien.

The element of truth in these characterizations should not lead us to confuse materialism with rationalism or empiricism. Indeed, a classical, archetypal Russian is neither a rationalist nor an empiricist, but is nevertheless a materialist, and the most unyielding materialism does not prevent him from proclaiming the mystic qualities of matter. Materialism proceeds from the ancient assumption about nature's priority over man, of its maternal rights over man, and the reciprocal duty of man toward Mother Nature.[20]

Yet it is well-known that Marxist-Leninist materialism is not merely worship of matter; it struggles in alliance with atheism against religion or (perhaps) against God himself. Materialism is a form of theomachy (*bogoborchestvo*) that rejects worship of the Father in favor of worshiping Mother Nature. Lenin announced that "all worship of a divinity [*bozhen'ka*] is necrophilia—be it the cleanest, most ideal, not sought-out but built-up divinity, it's all the same."[21]

In a single phrase, Lenin demonstrates two ways of vanquishing God: by transforming him into a child (*bozhen'ka*, "godlet"); and by transforming him into a corpse (*trupolozhestvo*, "necrophilia"). Of primary significance is the desire to declare in mocking tones with traces of a lisp that God is nothing important, to turn him from the Father into a baby, to eliminate the rival in this love-struggle for the mother. In this way, the child attempts in fantasy to trade places with his father. It is interesting in this context to compare two of Lenin's neologisms, in which the diminutive suffix *-en'k* and the augmentative suffix *-ishche* turn out to be antonyms not only on the grammatical plane, but also in terms of worldview: on the one hand, the contemptuous "godlet" (*bozhen'ka*), and on the other, the crudely elated "What a man!" The latter description of Lev Tolstoy—"What a full-blown man!" (*Kakoi materyi chelovechishche*)—attested to by Maksim Gorky in his sketch "V. I. Lenin," has often been quoted as an example of Lenin's "activist" or even "fighting" humanism. Inclusion of the epithet "full-blown" (*materyi*), derived from the root *mat'* and denoting the highest level of sexual maturity, also unconsciously points to the Oedipal subtext of Lenin's materialism. In his competition for the mother, the son imagines himself a "full-blown man" and the father, a powerless "godlet."

Any attentive psychoanalyst will identify this "militant materialism" and its furious scorning of a "damned God" as the Oedipus complex elevated to the stature of philosophy. The Oedipus complex is not limited to the framework of family relations; it can reveal itself in the relationship between man and nature, when the latter is identified as Mother.[22] Materialism, when coupled with atheism, is nothing but the conscious projection of this childish complex: the son's striving to take his mother away from his father by killing the father or, better yet, simply by announcing his death. This is why Lenin considered love for the Father to be a necrophilic perversion. Soviet materialism as a mother cult is, strictly speaking, not philosophy, but mythology.

A psychoanalytic interpretation of materialism can go still further to explain a paradox that cannot be solved in the framework of Marxist philosophy: Why did the consistently materialistic approach lead to an unprecedented violence of man over nature and over society in the Soviet era? Soviet ideology allegedly proclaimed the priority of matter, but, in actuality, such entities as the "planned economy" and "ideological and Party commitment" devastated living matter: Chernobyl is only one example. As early as the beginning of the 1930s, Andrei Bely remarked that the triumph of materialism had abolished matter itself. Now, in the early 1990s, we are able to witness the last stage of materialism's destruction of matter in the USSR: there is nothing to eat and no clean air to breathe, many natural resources are exhausted, and agricultural production is marginal at best.

All this can be explained again in terms of the Oedipus complex. In reality, the son kills his father, not to worship his mother religiously, but to master her sexually. In the same way, materialism-atheism dethrones God the Father, not for the sake of the maternal superiority of Nature, but for the son's superiority over his mother. For example, Stalin in his work *Dialectical and Historical Materialism* (1938) which for many years became the Holy Scripture of Soviet ideology, proceeds from Engels's assumption that "the materialistic outlook on nature means no more than simply conceiving nature just as it exists, without any foreign admixture,"[23] which means "without God" or "without spirit." In the same work, however, Stalin asserts that "men carry on a struggle against nature and utilize nature for the production of material values."[24] The son abducts Mother Nature from the Father ("foreign admixture") in order to intrude into the womb from which he was born and to become her master and her spouse. This is the incestuous essence of materialist civilization.

Probably the only solid monument to this epoch of militant materialism will be the underground palaces of the metro systems in Moscow, Leningrad, and other large cities. In Russian, the formal term for "metro" is *Metropolitan,* but this is not just a system of transportation, it is also the *Matro*politan, the city or even shrine of the Mother. The first metro stations were built in Moscow in the mid-thirties, while the antireligious political campaigns were reaching a climax, and Christian temples to the Heavenly Father were being destroyed all across Russia. To replace these temples, new ones were constructed that were dedicated to the earth and were built into, not above, the earth itself. These underground temples were symbolic both of the new predominance of materialism as an antireligion and of the reborn religion of the Mother.

Anybody who has descended into the Moscow metro has noticed the abundance of beautiful Soviet emblems that decorate its walls. Portraits and statues of Soviet leaders surrounded by the reverent masses, overflowing cornucopia of fresh fruits and vegetables, heavily armed men and women ready to protect the state, workers and peasants clasping hands in eternal friendship, representatives of various Soviet nationalities all seated together at one table, toasting their Party—such are the icons and frescoes of sacred events in Soviet history. In addition to functional transportation purposes, space was wisely reserved in these tunnels for transcendental, religious depictions, such as these.

It is fitting that stones removed from ransacked churches were deliberately used in the construction of these churches of the underworld. The destruction of the Father's temples and building of the Mother's temples essentially formed a single process. The first church of the Mother, the Revolutionary Square metro station in central Moscow, was partially constructed from the stones of the Danilov monastery. (Ironically, the latter is now a centerpiece in the current revival of the Father's church: the patriarch and hierarchy of Russian Orthodoxy have recently moved from provincial Zagorsk to this urban monastery.)

In his *Poeziia rabochego udara* (Poetry of the worker's blow [1918]), proletarian poet and thinker A. K. Gastev prophetically points to the new turn in civilization: from the heavens to the underworld.

> We won't strain toward these pathetic heights, known as the sky. The sky is a creation of idle, lay-about, lazy and timid people.
>
> We will dash below!
>
> . . . For long years we will go away from the sky, from the sun, from the twinkling of stars, and pour into the earth: she into us, and we in her.
>
> We will go into the earth by thousands, we will go in by millions, we will pour in as an ocean of people! And from there we will not come back, we will never come back. . . . There we will perish and bury ourselves in the insatiable rush and the laboring blow.
>
> Born of the earth, we will return to her, as the ancients used to say; but the earth will be transformed. . . . When she can bear no more and rends her steel armor, in an ecstasy of labor's outburst, she will birth new beings, whose name will no longer be man.[25]

Such is the frenzied erotics of labor: man's reentry into his mother's lap. He no longer wants to depend on the father, to cringe before the sky. Rather, he is filled with passion for his mother and determines to possess her, to pour into her the "ecstacy of labor's outburst," so she will conceive new, superhuman beings. "Born of the earth, we will return to her": precisely the formula of Oedipus' desire. The entire lexicon of this passage by Gastev, despite the ostensible topic of "labor," is filled with openly erotic metaphors reminiscent of whole works by such authors as D. H. Lawrence or Henry Miller. Further on we read: "Let us dig into the depths and cut them open . . . let us lay bare the under-earth caverns . . . in the insatiable rush and the laboring blow . . . she'll be full with an unquieted storm . . . moved to ecstacy by the outburst." Materialism, with its revulsion for the sky and frenzied love of the earth, shows its incestuous underside.

If we consider materialism a certain type of mythology, it might well arise of its own accord from the soil of any national culture on the basis of ancient pagan beliefs.

What were the sources of the Soviet materialist bias? Was it imposed on our society by foreign thinkers, by German scientific materialists such as Ludwig Buchner, Karl Vogt, and Jacob Moleschott? (They were admired by Chernyshevsky, Pisarev, and other revolutionary democrats.) Or did our materialism come from Marx and Engels, the founders of dialectical materialism, via Lenin and the social democrats?

Perhaps the roots of Soviet materialism are deeply native. Recall the furious curse with which Lenin condemned German professors, admonishing them to return to their mothers' vaginas. These grandiose materialist teachings, exaltedly accepted by the lower classes after the October Revolution, revert back to that favorite expletive, "F... your mother!" (*tvoiu mat'!*), which in Russian is a familiar and virtually all-purpose saying.

This curse of sending the son to the same womb that gave him birth originates in the ancient tribal practice of incest as an accepted type of relation. Marxism-Leninism teaches that the future of communist society will be to revive on the highest technological level the primitive communal structure. The importance of this statement has been underestimated: Does it not mean that patterns of behavior forbidden by civilized societies will also be revived under communism as accepted social practice?

In Russian, such foul language is called *mat,* which has the same roots as the words "mother" (*mat'*) and "matter" (*materiia*). In the late 1920s and early thirties a pun was in vogue among the Soviet intelligentsia: the party chiefs adore dialectical materialism, while the masses prefer the *maternyi* dialect. This pun is more than a simple joke: it does not so much underline the difference between the party's and the people's understanding of the basic category of mother-matter, as it stresses their essential unity. Is not dialectical materialism a philosophical modification of *mat?* Doesn't it worship matter in the same way that a son may abuse and denigrate his mother? Proclamations of the priority of matter over the spirit or the struggle of materialism against idealism may be regarded as equivalent to the obscenity of pushing a son back into his mother's womb.

Should the mother enjoy this rape, or writhe in pain and lose the will to live? The reaction of nature to the incestuous drive of Soviet man is the answer to this question.

It is commonly thought that incestuous relationships are taboo in civilized societies because inbreeding can cause genetic mutations. The Soviet Union seems to be the first instance of a civilized society that is founded on the concept of incest: an exception that proves the rule. The Soviet Union has retreated back to barbarism and has been overtaken by unprecedented forms of social, physical, and environmental degradation.

Medicine knows only too well the type of fruit that issues from the union of mother and son. Among the innumerable pathologies known to materialist civilization, suffice it to mention pathoeconomics, pathosociology, pathopedagogy, pathoaesthetics, and patholinguistics. Violence against nature and the exhaustion of her life-giving womb beneath the blows of an iron sledgehammer, causing continuous miscarriages, harvests hastily extracted from nature, without coming to term, and the despoiling of rich underground resources . . . Violence against one's own people through the mechanical division into classes and then infecting some classes with hatred for others . . . Violence against art, whereby images born of life itself are replaced by the artificial insemination of future homunculi with the abstractly correct ideas of socialist realism . . . Violence against language and its perversion into an instrument, a bayonet for the class offensive, fashioned of words that do not grow from the root but are mechanically stuck together from bits and pieces: "Komsomol," "kolkhoz," "partkom"—these are some of the consequences of this epoch-making and all-embracing incest.

It is not coincidental that the Bible of this new incestuous materialism is Gorky's novel *Mother* (1906). The hero of the novel turns out to be the son, Pavel, who subjugates the will of his mother, Nilovna, and leads her into revolution. At first, she is a Christian believer, but her belief in Father and Son gives way to passionate support for revolutionaries the world over, as if they were all her sons.

Pavel's father, the tyrant Mikhail Vlasov, appears in the first pages of the novel, only to die promptly from alcoholism. Gorky rejects faith in the Father, the opiate of the people, in order to position the son closer to his mother instead. Here they are, Pavel and Nilovna, alone, and what does their situation represent if not Pavel's attempt to dominate Nilovna and her willingness to submit to his will?

> She clung to his every word with fear. The eyes of the son burned beautifully and strongly. . . . "What choice have you ever known?" he

asked her. "What can you recall of your life?" . . . It was sweet for her to see that his somber blue eyes now burned so softly and gently. . . . He took her hand and firmly clenched it in his hands. She was stricken by the word "mother," which he pronounced with hot passion, and by this clenching of her hand, which was new and strange. . . . And embracing his strong, well-proportioned body with caressing, warm glances, she began to speak swiftly and quietly.[26]

This episode with its "strange groping" and "hot passion," is reminiscent of Turgenev's love scenes, but of course here the lovers are mother and son. "It's magnificent—mother and son together . . . !"[27] Soviet students learned these lines in school, year after year, without comprehending the perverse underlying meaning of such stirring episodes. We wrote compositions about how the thoughts and deeds of the son made his mother's heart overflow, and how, under Pavel's influence, her soul straightens and her body becomes young again.

Later on, Gorky let slip the secret of his worldview, as so often happens with dangerous, "repressed" erotic themes, in a reference to another writer. In Mikhail Prishvin's works, Gorky found and ardently approved the spirit of all-embracing incest with Mother Nature:

In your books, this sense of the earth, as of your own flesh, sounds to me remarkably comprehensible, as you are husband and son of the Great Mother.

Does this sound like incest? But, after all, that's just what it is: man, born of the earth, makes her fruitful with his labor.[28]

Here we see clearly stated what is subconsciously hidden in the image of Pavel Vlasov—"husband and son of the Great Mother"—and this image acquires archetypal depth. Gorky realizes that he has made it "sound like incest," but since this is already the ideological stereotype of the entire new Soviet civilization, any shamefulness disappears from his admission, written almost thirty years after *Mother*. On the contrary, pride takes its place in the man who attains to the level of "making fruitful" his own mother. Labor, thus, is considered not a form of obedience to the Father, not his curse laid upon the son in consequence of the first sin, but the piercing joy of copulation with Mother Nature.

Lenin's high regard for *Mother* as a "necessary and ultimately timely book" is known by every Soviet student. It is not by chance that this novel was written at almost the same time (1906–7) as Lenin's own treatise, *Mate-*

rialism and Empirio-Criticism (1908; published, 1909)—just as the first Russian revolution was being put down by the tsar. Actually, Lenin's treatise tries to argue in theoretical terms precisely what Gorky's novel portrays: that the Mother is completely independent of the Father (be he God or tsar) and would be infinitely happier in union with sons who are revolutionaries and materialists.

The Russian language is comparatively gender-conscious, and Lenin's philosophical views are highly charged sexually. Lenin denigrates those concepts that are masculine in the Russian language, such as God (*Bog*), spirit (*dukh*), sign (*znak*), symbol (*simvol*), hieroglyph (*ieroglif*); while matter (*materiia*), reality (*real'nost'*), nature (*priroda*), truth (*istina*) and factual data (*ob"ektivnaia dannost'*)—his terms of positive valence—are feminine.

In Lenin's view, nature is not just the spouse of man, but rather his mother. This view is the basis of the polemical chapter "Did Nature Exist Before Man?" in *Materialism and Empirio-Criticism*. Here Lenin attacks those empirio-monists and empirio-criticists who defended the simple "conjugal" relationship of the "central member," man, to the material world. They defended the "principal coordination" between the human sensibility and the material world, which in mythological terms is more similar to a spousal relationship than to that of a mother and son.

In a psychoanalytic sense, the materialistic teachings of Lenin represent a fascination with the mother's womb and lead to his formula of philosophical seduction: "Matter is a philosophical category for the designation of objective reality, which is given to a man through his senses."[29] A man, bereft of his Father, remains alone with undifferentiated feminine matter, which surrenders to him sensually. In Russian, every principal word in Lenin's definition, except "man," is feminine.

Thus we can understand the origins of Gorky's and Lenin's vindictive ideology of incest, which emerged as a reaction to the Father tsar defeating the sons (1906–8). Upon attaining power, they successfully avenged themselves on this earthly father as well as on the Heavenly one. All mechanisms of psychological and social self-restraint were destroyed and primordial polymorphous sexuality, lust in the broadest sense, became evident, as we have seen, in all types of social relationships.

And now we can begin to define communist labor not only as the promiscuity of collective ownership, but also as an incestuous attitude toward Mother Nature. Our labor was furious and frenzied, as if we were possessed by insatiable desire. The all-time favorite Soviet saying became the maxim of agronomist Ivan Michurin: "We cannot wait for favors from nature; to take them from her is our task."[30] I remember schoolteachers constantly repeating this sentence to us with a proud, ardent emphasis on the verb "to take." Labor became a sort of rape: taking by force from Mother Nature those favors she was not inclined to relinquish.

The translation of Marxist categories into the language of Freudianism and the interpretation of Soviet civilization in terms of psychoanalysis—these have become rather popular motifs of the humanities in contemporary Russia. The Oedipus complex, as presented in this chapter, is by no means the only key to the Soviet unconscious.

Georgy Gachev has worked out the concept of a "Rustam complex," whereby youth is offered in sacrifice to age, as the father kills his own son. In Gachev's estimation, this gerontocratic complex is characteristic of the Eastern unconscious, including that of Russia, whereas the Oedipus complex, with its cult of triumphant youth, characterizes European and, broadly speaking, Western civilization in which the new vanquishes the old. The archetype of filocide, as Gachev formulates it, explains Russia's perpetual return to archaic ways of life, from capitalism to feudalism and even the primitive communal system: the father "devours" his children, as elderly inertia wins out over the energy of the young.[31]

Boris Paramonov has worked out a different psychoanalytical theory, one that views Bolshevism as the perversion of natural relations between man and woman, man and nature, in preference for a homosexual Utopia. In this context "comradeship," the society of like-thinkers of the same sex, becomes the source of ideologically sublimated pleasure. Paramonov emphasizes the homosexual basis of Plato's "ideal republic" and finds corresponding motifs in the work of the leading Soviet writer Andrei Platonov.[32]

Nonetheless, the current trend toward psychoanalytical interpretations of Soviet phenomena has nothing in common with the Freudian-Marxist Utopias of Reich, Marcuse, Fromm and other New Left theorists of the 1960s. Freudian-Marxism was a typical manifestation of the modernist paradigm, striving to unite these two types of "radical critical" discourse in order to build a metanarrative of liberation. Social revolution was augmented by sexual revolution, as creative ecstasy and promiscuity were postulated in the economic and erotic spheres alike.

The aim of Freudian interpretations of Marxism in post-Soviet Russia is entirely different: not to strengthen but to annihilate these two discourses by imposing them on each other. On the face of it, contemporary Freudian interpretations of Marxism intend to substitute one discredited discourse for another that still appeals to contemporary Russian theorists because of its longtime repression under the Soviet regime. However, the far-reaching goal of these interpretations is not to demonstrate the superiority of Freudian discourse over Marxist discourse, but rather their essential similarity. Postmodern anti-utopian impulses are in effect: in these newest interpretations, one of which is offered here, Marxism and Freudianism mutually mock one another, revealing the contingency of their "liberating" and "unmasking" lexicon. Freudianism emerges not as a necessary addition but as a grotesque and laughable discreditation of Marxism. Translation from Marxist language into Freudianism serves not as a verification but rather as a falsification of both languages: precisely because they speak in the same way, they describe not so much reality itself as the very mechanism of such speaking, a model of deterministic prophesy. By harmonizing with each other they elucidate the interplay of sister languages, a double solipsism from which there arises no reality whatever other than that of language and metanarrative structures that reflect and repeat each other endlessly. Translatability is a sign of stereotypification, which becomes an object of theoretic irony; repetition and bare quotation are the device of parody. Marx and Freud unintentionally repeat, and thereby parody, each other's gestures; they are two great actors playing out one and the same comedy on the postmodern stage—the modernist project of the "liberation of humankind."

The concept of postmodernism in non-Western cultures has been fiercely
debated in recent times. Specifically, can there be such a thing as postmodernism beyond Western culture at all, and if so, is there one postmodernism,
common to the United States, France, Germany, Poland, Russia, Japan, and
so on? Or are there as many different postmodernisms as national cultures?

Over the past two or three years, this discussion has evolved in Russia as
well. As recently as the late 1980s, "postmodernism" was still a rather exotic term that served highbrow intellectuals as a kind of shibboleth. However,
it very quickly became a cliché to be repeated in nearly every critical article.
Judging by the frequency of its proclamation, one might think that postmodernism has become the most widespread and active movement in contemporary Russian literature. To cite one influential young critic,

> today, postmodern consciousness, while still continuing its successful
> and smiling expansion, remains probably the only live aesthetic fact in
> all of the "literary process." Today, the postmodern is not just a fashion,
> it constitutes the atmosphere; one may like it or not, but it alone is now
> truly relevant. . . . [It] is the most vital, the most aesthetically relevant
> part of contemporary culture, and among its best examples, there is
> quite simply some excellent literature.[1]

Moreover, several conferences in Moscow have now been devoted exclusively to postmodernism,[2] and many of Russia's most progressive critics
and writers now swear by this sacred concept.

Only one other instance of such unanimous public enthusiasm inspired
by a literary concept readily comes to mind: the official proclamation and
establishment of "socialist realism" in 1934, as the single, comprehensive

method for all of Soviet literary practice. I will attempt to show that this parallel is not arbitrary: what is called postmodernism in contemporary Russia is not only a response to its Western counterpart but also represents a new developmental stage of the same artistic mentality that generated socialist realism. Further, both of these movements, socialist realism and postmodernism, are actually components of a single ideological paradigm deeply rooted in the Russian cultural tradition.

I trust that my proposals will be understood not as strict theories, but rather as loose hypotheses that may prove especially relevant in understanding the turbulent state of contemporary post-Soviet culture, which itself is in a very hypothetical period of transition.

1

I have deliberately entitled this chapter after Nikolai Berdiaev's famous work, *The Origins and Meaning of Russian Communism* (*Istoki i smysl russkogo kommunizma* [Paris, 1955]). Communist teachings arrived in Russia from Western Europe and seemed at first completely alien to this backward, semi-Asiatic country; however, Russia turned out to be the first nation to attempt an enactment of these teachings on a worldwide scale. Berdiaev has shown convincingly that communism was intimately linked to the entire "communal" spirit of Russian history, going back to times long before Marxism could have been known anywhere in the country.

In my view, the same paradox pertains to the problem of Russian postmodernism. A phenomenon that seems to be purely Western in the final analysis exposes its lasting affinity with some principal aspects of Russian national traditions.

Among the diverse definitions of postmodernism, I would single out as most important the production of reality as a series of plausible copies, or what the French philosopher Jean Baudrillard calls "simulation." Other features of postmodernism, such as the waning of comprehensive theoretical metanarratives or the abolishment of oppositions between high and low, elitist and mass culture, seem to be derived from this phenomenon of hyperreality. Models of reality replace reality itself, which then becomes irrecoverable.

Indeed, earlier predominant movements in twentieth-century Western culture, such as avant-gardism and modernism, tended to be elitist, in that they pitted themselves against the reality of mass society, either because of their alienation from it (in the case of modernism) or because they aspired to transform it to revolutionary ends (in the case of avant-gardism). As for metanarratives such as Marxism and Freudianism, their main aim was to unmask the illusions, or ideological perversions, of consciousness, in order to disclose the genuine reality of material production, in the case of the former, or libidinal energy, for the latter. Yet once the very concept of reality ceased to operate, these metanarratives, which appealed to reality, as well as the elitist arts, which opposed it, began to wane.

The authority of a reality principle serves as the foundation of great traditions in Western philosophy, science, and technology and thus may be considered the cornerstone of all Western civilization. According to this principle, reality must be distinguished from all products of human imagination, and practical means may be used to establish truth as a form of correspondence between cultural concepts and reality. Science, technology, and even the arts strove to break through various subjective illusions and mythological prejudices in order to reach the substance of reality with the help of objective cognition, practical utilization, and realistic imitation, respectively. The last great metanarratives of Western civilization, those of Marx, Nietzsche, and Freud, are still pervaded by this obsession with capturing reality, as they relentlessly attempt to demystify all illusory products of culture and ideology.

During the twentieth century, however, an unexpected twist transformed these highly realistic and even materialistic theories into their own opposites. While Marxism, Freudianism, and Nietzscheanism all appealed to reality as such, they simultaneously produced their own ideologized and aetheticized versions of reality, along with new, sophisticated tools of political and psychological manipulation. Reality itself disappeared, yielding to these refined and provocative theories of reality and, moreover, to practical modes of producing reality. Now, in the late twentieth century, we produce objectivity itself, not merely separate objects.

In other words, what we now see as reality is nothing more than a system of secondary stimuli intended to produce a *sense* of reality: precisely what Baudrillard calls "simulation." In spite of any apparent resemblances, simulation is the opposite of what was understood as "imitation" during the Renaissance or the Enlightenment. Imitation was an attempt to represent reality as such, without subjective distortions. Simulation is an attempt to substitute for reality those images that *appear* more real than does reality itself.

The production of reality seems new for Western civilization, but it has been routinely accomplished throughout all of Russian history. Here, ideas have always tended to substitute for reality, beginning, perhaps, with Prince Vladimir, who adopted the idea of Christianity in A.D. 988, and proceeded to implant it in a vast country where it had been virtually unknown until that time.

Peter the Great ordered Russia to be educated and vigorously introduced such innovations as newspapers, universities, and academies. These institutions appeared in artificial forms, incapable of concealing their deliberateness, the forced nature of their origins. In essence, we are dealing with the simulative, or nominative, character of a civilization composed of plausible labels: this is a "newspaper," this, an "academy," this, a "constitution," none of which grew naturally from the national soil, but were implanted from above in the form of smoothly whittled twigs in hopes they might take root and germinate. Too much in this culture came from ideas, schemes, and conceptions, to which reality was subjugated.

In his *Russia in 1839,* the Marquis de Custine described the simulative character of Russian civilization in which the plan, the preceding concept, is more real than the production brought forth by that plan.

> Russians have only names for everything, but nothing in reality. Russia is a country of facades. Read the labels—they have "society," "civilization," "literature," "art," "sciences"—but as a matter of fact, they don't even have doctors. If you happen to call a Russian doctor from your neighborhood, you can consider yourself a corpse in advance. . . . Russia is an Empire of catalogues: if one runs through the titles, everything seems beautiful. But . . . open the book and you discover that there is nothing in it. . . . How many cities and roads exist only as projects. Well, the entire nation, in essence, is nothing but a placard stuck over Europe.[3]

One can ascribe this negative reaction to a foreigner's prejudice, but Alexander Herzen, for one, believed that de Custine had produced a fascinating and intelligent book about Russia.[4] Moreover, no less a devotee of Russia's national roots than Ivan Aksakov, one of the most sincere and ardent Slavophiles of the nineteenth century, held a similar view on the "Empire of catalogues." He recognized the concepts of "intentionality" and "counterfeit" as fundamental to his native civilization:

> Everything in our country exists "as if," nothing seems to be serious, authentic; instead, everything has the appearance of something tempo-

rary, false, designed for show—from petty to large-scale phenomena. "As if" we have laws and even fifteen volumes of the code of laws . . . whereas half of these institutions do not exist in reality and the laws are not respected.[5]

Even the syntactical constructions of de Custine and Aksakov's comments seem to coincide: the former states that "they have society . . . but as a matter of fact . . ." while the latter remarks, "we have laws . . . whereas in reality . . ." Both of these authors, from diametrically opposite standpoints, indicate the "halved" and chimerical character of Russian civilization. For de Custine it is insufficiently European; for Aksakov, insufficiently Russian. But the result is the same: the ostentatious, fraudulent nature of the civilization begets external, superficial forms, devoid of both genuine European and intrinsic Russian contents, and it remains a tsardom of names and outward appearances.

This civilization, composed entirely of names,[6] reveals its nature in post-modern Russian art, which shows us a label removed from utter emptiness. Conceptualism, for example, the prevailing trend in Russian art of the 1980s and early 1990s is a set of such labels, a collection of facades lacking the other three sides.[7]

2

The most grandiose simulacrum, or "concept" that expressed the simulative nature of Russian civilization was, of course, St. Petersburg: the city erected on a "Finnish swamp." "St. Petersburg [was] the most abstract and premedi-tated [*umyshlennyi*] city in the whole world," according to Dostoevsky,[8] who sensed that the reality of the city was composed entirely of fabrica-tions, designs, ravings, and visions, lifted up like a shadow above rotten soil, unfit for construction.

Instability was laid into the very foundation of the imperial capital, which subsequently became the cradle of three revolutions. The realization of the city's intentionality and "ideality," the lack of firm soil to stand on, gave rise to one of the first, and most ingenious, literary simulacra. In Dos-toevsky's words:

A hundred times, amidst this fog, I've been struck with a strange but importunate reverie: "And what if this fog were to scatter and leave for above, wouldn't this entire rotten, slimy city take off with it, wouldn't it rise up with the fog and disappear like smoke, and the prior Finnish swamp would remain, and, in the middle of it, *for beauty, I think,* the bronze horseman on his hotly breathing, exhausted horse?" (Emphasis mine)[9]

This vision might well have just come off the canvas of a conceptual artist, a postmodern master, such as Eric Bulatov, or Vitaly Komar and Alexander Melamid. Contemporary Russian conceptualism emerged, not from the imitation of Western postmodernism, but rather from the very same rotten Petersburg fog of Dostoevsky's "importunate reverie." For conceptualism, it is not enough to show that the "winter city," splendidly and proudly erected on the marsh, is a shadow and a phantom, concealing the authentic reality of the marsh itself as a densely congealed evaporation. Many contemporary Russian realists—not "socialist realists," but those of a strictly critical vein, such as Solzhenitsyn—limit themselves to this very task: to depict the swamp in which we all live, and to prove that it inexorably draws all of us into its abyss, only to burst open again, here in natural disasters, there in social catastrophes. Conceptualists, on the other hand, are more eccentric; they not only show us the quagmire beneath the evaporated city, but they also drive into it a sacred fragment of this city, the figure of the founder, upon whose forehead the monumental, state-creating thought is forever frozen.

What justifies such conceptual liberty, such disrespectful humor? Why, for beauty, I think! Such is the aim of the conceptual aesthetic: to demonstrate the complete reality of ideological signs in a world of spectral and annulled realities. There is an irresolvable paradox in the fact that a monument to the founder abides in a swamp that preceded the city and will survive it. Is this not the archetypal phenomenon of Soviet civilization, which has celebrated itself in the most grandiose projects and Utopias in mankind's history? These plans and ideas emerged from the heads of their creators only to return there cast in iron, bronze, or plaster, hardened into a heavy "thought on the forehead." And reality rushed past them, frenzied, like the unfrozen Neva, insane, like Evgeny, the hero of Pushkin's *The Bronze Horseman.* "Such a thought is on his forehead! Such strength he hides within!" These remarkable lines from Pushkin's narrative poem, describing the famous monument to Peter the Great, underscore a paradox: the inanimate monument can *think,* whereas the living hero *loses his mind* under its influence. An idea embodied in metal overwhelms and dissolves reality. The raving of rationality, the orgy of continuous organizational fever, like a little organ (*organchik*) in the head of the city-builder (recalling the supernatural personage of "Ugrium-Burcheev" in Saltykov-Shchedrin's *History of a Town*)—such is the self-perpetuating mechanism of conceptual creation.

It is not surprising then, that the specter wandering through Europe, as Marx and Engels characterized communism in the first lines of *The Communist Manifesto,* settled down and acquired reality in Russia. This country proved to be especially susceptible to mistaking phantasms for real creatures.

After the Bolshevik Revolution, the simulative nature of reality became even more pronounced in Russia. All social and private life was subordinated to ideology, which became the only real force of historical development. Signs of a new reality, of which Soviet citizens were so proud in the thirties and fifties, from Stalin's massive hydroelectric plant on the Dnieper River to Khrushchev's decision to raise corn and Brezhnev's numerous autobiographies, were actually pure ideological simulations of reality. This artificial reality was intended to demonstrate the superiority of ideas over simple facts.

Communist *subbotniks*[10] in the Soviet Union were examples of hyperevents, simulating "the celebration of labor" precisely in order to stimulate real labor. No labor was recognized in the Soviet Union except this artificial communist enthusiasm, which supposedly justified Lenin's ideas about "free labor." (Both meanings are relevant in this Soviet idiom: "free" from exploitation and also "free" in terms of not being paid.) Simulation is not a lie because the latter presupposes the existence of some external reality that may be distorted or verified. In the case of Soviet society, reality was made to coincide with those ideas by which it was described; it thus effectively became nothing other than the creation of these ideas. Even Solzhenitsyn did not uncover any radically new realities, because everyone in the Soviet Union was perfectly aware of the existence of "the people's enemies" and "socially alien elements" who were confined in Stalin's labor camps. Ideology did not lie, but simply re-created the world in its own image and likeness. Therefore, the ideological image of this world could not be anything but relevant and truthful. Ideology did not lie; it was the real world itself that tended to disappear and to dissolve in ideological signs.

Such is the conceptual bias of Soviet reality itself: in comparison with a name that "ideally" signifies a certain quality of an object, the object itself turns out to be warped and on the decline. The presence of the idea of a sausage confronts the absence of real meat therein. The presence of a plan for manufacturing confronts the absence of actual production. Cheese or sausage in Russia, far from being material facts, turned into Platonic ideas. Conceptual art plays upon this material devastation of concepts. Dmitry Prigov, a leader of contemporary Russian conceptualism, wrote in his poem about the American president, Ronald Reagan:

> Reagan doesn't want to feed us
> Well, okay, it's really his mistake
> It's only over there that they believe
> You've got to eat to live
> But we don't need his bread
> We'll live on our idea . . .[11]

And indeed for quite some time, the idea of bread was more nourishing in Russia than bread itself. A mystical shortage of some material elements disguised within an effective presentation of their ideal counterparts: this is the Russian enigma manifesting itself at all levels, from the everyday-existential to the sociogovernmental. Even if the presence of bread allows one to define the "idea" of a given store as a "confectionery," there still is no sugar in it. In the economic system there are producers and consumers, but the intermediary elements between them that constitute a market are absent. The "minus-system" in which Russians have lived emerged as if from the canvas of a conceptualist artist, where names and labels demonstrate their own emptiness and lack of meaning. Roads lead to villages that have disappeared; villages are located where there are no roads; construction sites do not become buildings; house-builders have nowhere to live. A civilization of this type can be defined as a system with a meaningful absence of essential elements, "a society of deficit." Specters are more real here than reality, which itself becomes spectral.

In Baudrillard's definition of hyperreality,

> [T]he territory no longer precedes the map, nor survives it. Henceforth, it is the map that precedes the territory—PRECESSION OF SIMULACRA—it is the map that engenders the territory, and if we were to revive [Borges's] fable today, it would be the territory whose shreds are slowly rotting across the map. It is the real, and not the map, whose vestiges subsist here and there, in the deserts which are no longer those of the Empire, but our own. *The desert of the real itself.*[12]

Today we can address this phrase, "the desert of the real itself," directly to what remains of the Soviet Union. This country is originally poor not in commodities, comfort, hard currency, but in reality itself. All its shortcomings and deficiencies are only symbols of this fading reality; and symbols themselves constitute the only genuine reality that survives.

Recalling the Potemkin villages of Russia's more distant past,[13] one cannot but think of their contemporary, post-Soviet adaptation: a phenomenon known as "presentations" (*prezentatsii*). This word was assimilated into Russian from English in, approximately, 1990–91 to denote the ceremony of an official opening of some public institution. In spite of the fact that Russia grows poorer and continues to crumble from day to day, such festive "presentations" are now widely fashionable. A stock-exchange or joint venture, a political party or new magazine formally presents itself (*prezentiruetsia*) to a select audience. For seventy years all of these institutions of Western civilization were banned from our society, but now it greedily absorbs them into the social vacuum. The necessity for such formal openings indicates the intrinsic limitations of these enterprises: they do not proceed organically from the national cultural soil. The overwhelming majority of these businesses and associations collapses within several weeks or months, leaving no memory of themselves other than their dazzling presentation. None of the cheerful participants at such lavish events, marked by long speeches, caviar, brandy, and oysters, would attest that the object of their presentation will survive even until the following morning, but most are fully satisfied by their inclusion in today's presentation and by the anticipation of more in the days to come. The entire life of society becomes an empty self-presentation. Neither political parties nor enterprises are really created, but rather *concepts* of parties and enterprises. Incidentally, the most real sphere, economics, is simulated even more than all others. Yet the only area in which this process of simulation might be truly beneficial is culture, since by its nature it is inclined to "present," to create images.

Prince Potemkin's villages of the late eighteenth century may still be considered a deliberate deception, but no one would identify our late twentieth-century "presentations" as either truth or lie. They are typical simulacra that do not claim to be veritable and thus cannot be reproached as deceptive. Such is the progression from "imitation" to "simulation" as revealed through major periods of Russian history. Even the Soviet regime was careful to maintain some presumptions of truth behind its evidently simulative ideological activities, but now that the communists are no longer in power, no one monitors events, and the simulative nature of the civilization is laid bare. Another difference is that under communism the category of *plan* prevailed, whereas postcommunist society celebrates *presentation,* implying that it is the present, not the future, that is simulated most of all.

"Presentation" in the post-Soviet period means a paradoxical lack of presence, the most genuine and tangible part of reality, which finally dissolves in a world of unabashed simulacra.

To sum up: throughout the course of Russian history, reality has been subjected to a gradual process of disappearance. The entire reality of pagan Rus disappeared when Prince Vladimir ordered the introduction of Christianity and briskly baptized the whole nation. Similarly, all reality of Moscovite Rus vanished when Peter the Great ordered his citizens "to become civilized" and shave their beards. All reality of "tsarist" Russia dissolved when Lenin and the Bolsheviks transformed it into the launching pad for a communist experiment. Finally, all Soviet reality collapsed in a few years of Gorbachev's and Yeltsin's rule, yielding to a new, still unknown system of ideas. Probably the ideas of capitalist economy and free enterprise now have a good chance to prevail in Russia, though they remain, once again, pure conceptions against the background of a hungry and devastated society. Personally, I am confident that in the long run Yeltsin or another leader will manage to create a simulated market economy in Russia. Realities have always been produced in Russia from the minds of the ruling elite, but once produced, they were imposed with such force and determination that these ideological constructions became hyperrealities.

3

It should be emphasized that conceptualism is tightly linked not only with the system of Soviet ideology, but also with the deep contradictions of the Russian religious identity in its role as a middle or intermediary point between the West and the East. Russia cleared a path in the middle of two great spiritual systems, one of which originates from empirical reality and explains all apparent illusions as its own handiwork, while the other asserts that all reality is illusory, a product interwoven of the many-colored veil of Maya,[14] which must be cast off to reveal Absolute Nothingness. It was necessary to combine these two extremes, even at the cost of an absurdity—the paradox of the Russian religious calling. The West realizes its calling in the forms of cult and culture developed by Catholicism and Protestantism, in their positive sense of the presence of God and in the totality of earthly entities, such as society, state, family, production, art. It stands to reason that all subversive, oppositional movements, from Romanticism to Existentialism, were directed against this positivity; nonetheless, they only underscore the fundamental fact of the positive religiosity of the West. The East, on the other hand, developed the most precise religious intuition of Emptiness, through its identification of life's highest meaning in the rejection of any and all positivities and, in drawing near to Nothingness, to its freedom and timelessness.[15]

Russia still has not made a choice between these global systems or worldviews, but has, instead, combined their contradictions both in "Orthodoxy," with its alienation from worldly culture, and in "communism," with its struggle against the "other world." Orthodoxy claimed to set aside all mundane activities in order to aspire to the Heavenly Kingdom, but in practice, it merged with Russian statehood to become a virtual synonym for political loyalty. On the other hand, the utopian practice of "communist construction," affirmed materialism as its highest principle, yet wreaked destruction on matter in practice, while lapsing time and again into the very idealism it so savagely rejected in theory. This closed system of self-negation is played out, entirely consciously, in conceptualism, which thus illuminates, at least in part, the mystery of Russia's religious calling.

I will cite Ilya Kabakov, a leading artist and theoretician of contemporary Russian conceptualism, whose vision depicts his native country as a huge reservoir of emptiness that swallows and dissolves all tangible constituents of reality:

> Every person who lives here lives, whether consciously or not, on two planes: 1. on the plane of his relations with other people and nature, and 2. on the plane of his relations with the void. These two planes are in opposition, as I have already said. The first is the "constructive" side. The second consumes and destroys the first. On the level of daily life this split, this bifurcation, this fatal non-contiguousness of the 1st and 2nd planes is experienced as a feeling of general destruction, uselessness, dislocation and hopelessness in everything; no matter what a person does, whether he is building or undertaking some other task, he senses in everything a feeling of impermanence, absurdity, and fragility. This life on two planes causes a particular neurosis and psychosis in every inhabitant of the void, without exception.[16]

Though Kabakov emphasizes the opposition between "constructive" and "destructive" impulses in Russian culture, it is clear from his description that they are basically one. Any object is deconstructed in the very process of its construction. In Russia, "nothingness" comes to light, not in its primordial and pure, "Eastern" emptiness, but as the self-erasure of a positive form, often one that has been borrowed from the West. The futility of positivity itself, which must nonetheless remain positive so as to demonstrate its futility again and again, forms the core of the Russian religious experience. Visible assertions conceal a lack of content while displaying an intrinsically illusory quality. Civilization is neither maintained nor annihilated, but abides as evidence of what civilization may be when there is none: a large-scale, very plausible and impressive simulacrum of civilization.[17]

Potemkin villages appeared in Russia, not simply as a political trick, but as a metaphysical exposé of the fraudulence of any positive cultural activity. This is a kind of outward appearance that scarcely conceals its deceptiveness, but also does not destroy it in any purposeful way, as Maya must be destroyed in Eastern traditions. Rather, it is anxious to preserve a semblance it in no way intends to ground or fill in. The intermediary stratum between "is" and "is not" forms an edge along which the "enchanted pilgrimage" of the Russian spirit slides.

The intermediary location of this religious experience, between East and West, creates semispectral constructions of the positive world that stand eternally in scaffolding, with wind blowing through them unimpeded, like the ubiquitous new suburbs (*novostroiki*) of Moscow, which impress foreigners with the feverish scope of constructive activity. These semiconstructions indicate by their entire appearance that they will never be finished, that they were not even undertaken so as to come to completion, but so as to dwell in this blessed interval between yes and no, existence and nonexistence, in the reign of a frozen moment. This is neither the emptiness of an already devastated place, like a desert or a wasteland, nor the completeness of creative endeavors such as towers or spires, but precisely an eternal would-be and not-yet construction, a "building long in-progress" (*dolgostroi*). Its walls and ceilings are every bit as significant and cherished as are the deficiencies and voids that can be seen between them. This is not only a typically "half-ruined" Russian landscape, but the duality of a people's character. The implicit motto of such activity is "it is necessary to begin, but it is impossible to finish": such is the intermediate stance of the free Russian spirit, which is as alien to the Eastern contemplative practice of world-negation as it is to the energetic Western ethos of world-organization.

Indeed, even our cities and buildings, those that manage to arise from the heaps of garbage, from the muddy grave prepared for them in advance, appear to be dilapidated and decrepit. Brand-new structures can scarcely survive: in a matter of days, they will be broken down, plastered with leaflets, and splashed with slops, as they return willy-nilly to a state of being under construction.

Of course, it is quite risky to put the disposition of a whole people into the narrow framework of a "national identity." Nonetheless, Russia demonstrates a consistent inclination to generate positive, tangible forms in order to feed the continuous process of their annihilation. This same process, however, may be defined in a different way: as a need to materially secure the very traces of this annihilation so that emptiness should not simply hang in the air as nothingness, but rather should appear as the significant absence of certain elements indispensable to a civilization.

Ilya Kabakov distinguishes Russian conceptualism from its Western counterpart by pointing to emptiness as the ultimate signified of all signifiers. In the West, conceptualism substitutes "one thing for another"—a real object for its verbal description. But in Russia the object that should be replaced is simply absent.

> In contrast with the West, the principle of "one thing instead of another" does not exist and is not in force, most of all because in this binomial the definitive, clear second element, this "another" does not exist. It is as if in our country it has been taken out of the equation, it is simply not there. . . . What we get is a striking paradox, nonsense: things, ideas, facts inevitably with great exertion enter into direct contact with the unclear, the undefined, in essence with emptiness. This contiguity, closeness, touchingness, contact with nothing, emptiness makes up, we feel, the basic peculiarity of "Russian conceptualism." . . . [I]t is like something that hangs in the air, a self-reliant thing, like a fantastic construction, connected to nothing, with its roots in nothing. . . . So, then, we can say that our own local thinking, from the very beginning in fact, could have been called "conceptualism."[18]

4

Almost all investigators of postmodernism cite America as a wonderland in which fantasies become more real than reality itself. America is not alone in this, however. Russia, in contrast to the rest of Europe, also developed as a dream realized in actuality. It is curious that when Nikita Khrushchev came to the United States in 1959, one of the first things he wanted to see was Disneyland. My guess is that he wanted to learn whether Americans had succeeded in creating as perfect a simulation of reality as the Soviet model, in which Khrushchev himself and all his predecessors, both tsars and general secretaries, were such skilled masters.

There are a variety of modes for the production of reality. One is the Soviet-style ideocracy that flourished on Marxist foundations and denounced all other ideologies as mystifications. Another is the American-style psychosynthesis, which includes a comprehensive system of mass media and advertising that flourish on the pragmatic principles of organizational psychology, while claiming to denounce all types of delusional consciousness.

In this way, Soviet phenomena may be estimated as no less postmodern than American ones. It is true that the postmodern self-awareness of Soviet reality emerged later than parallel philosophical developments in the West. Nevertheless, as early as the mid-seventies, conceptual art and literature, with their comprehensive reconsideration of the entire phenomenon of Soviet civilization, were becoming increasingly popular in the Soviet Union. In contrast to realistic literature of the type produced by Solzhenitsyn, conceptualism does not attempt to denounce the lie of Soviet ideology (moving from false ideas to a genuine reality); in contrast to metaphysical poetry of the type produced by Brodsky, it does not turn away from Soviet reality in search of higher and purer worlds (moving from false reality to genuine ideas). Conceptual painting and writing, as represented by the work of Ilya Kabakov, Erick Bulatov, Dmitry Prigov, Vsevolod Nekrasov, Lev Rubinshtein, and Vladimir Sorokin, convey ideas as the only true substance of the Soviet way of life. Paradoxically, false ideas constitute the essence of this genuine reality.

What is Soviet conceptual art, and why is it so named? First of all, one philosophical parallel, although remote in chronological terms, may be illuminating. As a school of medieval philosophy, contrary to realism, conceptualism assumed that concepts are self-sufficient mental entities, which must be distinguished from external reality. Throughout the new Middle Ages of the twentieth century, conceptualism took a similar critical stance, denouncing the basic realistic illusions of Soviet scholasticism, its identification of ideas with material reality. From the conceptual point of view, concepts have their own realm of existence in the ideological mind that differs substantially from the reality postulated by realist philosophy, or, in the case of the Soviet Union, by materialist ideology.

Turning directly to conceptualism in Russian art and literature, we find that, traditionally, any work may be simplistically reduced to some general ethical or political concept. For example, *Anna Karenina* could be reduced to a moral, such as: "A woman should never be unfaithful to her husband: she got what she deserved." Of course, everyone is indignant at such crude simplifications of great works of literature, but in the Soviet era, literature increasingly became nothing more than the fictional illustration of such simple ideas. Hence one of Prigov's "concepts" presents the following psychological scheme that could represent the conceptual framework of both *Anna Karenina* and, for example, Fedor Gladkov's construction novel in classical socialist realist style, *Cement* (1925), as well as a great number of other narratives.

> And married a general. He, returning from his foreign travels, meets her, now mature and wise, and his cold heart grows warm, but her heart is now like a piece of marble, impassive. He races around and around, throws himself into an ice-filled bathtub, but too late! too late! his heart is all surrounded by hellfire, all! and it burns the ice and his own flesh to ashes! if only he had the power to ignite her cold heart! DEATH! DEATH! All that remains to him is DEATH![19]

Narrative is reduced to the most simplified scheme and becomes a mere concept of narrative, the demonstration of an ideological code or a dictionary of literary motifs. Conceptualists readily elaborate such general themes as "the communist conquers his inner hesitations and boldly leads his comrades to increased labor productivity." Since no self-respecting Soviet writer would limit himself or herself to such truisms, he or she would try very hard to describe this communist and his comrades as real people, with many plausible details, including their foibles and personal weaknesses. Nevertheless, this character essentially remains only a vehicle for some predetermined idea or ideological tenet. Conceptualists grasped and unmasked the artificial nature, not only of Soviet literature, but of Soviet reality itself. Their works cannot be *reduced* to concepts, only because they are willfully and fundamentally *deduced* from them. The intention of an artistic work is advanced prior to the work and even instead of it. Conceptualists do not try to provide plausible illustrations of their ideas, but rather strive to convey them in a deliberately schematic manner, using the most ordinary and simplistic language. They create excellent works of bad art that purposely and often masterfully imitate the typical Soviet range of ideas. Classical Russian literature, with its emphasis on ideological, moral, and psychological matters, also provides an inexhaustible source for conceptual games. Artistic poverty becomes a distinguishing feature of conceptualism as a deliberate presentation of ideas denuded of their material referent.

Thus, conceptualists proved to be the first Russian postmodernists to stop opposing reality and ideas: whether it be opposing veritable reality to mis-leading ideas, as did Solzhenitsyn, Shalamov, and Grossman, or high ideas to low reality, as did our metaphysical and mythological writers. Concep-tualists have overcome both realistic traditions and romantic aspirations: they understand that in this country, no reality is more primary than that of ideas, and thus pastiche and parody of these ideas became their main artis-tic forms.

In conceptualist writings, all punctuation marks tend to be omitted, but if punctuation were to be used, the most frequently encountered form would be quotation marks. Since they refrain from proclaiming anything on their own behalf, conceptualists simply "repeat" what has already been said by others: by Pushkin, Dostoevsky, Mayakovsky, or what has been overheard from the neighbors in their communal apartment. Postmodernism is the world of quotations, but it is also a typically Soviet world, where all state-ments are pronounced either on behalf of the beloved leaders or the arch-enemies, but never as a form of self-expression. Under "real socialism," all people are supposed to think in impersonal, general ways, as if one's "own" thoughts were actually the articulations of someone else's ideas. Even in one's own mind thoughts emerge in the form of quotations.

Dmitry Prigov writes:

> The heroes of my poems have become the different linguistic layers (quotidian, state, high cultural, low cultural, religious and philosophi-cal), representing within the limits of the poetic texts corresponding mentalities and ideologies which reveal in this space mutual ambitions and pretensions. . . . In our times postmodernist consciousness is super-seded by a strictly conceptual virtual distance of the author from the text (when inside the text there is no language for resolving the author's personal pretensions, ambitions, or his personal ideology, but he, the author, detaches himself and is formed on the metatextual level). . . . The result is some kind of quasi-lyrical poem written by me under a feminine name, when I am of course not concerned with mystification but only show the sign of the lyrical poem's position, which is mainly associated with feminine poetry.[20]

Certainly, when Prigov composes verses on behalf of a woman, femininity also becomes a concept.[21]

The most representative genre of the Soviet epoch is not the novel or poetry, but metatextual discourse descriptive of cultural codes, such as the encyclopedia or textbook, in which an author remains anonymous in the midst of generally accepted opinions. The flow of time stops and categories of space become primary. The cessation of time is a common feature of both Soviet and postmodern reality, insofar as they become self-sufficient systems incorporating the exemplary, classical fragments of previous cultures and eras. Soviet culture was not thought to be a transitory phenomenon, but an accumulation and treasury of all human achievements, where Shakespeare and Cervantes, Marx and Tolstoy, and Gorky and Mayakovsky are equally valuable participants at the feast of great humanistic ideas. The encyclopedia, or textbook, collections of quotations or of unquoted, but highly authoritative and compelling judgments—these were the most lawful and comprehensive forms of "collaborative" thinking, as it flourished in Stalin's time.

The erasure of metanarratives is another important feature of postmodernism that is worthy of explanation. In the case of Soviet experience, we had an indisputably Marxist metanarrative. There is a common, though fallacious belief that Marxist teachings began dissolving into a variety of ideological positions only during and after perestroika. In truth, this dissolution began at the very moment Marxism was brought to Russia and progressed further as it was transformed into so-called Marxism-Leninism, or Soviet Marxism.

Perhaps more than any other metanarrative, Marxism relies on reality and materiality as the determinant of all ideological phenomena. When this teaching came to a culture in which reality had always been a function of the powerful State imagination, a strange combination emerged: materialism as a form and tool of ideology. Paradoxically, Marxism was a catalyst for the transformation of Russia into an enormous Disneyland, though one less amusing than terrifying. Before the Bolshevik revolution, not all aspects of material life were simulated, so that space remained for genuine economic enterprises. But once Russian ideology had assimilated materialism, all material life became a product of ideology.

Marxist teachings themselves also suffered a paradoxical transformation. On the one hand, Marxism became the only theoretical viewpoint to be officially sanctioned by the Soviet regime. Ironically, for this very reason, it expanded to incorporate all other types of discourse. Internationalists and patriots, liberals and conservatives, existentialists and structuralists, technocrats and ecologists all pretended to be genuine Marxists and pragmatically adapted the "proven teaching" to all varieties of changing circumstances. In the West, Marxism preserved its identity as a metanarrative, giving its own specific interpretation of all historical phenomena, because it was freely challenged by other metanarratives (such as Christianity and Freudianism). In the Soviet Union, however, Marxism became what postmodernists call pastiche, an eclectic mixture of all possible interpretations and outlooks. As an all-encompassing doctrine, penetrating even physics and theater, military affairs and children's play, Soviet Marxism was the ultimate postmodern achievement.

As for the rapprochement and integration of popular and elitist cultures, this tendency was stimulated by a Soviet cultural politics of universal literacy and ideological persecution. On the one hand, the masses were persistently and vigorously trained to perceive the value of high classical traditions, while base forms of mass entertainment were banned, such as pulp fiction, comics, the cabaret striptease, and so on. On the other hand, so-called elitist movements in the arts and philosophy, such as avant-gardism and modernism, surrealism and Freudianism were also strictly banned.

These attempts to homogenize Soviet society created a new culture of mediocrity that was equally far from both the upper and lower levels of a highly stratified Western culture. In the Soviet Union, this middling level was established even earlier than in the West, and the leveling process provided the ground for postmodern development.

5

One can readily anticipate a counterargument: How can we refer to Soviet postmodernism without a clear identification of Soviet modernism? In the West, postmodernism comes after modernism, but where is the corresponding progression in Soviet culture?

It is obvious that Russian culture of the pre-Revolutionary period was predominantly modernist, as indicated by such trends as symbolism and futurism. The Bolshevik movement and the October Revolution it fomented may also be seen as modernist phenomena, in that they are expressions of a thoroughly utopian vision. Rigidly consistent styles of modernist aesthetics were still dominant in the 1920s, as Mayakovsky's and Pilnyak's writings, for example, amply demonstrate.

In this sense, socialist realism, officially proclaimed in 1934, may be regarded as an essentially postmodern trend destined to balance all opposites and create a new space for the interaction of all possible stylistic devices, including romantic, realist, and classicist models. Andrei Siniavsky was one of the first theoreticians to be struck by this unbelievable and eclectic combination of varied modes of writing in "socialist realism," where, in his view, the first term of this expression contradicts the second:

> It seems that the very term "socialist realism" contains an insoluble contradiction. A socialist, i.e., a purposeful, a religious, art cannot be produced with the literary method of the nineteenth century called realism. And a really faithful representation of life cannot be achieved in a language based on teleological concepts. . . . They [socialist realists] lie, they maneuver, and they try to combine the uncombinable: the positive hero (who logically tends toward the pattern, the allegory) and the psychological analysis of character; elevated style and declamation and prosaic descriptions of ordinary life; a high ideal with truthful representation of life. The result is a loathsome literary salad. . . . This is neither classicism nor realism. It is a half-classicist half-art, which is none too socialist and not at all realist.[22]

Socialist realism was not a specific artistic movement in any traditional or modernist sense. It can be adequately understood only as a postmodern phenomenon, as an eclectic mixture of all previous classical styles, or as an encyclopedia of literary clichés. We should trust socialist realism's own self-definition, as the unity of a method attained through a diversity of styles: "[S]ocialist realism is regarded as a new type of artistic consciousness which is not limited by the framework of one or even of several modes of representation."[23] Socialist realism successfully simulated all literary styles beginning with ancient epic songs and ending with Tolstoy's refined psychologism and the futuristic poetics of placards and slogans.

In the Soviet Union, the thirties through the fifties clearly constitutes a postmodern epoch, even though the prevailing term at the time was "antimodernism," as Stalinist aesthetics mounted a furious struggle against "rotten bourgeois modernism." Antimodernism in relation to the West, however, was in fact postmodernism in relation to the native, pre- and post-Revolutionary modernist culture.

As a minimum, we can generalize the following postmodern features of socialist realism:

1. The creation of hyperreality that is neither truthful nor false but consists of ideas that *become* reality for millions of people.

2. The struggle against modernism as an "obsolete" mode of aesthetic individualism and linguistic purism.

3. The erasure of specifically Marxist discourse that then degenerates into

a pastiche of many ideologies and philosophies, even combining material-ism and idealism.

4. The erasure of any specific artistic style and ascension to a new "meta-discursive" level of socialist realism that combined classicist, romantic, realist and futurist models.

5. The rejection of "subjectivist" and "naive" discursive strategies and the transition to "quotation marks" as a mode of hyperauthorship and hyper-personality.

6. The erasure of the opposition between elitist and mass culture.

7. An attempt to construct a posthistorical space where all great dis-courses of the past should find their ultimate resolution.

Certainly, socialist realism lacks the playful dimension and ironic self-consciousness so typical of mature postmodernism. But socialist realism is only the first stage in the transition from modernism to postmodernism. Socialist realism is postmodernism with a modernist face that continues to wear an expression of absolute seriousness. In other words, Russian post-modernism cannot be fully identified with socialist realism, but also cannot be divorced from it.[24]

In the sixties and seventies, a second wave of modernism emerged in Soviet literature: futurist, surrealist, abstractionist, and expressionist trends were revived in literature, painting, and music. The era of the 1920s became the nostalgic model for this neomodernist phenomenon, as seen in the work of writers Andrei Voznesensky and Vassily Aksyonov.[25]

It is all the more significant that later, in the seventies and eighties, a second wave of postmodernism arose in opposition to the neomodernist generation of the sixties. For such postmodernists as Ilya Kabakov, Boris Groys, or Dmitry Prigov there are no figures more adversarial than Male-vich, Khlebnikov, and other modernists of the beginning of the century, not even to mention the latter's successors in the sixties, such as Voznesensky. Consequently, this explicitly postmodern generation feels a sort of nostalgia precisely for the typical Soviet life-style and the art of socialist realism, which provides them with congenial ideological material for their concep-tual works. Socialist realism is close to conceptualism in its antimodern-ist stance: both forms share highly conventional semiotic devices, sets of clichés and idioms that are devoid of any personal emphasis or intentional self-expression. This is why the well-known postmodern visual artists Vi-taly Komar and Alexander Melamid (both of whom emigrated to the United States in the mid-1970s) have called their method "soc-art": it is entirely oriented toward socialist realism and reproduces its models in the exaggerated mystical and simultaneously ironic manner that was envisioned by Siniavsky in his essay on socialist realism. For example, Stalin appears in their paintings surrounded either by Muses or monsters.

The postmodern paradigm, whose components appeared more or less simultaneously in the West, was much slower to mature in Soviet culture. The first wave of Soviet postmodernism—namely, socialist realism—accomplished the erasure of semantic differences between idea and reality, between the signifier and the signified, while the syntactic interplay of these signs was aesthetically adopted only by the second wave: conceptualism. Although it might seem that these two processes should naturally coincide, it took several decades for Soviet culture to pass from one stage to the next.

One important factor is that Western cultures have great respect for the reality that lies beyond signs themselves. As soon as signs proved to be self-sufficient, they immediately acquired a playful dimension. The Russian cultural tradition is much more inclined to view signs as an independent reality deserving of great esteem in and of itself. Therefore it was extremely difficult to accept the notion that signs, which substitute for another reality, might become objects of irony and aesthetic play.

There are two essential aspects to Western postmodernism: the actual substance of postmodernism, and the interpretation of this substance in postmodern terms. In the Soviet Union, these two aspects developed separately. The period from the thirties to the fifties witnessed the emergence of postmodernism as a specific substance in the form of cultural phenomena, including the ideological and semiotic dissolution of reality, the merging of elitist and mass culture into mediocrity, and the elimination of modernist stylistic purity and refinement. Only in the late fifties, in the works of such poets as Kholin, Kropivnitsky, Vsevolod Nekrasov, Vilen Barsky, and then in the seventies, in the works of Ilya Kabakov, Eric Bulatov, Dmitry Prigov, and Lev Rubinshtein, was the "substantial" postmodernism of Soviet culture interpreted precisely in postmodernist terms. Signs of heroic labor, collectivism, the striving for a communist future and so on, which were previously taken seriously as the signified reality itself, now were perceived to be valid or real only at the level of the sign, making them susceptible to all sorts of linguistic games. Soviet postmodernism finally discovered the second aspect and blossomed into a full cultural phenomenon, comparable to its Western counterpart.

Certainly, such postmodern phenomena as Jorge Luis Borges's stories, Vladimir Nabokov's and Umberto Eco's novels or Jacques Derrida's models of deconstruction have had a considerable influence on some contemporary schools of Soviet writing, including conceptualism and metarealism. What is much more striking, however, is that the earlier post- or antimodernist phase of Soviet literature still influences the contemporary American literary scene. For example, Tom Wolfe's recent manifesto "Stalking the Billion-Footed Beast" gained much attention with its attacks on modernism and calls for a social novel that would combine fiction with reportage. Wolfe unconsciously duplicates the very patterns that Stalin's ideologists used in their relentless political tirades against Russian pre-Revolutionary and Western bourgeois modernism.

While he criticizes the modernist and minimalist schools of writing, Wolfe recognizes the literary accomplishment of their members: "Many of these writers were brilliant. They were virtuosos."[26] Are these qualities not enough for a writer to accomplish his literary destiny? Not at all, since Wolfe discloses the glaring disparity between the artists' talents and the mistaken directions of their creative endeavors: "But what was the lonely island they had moved to?" It is curious how closely the targets of Wolfe's manifesto and Soviet canonic aesthetics coincide: he condemns "avant-garde positions beyond realism . . . , Absurdist novels, Magical Realist novels," and a variety of other methods.[27] It was in this very manner that Stalin's chief ideologue, Andrei Zhdanov, justified his attack in 1946 on two of the few remaining independent writers in the Soviet Union, Anna Akhmatova and Mikhail Zoshchenko:[28] "These works can only sow sadness, depression, pessimism, and perpetuate attempts to escape the important issues of social life, deviate from the wide path of social life and activity into a narrow world of personal experience . . . wretched private feelings and digging within their petty persons."[29]

One can easily amplify this severe accusation with the words Tom Wolfe addresses to contemporary neoromanticists, or, as he says, "neo-fabulists": "The action, if any, took place at no specific location. . . . The characters had no background. They came from nowhere. They didn't use realistic speech. Nothing they said, did, or possessed indicated any class or ethnic origin."[30]

Wolfe probably has never heard of, let alone read, Andrei Zhdanov's infamous denunciation of Akhmatova and Zoshchenko. Nevertheless, his main points and even his choice of metaphors are the same as Zhdanov's: both compare writing to engineering, for example. Wolfe also proposes that writers form brigades to pool their talents for an investigation of the amazing social reality of the contemporary United States, as was done in the Soviet Union of the 1930s.[31]

I do not go so far as to suggest that the aesthetic code of Stalinism directly influenced a postmodern writer like Tom Wolfe. Still, the terms of the post-modern debate apply equally well in such radically different conditions as the Soviet Union of the late 1940s and the United States of the late 1980s. The fact that Soviet and Western contemporary cultures mirror each other's past requires a new theoretical framework for interpreting these overlapping dependencies. The quest for a postmodern worldview must inevitably bring about opposition to the abstractness and individualism of modernist writing; it also causes a turn toward consciously trivial, even stereotypical forms of language, as imposed by the dominant social order.

Thus, postmodernism may be seen as a cultural orientation that has developed differently in both the West and the Soviet Union. The Western version came later chronologically, but was more self-aware from a theoretical standpoint. To isolate and identify a Western-style postmodernism in twentieth-century Russian culture proved difficult because the formation of a specifically Russian postmodernism is divided into two periods, as I have suggested.

The development of Russian modernism was artificially halted in the thirties, while in the West it continued smoothly up to the sixties. This accounts for the existence of a single postmodernism in the West, while two separate postmodernisms arose in Soviet culture, one in the thirties and another in the seventies. This obliges us not only to compare Russian post-modernism with its Western counterpart, but also to examine the two separate phases of Russian postmodernism: socialist realism and conceptualism. Perhaps it is the split between them that has made both versions so highly charged ideologically, although with opposing valences. The first postmodernism is explicitly heroic; the second, implicitly ironic. Nevertheless, if we identify them as two aspects and two periods of one historical phenomenon, these opposing tendencies quickly neutralize each other, constituting an utterly "blank pastiche," to use Frederic Jameson's term. The tendency to perceive socialist realism and conceptualism as mutually s[t]imulating aspects of one and the same cultural paradigm will undoubtedly find further support in the course of future reinterpretations of Soviet history as a whole. The two Russian postmodernisms complement each other and present a more complicated and self-contradictory phenomenon than Western postmodernism, which is concentrated in a single historical period.

PART III CULTURE

CHAPTER 7 · At the Crossroads of Image and Concept: Essayism in the Culture of the Modern Age

It seems to me that the essay (Montaigne) is postmodern, while the fragment (The Athaeneum) is modern.—Jean-Francois Lyotard, *The Postmodern Condition*

Despite the fact that the essayistic genre recently celebrated its 400th anniversary, it remains one of the least theoretically investigated areas of verbal art.[1] It has undergone endless renewals and changes of form in the process of passing from author to author, persistently defying the least attempt at a precise definition of its specific features. Essayistics represents a kind of supergeneric system, encompassing the most varied philosophical, historical, critical, biographical, autobiographical, journalistic, moralistic and popular-scientific compositions. "What the essay is has never been precisely determined," asserts one dictionary of literary terms and concepts, while another adds, still more categorically, "The essay is not to be cornered in a definition."[2] This "undefined," elusive quality is part of the basic nature of the essay, as I shall attempt to show, and it is determined by the creative premises that force this genre to consistently outgrow its generic boundaries. At the deepest level of the essay there abides a conception of man that endows the outward characteristics of the genre with a connective inner unity. The following are normally listed among the essay's identifiable characteristics: modest length, emphatically subjective treatment of a concrete topic, free combinations of compositional features, a fondness for paradox, a tendency to employ conversational language, etc.

The Self-Substantiation of Individuality

It rarely happens that a work by a single author can create an entire genre that subsequently develops over the course of ensuing centuries. The fact that the essay did have such an individual creator in Montaigne expresses an essential property of the genre, as seen in its orientation toward self-discovery and the self-definition of individuality. "Finding myself entirely destitute and void of any other matter, I presented myself to myself for argument and subject. It is the only book in the world of its kind, a book with a wild and eccentric plan."[3]

Indeed, it is in Montaigne's work that the human self first appears in all of its irreducibility to anything general or objective, to any given norm or model. The orientation of discourse toward the speaker himself, the conjunction of personality and discourse in the process of becoming—this is one of the definitive characteristics of the genre, making the Renaissance an appropriate era for its appearance. None of the works normally included among ancient precursors to the essayistic tradition—Plato's *Dialogues,* Theophrastus's *Characters,* Seneca's *Letters to Lucilius* and Marcus Aurelius's *Meditations*—are truly essayistic in the proper sense. These compositions lack the directly experienced correlation of the "I" with the writer's own self; rather the "I" is correlated with a particular understanding of man in general, of the necessary, the pleasant, the desirable. "You must live in such a way that you have nothing to confess to yourself that you could not confess to your enemy."[4] In their form (a verbal imperative) and content (the lack of distinction between oneself and one's enemy), Seneca's superlative moral injunctions brilliantly depict the normative nature of ancient thought on the subjectivity of man.

The paradox of essayistic thinking consists in the fact that underlying the very bases of the genre is an individuality that must find its basis for existence precisely in itself. A person is defined only in the course of self-definition, and the work and creativity of a writer is a means of embodying this mobile equilibrium between the self that is defined and the self that is defining. "I have no more made my book than my book has made me—a book consubstantial with its author, concerned with my own self, an integral part of my life; not concerned with some third-hand, extraneous purpose, like all other books" (Book 2: chap. 18, 504). An essay is a path without an end, because its end coincides with its beginning, just as individuality emerges from and returns to itself.

Such solar revolutions of thought are felt in each of Montaigne's essays, which develop in spirals, rather than in the linear progression characteristic of treatises, in which the author strives with all the powers of his mind to reach some unified and general thought, originating outside the bounds of personal experience. Montaigne describes the customs of various peoples, the contents of books he has read, all of which could easily become a desultory commentary, a set of excerpts and quotations (which is, in fact, what the "Essays" consisted of in their preliminary stages), were it not for the perpetual return to the source that lies in the image of a personality embracing and comprehending many things but not reducible to any of them and always unequal even to itself: "Even good authors are wrong to insist on fashioning a consistent and solid fabric out of us. They choose one general characteristic, and go and arrange and interpret all a man's actions to fit their picture . . . And there is as much difference between us and ourselves as between us and others" (Book 2:1, chap. 239, 244). It is precisely because personality defines itself in Montaigne's work that it cannot be completely defined: in the subject's role, it always turns out to be more than what it was in the role of object, and a moment later, it reobjectifies its own expanded being but, again, without exhausting itself in so doing. (At the risk of getting ahead of ourselves, we must note that this age-old property of the essay has made it especially popular in the systems of romantic and existential worldviews, which continue and deepen the movement of individuality to the point of self-substantiation.) It is because of the acquisition of general and eternal grounding through experiments in self-substantiation that personality, initially lacking in these things, did not become a self-pacifying entity, identical to itself, but rather revealed a new source for development within itself.

This explains the proclivity for paradox that is so characteristic of the essay. Logic tells us that a paradox arises when different types of judgments are conjoined, when the subject of an utterance becomes its object (suffice it to recall the well-known paradox of the liar, whose assertion "I am a liar" must be false, if it is true). Since an essay consists largely of just such judgments, in which one and the same person serves in the capacities of thinker and thought-about, paradoxes arise constantly. For example, in characterizing himself as a man of incautious generosity, our author immediately catches himself up with the realization that a miser is most likely to evaluate himself this way: "All contradictions may be found in me by some twist and in some fashion. Bashful, insolent; chaste, lascivious; talkative, taciturn . . . all this I see in myself to some extent according to how I turn" (Book 2: chap. 1, 242).

A still more essential feature of the essay, in the estimation of all encyclopedias and dictionaries, is the presence of a concrete theme, much narrower in scope than that of the treatise, for example. However, in looking at the titles of Montaigne's essays, we find among them such "general," "abstract" topics as "Of Conscience," "Of Virtue," "Of Names," "Of Solitariness," "Of Vanity"—which the most abstract moralist or systematic philosopher would hardly scorn. In the context of Montaigne's compositions, however, these themes are actually perceived as circumscribed, private topics. Virtue and conscience do not act the part of broad, self-sufficient concepts to which all others are reduced, but rather appear as individual moments in the self-determination of an integral whole constituted by the author himself. In principle, an essay could be devoted to the universe, truth, beauty, substance, the form of the syllogism; still these themes would lose their generality and instead acquire concreteness through the will of a genre that makes them partial instances on the backdrop of that all-embracing "I" which forms an endlessly expanding horizon of essayistic thought.

It is no accident that many essayistic works—including 87 of Montaigne's 107 essays—bear titles beginning with the preposition "of": "Of Smells," "Of Steeds," "Of a Thumb," and the like. "Of" is a formula peculiar to the genre, proposed as an angle of vision, invariably somewhat skewed, which presents the theme almost as a by-product. Appearing, as it does, in a prepositional phrase, rather than in subject form, the topic of the essay is examined, not head-on, as in a scientific paper, but from the side, serving as a pretext for the unfolding of thought, which describes a complete circle before returning to itself: to the author, its point of departure and arrival. "Of" lends the entire genre a certain optional, unfinished quality, whereby thoughts follow one another "from a distance," in Montaigne's words, looking at each other "with a side-long glance" (Book 3: chap. 9, 761).

The title of an essay often does not convey even a fourth of its content. Thus, in his chapter "Of The Lame or Crippled," Montaigne discusses the calendar and movements of the heavenly bodies, reason and imagination, miracles and the supernatural, witches and sorcerers, Amazons and weavers. He does not approach his topic directly, but strolls around it, so to speak, describing now wider, now smaller circles, in search of new approaches, bypassing the topic itself or only touching on things related to it. An essay is always "of," because its actual, if not necessarily its *ostensible* topic, always stands in the subject's position: the author himself, who as a matter of principle cannot discover himself completely, since by his authorial essence, he cannot be completed. Therefore he selects a partial, personal theme, in order to blur its limitations and reveal the limitlessness that stands behind it, or more precisely, reaches beyond it.

The fact that in an essay the "I" always sidesteps definition, not yielding to direct description, distinguishes this genre from others that would seem closely related to it by virtue of their similar orientation toward self-consciousness, such as the autobiography, diary, or confession. These three genres have their own specific features: the autobiography reveals that aspect of the self as it came to be in the past; the diary reveals its present process of becoming; and the confession, the future direction, in which a man settles his personal accounts in order to become a self deserving of forgiveness and grace. Elements of these three genres may be present in an essay, but the peculiarity of the latter is that its "I" is taken, not as something total and uninterrupted, able to be placed whole into a narrative, but rather as a break in narrative: the "I" is so highly differentiated from itself that it can appear in the role of "not-I," clothed as "everything under the sun," whose presence is revealed outside the frame, in whimsical shifts in point of view and sudden leaps from one topic to the next. At times the "first person" is entirely absent: the "I" is not manifest as theme in the manner of these other genres; it cannot be embraced as a whole, precisely because it embraces everything and brings all into communion with itself.

When Montaigne asserts that he writes only about himself, he is well aware of the difference between this "theme" and all others; he is anything but an autobiographer. "I cannot keep my subject still. It goes along befuddled and staggering, with a natural drunkenness" (Book 3: chap. 2, 610). The very nature of the self is such that it cannot be isolated in pure form from all other things and concepts of "my" perception and interpretation. Its objectness has a certain fluid boundary that allows it to enter into the description of any other thing—it is no accident that discussions of "I" as such betray a marginal compositional character in the "Essays," in that they are relegated either to the very beginning or end of a chapter, and on the scale of the entire book, they are relegated to the final chapter, "Of the essay," in which the author at last speaks almost exclusively about himself. All beginnings and endings are located within the "I," but between them lies all the world, which the "I" uses to raise itself up (as if with a lever) in an act of liberation from being equal to itself. The "I" to which an essayist returns after passing through the circle of all things is not the one he was at the point of departure; the opaque medium of objectness has refracted his "I" to create an indispensable intermittancy in his revelation of self.

Any order established in an essay is soon broken; one thing interrupts another to create the zigzag pattern of a thought picture in the contradictory intonations of spoken language. Montaigne's constant references to his own forgetfulness, his tendency to tire quickly, his lack of consistent education, inability to concentrate for long periods, etc., serve as the equivalent of content and as a justification for the formal properties of the genre. All of the weaknesses and imperfections Montaigne attributes to himself personally are actually the properties of an emerging genre, the psychological reality of a new form, highlighted on the background of previous, canonized genres, like a kind of "minus-form," lacking in broadly meaningful content, logical consistency, all-embracing erudition, and consisting instead of nothing but flaws.

Everything we have said about the essay indicates its closeness to another genre: the novel, which also owed the appearance of its contemporary form to new creative orientations of the Renaissance personality. Essay and novel are not only genres of the same age, both born in the sixteenth century; they are also comrades in arms, affirming the right of the present and the transient to intrude upon the world's established values and display their relative nature in relation to the individuality of author and hero.

> To depict an event on one and the same temporal and evaluational level as oneself and one's contemporaries (and, consequently, on the basis of experience and invention) means to accomplish a radical turn-about, to cross over from the epic world to that of the novel. . . . The zone of contact with the uncompleted present and, consequently, the future creates a necessity for the non-coincidence of a man with himself. There always remain in him unrealized potentials and unactualized demands . . . , the unrealized excess of humanity.[5]

Such is the basic stance of Renaissance humanism, as it was embodied in the novel and the essay, so that Bakhtin's characterization of the one genre can be extended to the other.

One might add that the orientation toward spoken language and the familiar, uninhibited tone characteristic of the novel also find reflection in the essay. For example, in his discussion of the creative process, Montaigne compares intellectual "movements" with everyday physiological functions, not refraining from the use of even the "lowest" terminology. Everything that exists in the realm of mental comprehension, everything lofty and generalized, is drawn by the essayist or novelist into the zone of "familiar contact" with the present. The opening lines of several pieces in *The Essays of Elia*, from the pen of Charles Lamb, are indicative:

> I like to meet a sweep . . . one of those tender novices . . .

> The casual sight of an old Play Bill, which I picked up the other day, tempts me to call to mind . . .

A pretty severe fit of indisposition which, under the name of nervous fever, has made a prisoner of me for some weeks past . . .[6]

Thoughts on human nature, art, sickness and similar things are included in a stream of live, uninhibited speech that does not disguise its source in the speech and existence of one man. The topics of thought and imagination enter into the flux of being as it spills over them and washes away their self-sufficient meaning to reveal their commonality with the human activity that freely creates them, as distinct from the pre-novelistic and pre-essayistic canons. While expressing itself in these forms, such creativity simultaneously shows a hint of its own inexpressible, genuine and inalienable existence, flowing onward through the here and now.

Integrative Discourse

However, in its assertion of the present as a temporal and axiological orientation point, as well as in its denial of any "absolute past," the essay has not simply followed after the novel, but has gone beyond it, beyond the limits of any verbal enterprise that divides the authentic world from one that it itself creates. The novel, after all, leads us away into an ideally transfigured reality, distant from the author's own, into a special time and space, and in this sense it develops the tendency toward "illusionism," which is proper to art in general, while further augmenting this tendency with an illusion of the author's direct and immediate presence, in sharp contrast to the epic. The essay stands on the ground of present reality, while the novel only approaches this reality to the extent that artistic convention allows. The essay does not lead away anywhere; on the contrary, it brings into this reality even the boldest inventiveness of thought, the most head-spinning fantasy, the most striking hypothesis or the most far-reaching conception, returning them to the place from which they emerged: the authentic time and uncompleted situation of the author's life.

For this reason, any specifications separating the complete, created product from its creator is alien to essayistics. An essay may be philosophical, artistic, critical, historical, autobiographical, but the essential fact remains that as a rule it is everything at once. These attributes may interconnect variously in any one instance, one will predominate, while another steps aside, but in principle, all existing realms of consciousness are able to become components of an essayistic work.

Any given genre usually belongs to one particular sphere in terms of its mode of assimilating experiences of reality into the integrative processes of intellectual comprehension. Thus, the article, monograph, review, and commentary are scholarly genres; the novel, epic, tragedy, and short story are artistic genres, while the diary, chronicle, sketch, and protocol are documentary genres. The essay includes among its possibilities all of these variable means for comprehending the world without restricting itself to any one of them, it continually oversteps their borders, acquiring in this mobility its own generic, or rather, supergeneric nature. Montaigne's "essays" belong, to an equal degree, to the history of literature, philosophy, and morals. The same cannot, of course, be said of Rabelais's *Gargantua and Pantagruel,* nor of Cervantes's *Don Quixote,* however great the place of honor these works occupy in the literary realm.

Of course, in the words of Mikhail Bakhtin, the novel also

> widely and substantively employed the forms of letters, diaries, confessions, the forms and methods of new legal rhetoric and the like. Building itself in the zone of contact with the uncompleted event of contemporary times, the novel often crosses the border of artistic literary specifications, transforming itself now into a moral homily, now into a philosophical treatise, now into a directly political speech or degenerating into a raw, unrelenting confession, a "cry of the soul" and so on.[7]

While this may well be true, it is correct that the novel precisely *employs* all of these nonartistic forms, subordinating them to its own artistic requirements, such that it succeeds as a novel to the extent that it preserves a generic nature that obliges it to enclose all events and meanings within an imaginary and conventionalized reality. Authentic, unappointed reality comes into play with the same rights as any other image (as, for example, the image of the author in *Eugene Onegin*). In a novel, "authenticity" itself obtains the character of an artistic device, bringing it into communion with the closed world of invention. The fact that *La Nouvelle Héloïse* is written in the form of a correspondence, or that *The Hero of Our Time* takes the form of a diary, and *The Possessed,* that of a chronicle, does not prevent them from being *purely* artistic works. The novel differs from the epic in its orientation toward the "uncompleted present," its opposition to the "finished past," but this is only a difference of *intra*-artistic emphases. Over the course of centuries, striving beyond the borders of the purely artistic has given the novel its unique dynamism and a wealth of generic nuances and variations, but these remain within its specifically artistic nature. Everything the novel has touched, has been transformed into "gold," even raw emotionality and shrieks of the soul; if the transformation fails, then the novel itself remains raw, underdone, and incomplete.

As regards the essay, it does not "employ" the aforementioned forms, but exists *in* them, as the basic manifestations of its own essence. Be it a "Moral Homily" or "philosophical treatise," an intimate admission or invented scene, a speculative construct or vignette of everyday life—all of these are among the possibilities of the essayistic genre, whose sole "obligation" is to simultaneously and alternately use them all, without absolutizing any single one, since to do so would transform the essay into an article, diary entry, short story, or homily. These multigeneric and even interdisciplinary qualities are not only the right, but the duty of essayistic creations. They emerge in their entirety from that same unconsummated present to which the novel aspires, as to an alien realm, but which it is fated to "complete" artificially.

The essay is situated precisely within the becoming process of reality, where it gathers together all possible forms of assimilating and gaining awareness of this reality. It seems to turn the contents of all spheres of social consciousness inside out—be they artistic, philosophical, moral, or historical—in order to extract them from the enclosure of self-sufficiency and bring them into the world of human experience that creates them. Artistic images and philosophical concepts, historical facts, and moral imperatives are the varied forms that consciousness embraces one at a time, but here also circles back to their originary premises, to face the author's actual presence in the world and the all-embracing situation of human being, as it engenders all of these forms without being reduced to any one of them. The paradox of the essayistic genre is that it cannot be included in any one global system or "discipline" of the human spirit, as the novel is included in the artistic sphere, the treatise in the philosophical sphere, and so on. Rather, the essay includes the methods and tools of these disciplines among its own components. While the novel represents one method of organizing artistic images, imagery itself is but one possibility for the essay. Simply because the notion of "surpassing" inevitably creates two levels, this in no way implies that the essay surpasses the creative achievements of the novel; to the contrary, the latter's narrower generic potentials effectively concentrate its creative powers. We could say, that the novel surpasses the essay in terms of their respective levels of development (is there a single essay matching the significance of *Don Quixote* or *The Brothers Karamazov?*)[8] while at the same time the novel falls behind the essay in terms of developmental type. The essay is not an interdisciplinary genre, but a superdisciplinary one, integrating the characteristics of those systems, into which other genres enter as elements.

All human methods of assimilating worldly experience can be unified and interchanged on the self-propelling basis discovered in the essay, because here the very capability for endless, multifarious assimilation is itself assimilated. The essay is nothing other than an "experiment" that includes all types of cognition and action at the moment of their most essential uncompletedness, whereas the results of these processes differ profoundly and belong to spheres of consciousness that seem to have little in common: literature, philosophy, history, etc. Commonality reveals itself in the impulse through which reality is established in the personal experiences that give rise to all further diversifications of understanding. The essayist comprehends reality as something whole and integrated, the possibility of all further possibilities, the impulse of impulses.

The very concept of "essay" presupposes an extended present, which draws the past and the future into an ongoing stream of becoming. After all, an "essay" is at the same time an "experiment" whose result belongs to the future and an "experience," which preserves the imprint of the past.[9] But in "essay" as such there are no results at all, only the process itself, the "eternal present," open in all directions. In the essay, man stands as having been tested by his past and actively testing his future: in transition from potential to reality, at the point of greatest co-incidence between his "I" and the present time: "I do not portray being: I portray passing. . . . My history needs to be adapted to the moment. I may presently change, not only by chance, but also by intention. . . . If my mind could gain a firm footing, I would not make essays, I would make decisions" (Book 3: chap. 2, 611).

The division into image and concept, fact and hypothesis, "protocol" and "fantasy," emotional outcry and moral imperative, confession and homily occurs later, in the realm of results, whereas within an essay, in the process of its generation from experience, they are almost indivisible, like a kind of live protoplasm, a spiritual first substance. The essayist must resort to all possible means of embodying this wholeness of

experi${}_\text{ment}^\text{ence}$

in order to convey its fullness. Metaphor and concept, fact and invention, hypothesis and axiom, hyperbole and paradox—only on the borderline and juncture of these diverse devices does that experience manifest itself that cannot be confined to any one of them: ever-growing "experimental experience," substantiated in itself, which must be established and lived through ever anew: "for the reasons have little other foundation than experience"

(Book 2: chap. 17, 497). All means by which man assimilates the world are employed in the assimilation of man himself, but still they are not equal to him. No matter what sum of definitions are applied to him who seeks to define, he is fated to remain indefinable.

Thus, indefinability enters the essence of the essayistic genre (unless we dare to call it in grandiloquent style a "supergenre" or "integrative form of consciousness"), which more closely and directly reveals the activities of self-definition proper to the human spirit. However, this indefinability in no way indicates a lack of specificity in the essay; on the contrary, specific traits are easily recognizable and intuitively felt in the majority of works in this genre. A dynamic alternation and paradoxical juxtaposition of various modes of understanding are essential to it. If any one of them—be it the figurative or the conceptual, the narrative or the analytical, the confessional or the ethnographic description—begins to predominate sharply, then the essay is destroyed as a genre, being transformed into a single one of its component parts. The essay is maintained as a whole through mutual transfers of energy, momentary transitions from a figurative system to a conceptual one, from the abstract to the everyday. Consider the following phrases from a single page of Montaigne's concluding essay, "Of the Essay." They would seem to belong to entirely different types of discourse:

[Philosophical speculation] We abuse Nature too much by pestering her so far that she is constrained to leave us and abandon our guidance.

[Diary notation] I am not excessively fond of either salads or fruits, except melons. My father hated all kinds of sauces; I love them all.

[Physiological observation] I am very fond of fish. . . . I believe what some say, that it is easier to digest than meat.

[Reminiscence] Ever since my youth I have occasionally skipped a meal . . .

[Mythological image] I hate above all things the stupid coupling of so healthy and sprightly a goddess with that little belching god of indigestion, all bloated with the fumes of his liquor. [Venus and Bacchus]

[Commentary on works by other authors] I say, like that same Epicurus, that we should not so much consider what we eat as with whom we eat.

[Aphoristic generalization] There is no preparation so sweet to me, no sauce so appetizing, as that which is derived from society.

[Practical advice] I think it is healthier to eat more slowly and less, and to eat more often. (Book 3: chap. 13, 846)

All of these quotations may be united under the thematic rubric of "food," but the principal similarity among them is the presence of a personal relationship to the given topic, the fact that nearly every phrase is accompanied by parenthetical expressions and pronouns proper to the first person, on the order of "I propose," "I am agreed that," "it seems to me," and the like. Here we have, in the genre of the "essay," a holistic experimental experience in the relations of a given subject to a given object in a given instance: Montaigne's relation to food; and insofar as the experience described is holistic, it makes use of all possible means of expression—those appropriate to high philosophy, as well as those appropriate to cookbooks, allegorical poetry, and diaries. Here we find practical recommendations along with theoretical conclusions and recollections of the past along with admonitions for the future: both general and specific, abstract and concrete. Certain things are lacking, to be sure, for instance, political opinion, physical characterization and psychological self-observations, all of which are abundantly represented elsewhere in the "Essays," but I emphasize that I have selected a single page for my examples, so as to demonstrate in concentrated form how elements of the most highly differentiated cultural subsystems coexist in Montaigne's work.

It is not at all necessary for an essayist to be a good storyteller, a profound philosopher, a pure-hearted conversationalist, nor a moral teacher; yet, at the same time, all of these qualities taken together are in themselves not enough. In the power of his thought he lags behind professional philosophers; in the brilliance of his imagination he lags behind novelists and artists; in the sincerity of his confidences, behind diarists and authors of confessions . . . For an essayist an organic linkage of all these capabilities becomes primary, in the multifaceted sense of cultural life that allows him to center all the various spheres of knowledge within his own personal experience, and also to extract them from their professionally enclosed and completed worlds into a directly experienced, observable reality. In the estimation of the English romantic essayist William Hazlitt, Montaigne's service consisted in his being the first to dare to say as an author, what he felt as a man.

The artist's world is one of invented images; the philosopher's, of abstract concepts; the journalist's, of sociopolitical ideas; and the diarist's, of day-to-day events and experiences. The essayist finds such specifications alien, even the most essential and kindred of them. In the essay, whatever is kindred (daily life, one's surroundings) is examined from a philosophical distance, while the most distant (past epochs, artistic styles, and philosophical ideas) enters the visual field of day-to-day existence. One is *measured* against the other, making essays exceptionally rich in measurable examples that reveal an analogical structure in their parallels with various levels of being. Moreover, in distinction to the parable, which unfolds in a kind of absolute time and space, an *example* (in its capacity as an element of the essayistic genre) is written directly into the context of concrete experience: it is still someone's judgment or an incident from someone's life. All that is essential in an essay appears as something essential to someone and, similarly, the *essence* of all things is revealed only in the *presence* of someone. In truth, nothing human is alien to the essayist, this is almost a rule of the genre, requiring a maximally broad unfolding of the theme, so as not to neglect any possible point of view. Since the author is neither a theologian nor a politician, neither a psychologist nor a historian, not a specialist of any kind, who should have acquired definite knowledge and skills, but simply a person, who tests himself in everything, it is precisely "everything" or "something," universality or indefiniteness, that can serve as the best definition of the genre: "something about everything."

Nonetheless, even such specifications of the genre as these, consisting in the subsequent erasure of specifications, pose not less but rather more strict requirements for the author than would a short story or article, a novel or treatise. In writing those works the author can trust himself to the definite laws of the genre, which itself becomes his guide and teacher. As he follows the consistency of plot images or logical ideas, the artist or philosopher keeps to the criteria intrinsic to the systems they develop, whereas the essayist must alternate and develop new criteria for each passage he writes. Every system must destroy itself, almost as soon as it appears; otherwise the essay itself is destroyed. Nothing is stricter or more exacting than freedom from genre, as it presents itself to the essayist. It must be bought with an unremitting search for generic laws in every paragraph and virtually every line, one after the next, because prior discoveries only persuade us that they themselves must be abandoned. A process of genre formation continues uninterrupted over the course of the whole essay; not only utterances are engendered, but so is their very typology, whether scientific, artistic or what have you. Behind every thought or image lies rupture, and everything begins again. Any stopover within the bounds of one genre, any attempt to catch one's breath is counterindicated for the essayist, who has chosen the most stern and merciless "law of freedom": inexhaustible wandering through the realms of the spirit. The essayist is a freelancer, bound by nothing, which is why he is also a relatively carefree author, who begins each fragment of his work from absolute zero, like one who has only just taken up the task.

In its essence the essay is pure verbality, composition as such, in the broadest and most indefinite meaning of the word. It is a genre for untried beginners. In the lower and middle grades at school, pupils write compositions on "How I Spent the Summer," "My Dog: A True Friend," or "The Most Interesting Day of My Life"—in essence, these are "experiments" in the undifferentiated interpretation and description of specific aspects of life from one's own point of view. Later on, in the upper grades, compositional genres become differentiated. In compositions on literary themes, critical, interpretative, and conceptual impulses come to the fore. At this age the passion for writing begins to develop in many young people, and they find themselves drawn to artistic prose, short stories, or poetry. Some keep diaries in which they plumb the authentic events and sensations of life. What the third or fifth grader composed all in one piece, is gradually broken down into independent generic components, marking the beginning of specialization. But the essayist is, so to speak, the professional in a dilettantish genre. He becomes a master of the "free composition," a representative of verbality as such. Dilettantism has neither an accidental nor a preparatory character, in this instance, but becomes a conscious principle: the essayist tries to remain within the bounds of holistic thought, which is proper to the school-child, but is normally lost before we leave our youth. The essay is a first attempt with the pen, before it even knows what it will write, but still longs to express "all, absolutely all" at one stroke. Even the most well-ripened examples of the genre preserve this quality of the "first attempt," which simultaneously knows everything, but yet is fresh and uninformed.

Essay and Myth

If the essay could only be formed in the Modern Age, thanks to the revolution that placed the human individual at the center of creation, then what analogue did it have in earlier culture?

We will first make an assertion and then take up its substantiation: the essay's proclivity for holistic unification and juxtaposition of various cultural elements arose on the site of that centralizing tendency which had formerly belonged to mythological consciousness. In the essay this synthesizing quality represents a rebirth on humanist and personalist grounds of the impersonal, cosmic, or theistically oriented syncretism that, in ancient times, was based on the indivisibility of the primitive collective. The paradox of the essay lies in the fact that, by means of its reflective and individualistic nature, it is opposed to myth and all types of mythologizing, but not after the fashion of a piece, which, breaking free, stands opposed to the whole; it is rather like a newly formed whole that stands opposed to its own original form.

Philosophy, art, history, and a great variety of sciences are also opposed to the mythology from which they originated, as the specialized is opposed to the syncretic or as independently developed components are opposed to an original, undeveloped whole. Essayistics attempts to realize such wholeness within a subdivided and developed culture, which, on the one hand, sharply distinguishes it from myth, while on the other hand placing it in an analogous position in the differentiated system of spiritual activity. From this position, it rejects the normative, superpersonal tendency of mythology, even as it inherits the synthesizing and centralizing capacities of the latter, so that they now may be realized in the consciousness of the individual.

A vast body of research exists on mythologism in twentieth-century culture, delineating its three primary types. First, there is the *authoritarian* mythologism of totalitarian ideologies, such as communism, fascism, and Nazism, replete with images of class and national leaders, mythologemes of soil and blood, propagandistic emblems, and the like. Second, there is the *vulgar* mythologism of numerous branches of mass culture, which is expressed in the images of movie stars, fictional heroes, advertising cliches and trivial catch phrases. And third, there is the *avant-garde* mythologism of certain twentieth-century artists, such as Kafka, Joyce, Artaud, Dali, Beckett, Ionesco, and others, which is expressed as the helplessness and insignificance of the individual personality before the onslaught either of alienating, superpersonal social structures or of one's own subconscious.

However much these "mythologisms" may differ, they share among themselves and also with ancient mythologies a self-sufficiency of figurative, ideational schemes that are either indifferent to the individual or directly oppose him, personifying the power to which he is subject at the hands of cosmic forces, social laws, or psychological instincts. The powers of the "collective unconscious" make themselves felt throughout these modes of expression. Mythologism's anti-individual and antireflective impulse, which is perceived as something positive, heroic, and even idyllic in its "authoritarian" and "vulgar" varieties, is no longer a beautiful and lofty thing in avant-garde depictions. Here, it becomes a negative, dreadful, and grotesquely monstrous force, arousing maniacal fear, hysterical laughter, or utter paralysis in the face of implacable absurdity.

Nonetheless, not one of these "mythologisms" satisfies the basic function proper to mythology itself, which, in the words of E. M. Meletinsky, is "oriented toward overcoming the fundamental antinomies of human existence, toward harmonizing the personality, society and nature."[10] The extrapersonal nature of ancient mythology gave it a harmonious resonance with the cultural state of the primitive collective. But in the Modern Age any attempt to produce or re-create a depersonalized, mass mythology fails to provide the basic property and value of myth: its holistic, integral character and capacity to embody the multifaceted spiritual life of a new cultural subject that is now the individual, rather than the human mass.

A remarkable peculiarity of the essay lies in that wholeness is created, not through the exclusion and alienation of the personality, as in neomythological forms, but through the gradual revelation of self in its assimilation of all the means it can muster for comprehending the world, as potentials for its own ever-growing being. Although it would appear to be an antimythological form, taking individual reflection as its basic point of departure, essayistics takes upon itself the function of unification and consolidation of the various cultural spheres that mythology fulfilled in antiquity.

The functional commonality of myth and essay rests upon their deep structural similarity, even as it bears the imprint of enormous epochal differences. One of the main qualities of myth, observed by virtually all researchers in this field, is the coincidence of a general idea and a tangible image. The same impulses are conjoined in the essay as well, although here they have been separated from the primal state of indivisible identity to become independent entities: the idea is not personified in an image, although it freely combines with images, whether in aphorism and example, or fact and generalization.

Thus, in the essay "Of Distraction," Montaigne considers the fact that it is through abstraction and distraction that we usually succeed in ridding ourselves of grief and overcoming obstacles, rather than through direct opposition and struggle. He formulates this thought in general form more than once and then takes it through a series of concrete examples, describing how he was able to use abstraction to comfort a bereaved lady, how a French military commander used false proposals to lull his captors to sleep, how Plutarch distracted himself from mourning his deceased daughter by recalling her childish pranks, and so on. Each image not only affirms his initial thought, but also contains something more in its own concreteness that leads into the thought that follows, bringing up a new image for affirmation, which in turn slightly changes the course of the discussion. This creates a fluid movement of the basic content from abstraction to concreteness: image and concept open their unknown, unassimilated sides to one another, augmenting one another, thanks to their mutual irreducibility.

In myth these components are more tightly linked; they cannot be separated and introduced into new combinations. For example, Hippomenes won his race against the unbeatable Atalante by dropping the three apples given to him by Venus, and thereby distracting his fair competitor. Montaigne's use of this ancient Greek myth serves to embody the already familiar idea of "distraction as a path to victory." In the mythic version this idea is totally dissolved in imagery, in the plot and personages of the event; only the essayistic approach extracts it and presents it in more or less generalized form.

In an essay, thought is refracted through several images and image is interpreted through several concepts; it is this mutual dynamism that contains the new quality of reflection and relativity, distinguishing the thought-images[11] of an essay from those of mythology. No matter how many images are deployed to affirm a given thought, they never become equal to it, and no matter how many concepts are deployed to interpret a given image, they cannot exhaust it completely. This becomes a source of energetic self-development: at every given moment the thought-image is incomplete, inadequate to itself, requiring new "displays" of the image and new "proofs" of the concept. Image and concept have thus emerged from the state of mythosyncretic identity and developed into independent elements that can now explain each other endlessly but cannot merge into each other once and for all.

A thought-image such as this—whose components are maintained in mobile balance, belonging to one another in part, but also open to new interconnections, entering into mental and imagistic combinations independently of each other—could be called an *esseme,* on analogy with *mythologeme,* whose components are syncretically connected and indivisible. As a unit of essayistic thought, an esseme represents the free combination of a concrete image and a generalizing idea. At the same time, fact remains fact, idea remains idea. They are not connected in an obligatory or exclusive way but rather through the personality of one who unites them in an experiment of self-consciousness.

Here emerges another primary quality of the essay that again shows its similarity to myth: its truthfulness. "The content of a myth is thought by primitive consciousness to be perfectly real. . . . Among those for whom the myth arose and 'lived,' myth is 'truth,' because it expresses the meaningfulness of a given and on-going reality."[12] In contrast to artistic fantasies and philosophical abstractions, the essay brings its thought-images out into the sphere of an authentic, directly lived and currently ongoing life. These thought-images are true, not in some conditional sense, but on the continual basis of example in the author's life. Like myth, the essay not only melds a general idea with a tangible image, but further melds them both with the flux of reality.

Again, however, this synthesis of the abstract, the concrete, and the real is more mobile and free in the essay than it is in myth. In the former case, we are dealing, not with "higher reality," common to all the members of a collective, but the reality of personal experience, which is reliable only insofar as it consciously emphasizes its own limitations and relative nature. As Montaigne states, "I like these words, which soften and moderate the rashness of our propositions: 'perhaps,' 'to some extent,' 'some,' 'they say,' 'I think,' and the like" (Book 3: chap. 11, 788). In place of "knowledge," Montaigne puts forth the epistemological category of "opinion," which establishes the approximate, fluctuating correspondence between the subject and the object of cognition. Knowledge *affirms;* opinion *supposes,* leaving room open for doubt. In contrast to myth, the essay unfolds in a situation of cultural differentiation, when an enormous variety of other opinions exist alongside the opinion of the author; these are also drawn into the essay as doubts or co-opinions, which either add a note of equivocation to the author's own opinion, or are simply presented as the contrasting opinions of others.[13] Doubt is the conscience of an opinion, the consciousness of one's own incompleteness and relativity, which are defined by a newly dynamic interaction between subject and object. Between them lies, not simple identity, but a space of supposition and potential, in which essayistic truth reveals itself. Objectivity is attained through the full recognition and manifestation of subjectivity, rather than through its denial. "Whoever is in search of Knowledge, let him fish for it where it dwells. . . . These are my fancies, by which I try to give knowledge not of things, but of myself" (Book 2: chap. 10, 296). But only thus is authentic knowledge achieved: by acknowledging its lack of fullness, through opinion subjected to doubt.

Montaigne attributed symbolic meaning to the words inscribed on the crossbar of his scales: "What do I know?" Indeed, this question is central to his thinking on the world, the only still point in all the "rollicking" system of his "Essays." "The world is but a perennial movement" (Book 3: chap. 2, 610). An essay is not the unity of thought-image-being, but it is an experiment in their unification, an attempt at striking a balance among them.

When the scales hold a fact in one tray and an idea in the other, they stubbornly continue to dip—only doubt remains firm like the fulcrum of the crossbar. The very word *essai* entered French from the Latin *exagium,* which means "an act of weighing something." Thus the mobile balance of the components permeates the name, as well as the essence of the genre.

The quality of wholeness in thought and image brings about another essential similarity between essay and myth: the paradigmatic method of organizing statements. In his well-known analysis of the myth of Oedipus, Lévi-Strauss demonstrated that myth should not only be read along the horizontal axis, as a sequence of narrated events, but also along a vertical axis of events as they reveal variations on an invariant meaning.[14] The paradigmatic structure of myth escapes the conscious awareness of its bearers, and can only be discovered through research. In an essay, this becomes the author's direct intention; from an object of research it becomes a conscious creative method. In terms of its original structure, an essay is at heart a catalogue, a listing of various judgments, all relating to a single fact, or it can be various facts, all relating to one judgment.

In Chinese and Japanese examples of the genre, the essayistic paradigm appears in its unadorned aspect, dispensing with temporal sequence. We offer an excerpt from Sei Shonagon's *Pillow Book,* as an example:

[73.] Things Not Worth Doing
A woman has taken it into her head to enter Court service, but she finds the life tedious and regards her duties as irksome. She is forever grumbling . . .
An adopted son-in-law looks at his new parents with a malicious expression on his face.
The parents of a girl have adopted a young man to be their daughter's husband. At first the girl was reluctant to have him, but now that she has resigned herself it is the parents who complain, saying that he is different from what they had imagined.[15]

The parts of the text are linked neither by temporal connections nor through those of cause and effect: rather, they are offered as variations on an invariant meaning that is presented in the entitling first line; here, "things not worth doing." The pillars of meaningful elements that researchers extract in their structural analyses of mythological plots, emerge graphically in the compositional scheme of these essayistic texts.

As the history of Montaigne's writing process shows, his "Essays" were originally judgments on a single theme copied down from various books, to

which the author then added his own thoughts; or they began as examples
dug up from various sources to illustrate a moral aphorism. Here we present
the scheme of the opening piece in the "Essays" (Book 1):

> I.0.0. "By diverse means we arrive at the same end" (Book 1: chap. 1, 3).
> (Here we have the invariant idea, as expressed in the title).
>
> I.1.0. One may touch the heart of the victor either by submissiveness,
> which arouses his compassion, or by firmness, which arouses his admi-
> ration (a concrete example of the invariant).
>
> I.2.0. Edward, Prince of Wales, spared an entire city when he encoun-
> tered the valorous resistance of three Frenchmen.
>
> I.2.1. Scanderberg, prince of Epirus, spared a fleeing soldier, who sud-
> denly turned and faced him with a drawn sword.
>
> I.2.2. Emperor Conrad III was so fascinated by the courageous conduct
> of the women of a city he had beseiged, that he had mercy on their
> husbands (examples as variants).

At the basis of Montaigne's essays lies the same structure that is found in
the Japanese *zuihitsu:* an invariant idea stands alongside a series of illustrations, or an invariant image stands with a series of interpretations.[16] Needless to say, this structure may be complicated endlessly: the idea-invariant
is replaced by an image-invariant; one of the variations is transformed into
the invariant of the next paradigm, and so on. For example, the second part
of the essay outlined above is constructed like a symmetrical addition to the
first: the issue of the first part is "different actions—one consequence,"
while "one action—different consequences" becomes the topic of the second part ("firmness on the part of the vanquished may arouse the victor's
compassion or his cruelty," along with appropriate instances). In sum, grandiose hierarchies of examples and generalizations are deployed with their
shifts and inclusions, amassing systems that rival mythology in their complexity. All the while, the essay's paradigmatic mechanism remains unchanged, inviting the application of Lévi-Strauss's definition of myth as a
machine for destroying time. Neither logical nor narrative sequences are
dominant here; rather, semantic analogies and parallels hold sway.

This, incidentally, explains the essential quality of briefness that defines
both essay and myth, as distinct from "linear" forms such as the novel or
epic, which unfold their development over time. If *event* (whatever happens at a given moment in time) is the basic unit of narrative genres, then
custom (what happens all the time, as proper to a person, a people, or a way
of life) is the basic unit of the "explanatory" genres. In this case it is not

essential how things were on a certain day, but how they were overall, as the regulatory principle of individual or collective behavior.

Scholars have long taken note of the connection between myth and ritual, even interpreting the former as a verbal record and explanation of the latter. In the same way, virtually the leading role in the essay belongs to description and interpretation of secularized rituals: the customs, habits, inclinations that are proper to various peoples and personalities. In first place among them is the temperament of the author himself, which is also described as a series of rules, vagaries, and particularities. His little essay "Of smells" contains a dozen ethnographic descriptions of such customs as how the Scythian women oiled and powdered their bodies; how a certain Tunisian king's meals were packed with fragrant sweetmeats; how various aromas are used as incense in churches; and finally, Montaigne's own predisposition: "Whatever the odor is, it is a marvel how it clings to me and how apt my skin is to imbibe it" (Book 1: chap. 55, 228). All of this is said and thought in the "usual" present tense—any occurrence or utterance, even those that happen only once, are translated into the mode of frequency, repetition, emerging as manifestations of persistent qualities. Even recourse to the past only serves as an explanation and affirmation of certain patterns effective at present. "I find myself little subject to epidemics, which are caught by communication and bred by the contagion of the air; and I have escaped those of my time, of which there have been many sorts in our cities and our armies" (Book 1: chap. 55, 229). If myth operates primarily through "precedents," which the past poses as models for the present, then the essay operates through "examples," which the present draws to itself as a service of the past. In myth, descriptions of ritual act as a norm for regulating collective behavior; in essay, it is as if the author's personality effects its own self-regulation, not so much by making its own temperament a model, but by examining and transforming itself through comparison with the ways of other people, times and nations, as it reveals itself in incompleteness and openness before the future. But for all their differences, myth and essay are united by their orientation toward the integral category of custom, which embraces all the multiple and transient manifestations of the collective and individual.[17]

And so we have noted a number of characteristics connecting the essay with myth: (1) epistemologically, we find the combination of tangibly concrete with generally intellectual impulses in the *thought-image;* (2) the presumed reliability and truth of these thought-images is ontologically presented through their grounding in *being;* (3) structurally, we note the *para-*

digmatic organization of the utterance as a whole; and (4) thematically, there is an orientation toward *ritual* and *custom* as the most persistent and holistic forms of human existence.

Nonetheless, even at the closest points of correspondence between essay and myth, we find an essential difference conditioned by the synthetic nature of the one as opposed to the syncretic nature of the other. First, the components of an essayistic thought-image are freely interchangeable; one thought combines with various images, whereas in a mythologeme these are inseparable. Second, in myth the thought-image correlates with a higher, absolute reality, while in an essay it is immersed in a reality of becoming, from which it acquires its reliability of being only at the point of present time in the personal experience of the author. Third, the paradigmatic structure of myth remains unconscious, hidden beneath its plot composition, whereas the essay is consciously built, not unlike a catalogue, of variations on invariants, creatively employing the model that researchers discover in myth. Fourth, that which appears in myth as a ritual established since ancient times, a sanctified model and precedent, is interpreted in the essay as a custom (one among many), in contrast to or by analogy with which the ways of the author himself may emerge. A comparison of different customs allows for the realization of the moral self-regulation of personality.

In the Modern Age the essay takes upon itself the function of myth. It functions for wholeness, mediating between the philosophical, artistic, and historical spheres, between thought, image, and being. It finds realization precisely in the spirit of the Modern Age, which acquires wholeness only in the experience of its attainment, in the mobile and wavering balance of components: not as a given, but as a task.

Esseme and Metaphor

We will show how this new set for wholeness, specific to the thinking of the Modern Age, operates in the prose of Marina Tsvetaeva, one of the twentieth century's brilliant essayists. Her well-known reminiscence of Maximilian Voloshin, "A Living Word About a Living Man," begins as follows: "On August the 11th, in Koktebel, at twelve o'clock noon, the poet Maximilian Voloshin passed away."[18] An empirical fact is stated with the stern dryness of official protocol, even down to the hour of death. Thereafter, without ever departing from this fact, Tsvetaeva proceeds to endow it with such breadth of meaning that it simultaneously becomes a universal of her thought, requiring no invention for its embodiment, living on in the flesh of that singular and utterly real event. "Upon reading these words the first thing I felt, after the natural blow of death, was gratification: it happened at noon, at his own hour." The hour of death turns out to be not coincidental; this hour was a part of Voloshin, a part of his personality, which, so far, is affirmed only by the power of Tsvetaeva's loving and understanding feeling. At this point she introduces the "evidence," and noon is transformed from an hour of day into an hour of nature that Voloshin loved, an hour of place where he made his life. In a headlong procession of self-variation, the motif is strengthened through the significance of its supertemporal and superspatial invariant:

> At noon, when the sun is at its zenith, that is, at the very crest of the sky, at the hour, when body vanquishes shadow . . . at his own hour, the Voloshin hour.
>
> And in truth—at his favorite hour of nature, for August the 11th (by the New Style—the old would be late July) is surely the noontime of the year, the very heart of summer.
>
> And in truth—at his *own* hour of Koktebel, as all its countless visages, impress us in the visage of the noonday sun . . .
>
> And so, at his own hour of 12 o'clock noontide—a word, by the way, he'd have been pleased to notice, as he loved the out-datedness and weight of words—at his own hour of the day, of nature and of Koktebel.

The image broadens with new additions and ascends gradually to the generality of a concept: the noon hour belongs to both day and year, to both time and place; it is both beloved nature and a beloved word. Through all of these layers there emerges a category "of the noon" as an all-embracing type of existence personified by Voloshin himself. And finally, Tsvetaeva extends this generalizing construct with its meticulously retained levels of imagery to its logical, even "mythological," limits:

> The fourth and main thing remains: at the hour of his essence. For Voloshin's essence was of the noon, as noon—of all the day's hours—is the most bodily, the most tangible of bodies without shadows. . . . And at the same time it is the most magical, mythic and mystical hour, just as magi-mythi-mystical as midnight. The hour of the Great Pan, the French "Demon of Noon," and our own humble Russian noon spirit (*poludennyi*) . . .

Not only Voloshin's natural surroundings, but he himself is entirely "of the noon," to the depths of his personality and creative abilities. Thus the image gradually reveals its generalizing properties. But the question remains, what type of image is this? Clearly it is not a purely artistic one, since it contains no invention; everything is just as it was, authentic and untransformed, down to the minutest detail ("sail-cloth, wormwood, sandals"), and not in vain does Tsvetaeva repeat, insisting: "And in truth . . ."

It may seem that the best possible definition of Tsvetaeva's discussion would have to be "myth," particularly inasmuch as the author herself draws the parallel when she speaks about the Great Pan, the French "Demon of Noon," and Russian images of the "noon spirit." Still, it goes without saying that we cannot simply insert Tsvetaeva's Voloshin into this mythological company without equivocation. His image brings with it a historical and biographical reality (which Tsvetaeva gradually reveals) that is not reducible to the idea of Noon, just as the idea of Noon is not reducible to the personality of one poet Voloshin. This is "myth" renouncing its own collective and syncretic nature, "myth" as created by a single person and about a single person, displaying the very process of its creation: a "living word about a living man." And only such an image as this, at one and the same time "myth" and "nonmyth," can be considered organically whole and truthful for the consciousness of the Modern Age. If Tsvetaeva had cut out of her Voloshin all that did not fit into her quasi-mythological image of the "man at noon," she would have uttered not a living word but a dead one. Organic wholeness lives by knowing and surpassing its own finality, its own unmitigated identity with itself, where ancient, traditional, syncretic myth remains.

The open type of construction found in the thought-image is unique to essayistics; for this reason I propose to call it an "esseme" (following the formative principle employed in terms on a variety of structural levels, such as "mythologeme," "ideologeme," "phoneme" and so on). This term may serve to fill a lacuna in our theoretical work by giving a name to the notion of a quasi-mythological image that is already widespread in contemporary writing. This notion normally goes by the name of "mythologeme" both in Russia and the West, but it would be more appropriate to distinguish the structural units of authentic, syncretic mythology from those of essayistics, in which image, concept, and being are reassembled on a developed and differentiated cultural level.

The esseme is a thought-image that may come infinitely close to the mythologeme, as to its own definitive boundary, without ever becoming identical to it, in that it invariably manifests itself as the product of an individual consciousness perfectly aware of itself as such. It will not attempt to pass off concept as image, nor image as reality; it will not assert their identity as an axiom, but will allow it as a hypothesis. While remaining open and creative, essayistic consciousness resists the temptations of pseudomythologization by exposing the very process of its own activity. At the same time, it does not fall into the trap of endless self-reflection, but rather escapes it in images pushed to the level of generality. Intermediate steps in this process are not concealed as they mediate between the ultimately personal and the ultimately general. An esseme is a mythologeme "in potentia," displayed in the process of growth. In our excerpt from Tsvetaeva's essay, the stages of ascent unfold from empirical fact, through varying degrees of generalized imagery, to a synthetic thought-image, and this exposed dynamic serves to distinguish the esseme from both the ready-made, enclosed, and unchanging mythologeme of ancient times and the pseudomythologeme of our time (as in totalitarian or mass-media myths of the twentieth century).

We should add that, in many ways, the creation of an essayistic thought-image reproduces—but this time in reverse order—the process begun in antiquity, whereby the different arts and sciences first arose. A crisis in ancient syncretism expressed itself in the gradual metamorphosis of myth, which was thus transformed into allegory, its meaning detached from concreteness, so that it became increasingly speculative and abstractly conceptual. In the words of Olga Freidenberg, a major Russian specialist in ancient mythology,

> The old image is mythological and concrete, located in an unrepeating, one-dimensional time and an unchanging space; it is immobile, without differentiated qualities, and resultative, that is, "ready-made," without cause or development. But this image begins to take on a second meaning as well, "another" one. . . . An allegory of the image bears a conceptual character: concreteness takes on abstract traits, singularity—the traits of multiple repetitions . . .[19]

As it is transformed into metaphor, myth loses the unconditional linkage of its components. Its literal meaning becomes ever more self-sufficient until it outgrows itself to become a statement of fact; its figurative meaning becomes the increasingly abstract formulation of a concept. The essential linkage of two meanings, now symbolic and playful, acquires the properties of a comparison, trope, or allegory. Thus, there arose three independent types of thought, which mature antiquity opposed to the mythological: the historical, philosophical, and artistic (embodying literal meaning, abstract meaning, and their metaphorical connection, respectively).

In its new quest for wholeness, so characteristic of the twentieth century, metaphor continues to fulfill an important role as the dual unity of meanings, but this is accomplished in the reverse direction, not as a splitting in two, but as a new unity of previously divergent components. As we have seen, in Tsvetaeva's essay, metaphor does not abstract the general from the singular; on the contrary, it draws one to the other, working for their reunification. Noon becomes the embodiment of "Voloshinness," and Voloshin, the embodiment of "the noon." We might say that the esseme is a metaphor in the process of transcending its own symbolic and figurative nature, as it again imbibes fact, on the one hand, and concept, on the other: those things that had once been extracted from myth.

If a mythologeme is the distant past of metaphor, then the esseme is its potential future. Metaphor represents the historically intermediary cognitive step at which the earlier identity of concrete specificity and conceptuality is annulled, and a new premise is created, proposing a freer unity between them. The esseme is a first hint of the growing postmetaphorical wholeness of concept, image, and being, in which we sense the sign of mature times, moving toward inner completeness and spiritual fullness: a "pleroma," to use an eschatological term coined by the Gnostics. At the present time it is given to us to bear witness only to the very inception of an epistemological process whose results may be as enormous as the metaphorization of myth and the birth, on this ground, of history, philosophy, and art.

The Essayization of Literature and Philosophy

Essayistic consciousness could not be holistic if it did not somehow draw into its orbit other, more specialized areas, each of which assimilates reality in its own way. Much as image and concept combine and interact in the esseme, essayistics as a whole proves to be the sphere to which the creation of pure imagery and the development of conceptual thinking are drawn ever more overtly.

This process of jarring the traditional epistemological partitions between genres found its preliminary expression in what has been called "novelization." According to Bakhtin's multifaceted description of this process: "In the epoch of the novel's dominance nearly all other genres are 'novelized' to a greater or lesser extent. The novel introduces a problematic, a specific yet uncompleted semantic, and living contact with unprepared contemporaneity in the process of becoming (the uncompleted present)."[20] Bakhtin relates these changes headed up by the novel to possible shifts in the bound-

aries between the artistic and nonartistic, between literature and nonliterature, and generally all types of "specifica" not established over the ages and
for all time.

And indeed, the novelization of various genres has been extensive, beginning, roughly, in the mid-eighteenth century. But as a parallel, the twentieth
century, which has addressed the "crisis of the novel," gives way to another
process that clearly outstrips the previous one: the *essayization* of various
literary genres, primary among them the novel itself. Essayization develops
and gives new depth to novelization. One of the most significant properties
of the novel, which Bakhtin considered the basis of its generic expansion—
the "living contact with unprepared contemporaneity in the process of
becoming"—is most consistently and purposefully embodied in the essay;
within the novel itself, it essentially represents an essayistic zone of contact
with the extranovelistic world. After all, the novel's generic dominant is the
creation of a particular, self-enclosed, and invented reality that can only
take on a transformed contemporaneity, blocked off from the authentic flow
of contemporary life outside itself. This is why the novelization of literature, the contemporization of its artistic world, shifts over to essayization as
the next consistent stage of its development, stepping over the very framework of artistic conventionality. In its devotion to present time, the essay
outstrips the novel and reveals to it new creative perspectives, in that it does
not invent a self-enclosed reality, does not specify its image as an artistic
one, but rather moves it out into the expanse of reality where the author and
his readers reside.

In this way the "uncompleted present" first intruded into an aesthetically
complete reality "novelistically," in order to then open it essayistically and
draw it out into the uncompleted world of the extraliterary environment.
The novel was not essayized as a result of influences directed at it from
within essayistics, but as a result of its own process of movement toward
reality, as it overstepped the borders of traditional artistic conventions one
after the other. The novel overcame the mythological orientation and devotion to the past that were characteristic of the epic, but to finally affirm itself
in the present, to open itself to the new, it had to overcome itself to a certain
extent as well—its obsession with fictions, illusionist remnants of the mythological worldview. That self-sufficient world of imagination, which was so
dear to traditional novelists who strove to immerse the reader up to his
eyebrows, gradually began to stand up and reveal its own underpinnings,
for instance in Sterne's *Tristram Shandy* and Pushkin's *Eugene Onegin*.
Here, little novelistic islands are already washed on all sides by restless

surges of self-reflection that bring the image of the author onto the page, showing that other reality which creates invention and surrounds it on all sides.

The wealth of so-called lyrical digressions that grace Pushkin's novel are, for the most part, not lyrical at all; the sense of spontaneous self-expression characteristic of the lyric mode is absent. These are rather the essayistic threads of the novel's fabric, woven of one cloth with the surrounding, greater reality, primarily the author's own biographical experience. In the lyric, the "I" expresses itself directly, whereas in the essay it emerges as both the subject and object of utterance, as its relation to itself is mediated through analysis and reflection. In *Eugene Onegin* there is no "lyrical hero," to use generally accepted terminology, but there is an "image of the author"—an essential difference indicating the essayistic rather than lyrical mode of Pushkin's presence in the novel. A more detailed historical analysis might well show how the peculiarities of European and especially English essayistics, at the height of their flowering in the era of romanticism, are refracted in *Eugene Onegin,* through the intermediary of Byron's *Don Juan.*

As essayism permeates the novel, it definitively demythologizes the latter's imagery, leading it back to the foundations in life from which it developed. But this is only one function of essayism: the analytical function, most thoroughly worked out in the English tradition going back to Sterne. Its most characteristic device is a running commentary on "events" from the standpoint of how they are made, as well as recourse to addressing the reader directly, and the like.

Essayism also has a capacity for synthesis. It not only demythologizes the artistic image by bringing it into extraartistic reality, but also universalizes this use of imagery by raising it to the level of superartistic generalization. At the same time, the image is not "made strange" to the point that it becomes an object of self-reflective play; rather, it becomes overgrown with an outer facticity and abstract-logical functions that it assimilates along with acquiring the heightened ontological status of a kind of ideoreality, something maximally generalized, yet also true to life. The German romantics oriented the verbal arts in this direction, appointing a role for them in the future as a new form of mythology, fully incorporating history, philosophy, and religion. As these mythological potentials of literary creativity were progressively realized (as opposed to regressively), this led, not to the stylization of ancient syncretic forms, but to a new type of organic wholeness. Thus the mythologization of the verbal arts essentially meant their essayization, as is evident in such typically romantic genres as the essayized novel or tale: Schlegel's *Lucinde,* Novalis's *The Apprentices of Sais,* and others.

In Russian literature, the synthetic type of essayization can be found in Gogol's works, for example in the three constituent parts of "Nevsky Prospect." The first part presents Nevsky Prospect as a reality well known to every resident of Petersburg, depicted in the fullness of its everyday conditions, in the manner of the physiological sketch:[21] "here you will meet . . . at 12 o'clock . . . after 4 in the afternoon . . ." The second part tells the story of two young men whom the author picks out of the crowd as they stroll along the prospect. In this segment Nevsky forms the space of an invented reality, a place where fatal passions and deceptive hopes are destined to be born. Finally, in the third part, Nevsky emerges as a higher reality belonging to the metaphysical realm. This idea is revealed in the broadest possible terms, even drawing upon mythology:

> O, don't believe in Nevsky Prospect! . . . All is deception, all is dream, nothing is what it seems! . . . It lies at every moment, this Nevsky Prospect, but most of all, at that hour when night descends upon it in a fast congealing mass . . . and when the demon himself is lighting the lamps—only to show everything *not* in its natural light.

Gogol's Nevsky Prospect is a holistic thought-image, in whose complex dialectic the properly artistic episode (the story of two young men's romantic delusions) turns out to be a transition mediating empirical reality and the universal idea of Nevsky Prospect.

Of course from the traditional point of view, the sketchlike exposition and philosophical-mythological finale are but the supporting elements that serve to reveal the basic idea of an artistic narrative. But the opposite assertion is equally correct: the story of the artist Piskarev and the lieutenant Pirogov is one variation played out on the overall theme of "the street as lie," "the city as deception." Within the essayistic paradigm of the given work, the narrative is one of the proofs that "it lies at every moment." The essayistic system is built into the literary system in such a way that each of them may be seen as an interpretation of the other. It is no accident that "Nevsky Prospect" was included in Gogol's *Arabesques,* an anthology with great breadth of content in which artistic works stand side by side with sketches and articles: in "Nevsky Prospect" this combination is contained within the borders of a single work.

This quality of interinclusiveness, the interrefractedness of two impulses, becomes especially characteristic of twentieth-century literature. Many works traditionally considered to fall within the category of verbal artistry, have come to appear as literary essays, which can simultaneously be interpreted as essayized novels or tales. Thomas Mann characterized his "Story of Jacob" (the first part of his tetralogy "Joseph and his Brothers") as a "fantastical essay" (*ein phantastischer Essay*),[22] and this capacious generic definition, including fictional elements within the system of holistic thinking, may also be applied to other major creations of the German literary tradition: Hermann Hesse's *The Glass Bead Game* and Robert Musil's *The Man Without Qualities*.

It is to Musil, after all, that we must give the honor of having coined the word and concept of "essayism," which he views as an experimental means of existence, a special mode of assimilating reality, of higher value than science and poetry, and even as a utopia summoned to encompass the unity of what is and what is possible: "It was approximately in the way that an essay, in the sequence of its paragraphs, takes a thing from many sides without comprehending it wholly—for a thing wholly comprehended instantly looses its bulk and melts down into a concept—that he believed he could best survey and handle the world and his own life."[23]

Generally speaking, it is not easy to name major figures of world literature of the twentieth century whose work has *not* absorbed the essayistic impulse, to a greater or lesser degree, in the construction of imagery whose artistic wholeness is simultaneously dismembered analytically and incorporated into a synthetic wholeness of a higher order. Thomas Mann and Hermann Hesse, Paul Valéry, and André Gide, André Malraux and Albert Camus, André Breton and Antoine de Saint-Exupéry, Gilbert Chesterton and J. B. Priestly, Miguel de Unamuno and Elias Canetti, Henry Miller and Norman Mailer, Kawabata and Kobo Abe—through the work of these and many other writers, essayistics emerges from the confines of one genre into the main thoroughfare of literary development, broadly entering into all verbal genres and types. In Proust's work it is the *epic* that undergoes essayization, as images are born before the reader's eyes from the author-hero's contemplations and reminiscences. Elements of an analytical essayistics, commentary, literary criticism, and scholarship find their way into Thomas Mann's *novels*. With Kafka, the *novella* is often constructed like a business account or a scientific report, including classifications and elements of typological thinking. For George Bernard Shaw the *drama* acquires traits of a debate or intellectual duel; and in T. S. Eliot's *poetry* self-commentary becomes an organic supplement or even a basic component.

In this process, the analytical directedness of essayism predominates in the work of some authors, while the synthetic predominates in the work of others. Thus, in Gide's *The Counterfeiters* the reflective play of images dominates, emphasizing the experimental quality of their artistic symbolism, but in Hesse's *Steppenwolf* (created at almost precisely the same time) the conceptual intensification of images manifests their hieratic, extratemporal meaning. But more often these tendencies—the "reflective" and the "mythologizing"—are interlinked, as in Joyce's *Ulysses* and Mann's *Magic Mountain*. The same thought that breaks down the immediacy of the artistic image also expands it into a holistic thought-image. The paradox of essayism lies in the fact that it brings out the separate elements of an image, while at the same time bringing it together with concept and being; it destroys a specifically integrated artistic whole, only to re-create in its place a broadly cultural whole that is both integrated and creatively universal. Indeed, that which is normally called an "artistic whole" is, in actuality, decidedly partial and incomplete in its derivation from the originary syncretic state. The partial nature of artistic convention must be further exposed and expressed, in order to be fully integrated into a newly growing, unconventional whole.

Turning to Russian literature, we discover fruitful examples of essayization here as well. From the perspective of the present, we must concede that the greatest creative achievements of such outstanding writers as Mikhail Prishvin, Iury Olesha, and Konstantin Paustovsky are connected not so much with these authors' properly literary works, to which they gave the greater part of their conscious efforts, as to essayistics, which emerged from their pens as easily, naturally as breathing. Paustovsky explains that "the result is something crazy and free," in reference to his work on "The Golden Rose," which was written "about myself"—about his own experiences and that of other writers.[24] If we compare Prishvin's novel *The Tsar's Road*, which he worked on long and tortuously toward the end of his life, with the diaries he kept through the same years, we are struck by the fullness and depth of content that emerges in the latter unburdened by literary form, by the weight of a plot, and invented characters. We sense a lightly borne load of contemplations and truthful events that directly accompany a life, without needing to be shifted onto the shoulders of some "inserted" personage.

"It seems to me that the only work I could produce that might be meaningful and necessary to people would be a book about my own life. . . . Contemplations or recollections of some twenty to thirty lines—a hundred at most—this *is* the contemporary novel."[25] Thus, Iury Olesha explained his attraction to what may be called "life-thought-wording." Only in his later years, worn out by fruitless attempts to create something "artistically complete," did Olesha find the type of open genre necessary to his inclinations. In his book of jottings *No day without a line,* what could not be accommodated within a "novel" turns out here to possess its own complexity, perhaps of a higher order.

At the same time, the essayistic works of Prishvin, Paustovsky, and Olesha are not in any way poorer in artistic imagery than are properly literary works, although in this case such imagery is not self-sufficient and does not become purely depictive. Where image borders on idea and fact, an energy of tension and struggle is born that often burns out in the epistemological monotony of a world picture that links similar with similar, thought with thought, fact with fact, image with image, all subordinate to the monosemantic logic of a philosophical system or historical or literary narrative. In essay, the energy of tension among heterogeneous components overcomes the entropy of purely fictional or theoretical design. Thus, once it is incorporated into a superartistic whole, artistry does not fade away in the least. However paradoxical it may seem, the specific nature of artistic methods are actually etched more sharply on a contrastive background.

Still, the essayization of literature is but one aspect of the integrative processes of twentieth-century culture. Another related aspect is the essayization of philosophy, which in subordination to the logic of its internal development, has begun to lean toward the figurative, just as art leans toward the conceptual.

The classical systems of German idealism defined the furthest extent to which philosophical thought could go, moving within the purely discursive sphere of self-developing concepts. Post-Hegelian, and in the broad sense postclassical philosophy, discovered a reality opaque to logic and requiring the grounding of thought in the process of being that gives rise to it. If in the seventeenth century and the beginning of the eighteenth essayistics remained on the periphery of that general philosophical development defined by the discursive systems of Descartes, Leibnitz, Spinoza, Kant, and other "pure" thinkers, then roughly in the middle of the nineteenth century such thought loses its "innocence," its self-enclosure, and begins to seek substantiation outside of thought itself. This area beyond the boundaries comes to define the growing process of essayization. In order to "think the unthinkable"—life, singularity—thought must enrich itself with imagery and enter into the movement of concrete entities, thought-engendering situations, from which it once set off in pursuit of generalization. Kierkegaard and Nietzsche, who in many ways defined the path of Western philosophizing of the twentieth century, wrote not systematic treatises, but metaphysical literary experiments in which thought works its way through imagery and remains inseparable from it. Kierkegaard's Don Juan and Abraham, and Nietzsche's Dionysius and Zarathustra certainly are not artistic images but still less can they be called logical concepts. Rather they are a particular type of esseme in which thought strives to coincide with image and, failing this, sacrifices a part of the latter's plasticity along with a part of its own logic. Mann characterized Nietzsche precisely as an essayist of the Schopenhauerian school, a school that grew out of the conviction that will precedes representation, and being assigns thought its path. From this it follows that, in terms of the style of philosophy itself, systematics must immerse itself in essayistics, just as thought must immerse itself in the stream of life, which thereby grows more dense, without breaking off.[26] On this principle are built such important thought-images of twentieth-century Western culture as Camus's Sisyphus, Marcuse's Orpheus, and Saint-Exupéry's Citadelle.

The tendency toward essayization arises in a variety of philosophical orientations, but is not reducible to any of them, in that it possesses its own patterns and laws within the overall development of culture. The fact that a novella, for example, may be realistic, romantic, symbolistic, or expressionistic does not negate the necessity of analyzing "the novella" as a unique generic formation. In the same way, thinkers of vastly differing views may adhere to a similar stylistic-generic orientation, whose relatively independent logic requires its own explanation.

The expansion of imagery into the sphere of philosophical thought received stimulation from such polarized teachings as psychoanalysis and phenomenology. Freud's psychoanalytic work and, even more so, that of Jung bear a noticeable imprint of essayism, predetermined by the very project of penetrating the unconscious, that "boiling cauldron" of psychic energy where all cognitive impulses are molten and merged. Thus, we have psychoanalytic "concepts" of the thought-image type, such as "Eros," "Thanatos," the "Anima," "Persona," "Mask," and "Shadow"; essayistic reworkings of the mythological images of Oedipus and Narcissus, the fantastic images of dreams; and the psychoanalytic interpretations of such concrete symbols as "door," "key," "tablecloth," "cup" and so on.

As for phenomenology, which gives priority not to the unconscious but, on the contrary, to "pure consciousness," it also proclaims the return of philosophy from speculative abstractions to "things themselves" in their direct manifestation to the consciousness. According to Husserl, one should "take phenomena as they are given, i.e. as the present fluctuating awareness, opinion, disclosure which phenomena actually are."[27] In so doing, philosophy becomes "eidetics"—the intellectual contemplation and description of mental schemata as if they were concrete images graphically arising in the mind. The "intentionality" of consciousness, which is always directed toward some certain, external object, rendering it "consciousness *of*," finds its analogue in the structure of essayistic discussion which, as we pointed out above, is also "of." The unfolding of various opinions and approaches, dispositions and intentions in relation to given things—this is a mode of reducing the issue of their "extraphenomenal" essence. Montaigne's postulate to the effect that "the opinion I give . . . is to declare the measure of my sight, not the measure of things" (Book 2: chap. 10, 298), could be accepted in phenomenology, with the refinement that one's "sight" of things is itself an act of revealing their measure. The task posed to philosophy in Husserl's later works—to describe originary self-evidentness, to return to the "living world," which "is nothing else but the world of a simple opinion (*doxa*), which traditionally began to be regarded so contemptuously"[28]—this is a task that implies a consistent essayization of the philosophical method. For Husserl, as for Montaigne, opinion proves to be a more authentic form of understanding than speculative knowledge. The thought of a phenomenologist, like that of an essayist, is always written into the horizon of his being which it cannot and should not overstep, since to do so would be to distance itself into the objectively logical, abstract world of ideal conceptions.

The essayization of philosophy is even more consistently realized in work by the existentialists than in that of the phenomenologists. For the former, thought comes into direct contact with the creation of image and often merges with the process of literary composition. The hypostases of thinker/writer cannot be divided within the framework of an individual composition by such leading representatives of existentialism as Sartre, Camus, Simone Weil, Simone de Beauvoir, Gabriel Marcel, Heidegger, Unamuno, and Lev Shestov. Novels, dramas, treatises, and articles become variations on the essay, in that the ideas which serve as manifestations of the priority of existence over essence follow their own logic in unfolding as modes of existence in and of themselves, as "existentials," consciously harking back to mythopoeic unity. Consciousness recognizes the primacy of being, but this primacy is deduced from the demands of consciousness itself. In phenomenological and existential philosophies, thought and image, "idea" and "view" form a closed circle, as if conjoining within one point of "eidos" from which they went their separate ways in ancient times. Concept substantiates itself through inclusion in an image, an act of thought aimed in a direction opposite to that of Plato's deduction, which abstracts "idea" from "view." If for Plato authentic thought was opposed to the "inventions of poets," then for Heidegger to think meant actually to *be* a poet. This indicates the reverse motion of philosophy back to its own source, so that idea, in returning to the bosom of image, might recover the lost unity of a mythologeme. But the authentic result of such a reverse motion, regardless of the many illusions surrounding it, is not a mythologeme, but an esseme, not a syncretic but a potential, internally divided unity, mediated by the entire preceding course of development of abstract ideas.

The multifarious manifestations of essayism may be discovered in the work of such outstanding Russian scholars as Aleksei Losev, Sergei Averintsev, Georgy Gachev, and others.[29] Here essayism is primarily a result of the cultural multiplicity intrinsic to Russian traditions in the humanities, as found, for example, in the work of the nineteenth-century critics Belinsky and Herzen, who combined philosophical and philological, critical and artistic impulses at a time when these were divided into much stricter specializations in the work of their Western colleagues. The contemporary significance of this tradition, the complex interrelation of syncretic and synthetic elements that it entails, may not be immediately apparent and deserves special examination.

Essayism as a Cultural Phenomenon

The examples offered above show that both artistic-literary and conceptual-logical forms prove excessively narrow for the creative consciousness of the twentieth century, which seeks realization in composition as such, in the extrageneric or supergeneric thought-writing that was first developed in the essay. We have used the name "essayization" for the expansion of the principle of essayistic thinking into other genres and types of creativity; "essayism" is our term for the totality of this trend as a unified cultural phenomenon. Essayism is an integrative process taking place within culture as a movement toward the synthesis of life, thought, and image, in which these components—originally coexistent in myth but long since divorced from one another in the differential developments of culture—come together again in order to test their experimental kinship to each other along with their commonality in an as yet unnamed and unrevealed whole.

The peculiarity of essayism as well as its significance in the Modern Age is determined by its position in a deeply and increasingly specialized culture. The nucleus of this culture divides continuously and at an increasing rate of speed to form ever new and independent organisms. The arts and sciences continue to divide into disciplines, subgroups, branches, and varieties from which sprout entire new sciences and arts. The tendency toward specialization has gone so far that representatives of different cultural areas cease to understand each other. We are no longer dealing with only "two cultures," the artistic and the scientific, as C. P. Snow supposed in the late 1950s, but with a multitude of microcultures, of new cultural provinces that take shape in the place of what was once simply "human" culture: we now have literary, musical, mathematical and athletic cultures, even "the culture" of chess or of soccer. Moreover, these no longer quarrel among themselves as to which one came first (like physicists and lyricists did in their time), because to quarrel would require at least a minimum of mutual understanding and interest.

Nonetheless, within each system processes are at work to balance the basic developmental tendency toward proliferation and prevent decline and destruction. The centrifugal forces of modern culture engender their own opposite in centripetal processes, as a means of self-preservation. At times this centripetal tendency may appear to be overly rigid—as when it seeks to create a new mass mythology and force millions to submit to it, while at other times appearing to be overly soft—as in the case of many individual experiments in integrating different areas of cultural enterprise. Essayism is this softer form of gathering and condensing culture; here the common denominator of all the dispersed fragments of culture is an indivisible unity of individuality. Like mythology in ancient cultures, essayism fulfills the mission of linking what is separated but this time on the grounds of that most precious acquisition of the Modern Age: the value of the separate human personality, as affirmed in the Renaissance. Essayism is the synthesis of varied cultural forms on the basis of the self-conscious personality that ascends through this practice to a higher level of spiritual universality.

Essayism is one manifestation of a consistent "homeostasis" of the open system that is modern culture. Its intent is to maintain balance by realizing, with the centralizing consciousness of personality, the connections among all peripheral units, even the most remote and refined specializations—without, however, closing down the total system. Otherwise the preservation of organic wholeness in culture would require the sacrifice of its founding value and meaning: openness.

For this reason it is appropriate to reemphasize that essayism is *not* a reborn mythology and makes no attempt to affirm itself as such. This distinguishes it from all "twentieth-century myths," which renew archaic forms of syncretic wholeness for use as instruments of domination over mass consciousness. In relation to this type of mythologizing, which is reactionary and rudimentary in the literal meanings of those words, essayism emerges as a force for separation rather than gathering. Suffice it to recall once more Thomas Mann's remarks on *Joseph and his Brothers:* "In this book myth is knocked out of the hands of fascism, it is humanized up to the last cell of the language, and if future generations are to find something remarkable in the novel, it will be the humanization of myth."[30]

Essayism is a kind of "humanistic mythology," not merely a "humanized" one, since it was born in the bosom of humanism, in the heart of that epoch in which the last organic remnants of the old, prepersonal mythology finally came apart. The essential preconditions for that complex wholeness born in essayistic creativity were the differentiated quality of both the author and the cultural world around him. Between image, concept, and reality—as between subject and object—there always remains a zone of noncorrespondence, an essential miscontact that takes the form of self-reflection, criticism, commentary, the tragic consciousness of alienation, or the ironic play of estrangement. The previous syncretic identity of individual and mass, of logic and vision—the preconditions of ancient myth—can no longer be fully restored other than through force and falsehood, as witnessed by experiments in totalitarian ideology, which adapts logical thought to the task of proving the "obvious," and subordinates artistic imagery to the vulgarity of propagandistic schemes.

Essayism does not erase the boundaries between image, concept, and experience; on the contrary, it sharpens them to re-create the full multidimensionality of the human phenomenon. The presence of a human self that stands with all its opinions and doubts at the point of intersection of all unifying constructs is essential for a "humanistic mythology." And it is fitting that the analytical-mythological style of essayistics, as in Mann's tetralogy, is born of an artistic task: to "tell of the birth of 'I' from the primitive collective," to convey "a gentle but proud assertion of 'I.' "[31]

However, in emphasizing the demythologizing character of essayism on the one hand, we cannot fully accept Theodore Adorno's position on the essay as a form of "negative dialectic" and total denial. Within the framework of this conception, the essay's intention is to demonstrate the relativity of all absolutes, to dismember any and all political and cultural "alliances," to relativize the meanings of words, depriving them of their common status, as well as the judgments intrinsic to their petrified propagandistic usage. And indeed, from the moment of its origins beneath Montaigne's pen, essayistics became a method of critical reflection on manners that had lost their normative power and entered into contact with the exploratory acts of an inquisitive individual consciousness. In the later development of essayistics, however, this consciousness itself became the new global form of "commonness" that allowed for a free and dynamic interaction of relativized values. In Adorno's view, the essayistic personality is skepticism personified, with the oppositional quality of alternative thinking as it stands against the "establishment" and its canonization of ritual objects. But "alternative thinking" is only a historically and logically necessary stage in the becoming of "holistic thinking." One could say that the essayistic personality lives by its premonitions, guesswork and efforts at embodying a whole it will never possess in totality, as a ready-made, positive object for affirmation. This wholeness enters the horizon of consciousness while simultaneously remaining outside its boundaries. It is revealed in the form of suppositions, rich in many modalities of judgment, which the essayist does not transform into categorical, finalizing affirmations.

This basic property of essayistic thought—to remain always within a mode of openness—might be called *antitotalitarian totalization*. In a single act of consciousness, an essay can shatter the falsehood of a petrified whole and then re-create from its pieces a new whole possessed of internal dynamism. An essay always seeks the median, the intermediary. It avoids both the purely positive and purely negative: "[A] mean may be found between that base and sordid concern, tense and full of anxiety, which is seen in men who plunge themselves deep into it, and that profound and extreme negligence, letting everything go to seed, which we see in others" (Book 1: chap. 39: 180).

Montaigne's "a mean may be found" is a precise formula for the balance of judgments that characterizes essayistic writings. A sense of mediating among all manner of extreme ideas flows from the centered position of personality in this world. This is not a form of mediation that freezes up within itself, but rather a striving to discover openness even at the point of greatest concentration of all things: to be "between," neither opposing nor identifying with any of them. Neither positive nor oppositional, essayistic thinking is rather "interpositive," in that it reveals the meaning of lacunae, the unoccupied and intermediary positions in existing cultures.

The set for mobility, rather than rigidly fixed and centralized meaning is evident even in the smallest "cells" of essayistic language: any word can be transformed into the founding term on which an entire original system of word usage may be built. This practice endows the most ordinary, everyday words—those normally passed over by traditional metaphysics, such as *noon, snow, razor, smoke, sticky*—with profound significance. The more "far-fetched" the ideas and spheres of consciousness we attach to an ordinary word, the richer its inner life and creative potential.

Pascal's description may justifiably be applied to the essayistic world: its center is everywhere, and its surroundings nowhere. Any point may come into focus, and become the center of a system of dependent concepts. Thus, in Charles Lamb's well-known essay "A Dissertation upon Roast Pig," the dish named in the title develops from a founding concept to a kind of metaphysical absolute, from which are derived such secondary terms as "burnt," "scorched skin," "crackling," and so on.[32] As distinct from speculative philosophical systems, this type of focus is highly mobile and may shift from word to word, from concept to concept, without granting dominance to any one element over the others. A world in which each entity is central and peripheral at the same time actually consists of a multitude of worlds, all serving each other as both premise and conclusion, basis and superstructure—and in this mobility of its very foundations, the notion of an *open, integrated whole* has its foundation.

Thus, essayism can become the conductive wire between opposed tendencies—integrative ones as well as differentiating ones—and in the struggles between them, it takes both sides, defending the intermediary position of culture itself and its interests in a multiple and complex unity. Depending on the concrete historical situation in which essayistic thinking unfolds, it is bound to express the predominance of one tendency over another, so that culture might preserve its openness while acquiring wholeness, or preserve its wholeness while acquiring openness. Such thinking acts as a two-edged instrument, capable of analysis and synthesis, of dismembering monolithic, syncretic cultural forms that have outlived their time and of reuniting the broken fragments of overspecialized forms.

Many artistic, philosophical, and scientific movements have arisen in twentieth-century culture: expressionism and cubism, existentialism and structuralism, vitalism and behaviorism . . . Essayism cannot be grouped with any of these "-isms" because it is not a movement within a single branch of culture, but a quality of culture as it is drawn to wholeness, to the intergrowth not only of the conceptual and figurative impulses of culture, but also of culture itself with the realm of being that lies beyond it. This is not an artistic, philosophical, or scientific phenomenon, but precisely an all-cultural one, a mechanism for the self-preservation and self-development of culture as a whole: a lever for balancing centrifugal and centripetal tendencies, either of whose predominance could lead to cultural perdition.

This is not to say that all of contemporary culture can or should become essayized. The prospect of a culture in which everything would be mixed in with everything else is a nightmare worthy of an anti-utopia. Thus far, fortunately, everything remains in its appointed place: literature remains literature, a novel is a novel, science remains science, and a monograph is a monograph. It is also fitting that each branch of culture should continue to branch out, producing new fruits of artistic and scientific refinement. Experiments in integration have meaning only in the context of highly developed and deeply differentiated culture. Essayism does not extend over all types and genres of verbal art, but rather lies on the periphery of all of them, in the spaces and gaps between them. Very few works come into being on a new level of cultural commonality, not as artistic, philosophical, or scientific works, but directly in the genre of *culture itself,* where intracultural oppositions, such as those of concept and image, abstract and concrete, or general and singular, fall away or are mitigated. The particular flexibility and alacrity of what we have termed "essayism," as it moves freely among different types of cognition, is a necessary addition to contemporary culture, answering its need for variety and multiplicity.

A peculiarity of culture in the Modern Age is its aspiration toward the future, toward a finality that would accommodate infinity. Today it is clear that this is the only culture in history to seek its justification not in the past, but as something yet to come. It gives rise not so much to the development of a certain idea, as to the very idea of development. This culture is an experiment in self-creation; it tests creative inquiry into the potentials of culture itself. Broadly understood, essayism is the moving force of modern culture and the mystery of its unceasing newness.

CHAPTER 8 · Thing and Word: On the Lyrical Museum

. . . oh, for such saying as never the things themselves
hoped so intensely to be.

. . . fleeting, they look for rescue
through something in us, the most fleeting of all.
—Rainer Maria Rilke, *Ninth Duino Elegy*

What Is a Lyrical Museum?

Normally, things are selected for museum display for one of three reasons. Either very old and rare things are selected by virtue of being one of a kind or intrinsically valuable, in which case we have a thesaurus-museum, a treasure trove like the Kremlin Armory or exhibits from the Diamond Fund.[1] Or things possessing the significance of typicality are chosen for their ability to represent an entire class or category of similar things—in this case we have a catalogue-museum, a systematic collection on the order of most museums of technology, minerology, zoology, and the like. Finally, things may be neither especially unique, nor especially typical, but derive their interest from the fact that they belonged to some remarkable person. In this instance we have a memorial museum, which re-creates the surroundings of a famous writer, scientist, military leader, or whomever. Of course, these three functions of a thing—as rarity, as example, as relic—may intersect and combine in actual practice, but traditionally any one of them could guarantee the museum status of things; they elevate things to the category of display items.

The museum I plan to discuss here, however, does not belong to any of the types listed above. Its displays are composed of the things of everyday life,

lacking any material, historical, or artistic value. These are things of universal distribution that are available everywhere, without ever arousing the
slightest attention or surprise. At the same time, there is an essential individuality, rather than typicality, in the being of these things, which preserves the imprint of their owners' lives and worldviews. Yet this does not
serve to endow the items with memorial value, insofar as their owners are
ordinary people, whose names enjoy no fame, and of whom it would be
premature to take final stock.

And so, what kind of museum is it that displays ordinary things, and by
what right is attention called to them? The explanation lies in that, along
with the material, historic, and artistic values that are characteristic of very
few things, *every* thing, every object, even the most insignificant, can possess a personal, or *lyrical* value. This value is derived from the degree of
experience and meaning that the given thing has absorbed, the extent to
which it has been incorporated into the owner's spiritual activity. If we can
discern in it a significant meaning, or if we find a signature or commentary
affixed to it, then this is an item worthy of inclusion in a lyrical museum.
The intent of the museum is to reveal the endless variety and profound
significance of things in human life, the wealth of their figurative and conceptual meaning, which can in no way be reduced to a utilitarian role.

The whole of human life consists of things and is preserved in them, like
so many geological layers, through which we can trace a succession of
ages, tastes, attachments, fascinations. Children's toys—a ball, doll, hand
shovel. . . An eraser, a pen, pencilcase and bookbag. . . A ruler, skis, tennis
rackets. . . A table lamp, book, and notebook. . . A pocketbook, coinpurse,
mirror, and fan. . . A wallet, cigarette case, keys, various documents. . .
Scissors, knitting needles. . . A spade, pliers and a hammer. . . A compass,
watch, thermometer, magnifying glass. . . Cups, plates, and a well-worn
chair by a window. . . A simple stone, collected by the sea at one time, now a
frequent resting place for someone's gaze. . . Each thing is contained in
the integral magnetic field of a human life, charged with the meaning of
this life and oriented toward its center. Each thing is connected to a particular memory, experience, habit, loss, or acquisition, an expansion of life's
horizon. The ordinariness of things bears witness to their particular importance, their capacity to enter into the order of life, to grow as one with the
qualities of human beings to the point that they become a fixed and meaningful part of human existence—all of this is denied to things which are
"extra-ordinary."

The world itself is articulated, is "spoken" in things. It is not coincidental that the Russian word *veshch'* (thing) is etymologically related to *vest'* (news, a message) and *veshchat'* (to prophesy) and originally meant "that which is said, pronounced" (compare to the Latin word with the same root: *vox,* "voice"). To hear the voice contained within a thing, prophesying from its depths, is to understand both the thing and oneself. The very dichotomy of "thing" and "human" can at best be arbitrarily established within the framework of "human-thingness," which, ultimately, is as indissoluble as soul and body. "Thingness" derives its "head" from humans, while acting in turn as an extended human "body."[2] Wherever there is a thing, there is also a special exit for a human being beyond his body: to nature or art, space or thought, activity or quiet, contemplation or creativity. All of the basic components of human life find their correspondences in things, which act as letters, spelling out the meaningful words of actions, situations, interrelations. There is no such "thing"—be it an automobile or a button, a book or a candy wrapper—as a thing that lacks its own place in culture, or fails to bring its owner into communion with culture while demanding his reciprocal attention and understanding. After all, his very position in the world, the sense of his existence, is defined by the entirety of things surrounding him. A thing that falls away from meaning puts man in rupture with the system of surrounding connections and with himself.

It is here, around the things we encounter with every step we take, that an area has taken shape which now awaits its researcher, even demands the creation of its own academic discipline. This discipline could be called *realogy* (from the Latin *res,* "thing").[3] At the present time, the words "realogy" or the "science of things" are unfamiliar to the ear, but they had to appear eventually, inasmuch as the vast majority of things that surround us everywhere and every day do not come under the rubric of any theoretical discipline devoted to the study of things: neither industrial technology, technical aesthetics, commerce, art studies, nor museum practice. Of course, prior to reaching the hands of its owner, a thing normally must pass through the factory production line and the commercial distribution network; some also pass through a design bureau or a craftsman's workshop. But realogy looks at that essence of the thing that cannot be reduced to the technical qualities of a *product,* nor to the economic qualities of a *purchase,* nor even to the aesthetic aspects of a *work.* A *thing* possesses a particular essence that gains in significance in reverse proportion to the technological novelty, commercial value, and aesthetic appeal of the thing per se. This essence, involving the capability of a thing to become kindred, to enter the life of a human being, is revealed more fully as other qualities diminish and lose their value or newness. The one property of a thing that increases over the course of its incorporation into a life is its ability to absorb personal attributes, its quality of *belonging* to a person. Each and every thing has this essence by virtue of its very existence, but it remains for the person to reveal it through experience and attention, transforming intrinsic value into value for someone. This is precisely the task of realogy as a theoretical discipline and of the lyrical museum as the experimental foundation for a science of things: to comprehend the proper, nonfunctional meaning of things, independent of their commercial and utilitarian intent as well as their aesthetic qualities.

It seems wise to suggest a preliminary distinction between the terms "thing" and "object," which occur in very different contextual combinations.[4] "Object" requires an inanimate noun complement, while "thing" requires an animate one. We speak about the "object of what?"—of industry, of consumption, of export, of study, discussion, examination. But we ask, "whose thing is this?"—his, hers, mine, ours, my father's, my wife's, my neighbor's. In this instance, language shows better than any theoretical explanation the difference between object and thing, between the status of belonging to the world of objects and that of belonging to the world of subjects. A thing is not an object by its very nature as the property of a subject, a person. It is always "mine" or "someone's own." "Products," on the other hand, "goods" and even "rarities" are all varieties of objects, objects for industry, consumption, buying, selling, collection, or contemplation. Between "object" and "thing" approximately the same contrast exists as between "individuality" and "personality": the first is but the possibility or substratum of the second. An object only becomes a thing when it is spiritually incorporated into someone's life, just as an individual becomes a personality through the process of self-awareness, self-definition, and intensive self-development. To compare further, let us consider "he made a fine object" and "he did a fine thing."[5] The first means that he produced something with his hands; the second, that he performed an action. In Old Russian the word *veshch'* (thing) originally meant "spiritual matter," "deed," "achievement," or "word"[6] and this meaning, intuitively felt in the contemporary use of "thing," must be more fully revealed by theoretical work. Within every object there slumbers a portentous "thing," the trace or potential of a human achievement.

A lyrical museum is thus an experiment in de-*object*ifying things, starting with those that are closest to each of us, rather than those that are removed from us by historical time or associated with other natural surroundings or ethnic ways. Such a museum is the test of things' authentic assimilation into our lives. Do we really understand what these things mean for us? How they enter our immediate surroundings, bringing with them distant, all-embracing meanings, connecting us to the integral system of culture with its traditions and possibilities? How the line of personal fate and hope of inner becoming is drawn through them? All of this can be expressed subjectively to the extent that the lyrical "I" of the exhibitor determines the mode of expression in the exhibit. It is the sheer possibility of expression that is important, the presence of a lyrical impulse deep within the thing itself, its nonalienness, its kinship to the human "I" and human self-definition in the world.

In traditional museums it is essential to maintain a certain epic distance between the thing and that reality from which it is extracted and which it represents as if from afar, aloofly. This distance is necessary in order to establish the objective significance of things, to subject them to the test of time and of social recognition. It is necessary for the scientific investigation of their authenticity and representativeness. But another type of museum work is just as necessary—a type that will bring out the lyric, rather than the epic, nature of things. This must be revealed, not from the external view-point of the erudite specialist, but from within the spiritual and cultural situation in which these things act and live, inseparable from the life of their owner. To exhibit and offer commentary on a thing belonging to me per-sonally—this is the opportunity that a lyrical museum gives to each of us. Here the meaning of things unfolds from the standpoint of their real-life implementation as something present in the here and now, within the hori-zon of that consciousness which uses them and embodies itself in them.

These things may not be so significant as the ones displayed in historical or artistic museums, since, after all, lyrical poems do not usually commem-orate grandiose events—like the fall of Troy or the burning of Moscow—rather, they convey a "marvelous moment" (Pushkin), the flash of a smile, a breath of air, or a "speck of dust on a pen knife" (Aleksandr Blok). A thing can serve in the capacity either of metaphor or metonymy, conveying the spiritual through the physical or the whole through its parts. A lyrical thing on display is like a poetic trope, whose literal meaning coincides with its material existence and everyday function, but whose figurative meaning embraces the entirety of experiences and conjectures expressed in it. The lyrical museum also has historical relevance, inasmuch as that personal essence of things, which it is called upon to comprehend, has only recently been fully manifested, in the era of increasing depersonalization.

Between Warehouse and Landfill

The problem of reification is one of the most crucial facing twentieth-century culture. The very words "thing," "material," and "materiality" have come to be perceived with suspicion, as if they posed a threat to spirituality.[7] But a thing is not guilty of reification; that is the property of a person who reduces himself to a thing, whereas a thing proper always has the potential of rising to the human level and becoming animate through contact with a human being. It is not necessary to return to hand production for the realization of these potentials of things, as various thinkers including William Morris, Gandhi, and Heidegger seem to suggest. A thing can be domesticated by man even if it rolls out of the factory on the most impersonal and technologically advanced conveyers, since it nonetheless ends up in someone's house, where a person assimilates it into his private way of life, endowing it with numerous general, practical, conscious, and unconscious meanings. Putting a thing to use—be it sitting on a chair, watching a television set, wearing glasses, or reading a book—deteriorates into consumerism only when the item is not fully consumed, not assimilated to a person's complete existence, however paradoxical this seems. As a banal example, consider the book which is "used" only for the pretty color of its cover, or, at best, for the topical information it contains. Consumerism arises when a thing arrives in the home of its owner only to remain alien and underconsumed, as if it were still just a pretty object in the store window or on a shelf.

The twentieth century has created two grandiose symbols of the alienation that separates things and man: the warehouse and the landfill. In the former are housed things that have not yet come into human life and do not even seem to need to, as their bright labels glint haughtily beneath impeccable plastic wrappings. Meanwhile, in the case of the latter, things that have lost the attention and care they once enjoyed, are thrown out, abandoned to the ravages of dust, smut, rot, and rust. Acquisitiveness and "disposingness" are opposite tendencies, but they are interrelated in their common cause: the incomplete assimilation of things, things for which someone did not have enough soul "to spare." If a thing does not enter completely into a person's life, but remains essentially a warehouse or store-window item, then its unneeded potential is condemned to purposeless decrepitude and collapse. In one sense there is no fundamental difference between warehouse and landfill: if we leave aside the space of human assimilation, the one passes directly into the other, from jewels to junk.

The image of "soulless things" has found repeated embodiment in twentieth-century art. We can readily recall pop-art portrayals of massive heaps of natural or naturalistically reproduced things, with their garish, store-bought exterior, which seems to have never *yet* been touched by human hands. At the other extreme, certain styles of avant-garde art, particularly conceptualism, have given meaning to the poor, worn, thrown-out things that will never *again* be touched by human hands. Yellowed papers, old documents, broken pencils, tattered remnants of books and newspapers, injured chairs, tottering on three legs—such is the ironic-grotesque, or sometimes the elegaic-grotesque, assemblage of many conceptualist works, in which words usurp the place of worn-out and neglected things.

Needless to say, these two extremes do not exhaust the artistic treatments of the "ready-made thing" in twentieth-century art. But if we consider the other trends that rely on "ready-made" motifs in eclectic combinations, the majority of which originated in the years between 1910 and 1920 and still retain their popularity to varying degrees, here, too, we discover that attention is turned primarily to the impersonal, object side of things. Constructivism was primarily interested in the technical and pragmatic aspects of things; dadaism, in their absurd logic and metaphysical properties; surrealism, in the symbolic coding and decoding of visual elements. A thing was perceived and displayed as an attribute of the production process or the comforts of modern life; as a mysterious item situated in the boundless emptiness of the cosmos; as a sign of the invisible deeds of otherworldly powers; as an unstable daydream that shifts its shape even as we gaze upon it, and as a vicious trap, ready to snap shut on the trusting observer. In all of this there was much poetry, but none of it was lyrical. The connection of the thing being displayed to its owner, its inclusion in a circle of concrete concerns and attachments, the deep meaning hidden in its singularity—none of this was developed in relation to real things to the extent that it was developed in the literary and painterly images of things in Rilke's lyrics, for example, or the still lifes of van Gogh.

Word and color are less tangible than an actual thing; for this reason they can express its spiritual essence very well, but only at the price of separating the thing itself from the artistic plane of the book or painting. The "lyricism of things" always turns up on the delimiting borderline of art: the lyrical is dematerialized, and the material is depersonalized. These are divergent extremes that cannot easily be mediated or combined. The lyrical meaning of an authentic and singular thing remains unrevealed. It may be transferred into words, colors, or photographic and cinematographic images, pulling away in the process from the thing itself, from its full, truthful, and irreplaceable presence. Or we may take a thing in and of itself, in all the wealth and variety of its potentials and plasticity, its decorative forms and visual symbolism, but in this process the thing pulls away from its own inner history, from the meanings accumulated in its former lives, "offstage," through its interactions with a person. For an artist working with "ready-made" objects, the decision to include, say, a chair in an installation does not take account of where the chair may come from; who has been seated on it, carrying on a conversation; how it may have been moved about to provide a better view of other people. For the artist all that matters is the construction and material of the chair.

To combine the personal importance and the everyday presence of things, to show, as far as possible, how these attributes are intertwined—this is the task of the lyrical museum. Here the spiritual life of the lyric "I" is not torn away from those concrete things in which it poured itself forth, concentrated its activity and its embodiment; nor is it dissolved in purely verbal or visual imagery. Furthermore, things are not torn away from their singular fate, from participation in the lives and concerns of the specific people among whom they acquired their "face." They are neither frozen in pure objectivity, nor transformed into material for graphic constructions. The words of each individual exhibitor, our "lyrical hero" in this case, come together with his things, as they mutually complete each other in a holistic work of art: a "verbject" (in Russian, *veshcheslov*), which should be recognized as a new genre in spiritual-material culture.

It is well known that twentieth-century history exerted considerable effort to disengage things from their meanings and to place man's surroundings in opposition to him. Twentieth-century art could not help reflecting this alienation in fearsome and pathetic images, in the sheen of things untouched like idols, and in the rot of things untouched like lepers. But while the store window and the dump are extreme points between which things move, they do not exhaust the proper essence—mobile, changeable, wandering—of any given thing. The path a thing traverses runs through the hands of people, through innumerable contacts with their meaning-engendering fates. Even if we accept that the store shelf is the point of a thing's origin, and the trash heap its final destination, still, the center and heart of the thing's existence is its stay in someone's home, broadly understood as the world inhabited by man. Here the thing may lose its cold glitter, but it doesn't fade into oblivion so long as the fingers whose touch dulls its shine keep it free of dust. It consists entirely of touches that invisibly carve out its essence. It is not at all their separateness, their counterposition to man that defines things, but rather the "contactability" that earmarks them for being touched, taken, carried. After all, many things have knobs and handles and are specifically structured for the human hand, almost as if they themselves reach out for someone. Such items as these, though their construction depends on machine work, express the warmth and essence of sculpting fingers; in the lyrical museum they are displayed as works of *everyday spiritual creation.*

Culture now faces the task of "dis-enchanting" things, of setting them free from estrangement and oblivion; in this undertaking, the *domestic* emerges as a vital social and cultural category, one that heralds the complete incorporation of things into body and soul, their full communion with our lives. Of course, the home can also be transformed into either a landfill or a warehouse (or even into both at once), but in that event, it ceases to be a home, a place where all things and creatures present belong together. In this sense, the lyrical museum is an experiment in the self-consciousness of *domestic culture,* which is deserving of the broadest display, and should be brought outside the boundaries of private practice into the larger world, so that the latter may benefit from following this prototype by becoming increasingly domestic.

A New Memoriality

In our time, the commercial value of a thing as an attractive "novelty" for consumers represents a normative significance that takes precedence over all its other values. The prominent role of the display window comes into play in this system of material culture as the point of origin from which things enter into life, sent off with the best wishes of advertising copy. The entire social complex of commercial signs serves to increase the status of novelty, emphasizing its practical superiority, its convenience, fashionability, reliability, and all manner of advantages. Methods for describing and recommending new things have been developed down to the minutest detail: outlines, annotations, instruction booklets, guarantees, trademarks, quality control slips, and etc., etc.

But any interpretation of those things that have served out their term is altogether lacking. For this we need a kind of "anti-display window," where used things could find shelter, and where appropriate descriptions and attestations could be attached to them—not of the advertising type, of course, but rather a lyrical, memorial kind of meditation. Here would be depicted not the product's price, but the life's worth of the thing, the meaning it acquired from people, over the course of time spent serving them. If so many approving and laudatory words can be found for unused things, then why can't we find words of understanding and sympathy for old things that have stood up to trials and given use to their owners, becoming kindred to them in the process?

Of course such "anti–display windows" could not be set up behind sparkling glass in well-trafficked areas, but a place could be found for them within the very house where the thing spent its life. Before relegating the aged thing to the attic or landfill, where it will ultimately mix in with dust and rubbish, dissolving into undifferentiated muck, why can't it be kept in a specially maintained memorial space in the home, like a part of one's life, once embodied and now passing away? If in the space of the display window each advertised model stands in its unique integrity, then how much more deserving of such dignity is the thing that has served out its usefulness? It is no longer just a standard or a type among hundreds of identical examples; it has become unique in its essence and fate, representing nothing other than itself. It might indeed prove worthwhile to keep such dear and deserving things hanging on the walls to give the room a dimension of depth, of "eternity," where time already-lived-through abides in a single space with the ongoing and the incipient.

I will attempt to describe the impression produced by a lyrical museum organized once in the Moscow apartment of my friends in 1984. The things that were hung all over the walls seemed suspended between life and death, as if frozen in endless expectation or in some kind of otherworldly service. They had left that part of the room devoted to active life, where they had once played a useful role, but had not gone beyond its walls into the useless clutter of storage, nor yet further, beyond the borders of the home, into a garbage dump. The wall thus became a particular kind of mute, impenetrable curtain between two worlds, from which departing things take a final look at what they're leaving behind. They had already lost the appearance of substance but retained sharp, sunken features that resembled faces, protruding from the surface of the wall like a memorial bas-relief. These sculptured masks looked into the space of the room upon their living doubles: a bottle looks down upon a bottle, a saucepan on a saucepan, a pair of glasses on a pair of glasses, as if trying to remind them of the most important thing in their existence. The flat surface of the wall is a spatial analogue for death; it cuts every thing into two sides, "this" and "that," baring the heart of the matter on an accompanying label, so that what was once just a "thing in itself" is now revealed to us in word traces on a magical plane.

Needless to say, the presence of such a museum on the wall lends a good deal of weight to the room, just as a case lends a sense of enclosure and value to any object it contains. When we place mirrors in a room, we attempt to close off the living space, directing the gaze inward to illuminate the soul, but the brilliant reflective surface leads only to the level of the empirical being of things, where they are splintered, changeable, elusive. Decrepit hardware hanging from the walls, on the other hand, can become a kind of mirror of the semantic eidos, reflecting the consistent and lasting essence of things. Looking into this depth, the whole room recognizes its prototype, shifting in time, so that together they may house a growing share of immortality. Such museums on the wall become mirrors of memory, capable of inspiring in each home a more respectful and less exploitative attitude toward things; they can help to overcome consumerism, which values only the new.

The very category of "memoriality" must now be viewed with due consideration for the changing status of things in an age of mass production of objects destined for consumption. Traditionally, a memorial museum assumes that a thing is longer-lived than a human being and can therefore be appointed to preserve his or her memory. This was the predominant situation in all previous epochs: one and the same thing—an armoire, a trunk, a book, a set of dishes—was used for several generations. In our epoch the relationship has been reversed: many generations of things can pass through a single human lifetime. The owner of useful things, still in their prime, buries his short-lived commodities at the landfill, replacing them with more fashionable and convenient items. This is a source of difficulty for those who wish to found memorial museums in contemporary society: there is a scarcity of things that fully reflect the life of their owner, that fully "answer" for him.

This represents a new sociohistorical phenomenon: it is no longer things that change ownership, it is owners that change things. The situation calls for a reevaluation of the traditional understanding of memoriality. Who is to preserve the memory of whom? Who will take the responsibility for bearing witness? In reducing the useful time span of things, we eliminate their burden of memory. In so doing, we place this burden on ourselves.

In that system of ephemeral and lasting values that is culture as a whole, an increasingly episodic, passing role is relegated to things. If at an earlier time our material surroundings represented the most stable, "immovable" elements of an existence, in which a person could leave brief traces, now it is human consciousness that has become far more long-acting, as it draws into itself a multitude of changing material conditions. We can say that a thing bequeathes the consciousness of its owner to another thing that comes after it, making consciousness a mechanism of continuity between them. As a given group of things subsides and casts off the load of meaningfulness and hereditary memory that it has borne over several generations, the difficult task of endowing culture with meaning and weight passes to personal memory.

A contemporary memorial museum, in contrast to a traditional one, may be characterized by the fact that things do not tell the story of a person they have survived; rather, a person tells the story of things that were somehow dear and close to him, so that these short-lived items should not be consigned to oblivion. That which is lasting assumes the burden of concern for the ephemeral, so that what has once entered the sphere of culture, may remain there as long as possible, if not forever. Along with memorial observances in which things traditionally preserve the memory of people, there should now be established observances whereby people, with a full sense of their responsibility toward culture, bear lyrical witness to and preserve the memory of things. Thus, a lyrical museum could also be called a memorial to things. Individual memory is the most important factor in creating a museum that displays in space the things memory has saved from time.

In all of this we are not calling for a renewal of the "antiquated," benevolently accepting attitude toward things with its unshakable consciousness of their meaningfulness as rooted in a traditional way of life. It is unlikely that our ancestors would have taken a notion to ponder intensively the things near at hand to them and to create some kind of memorial, but this is because the very homes they inhabited were, in fact, "memorials" of this kind.[8] A thing was possessed of meaning from the very beginning, insofar as it had been received from one's ancestors, and in the final analysis it had meaning by virtue of being passed on to one's heirs. This was a peaceful, epic-style appeasement, giving things their meaning without lyrical outbursts.

In our time these beginnings and endings have been disconnected; the ancestor's position has been usurped by the point of sale, while the heir's position is now the disposal site. But for that reason the midpoint becomes all the more significant, as that brief interval in which a person must create in personal experience the entire fate of a thing, compensating in the present for a lack of both past and future. Meaning is no longer accepted and passed on, it is created here and now, just as lyric takes the place of epic. The epic culture of things has broken down and is not apt to be resurrected, but in its place a new lyric culture is arising with its own psychological and aesthetic potentials. Because a thing is not originally one's own, the process of assimilating it can lead to failures, confronting us with faceless mechanical objects. A certain lyrical "daring," however, inevitably treads upon the ruptured epic linkages of things, bringing together at risk to itself the sundered ends and beginnings, as it creates a new, more dynamic and "uncertain" meaning along the borders of an encroaching meaninglessness and loss of memory, characteristic of objects with neither roots nor shoots. The great accumulation of things confined to realms outside of consciousness, whether they be vast stores of ready products or burying grounds for garbage, necessarily activates a compensatory cultural mechanism that counters with the intentional safekeeping of certain things in consciousness and for consciousness.

The Significance of Singularity

This type of safekeeping entails a far-reaching consideration of self-interest and even a sense of thrift, which Andrei Platonov accurately called the meagerness or thriftiness of empathy. The following characteristic passage from Platonov's work elucidates the aim of our project.

> Voshchev picked up the dried leaf and hid it away in a secret compartment of his bag, where he used to keep all kinds of objects of unhappiness and obscurity.
>
> "You had no meaning in life," Voshchev imagined to himself with meagerness of sympathy. "Lie here, I will learn wherefore you lived and perished. Since no one needs you, and you are straying about in the midst of the whole world, I will preserve and remember you."[9]

This bag—in which the hero stows things that have not yet obtained their own meaning in life, so as to bring them to consciousness and commit them to memory—is the prototype of the lyrical museum. Here we see that the human mind has a need to test even the smallest, most trivial thing to determine its meaningfulness; without this we cannot be at peace. Our contemporary situation, with its harsh questioning of the meaning of "unknown and orphaned" things, leads us to a problem that has troubled minds since time immemorial: the problem of cosmodicy. Can the world endure if so much as a single grain of dust falls "out of line," turns out to be inessential, unnecessary? Can a single antimeaning destroy, like an antiparticle, the rational mechanism of the universe? The world can only be justified for man in good conscience if everything it contains is neither random nor worthless. It would seem that there is little difference, whether a certain dry leaf exists in this world or not; this tiny problem, however, contains a decisive test for human understanding, which tests on such insignificant things as these the rationality or irrationality of the entire great Whole, thereby deciding whether to accept or reject it. Of course, it's not enough simply to "see through" a thing in one's mind; we have to pick it up, like Platonov's hero, carry it about in a bag and pass it through our lives, in order to somehow make it kin to us. In return, a single such "unfortunate and unknown object," healed through our saving and remembering, could become a blessed messenger of the deeper substantiality of everything that is.

A memorial to things may be seen as a potential experiment in cosmodicy, a justification of the world in its most minute components. That this is a collection of the unlavish things of unfamous people not only does not negate, but to a certain extent enhances the value of their meaningfulness. In order to comprehend the nature of matter, a physicist turns not to many-tonned chunks of it, but to its most minute particles. And so comprehension of the structure of meaning in the world also requires intent and detailed examination, microscopic penetration to the depths where large meanings disappear and the most minute ones are discovered. It is not in the fabulous Koh-i-noor diamond, nor in Napoleon's three-cornered hat, nor in a violin by Stradivarius, but in some little thread, a scrap of paper, a pebble, or a matchstick that the indivisible, "elementary" meaning of things is revealed. Investment of meaning in the smallest thing brings the greatest justification into the world.

Furthermore, the meaning that a thing acquires is gratefully returned to man, affirming anew that he himself does not exist at random: cosmodicy becomes a prologue to anthropodicy. To quote Platonov once again:

> Voshchev sometimes bent down and picked up a pebble, or other sticky bit of trash, and put it for safekeeping into his trousers. He was gladdened and worried by the nearly eternal presence of a pebble in the midst of clay, in the condensation of darkness; that meant that it had reason to be there, hence there was all the more reason for a person to live.[10]

Platonov's hero is one of those perspicacious eccentrics who come to know the measure of their own essential place in the world through a serious, painstaking sense of brotherhood with the lower forms of existence. A little stone that reveals some kind of "reason" as it is lifted from the earth becomes the foundation of man's hope to himself be justified, time and again, in a world of singularly justified entities. And so we see a mutual approach to one another of man and things, along with an increase of meaning. Perhaps the main thing that a visitor should derive from the lyrical museum is not just a new sensation of closeness to the objects that surround him, but also a new level of self-assurance, a kind of metaphysical energy, strengthening him in the knowledge that his existence is not worthless.

This author knows from experience that to give meaning to a single thing is a very difficult task: it is singularity itself that defies definition in thoughts and words, because these are intended rather for comprehending the general. It is easier to comprehend the significance of an entire class or type of item than of a single representative: "foliage" or "stone," rather than *this* little leaf or pebble. As we draw nearer to the singular, attempting to ask it, not a functional, but a philosophical question of worldview: "Why are you alive?" we clearly feel how this question is grounded in the secret of all creation. Only along with it or in its stead can the singular make an answer.

It is well known that in the course of its historical development, abstract thought ascends to the concrete level. It may well be that thinking in singularities is the highest level of ascent. In this process the general categories that lie at the basis of any theoretical contemplation are not canceled out, but are tested in the movement toward an ever more complete, multifaceted and integrated re-creation of the thing as a synthesis of the infinite multitude of abstract definitions. Logical abstractions, which over the course of historical development raised human reason above the empiricism of simple sensations, seem to return once again to their point of departure—the singular thing—in order to reveal within it the condensed wealth of all human culture and universal meaning. The singular "this" is most directly connected with the one, the "all," in the same way as the elementary particles (and not mountains or whales) reveal the unity of material creation. Thus we find reason to hope that realogy will come to comprehend reality, not only in terms of general concepts, and not even in concrete images, but in actual, singular things, finding the most excellent means of describing and interpreting the meanings of countless "this-nesses" that surround us, leading directly to the unitary foundation of being.

In the meantime, it is obvious that since the singular does exist, it is essential and meaningful. To "think" it is difficult, to comprehend it fully is no doubt impossible: thought is always deflected toward the abstract, bypassing "this" and encompassing a whole class, type, or variety instead. But the mere approach to a singular thing, with its lasting and yet unrepeatable meaning, gives us the important and encouraging knowledge that nothing, not even the smallest and most insignificant, is doomed to pass away without a trace.[11]

Experiments in the Description of Things

Let us imagine how a lyrical museum might look. Its physical space is divided into a series of partially enclosed cells, separated by opaque or semi-opaque partitions, not unlike rooms in a many-chambered house.[12] In each of these "rooms" one participant sets up his own exhibit and hangs up sheets of paper with a commentary on each item—this is his personal space. The things displayed are authentic, taken directly "from life," and each is accompanied by a lyrical meditation-description. Each of the small enclosures, constituting the exhibition space (not only like a house, but also like a labyrinth where one can and even should lose one's way at least a bit), is intended to be occupied and viewed by only one visitor at any one time. The nature of lyrical space does not allow for broad expansion of the exhibition, simultaneously attracting the attention of all visitors to a certain spot; on the contrary, it demands individual concentration, deepening the contact between the viewer and those items, on which his gaze is fixed. The encounter with things takes place one-on-one, in the spirit of "singularity" that makes itself felt in both the intellectual and the spatial approach to things, a narrow yet in-depth approach, that makes its way to the heart.

It is in no way mandatory, and indeed scarcely possible, for a viewer to look at all of the exhibits and read all of the commentaries on a single visit. It's actually more important that he should feel the unencompassability of this multifaced and many-personalitied environment, stretching out all around him. A lyrical museum does not assume the creation of special items for exhibition; rather it re-creates an authentic reality of things that always reaches beyond the horizon of perception. All things lie together in one field of vision only at the warehouse or the dump, in the overgrown and deteriorated remnants of a bygone, epic panorama of the world. In the domestic realm, one point of view captures only a small portion of reality at any one time, which is why this viewpoint must be mobile, so as to follow a path whose course cannot be determined in advance. One can wander through the labyrinth-house for quite some time, everywhere coming upon unfamiliar exhibits or coming up to familiar ones from an unexpected angle. The inner world of each personality is open before us, but only from the point of view at which it is closed to all others. In this way the museum creates an image of an infinitely large and voluminous world, in which there is no one door common to all, only numerous entrances, and in which no one can meet everyone, but each can meet with each other.

Within the individual exhibits the most widely varying lyric focus is possible, including a meaningful violation of the lyric mood, which also tends to emphasize the overall focus of the museum. One may display detailed commentaries on nonexistent or absent items. Items can be "provocational"; that is, intended for use in some type of action whose result will make the item fit its description as an exhibit. Descriptions may be either of the everyday variety or highly philosophical, either serious or humorous, precisely corresponding to the item displayed or emphatically and grotesquely not corresponding to it. Ideally, participants in the museum should include persons of various professions, ages, and interests, so that the world of things in which we live and which lives in us may take shape to the fullest possible extent.

Below, I offer to the reader's attention two commentaries on my own display items as experiments in the description of things.[13] I would like to lead the reader into the atmosphere of this imaginary museum, insofar as a text can accomplish this in the absence of the actual things intended for display. Needless to say, these descriptions should be accepted in accordance with their own laws, although they appear here within an article, rather than in their proper "lyrical museum" genre. As an introduction I offer the following words of Montaigne, a worthy epigraph to the entire lyrical museum: "I speak my mind freely on all things, even on those which perhaps exceed my capacity . . . and so the opinion I give of them is to declare the measure of my sight, not the measure of things."[14]

A Fantik *(Candy wrapper)*

What is there to say about this candy wrapper bearing the sonorous title of *"Bylina"* (Epic Song), that somehow wound up stranded on my desk among much lengthier papers and books full of import and intended for serious reading? Who will hear this solitary word, shouted out in haste, but promptly, abashedly cut off? This minute, shabby scrap of paper, not even of a moment's, only of an instant's usefulness, with a millenial memory: bylina!

Things have their own service entrance and ladder of social status that leads them to a human being, and a candy wrapper has its place very near the bottom. Pitiful is the fate of things that serve only other things: all manner of wrappings and packing materials, boxes and sacking that don't have their own value, but merely clothe more important articles, deserving of preservation. But even in this secondary category a candy wrapper takes last place. A box or packet of some kind can always be reused in its original function, but a dock-tailed wrapper, emptied and unfolded, has reached the point of offering no further use to anyone.

Nonetheless, there is something attractive about it, something that a person can recognize as a tiny but significant part of his own fate. We see before us two bits of paper, one white and the other colorful, like under- and outerwear, a T-shirt and a dress shirt for a piece of candy. It's as if a general law of multilayered coverings were in effect here: the inner layer is colorless, repels dirt, and is intended mainly to protect purity, while the outer one is gaudy and bright, intended to attract the eye. (It is also possible to have a middle layer that would be the most substantial and protective: among human coverings this would be a coat of mail; among candy wrappers, a layer of foil.) It would seem that these two functions are opposed—to enclose and to attract—but together they shape the essence of a covering, through which a thing at once reaches into the depths and emerges onto the surface, abides within and also outside itself. The luxuriant double—and, moreover, triple—wrap gives a piece of candy the alluring and mysterious air, both challenging and unattainable, proper to any kind of sweetness. Thus, the many layers of the candy wrapper indicate the presence inside it of something secret and tempting, transforming the process of unwrapping into an extented, sweet anticipation of something that otherwise would just be swallowed, quickly and crudely. A candy wrapper is the sweet within the sweet, the covering of its physical nature, but also the kernel of its psychological content. "Sweet" is here removed from the class of simple sensations of taste into the realm of internal states of being, of expectation, a kind of languishing. It would seem that children sense this more sharply than adults and therefore save candy wrappers not only for the sake of their colorful appearance, but also because they are an extract of sweet expectancy that the tongue can never know.

Yet simultaneously this "pure," nonphysiological sweetness does find expression on the tongue: in the name written on the wrapper. If the paper is the material covering of sweetness, then the name of the candy is an expression of its "ideal" meaning. This one is called "Bylina," but many other names—"Masque," "Muse," "Enchantress," "Kara-Kum," "Lake Ritsa," "Southern Night," "Evening Bells," "Flight," "Firebird," "Golden Cockerel"—are also unusually beautiful and expressive of a fairy-tale quality that leads us away to distant lands, exciting our imagination. The candy's sweetness seems to be not of this world; it must be sought beyond the thrice times nine lands, in the kingdom of seductive dreams. The name on the wrapper corresponds precisely to its concealing and attracting essence, in that it seems to contain an alluring secret. It is surely not by chance that *fantik* ("wrapper") sounds so much like "fantasy" and "phantom": there is not more than one word inscribed on such a tiny bit of paper, but it almost always belongs to the world of imagination. A *fantik* must be the minimal page of a fantasy, and a candy is a double fairy tale, known *in* the tongue of the dreamer and *on* the tongue of the eater.[15] The "sweet" fantasy brings itself down to the immediate material reality of that tongue, whose idealizing capacity is designated by the word on the *fantik*.

And so two properties of the tongue, diverging to the far reaches of culture and nature, coincide once again, like the two sides of a piece of paper, recognizing in a candy wrapper—in this little bilingual dictionary that translates from the tongue of the speaker to the tongue of the eater—their forgotten kinship with each other. The covering for a candy is the tongue's address to itself: its flesh addresses its sign system, by way of conversing with itself and reestablishing the unity of its abilities. It's not such a small thing, this candy wrapper: in it the most abstract dream and the most sensory reality come together as nature enters into culture and teaches us to cultivate the beautiful on the tip of our tongue.

A Kaleidoscope

Only once did I gaze long and hard into this toy kaleidoscope. It was at a difficult and weighty moment of my life. Perhaps for that reason I came to associate with it certain general thoughts, which I would like to share.

The most random combinations of bits of glass reveal proportion and purposefulness, when they are reflected in the mirrored purity of a kaleidoscope. Order, after all, is nothing other than symmetry: randomness becomes a pattern when it is repeated on the left and right, above and below. The kaleidoscope's magic is this momentary ordering of any chance caprice, its transformation into a law, in accordance with which an entire iridescent and crumbly world takes shape. Through the dark tube we stare as through a metaphysical microscope at the mysterious essence of life, perceiving order in the teeming movements.

The selfsame stone that falls from a hill into a valley in Tiutchev's poem "Problème," cast down by its own will or perhaps by an unseen hand, is here broken up into many little stones that give an answer in their contours to the eternal question of free will. The future lies before me. I am free to become one thing or another in it, to act like this or like that: everything depends upon a free decision. But no sooner is my act performed, than it turns out that I could not have done otherwise, that an entire chain of preceding actions led up to this singular act and made of it an essential link in a life progression. In the moment of transition from past to future, at the point of the present, a fatal leap "from freedom to necessity" takes place, and utter arbitrariness suddenly reveals itself as providence.

It is as if mirrors were set up in the depths of creation, lending symmetry and order to our every act as soon as it is performed. Any one piece of glass may turn up any which way, but with each turn it reveals the stunning wholeness and meaningfulness of the entire, consummate picture of the world. In any design once obtained, it is too late to make a replacement of parts, to poke another bit of glass in with the rest, out of time with the multiply affirmed and "symmetrized" selection. Past and future are like mirror-covered walls around the present in which anything can happen, but the whole of life changes with each happening, as if a new design of meaning passes through time, although life remains whole and integral at every moment, just as a picture in the kaleidoscope cannot possibly be asymmetrical, or taken in isolation.

The law of the continued wholeness of the present, in all its free and mobile fulfillment, is one of the most basic in life. A man may commit a crime or sacrifice himself; in that very instant all his prior life and all his life to come is rebuilt in a new, finished and strictly shaped configuration. Our every act newly crystallizes not only the forms of the future, but also those of the past; a symmetrical formation extends from it on all sides.

True, the sides of the kaleidoscope are not so pure and bright as the triangle at its center, and the reflections upon them are more blurred and distorted, the closer they come to the opening, until their illusory nature becomes obvious. But, after all, in life itself, in broad daylight, within the strict confines of everyday consciousness, only the present appears to us clearly, while its symmetrical reflections grow dimmer and more ghostly in the far reaches of the past and future; in this final, indiscernable distance, Someone looks on these myriad details with an all-seeing eye.

A word of warning for those who wish to take a look into the kaleidoscope: it has gotten slightly broken in the course of children's play. The outer glass, which protects the eye, is missing. Between the inner walls a blue particle has gotten loose, so be careful that it doesn't fall into your eye; don't tilt the kaleidoscope too sharply. There is no guarantee that other bits of glass won't also fall out. There is no impassable boundary between the illusion that delights the eye and the reality that can injure it.

Thing as Word

The texts presented above are intended to be perceived along with and in relation to the items described in them. And here arises the final question: Is such a doubling of the word by the thing really necessary? Anyone can easily imagine a candy wrapper or a child's kaleidoscope, so why put the actual object alongside—almost *in*side—the verbal description, where the reader's gaze has to stumble over it continually? If we endeavored above to establish why it is necessary to endow things with meaning, then in conclusion we shall attempt to understand why the thing itself is indispensable to meaning.

As a rule, text exists so that the reality it describes should not necessarily have to exist immediately alongside it. A sign is the replacement, the substitute for a thing. If a thing is presented *along* with the sign that refers to it, this means that its being is incomparably more meaningful than its meaning, and is important as such. In the lyrical museum, words make an intense effort to express the essence of things in order to show that in the final analysis this essence lies outside, beyond words. In this sense words strive to point out the thing itself.

And now an author has said all that can be expressed, and a viewer has read all that can be perceived in words. There remains only the thing itself, resting wordlessly on its stand. And now it is possible that in the uncapturable part of a second the most important event will occur: the inner contact of the viewer with the silent thing which is more than all the words that have been said about it. Now its own being continues speaking to you and acting upon you. In its silence and immobility some sort of special, unutterable word comes through, an inner movement arises that seems to rock the layers of space enveloping it—but even if we should succeed in describing all of this, the thing would still move away, beyond the framework of description, to turn up again on the far side of all words and all ideal representations as pure being, irreducible to anything but itself.

The touch of this being yields an incomparable joy, no weaker in force than aesthetic joy, but different in quality. In it we enjoy not the creative transformation of a thing, its turning into something else, as in a painting, but precisely the presence of the thing in its basic "is-ness," in all the authenticity of its own existence, which communicates with ours directly and without mediation, expanding the volume and strengthening the basis of our own. The "is" of a thing rings with affirmation of our "am." In distinction from aesthetic joy, this joy can be called existential, in that it embraces the existence of things so fully that it does not require their reembodiment in imagery.

It would be incorrect, however, to suppose that such perception of the primary truth and self-value of things comes to us in and of itself, without the preliminary work of their meaningful and verbal assimilation. Despite the primacy of being in significance, it is ultimate in sequence. If we glance at a thing simply and without "mediation," we will merely see its poor objectness, reduced without remainder to some practical function. Chair for sitting, cup for drinking, key for opening the door, candy wrapper for wrapping candy: the significance of the thing in this empirical context is reduced to a tautology and identified with a use. The contemplation of a thing on this "first" level is unbearably trivial and dull; one must simply pick them up and use them.

As we endow the thing with meaning by creating its conceptual description, we transfer it to a second, deeper level, where it emerges from the state of self-equivalence, not as tautology, but as metaphor. The thing is included in a verbal context, in which the direct function of its being receives a generalized, figurative meaning. The function of a candy wrapper in covering sweetness or of a kaleidoscope in entertaining the eye with multicolored designs receives an interpretation on the scale of personal experience and fate, in the language of philosophy, psychology, morality. On this level the lyrical museum represents a set of texts that derive, "draw out" all possible meanings from things—historical, biographical, symbolic, associative meanings. But the final task is to "return" all these meanings to the thing, to pour them back into their source.

It is only after the thing has been removed from the narrow confines of functionality into conceptual open spaces that the third level of its existential depth can begin to emerge. Here the thing is neither used as an object nor interpreted as a sign, but fulfills itself as being, in all the fullness of meanings enclosed and dissolved in its objectness. All that is proper to it, all that has been drawn out of the life around it and laid into it by thought, is *now here,* pointing to its presence. On the third level the significance of the thing is no longer tautological or metaphorical; rather, it can be called mythological, in that the thing now becomes what it means and, moreover, *means what it is.*

This is why, on the third level, a thing cannot be made to yield up its final meaning; in so doing the meaning of its being would be lost. One can approach the task endlessly and laboriously, but in the end we will meet that selfsame thing, which does not give up its full meaning and therefore cannot be annulled in its own being. No matter how lyrically penetrating or philosophically significant the text, it must yet include at the limit of its comprehension the whole, actual thing, which alone manifests the higher degree of concreteness that thought aspires to. This thing will become, not an object, but an act of thought. It will enter the text with the rights of a fundamental, axiomatically undefinable concept that will be brought into the definitions of other concepts. Filled with meaning to the brim of its essence, the thing begins to think by means of its existence. To indicate "this," means to employ the most authoritative and indisputable documentation.

And so a memorial to things is necessary not only because things require meaning and interpretation, but also because they can never be interpreted to the end. If that were possible, then the most important part of the memorial could be left out: the things themselves. This dialectic of necessity and impossibility unfolds within the exhibition, where words need things as much as things need words.

Usually it is words that speak, while things keep silent. But when words approach the boundaries of silence, this silence of things begins to speak for itself. The greatest challenge is to find the words that will set off the thing itself as its own singular, sought-for, and irreplaceable word. Only then does it become itself—a message (*vest'*), a voice sounding in silence, in answer to all the words uttered on its behalf.

In conclusion—a few more excerpts from the lyrical museum, but this time rather than descriptions of individual things, some observations on the wisdom of things, the depth of content in their messages addressed to people. Rather than attracting us as a source of riches and external plenty, the world of things can be our reminder of a long forgotten bliss.

> First of all, a thing is a lesson in humility and acceptance of the world. "Things are meek. On their own, they never do evil. They are sisters to the spirits. They receive us, and upon them we place our thoughts, which have need of them, as fragrances have need of flowers to settle on. . . . I, who could not bend my soul before men, prostrated it before things. A brightness emanated from them . . . like the vibration of friendship." So wrote the French poet Francis Jammes in "Des Choses" (1889).

Try to sense in yourself this tiny paradise, where each and every thing harkens from beginning to end to the voice of its creator. Refusing no request, it nonetheless keeps faith with its appointed purpose; a cup refuses drink to no one, but it will not allow itself to be used for wiping hands. Man has not yet "matured" to such a point of faithfulness to his own purpose coupled with responsiveness to all that surrounds him. He is harsher on others and softer on himself, when it should be quite the other way around. From things he can learn the perfect art: to combine infinite obedience to each who needs him with infinite devotion to the purpose placed in him by the creator.

If the greatest temptation for profit and gain comes from things, then the greatest lesson in renunciation of these vices comes from them as well. Things, like saints, bestow everything they have upon us without recrimination, keeping nothing back for themselves. Wretched and poor, they fulfill the commandment "give of what you have," literally and completely. All that we have is made up of things, while they have absolutely nothing. Things are not able to want or to take anything from us, since, after all, nothing can be given or taken but things themselves. An animal may have a den and a plant the soil, but property can have nothing at all. It is the truest have-not. In giving themselves to us as possessions, things teach us not to possess.

The human calling is not to amass wealth in things, but neither to refuse them altogether. Rather we are called to be with them and share in their qualities of silence, lack of malice, impassivity, freedom from envy. People could resolve the problem of property in a new way: not by sharing things out among themselves, but by sharing the very fate of things. In other words, by taking a vow of poverty even as we take things into our property: by becoming poor, as they are, for the sake of our spirit and thereby enriching ourselves. Our ownership of things should not be thought to give us unlimited power over them; we are only their stewards or, in the best instance, the ones who help them manifest their purpose. This means we must come to see in the worldly luxury of things a manifestation of their genuinely monastic poverty and readiness for self-sacrifice. There is no way out in obtaining and distributing things, but there can be one in sharing their poor state and their obedience, and in taking a lesson from them in giving service to people. For each thing there is a special service, to which its life is unstintingly devoted. He who loves things for the poverty in which they abide, rather than for the wealth they provide, grasps the wisdom of love.

A plant is more quiet and obedient than an animal, a thing is more quiet and obedient than a plant. The feeling of peace and quietude we experience in the forest or field must surely be still more profound in a gathering of things. We should conduct ourselves in the presence of things as we do at the bedside of a sleeping child, listening in silence. Some people become attached to the materiality of things with all their hearts; others spurn this attitude as materialism. Is not materiality just another name for fate, that things accept and bear far better than humans do?

All that a man has is taken from things—to things remains only pure being. In measuring himself against things, which have nothing except being, man can achieve authentic humility. Passing down the entire path of evolution, he returns to the place where not even a plant can be.

"Man is the measure of all things," said Protagoras. But it is just as true that a thing is the measure of all humans.

Rilke wrote that God is the thing of things, and boundless presence. At the limits of minutiae, the same pureness of being is reached that exists at the limits of greatness, and the one serves as a model for the other. No one is denigrated so much as things are, and no one is so blessed as these "little ones," with a blessedness that man can never know. Even a monk, according to Rilke, is too insignificant, but still not small enough to have the likeness of a thing before God.

The world of things is a monastery, sunken in silence and patience, where people come and go as pilgrims, learning obedience.

And so we see that it is not only for use that things are given to man, but also for learning. We learn from those who serve us. When we receive something good from things, we should perceive it as an act of generosity and as an injunction to carry on the service in the human world. Only thus can a thing reveal its hidden nature as a meek, voiceless Word, tirelessly teaching us.

The lyrical museum is a project born within the framework of conceptualism and at the same time leading beyond it. Conceptualism revealed the vacancy of reality standing beyond words. The next step brings us to a realization of the vacancy of words themselves, beyond which stands the silent reality of singular things. The lyrical museum brings us out into trans-semiotic space where signs designate the limits of their own contingent nature and point to something external to themselves, something uncondi-tionally existent.

Thus, there occurs a self-exhaustion and self-erasure of the postmodern paradigm that focuses on the reality of signs in their differing from each other. But if difference is the constructive principle of sign systems then it should include the possibility of something differing from signs them-selves. This is precisely what is now radically reconstructing post-Soviet Russian culture, where conceptualism, the boundless play of signs, gives way to a new feeling of authenticity that might be defined as the realm of singularity (ungeneralizability) and silence (unspokenness).

Some forty years of predominance of sign systems (since the mid-1950s) in the self-consciousness of Western culture and in the methodology of the humanities is not only drawing to an end; it is now being understood as a necessary movement beyond the bounds of sign systems. We have no other means of talking about the world than through words or signs, but in post-modern space signs bare their own contingent nature, emphasizing it and thereby implying the possibility of an existence external to themselves. Postmodernism was a powerful warning that signs are only signs and should not be confused with reality. But from this it follows that reality should also not be confused with signs. Reality is the conceivable limit of all sign differences, the most radical of them all: the point of crossover not from one sign to another but from sign systems as such to that which lies beyond them.

Needless to say, this "beyond" can only be designated, but in so doing, it is precisely the trans-semiotic existence that is designated. At the limit of its contingency the sign opens a door to the existential realm, indicating the boundary of postmodern semiotic relativism. To follow the sign means to overstep the limits of the sign. Postmodernism was a necessary introduction to this realm of wordless singular existences: self-criticism of language served as a starting point for the movement of culture beyond language. The lyrical museum is an experiment in reading things, so that the signs for things are gradually replaced by things themselves, as the ultimate and maximally accurate signs of themselves. The chain of signs closes on that which is not sign.

This is no longer the naive realism that believed in a transparency of signs, in the truth of signifieds, but an experienced realism that doubts the correspondence between language and reality. This is a reality understood as transcendent to language and comprehensible only through its radical difference from language. Although we cannot get along without language for comprehending reality, we must use language precisely to the extent of its noncorrespondence with reality, as a series of self-unmasking speech acts that bare their own semiotic contingency.

In other words, reality is restored to its rights, but no longer as something positively denoted by language; rather it is the self-negation of language, revealing its own constructed limits and lapsing into silence as it approaches that of which it speaks. Postmodernism may be seen as the negative, apophatic stage of development of Western culture, as the epoch of its linguistic self-consciousness, beyond which opens a space of nonlinguistic existence. The lyrical museum is a world of nonreproducible reality in which the object of perception (a thing) is just as singular as the subject of perception (a personality).

CHAPTER 9 · Culture—Culturology—Transculture

For the past two decades, the concepts of postmodernism, poststructuralism, posthistory, and postindustrialism have dominated the theoretical scene in the West. I would like to suggest that this "post-" paradigm itself may now be a thing of the past. The present era, which seems to have begun with the collapse of the Berlin Wall in 1989, needs to be redefined, probably in terms of "proto-" rather than "post-."[1]

As far as theory and the arts are concerned, the twentieth century began well before the year 1900, and the twenty-first century may be under way already. One of the major factors that will determine its cultural identity is the idea of pluralism, which has gained recognition throughout the world, acquiring particular importance in the former Soviet Union. Paradoxically, the worldwide dissemination of pluralism has served to break down its character as a specifically Western, liberal idea, while also serving to revive the value of cultural unity or integrity. We live in a more pluralistic world, but it is a *single* world, which was previously divided into East and West (along with other internal divisions as well).

Moreover, the type of pluralism that predominated in Western culture of the 1970s and 1980s contained strong elements of relativism, and tended to ignore or even undermine the very notion of unity. Some postmodern thinkers have theorized "culture" as something specific to each separate nation, race, gender, age group, and so on. Now that a pluralistic worldview has increasingly come to prevail from Moscow to Berlin and, hopefully, also to Beijing and Havana, the promising perspectives of transcultural human identity become ever more tangible. To define the patterns of this new unity based on pluralistic values should be, in my view, the most immediate aim of the contemporary humanities. (If the reader will kindly bear with me in the more or less simultaneous exposition of various aspects of a few key ideas, I will come to a definition of what I mean by "transculture" after first focusing on more basic notions.)

The notion of "proto-unity" emphasizes the positive values of spiritual "totality" that were so monstrously perverted by Eastern totalitarianism. The concepts of "organic collectivism" (*sobornost'*) and "integrative knowledge" (*tsel'noe znanie*)[2] have long been intrinsic to traditional Russian culture, so that it was almost natural for the political authorities to exploit these concepts in pursuing their own ends. It is not surprising that one and the same set of ideas may be pressed into the service of essentially incompatible philosophies if we recall, for example, that Russian intellectuals of diverse persuasions have always argued for the inner unification of a human being's various capacities. How will this essentially Eastern tenet be assimilated into the proto-unity of future civilization?

Furthermore, one must question whether the multiple cultural types—ethnic, local, sexual, professional, that are emerging in the United States as well as postcommunist Russia and many other places—are really self-sufficient, or do they depend upon one another to provide the foundation for a future cultural unity? How can diverse cultural identities merge without relinquishing their individual peculiarities?

These problems have been posed in the past by German romanticists, American transcendentalists, and Russian religious thinkers, and now, on the eve of the twenty-first century, they regain their vital significance. Not only multicultural, but transcultural consciousness promises to be a defining characteristic of this new age, as numerous existing cultures search for the broadest possible framework to shape their interactions. This search calls into question such conventional assumptions as "East and West," and "integration and pluralism," which have often been distorted and interpreted as polar opposites. A theoretical model is needed that will (1) disentangle the concepts of "totality" and "totalitarianism," (2) free pluralism from indifferent or cynical relativism, and (3) demonstrate how pluralism and totality need not be construed as contradictory values.

My primary focus will be the formation of a mentality I call "transcultural consciousness," as it has evolved in Russia over the course of the past twenty-some years. In conclusion I will also draw a number of parallels with the American concept of multiculturalism.

Culture and Civilization

Although the question of culture and civilization may seem to be long out of date, it has arisen anew in contemporary Russia. The crucial, transitional state of our culture today suggests that this is not merely a question of shifting phases in a process of intracultural evolution, but one of much larger scope. Perhaps we are witnessing the birth of a new type of culture from the womb of Soviet civilization. Therefore, it may be useful to recall the historical correlation of these two global concepts as well as the differences between them.

According to Oswald Spengler, civilization is the twilight and decline of culture, a time when governmental and technocratic mechanisms equalize all specific ways of life on a mass scale, eventually supplanting traditional cultural forms of organic spiritual activity. Spengler wrote that "civilization is consummation. It follows culture, just as completion follows commencement, as death follows life and as rigidity follows formation. . . . It is the inevitable end; all cultures come to the state of civilization with a deep, internal necessity."[3]

However, another vector or route of evolution may be just as valid. Russian and American history demonstrate that the opposite of Spengler's process is also possible: culture can be born from civilization. In the United States of the nineteenth century, there existed a powerful bourgeois-democratic civilization that had achieved high technological and economic developmemt, while remaining almost destitute in terms of culture, importing all of its viable forms, genres and so on from Europe (with a few exceptions). The appearance of American *culture,* as an original, spiritually rooted, national organism capable of exerting worldwide influence, is a fact of the twentieth century, determined after the end of the First World War. The same is true of Russia. Here, the eighteenth century was a time of intensive development of civilized institutions under the influence of West European models and spurred by Peter the Great's reforms. The resulting Russian civilization was a weighty edifice that pressed down upon a friable and unstable soil. Only during the following century, beginning in the 1820s, did our civilization manage to put down real roots into this national soil and thereby develop a unique modern Russian culture achieved through suffering. Alexander Herzen's well-known observation expresses this very idea: one hundred years after Peter's reforms, Russia answered with the dazzling phenomenon of Pushkin. In this view, culture becomes a nation's answer through self-development to the challenge of other nations' civilizations.

Spengler's analysis may be more appropriate to those organic cultures that developed on firm national soil, with consistent ethnic characteristics. According to this model, such cultures as those of India, China, and Western Europe gradually degenerate into civilizations. But the opposite process would seem to characterize regions that have fallen under strong foreign influences. In those places where civilization has intruded from the outside, where it appears borrowed or amalgamated, as in America or Russia, it may actually precede the development of culture. Here, civilization evolves into culture as a natural extension of its own ripening and demise.

In those nations where the cycle of development proceeds from an already civilized condition, characterized by the ascendancy of social and political interests, the central ideas of citizenship and the state, culture represents the twilight of this world, in whose dusk a multitude of secret, intimate, spiritual worlds take on new form. The civilized "day," with its hustle and bustle of activity, has faded, and in its wake, rays disperse in complex patterns in all directions, refracting varied and fantastic hues, the blossoms of colors in decline: the wealth of obscure cultural metamorphoses spawned from a once clear and predictable day. Everything earthly has already been claimed, and everything historical has been achieved, so as civilization approaches its mysterious end, shrouded by dusk, it regains the transcendental vision and intuition of the beyond that belongs to culture. As Hegel loved to repeat, "The Owl of Minerva flies out in the dusk."

Each civilization feeds on an idea of history and progress that is eventually exhausted over the course of time, until it inaugurates a golden age of metaphysical ideas. As it lives out its planned existence, civilization eventually overruns the time granted for its own fulfillment. After coming to an end, civilization continues to exist in an afterlife that turns out to be culture. In realizing its own finality in an epoch of decline, civilization acquires the sharpened night vision characteristic of culture. It generates a vision of the next world, as its sensitivity to the final questions of existence grows more acute. As a prevailing sphere of civilized activity, politics gives way to religion, philosophy, and art. Thus, over the course of the last century, the "twilight" of Saint Petersburg civilization (from Nicholas I to Nicholas II, from Pushkin to Blok) generated the striking phenomenon of Russian classical culture, as creative intuition was intensified by the feeling of a growing crisis in social relations. Culture is the dusk of civilization, the fermentation of distilled liquid, and the conversion of water to wine—a miracle of transfiguration.

The most important moment in the transition from civilization to culture is the eruption of an internal split, not unlike an individual's ability to see him- or herself from without. With very rare exceptions (primarily in the work of Radishchev and, in part, Derzhavin),[4] Russian civilization of the eighteenth century was monolithic, devoid of the organic "defects" of self-reflection. Only in the 1820s did the ruling class split in two, giving rise to political opposition, in the form of Decembrism, and the psychology of the "Outsider," in the form of "superfluous people."[5] As a result of this internal split in the nobility and, hence, in the social foundations of this civilization, the remarkable culture of nineteenth-century Russia was created.

Thus, culture is civilization that has realized its end and embraced its own limit in the perspectives of self-destruction: political opposition, economic crisis, environmental catastrophe, or a cultural metalanguage capable of using "civilized" language in a practice of self-analysis or self-critique. The feelings of pain and death at work within civilization express its potential for becoming culture. We do not need to hide from ourselves, to artificially dull the pain, to resist the coming metamorphosis. Civilization must die so that from the shell of this voracious, metallically monotonous caterpillar that has sunk into the state of hibernation, immobility and pupation, an immortal soul may suddenly emerge: culture, the butterfly of the night.

A decisive indication of culture's ability to reflect upon itself is the formation of a specific discipline that unlike all others, encompasses the entire culture as its integral object. This is what gradually arose in Russia in the 1970s and 1980s under the name of "culturology."

What Is Culturology?

The closest English equivalent of "culturology" is no doubt the term "cultural studies." The contemporary Russian meaning, however, conveys the essential concept of a whole, indivisible discipline that cannot be reduced to a number of special studies. The object of study in this case is culture as the *integral* system of various cultures—national, professional, racial, sexual, etc.

Since the postcommunist culture of a newly emerging Russian state has only recently been born from "Soviet civilization," culturology long remained a blank spot on the map of the Russian humanities. What was termed the "theory of culture" in the Soviet Union was taught to future librarians and club workers: the theory of political management of cultural affairs and the administrative organization of its institutions. Yet politics is one of the constitutive parts of culture and is itself subject to culturological analysis and justification.

The poorly developed state of our culturology by no means implies a dearth of outstanding culturologists. It is sufficient to mention such names as Mikhail Bakhtin, Aleksei Losev, Sergei Averintsev, Georgy Gachev, Iury Lotman, Viacheslav Ivanov, Vladimir Toporov, and Vladimir Bibler. But such is the paradox of our newborn culture: the presence of very gifted writers does not necessarily make a great literature, and the presence of gifted scholars does not guarantee a high level of scholarly research. In the same way, culturology presupposes a social mode of thought, action and ideas that cannot be enacted through the efforts of individual thinkers working in isolation. It is not surprising that all of our culturologists are "migrants" from other, more specific fields of study—most often philology, literary criticism, and the general history of art—who "illegally," at their own risk, have overstepped the boundaries of their narrow disciplines. But the question remains: When will it be possible for culturology to develop on the basis of its own object of study, on the scale of an all-encompassing system of knowledge? This integral area requires specialization in its initial stages, but at the present point in time, we must have *specialists in the universal.* Only in this way can the universal take its place amid the many faces of particularity and begin the work of transforming and synthesizing them. Today we need culturologists not only from the fields of ancient philology, general Slavistics, or the history of Russian literature, but from culturology as such.

The fact that culturology could not exert a tangible influence on the development of "Soviet culture" reflected the latter's arrogance and one-dimensionality. Official culture resisted intimate scrutiny or comparison with other cultures, claiming for itself a kind of superhistorical and supercultural status. It failed to develop the need or capacity for self-reflection, and it is precisely this that constitutes culturology. For many decades, Soviet civilization assumed the right to judge and not be judged, as it described itself in a language of evaluations without objective concepts, which it denigrated as "ideologically harmful and alien." It did not need culturology but rather "culture-apology," and so it lost the true attributes of culture, which needs a zone of distancing, nonparticipatory, or alternative thought.

As Russian culture gradually revives from the self-hypnosis and paralysis induced by the Soviet state's delusions of grandeur, it becomes what it always should have been: *only* culture and for this very reason, *truly* culture— a realm of active, objectified, and multifaceted freedom, which characterizes the individual's attitudes as well, in terms of the freedom to accept or reject various cultural forms, to participate or to decline participation. The influence of culturology is now free to grow, since it represents our culture's self-determination, including its ability for self-criticism, self-denial, and the formation of various countercultures. Indeed, countercultures become possible only within the context of a highly developed culture, as evidence of its ripeness and sacrificial fullness, like an individual who has reached the highest level of attainment and can do nothing more than give of him- or herself to others (a thought of Dostoevsky's). Similarly, a developed culture repays debts to nature and faith, sacrificing itself for the sake of spontaneity, immediacy, originality, general harmoniousness, and love. An "escape to nature," with physical survival guaranteed, is only possible thanks to a culture so generous and firmly established, it can allow itself to be ignored.

Such self-estrangement without loss of unity is only possible within the intermediary realm of culture, which corresponds to the intermediary position of the human being between the realms of Nature and Spirit. I venture to add one more definition of culture to the hundreds that have been formulated already: culture is everything humanly created that simultaneously creates a human being. Nails or machines are certainly created, but to the extent that they serve only to produce other objects, they do not belong to culture. Trees and flowers may mold the human soul in a certain way, but they are not themselves humanly created. Culture, in the broadest sense, is humankind's self-creation: it is only in cultural activity that the human being appears as both creator and creation, balancing the attributes of the divine Creator and the humble creature. To use the terms of information theory, nature is a text whose receiver is the human being, while the sender is Someone Other; cult, on the contrary, is a text whose sender is the human being while the receiver is Someone Other. Culture, however, is a text whose sender and receiver is humanity; thus culture is the council of all nations and all generations, of humanity's internal affairs.[6]

While culture is humanity's message to itself, culturology is the objectified self-consciousness of culture; it explores the perpetual self-estrangement of the human spirit (in its almost compulsive production of external objects) as well as its self-acquisition (in its ongoing interpretation and appropriation of these objects). Culturology is for culture what culture is for humanity—a means of self-knowledge and self-regulation. If culture is the cultivation of nature, then culturology is not merely the study of culture, but its further cultivation. In the process of self-reflection and self-estrangement, culture becomes an object of its own intellectual activities, and culturology is the locus of this activity.

Thus, the cultural sciences may be distinguished from the natural sciences in that the former play a key role in constituting their subject matter: physics and biology are not parts of nature, while philology and psychology are parts of culture. Culturology offers *integrative* knowledge of the various *parts* of culture. Culture includes many crafts, sciences, occupations, arts, professions, and beliefs, all of which develop within their own spheres with little awareness of one other. Culturology studies the whole that is present in each of these spheres as an unrealized other, as a fundamental unconscious, uniting all types of social consciousness: aesthetics and ethics, art and science, politics and mythology. Culturology's subject matter extends beyond the confines of all individual areas of the humanities. Within its proper limits, for example, aesthetics knows nothing of the relation between avant-garde art and the religious, eschatological consciousness of the twentieth century; the same is true of theology. Culturology is called upon to realize the ideal of cultural wholeness, as it reveals connections and relationships unknown to separate disciplines. The relationship between culturology and the humanities is similar to that between mathematics and the natural sciences: both are spheres of metalanguage, of metascientific consciousness and description. The broadest and most comprehensive concept corresponding to that of "nature" is precisely that of "culture."

As for the relationship of culture and society, there has long been a bias toward the latter, so that culture was perceived as a by-product of certain stages of social development, that is, as something secondary and contingent. Moreover, this fostered the inclusion of culture studies within the confines of social inquiry, precluding culturology in favor of a sociology of culture. Yet this is tantamount to replacing aesthetics with a sociology of art, or physics with a sociology of science. To be sure, certain features of a social order enable or prevent certain elements of content in culture, but this does not imply that content itself is a mere derivative of social relations: it possesses its own source of creative energy, which provides the essential stimulus and perspective for social development. The scope of culture is much broader and deeper than that of society as such. While society encompasses all living people in their combined activity and the interrelations of their roles, culture embraces the activity of all previous generations accumulated in artistic works, scientific discoveries, moral values, and so on. The social level is but one horizontal section of culture, which in its totality permeates all historical worlds, as we see in the perpetual migration of texts and meanings from country to country, from generation to generation. Culture is the totality of objectified relations of human beings among themselves. And therefore, as the individual becomes part of culture, growing in the knowledge of multiple levels of cultural heritage, s/he discovers ever more facets of humanity *within* him or herself.

Of course, culture necessarily includes the social dimension, but it cannot be reduced to it. To live within society *and* to be free of it—this is what culture is about. It enters the blood and bone of society, in order to liberate individuals from the constraints of their social existence, from its repressive tendencies and historical limitations, much as spirit is not free from body but represents a liberating force able to transcend external obstacles. Society can develop only with the nourishment of nonsocial, metasocial, and trans-social elements, such as those contained in the cultural products of different epochs, in their mystical revelations, artistic imagery, and ethical imperatives. Culture is the porous and spongelike quality of a social body that enables it to breathe the air of all times.

As a force for liberation, the ideal of culture—rather than that of politics or technology—is predominant in truly democratic societies. Enlarging upon the definition proposed above, I would add that culture is the creation of a human being insofar as s/he is free from physical, social, and other needs; at the same time, culture functions for the liberation of other human beings as well. It is an objectified form of freedom, passed down through times and spaces, so that a single person may become the representative of all humanity in its past, present, and possible future.

Social cataclysms and revolutions of all kinds (such as Russia is experiencing today) reemphasize our need for the deepest possible perspectives on liberation, the kind of cultural perspectives that open up following a political coup (and often in opposition to it) and leading far beyond the confines of politics. This is the reason that the following words written by Osip Mandelshtam in 1920 are so relevant to our present context.

> In a state of divine madness, poets speak the language of all times and all cultures. Nothing is impossible. As the room of a dying man is open to all, the door of the old world has been thrown open to the crowd. All at once everything becomes common property. Go and take it. Everything is within reach: all the labyrinths, all the hiding places, all the secret passages. The word has become not a seven-barreled flute, but a thousand-barreled one, enlivened by the breath of all ages at once.[7]

In genuine cultural activity one cannot take without giving or creating something new in return, yet in Russian libraries, when one looks in the subject catalogue under "culture," one finds a bibliography on libraries, museums, historical monuments, collectors and restorers, clubs, circles and societies of culture, institutions and agencies concerned with culture. This indicates the popular misconception that culture consists in the activities of collecting, preserving, and restoring cultural products, or else it equates culture with the work of propaganda, education, and popularization—as if the chief treasures of culture have all been created in the past, and the only remaining task is to distribute them among the masses in a fair and equitable way. The West is often called a "consumer society," and while this may be accurate in a sense, it is just as obvious that to consume in increasing quantities requires that one first produce what is to be consumed. Soviet society, on the other hand, may be called the society of *distribution,* for this problem lies at the center of interest: who gets how much, and not who creates how much. Consumption is not necessarily a vital issue, particularly since the quality of what is produced is often such that it is not really meant to be consumed, whereas regulated distribution provides the key to achieving equality at the lowest possible level of both consumption and production. The "distributional complex," or neurosis, also functions within the Russian cultural sphere: while little effort goes into producing anything genuinely new, the main concern is to distribute what there already is, most of which was created (not necessarily by us) decades and centuries ago. Hence the emphasis on such retrospective activities as "cultural" applications of one's leisure time, "cultural" events, "mass-cultural" work, "cultural field trips," *kultorg* (a cultural organizer in the work place), *kulturnik* (a cultural organizer at vacation resorts), and so on. In the popular understanding, culture is equated with a variety of ready skills, a mastery of traditions, reflected in the coinage of a unique expression: "the cultured person"—which means, roughly: "well-read," "well-informed," "polite," "considerate." But culture is not the sum of habits and skills, no matter how noble; rather, it is a sphere of creativity and freedom, where the person becomes both creation and creator. Culture is essentially a laboratory where creative possibilities are tested.

The Laboratory of Culture

For these reasons, culture needs not only libraries, museums, and schools (although these, too, are often lacking), but above all laboratories, focusing on experimental production of cultural objects and ideas in small quantities, but of genuinely new quality—an approach that precludes the distributional emphasis. After all, the culture of the Modern Age was born in craft workshops, alchemists' laboratories, and artists' studios. Each epoch of cultural tumult (an important part of which is always some type of political perestroika) renews our perennial need for "minor," socially unconnected forms of intellectual production, conspicuously discrete from the dominant ideologies of the time. By its very nature, culture is an alternative form of consciousness: in the fifteenth century, it offered an alternative to religion; in the twentieth century, to politics; in the twenty-fifth century, perhaps it will offer an alternative to science. Yet an alternative to culture itself is hardly possible when we conceive of culture as the totality of alternatives, rooted in human freedom.

Society has need of culturology in order to concentrate within itself effectively the genuine totality of human capacities. By the same token, culturology should not only be an indispensable part of an individual's consciousness, but should also represent the wholeness of this consciousness as it integrates all aspects of life and cultural participation. If the whole of culture is usurped by any one of its components, such as politics, technology, or ecology, then a distinct type of totalitarianism reasserts itself and will inevitably seek to reign over all others. In a post-totalitarian country, no new type of totalitarianism can be productive except that of culture in its role as the *free totality* of all types of political activity, artistic endeavor, scientific inquiry, and so on. To the extent that they all work to liberate the human being, philosophy, art, science, and politics mutually check one another's power over the individual and society—power that, if unchecked, could become monopolizing and enslaving. Thus, it is only through the mutual limitation of its various alternatives that culture remains a force for liberation from religious fanaticism and political authoritarianism, from scientism, aestheticism, moralism, technocratism—all of the usurping pretensions of each separate cultural realm, as they attempt to rely on themselves alone.

This is not to say that culture functions on the principle of divide and conquer. Rather it aims to "liberate by unifying": it does not so much rule over its constituent parts as it frees them from their innate restrictions by unifying them into a more truly complete entity. Culture liberates us from the dictates of each specific sphere of consciousness, from the restrictive fate of being only a "political," or a "technical," or a "moral" human being.

Science and art, philosophy and religion—all taken as a whole form the central concern in the Laboratory of Contemporary Culture (see introductory note to this chapter) to the extent that it finds its own center and its unifying conception in a liberating vision of culture. Mikhail Bakhtin emphasized that "the most intense and productive life of any culture occurs on the borders of its various realms, not there and then, when these realms retire into their specificity."[8] This primary intuition of Russian culturology was further elaborated by Bakhtin's follower, philosopher Vladimir Bibler: "Culture can live and develop, as culture, only on the borders of cultures.... Culture is the form of the simultaneous being and communication among peoples of various cultures—past, present and future—in the forms of dialogue and mutual generating of these cultures."[9] Thus, culture is never self-identical: it exists in the overstepping of its own borders, the interaction of various cultures, diverse in terms of age, social status, profession. It is the interaction of youth and "adult" cultures, the traditional and the avant-garde, mass and elite, political and artistic. The goal of the Laboratory is to interrogate the depth of these interrelations, their hidden basis for kinship, and the increasing openness of the Whole.

The term "contemporary" must not be understood too narrowly. The contemporary is *something whose time has come.* For us in Russia today, the epoch of early Christianity is more contemporary than that of the Enlightenment. It is precisely because we are severely behind in time, that for us the borders of the contemporary extend themselves to include an entire century that produced the as-yet-unread Soloviev and Nietzsche; to encompass a century and a half, within which appear the unknown Chaadaev and Khomiakov, Kierkegaard and Schelling; and even to reach back a thousand or two thousand years separating us from the crucial turning points of our own and world culture.[10] All of this may be "con-temporary" as never before, perhaps more so than in its own time, for the irreversibility of what we have missed grows with every year and epoch missed, as does the urgency of its entry into our life. Therefore, we cannot limit our definition of the contemporary in chronological terms. The program of our Laboratory includes the study of cultural traditions that nourish contemporaneity and are perceived as its anticipation, as the interresonant con-temporaneity of different times within the present day.

With its compact research collective, the Laboratory is a microculture that models the processes and patterns of macroculture, developing and forecasting its main tendencies in a compressed and accelerated manner. The products of such culturological investigation are themselves a part of that same contemporary culture, although they are reconstituted at a new level of reflection that comprehends itself as a whole, as a spiritual synthesis of different cultures. Culturology becomes the point of departure for cultural genesis: conscious interdisciplinary creativity aims to produce not only individual works of art or science, but also creations in the genre of culture itself. Thus the task must be understood in a dual sense: ours is a laboratory for both the *study* of contemporary culture and the *development* of its new, experimental forms.

Ideally, of course, it would be desirable to speak not only of one or two laboratories, but of an entire laboratory movement that would simultaneously carry out both analysis and synthesis of different cultural forms, varieties, and orientations. In Russia we have a tradition of staunch bias against self-consciousness, reflection, and self-reflection—which have been presumed to destroy the intrinsic wholeness of an individual entity. In actuality, it is only self-consciousness that can provide such wholeness: it allows the individual, an ensemble of diverse habits and character traits, to become "someone for oneself." In the same way, culture stands in need of self-consciousness, since it represents a vast, unimaginably dispersed aggregate of different sciences, arts, traditions, contingencies, texts, and professions. The laboratory movement in culture may be seen as a path toward self-consciousness, the self-discovery of wholeness and creativity in the forms of wholeness.

Why should science and art, politics and philosophy be spheres of creativity, but not culture as such? With the increasing integration of human reason, its powers will move into precisely the realm of such transcultural creative work, in the sense that transculture is a mode of culture created not from within its separate spheres, but organically in the holistic forms of culture itself—within the field of interaction of all its constituent parts. Our entire postcommunist culture can become a laboratory in which all previous cultural forms and styles are rediscovered and intermingled into a new *nontotalitarian totality.*

Culture and Religion

No doubt the most painful issue in this emerging totality is the relationship between culture and religion. Both sides of this theme were utterly neglected in the Soviet Union. From the standpoint of official culture, only humanistic and atheistic values received recognition, and from the standpoint of the Orthodox Church, believers were enjoined not to interfere in "cultural" activities. Now it is time to get rid of the prejudice that, strange as it may seem, many believers share with nonbelievers: that only the past tense of culture belongs to religion, whereas the cultural future has nothing to do with faith.

I would like to emphasize that both pre- and post-revolutionary relations between culture and religion were predisposed to mutual indifference or even incompatibility. It is well known that the great Russian poet Pushkin and the great Russian saint Seraphim of Sarov[11] lived at the same time, but knew nothing about one another. Such ignorance as this could prove fatal for Russian culture as a whole. This estrangement may be rooted in certain peculiarities of Orthodox spirituality, with its traditional suspicions of the mundane and profane aspects of cultural life. When Gogol and Tolstoy attempted to devote themselves to a religious calling, they expressed an emphatic aversion to culture, including their own previous artistic work. Conversely, when culture declared its freedom and independence, it aggressively challenged religious values: Soviet atheistic propaganda is the hyperbolic extension of this Renaissance-like, anticlerical gesture. So far we have seen convincing evidence that this division is disastrous for both sides. Culture loses its spiritual and, indeed, its etymological root, which is "cult," and devolves into a sort of literacy, a technology that Stalin called "the engineering of human souls." As for religion, it loses its vital élan, grows decrepit, and devolves into ritual, a technology of salvation that appeals exclusively to the elderly.

This period of mutual estrangement of religion and culture can now come to an end. The aspirations of such major Russian thinkers of the early twentieth century as Vladimir Soloviev, Dmitry Merezhkovsky and Nikolai Berdiaev[12] who contemplated the comprehensive interaction of religion and culture as two sovereign realms, can now, at the century's end, become a vital, broadly evident imperative. Religion and culture are two indispensable parts of one whole, its ascending and descending aspirations, breath and exhalation.

There is, however, a move expressed in various nationalist and quasi-Orthodox writings to reestablish the medieval patterns of spiritual life in order to reassert ecclesiastical controls over culture. But were such a disbalance reproduced at this point in time, culture would certainly demand revenge at the next point, and so on ad infinitum.

I believe that a new sort of relationship between these two global systems of human life and thought must be elaborated with the help of culturology. To illustrate this argument, I would draw a parallel between the relationship of material culture to nature and between the relationship of spiritual culture to religion. From ancient times and into the Middle Ages, man was almost totally dependent on nature, but beginning in the Renaissance, he has tried to gain freedom from his living environment. As a result, he violated and subdued nature to such a degree that he exhausted many vital resources and began to suffocate from the poisoned air and to die of thirst near the poisoned stream.

The same occurred in the spiritual sphere. When God was removed from the center of the universe, dethroned as the Creator of all things seen and unseen, what did we put in his place? At first, it was the collective egocentrism of all humanity; then social criteria prevailed, and the "center of the universe" came to be identified with exploited humanity and the oppressed classes. Still later, political parties and the "party spirit" declared themselves the measure of what could be considered "spiritual," until culture degenerated into a cult of party leaders and "fuhrers." Thus, in its search for total autonomy and independence from God, spiritual culture lost its vital sources and humanistic creed, just as technological culture, having achieved dominance over nature, lost its capacity to serve humanity.

Where can we find a way out? Should we return to the supremacy of nature or the supernatural over weak and trembling human beings? I think the *transcultural* approach to both material and spiritual culture is the most promising. This means that culture, overstressed by its yearning for autonomy over the past four centuries, may gradually rediscover cultural values *beyond* culture in the realms of both the natural and the supernatural. Ecology, or the relationship of material culture to nature, must be complemented by the analogous approach of spiritual culture to the supernatural. Cultural egocentrism must yield its place to *eco*centrism, as culture transcends its own boundaries in descending to nature and ascending to God.

What I propose is neither the ancient model of nature-centrism nor the medieval model of theocentrism, but a stance consonant with the new dimensions of culture itself. Arriving at the dead end of its autonomous development, culture must now recognize its dependence on the natural and the supernatural, must reconsider its arrogant opposition to the environment and to religion. Culturology, as the advanced self-consciousness of culture, leads beyond these narrow, "narcissistic" limits, giving rise to transcultural consciousness, which seeks to assimilate the values of nonculture.

The Way to Transculture

The twentieth century is the century of diverse independent cultures, each with its own unique value. As these values made their impressions on twentieth-century consciousness, the development of culturology became a natural result. Culturology arises when a culture is able to take a detached view of itself, presupposing the existence of another culture beyond its own boundaries. One of the achievements of culturology is the very possibility of using the word "culture" in the plural; previously, this entity was construed as exclusively singular, as a model, norm, or ideal common to all nations. There was only one culture, which presumed itself to be *the* culture. The diverse traditions of various peoples or nations could be regarded as more or less "cultured" insofar as they belonged or did not belong to this single culture, identified with the standards of Western civilization.[13] Today, however, it is widely recognized that there are *cultures,* not only different national and racial cultures, but youth cultures, feminine cultures, and so on. Culturology arises in the space between these cultures, as their ability to distance and objectify each other's existence. Culturology is inherently connected with democratic and pluralistic mentalities because it takes its starting point from the gap between various cultures.

In Russia as well, we can now observe and experience the multiplicity of cultures that have entered the spiritual space of the twentieth century and have come to occupy our consciousness impetuously over the course of just two or three years. The twentieth century appears overhasty to us, with its inexorable acceleration of the urge to grasp and embrace everything discovered and devised in many epochs and nations. But now Russia has to assimilate this abundance of inventions and discoveries in a period of several years. The Russian cultural situation of today is a condensed replica of the twentieth century's multicultural situation.

"Past shock" is now the dominant feeling of the former communist world, analogous to the "future shock" that dominated the Western world in the 1960s. This is the shock of meeting one's own unfamiliar past as well as that of all humanity. We managed to bypass future shock (borrowing Alvin Toffler's term), but now the inevitable stress of adjusting to time overtakes us in another form, as we are shocked by the sudden encounter with the whole of twentieth-centry culture, much of which has already become a thing of the past for Western countries. The cultural past of all humanity is now our only future.

At the same time, we are colliding with our own past face to face. During the seventy years of our Soviet "brave new world," we essentially had no past; we existed in the present and hoped to endure into the future. The pre-Revolutionary past was not our own, but belonged to the dead, exterminated people of "damned tsarist Russia." Now, however, the communist "future" and the socialist "present" have become our genuine past, so that all of our history opens to us simultaneously, along with all the historical layers of twentieth-century humanity. The present may be chaotic, unstable, and unreal, but we have finally come into possession of the past, or, more precisely, it has come forward to possess us.

To some extent, the current situation may remind us of the period of the first five-year plans, when Russia endeavored to catch up with the advances of Western industry, which had been developing consistently for centuries. The implicit task of the current period could be formulated in such a slogan as: "To master twentieth-century culture in five years!"

This situation strongly aggravates the danger of cultural schizophrenia. We are dizzy with the abundance of new literary periodicals and creative organizations, with the process of interference when one cultural stratum accumulates on top of another. Nabokov becomes for us a contemporary of the early Gnostic writers, and Solzhenitsyn may be read in one portion of time with the *Kama Sutra*. In a single magazine, photographs of nudes appear alongside the blessings and admonitions of the Orthodox Patriarch.[14] A young man may attend lectures on the arts of antiquity, performances of avant-garde theater, exhibitions of medieval icons and of abstract paintings; he may read Henry Miller and the life of Saint Sergy of Radonezh, may listen to rock music and participate in psychological groups for interpersonal communication. Taken separately, all this can split and empty one's personality rather than enrich it. How should we respond to the threat of cultural schizophrenia? Transcultural development is necessary to bring humanity into the wholeness of culture and the interrelation of its main branches and meanings. Otherwise we may end up with hundreds of books, concerts, exhibitions, ensembles—but no culture at all. The transcultural approach inspires us to search the diversity of educational and professional spheres for some center that is culture itself.

What is the relationship between culturology and transculture? I call culturology the discipline that investigates the diversity of cultures and their common underlying principles. Transculture, however, is not just a field of knowledge; rather, it is a mode of being at the crossroads of cultures. A transcultural personality naturally seeks to free his or her native culture—be it Russian, Soviet or any other—from self-deification and fetishism. If all other specialists work inside their own disciplines or realms of culture, unconsciously abiding by all their rules and taboos, a culturologist makes the native culture an object of *definition* and thereby surpasses its finiteness, its limitations. In so doing, s/he exhibits a transcultural awareness that derives from this calling. A culturologist is a "universalist," participating in the diversity of cultures. This presupposes some emotional openness and a scope of knowledge that can free a person from the limitations imposed by any particular cultural heritage. Transculture offers, moreover, a mentality capable of therapeutically benefiting those possessed by manias, phobias, and obsessions attendant upon their belonging to a specific cultural group.

The quality and merit of culture is its capacity to free man from the dictates of nature, its restrictions and necessities. But it is the merit and capacity of transculture to free man from culture itself, from its conventions and obsessions. Normally we live as prisoners of culture. We feel obliged to act and think in full accordance with the presumptions established in our native traditions. If one is a truly "Soviet" man, he should consider Lenin's mausoleum, with its well-preserved corpse of the great leader, to be the sacred center of a kind of ideological universe. He should believe, along with Lenin and Chernyshevsky, that the duty of literature is to teach people how they should live. But when he learns to participate in other forms of worship and other modes of creative writing he stops being a purely "Soviet" man and becomes a more truly whole personality, without narrowly specified attributes. This is the merit of transcultural consciousness.

In his article "Party Organization and Party Literature" (1905), Lenin asserted that it is impossible to live in society and to be free from society. But today we can see that the multiplicity of cultures creates this possibility, makes a social being free of society while also giving new impetus to social development. One can agree with Lenin: you are not free from your car when driving it, but, nonetheless, you drive it only because you are free to do so. Society is also driven—primarily by those people who are free from society, from its limitations and taboos.

Although it overcomes the limitations of culture, transculture does not mean simple negation. This temptation is too familiar to the Russian people, with their many past experiences of cultural nihilism. Some obvious examples are the "senseless and merciless Russian revolts" (in Pushkin's words) of *razinshchina* and *pugachevshchina,* as well as the great October Revolution, *leninshchina* and *stalinshchina.*[15] Like barbarism, such movements overstep the limits of culture, but in this they reveal their *anti*cultural, not *trans*cultural foundations. Transculture is a transcendence of culture that has nothing to do with the barbarous destruction of cultural objects and traditions. The latter derives essentially from precultural conditions and becomes an anticultural force; although it attempts to liberate the personality, it ends by subjecting it to the even harsher laws of the tribe, or of the mob. Thus the cultural nihilism of Mao or Sartre seems to be a mere illusion of liberation. When he destroys culture, man is taken prisoner by nature, and returned to the world of hunger, terror, and oppression: the struggle for survival. All the facts of modern barbarism bear witness to this.

By sharp contrast, transculture does not regress to the far crueler realm of "natural law" as it exceeds the bounds of culture; rather, it moves on to new degrees of freedom. Liberation from culture through culture itself and its endless diversity is the fundamental principle of transcultural thinking and existence.

There may be certain points of correspondence between transcultural consciousness and the concept of supramental consciousness, as described and promoted in India by the great sage Sri Aurobindo.[16] In principle, however, supramental consciousness can be attained by an isolated individual in complete privacy through the process of inner contemplation, whereas transculture is not reached by a purely psychological process. Russians, for example, are oriented more toward the West, than toward the East; for them, consciousness has real importance only in its relation to the material culture of humankind. Though transculture depends on the efforts of separate individuals to overcome their identification with separate cultures, on another level, it is a process of interaction between cultures themselves in which more and more individuals have found themselves "outside" of any particular culture, "outside" of its national, racist, sexist, age, political, and other limitations. I would compare this condition with Bakhtin's idea of *vnenak-hodimost',* which means being located beyond any particular mode of existence, or in this case, finding one's place on the border of existing cultures.[17] This realm *beyond* all cultures is located *inside* of transculture and belongs to this state of not-belonging (*nakhoditsia v meste vnenakhodimosti*).

Transculture is the mode of existence of one liberated from nature by culture and from culture itself by culturology. This transcultural world has never been extensively described because the path that leads to it—culturology, or the comparative study of cultures—was opened only recently. Some great insights are found in the work of Oswald Spengler, Herman Hesse, Thomas Mann, and Jorge Luis Borges, but even here transculture is often presented in oversimplified form, as a sort of caricature. Transculture is not a rarified and isolated construct that stands separated from real historical cultures, as Hesse suggests, for example, in his novel *The Glass Bead Game.* Hesse imparts a somewhat satiric tone to his description of "transcultural" Kastalia, even though he criticizes the same "light literary," "feuilleton" quality as a trait of pre-Kastalian culture. As distinct from Hesse's conservative and escapist Game, which is essentially derivative and forbids the creation of new signs and values, transculture aspires entirely to the sphere of creativity.

The transcultural world lies not apart from, but within all existing cultures, like a multidimensional space that appears gradually over the course of historical time. It is a continuous space in which unrealized, potential elements are no less meaningful than "real" ones. As the site of interaction among all existing and potential cultures, transculture is even richer than the totality of all known cultural traditions and practices.[18]

Through the signs of existing cultures, a "transculturist" tries to restore the mysterious script of the simultaneously present and absent transcultural condition. In essence, s/he both discovers and creates this realm. While scientists, artists, and politicians make significant but separate contributions to culture in their respective fields, the transculturist elaborates the space of transculture using various arts, philosophies, and sciences as tools to develop the all-encompassing genre of cultural creativity. From existing materials new cultural possibilities are invented, so that the "art of the possible" is truly the most necessary skill.

In Borges's great story "Aleph," the brightest point of the universe is described as a place where all times and spaces may be present together, without hiding or overshadowing each other. In the typical terms of physical reality, Aleph is a pure fantasy, but culture is, after all, a *symbolic* reality that can be condensed indefinitely by the increasing scope of its meanings. We may imagine transculture as the Aleph of the entire cultural world.

Transculture and Multiculturalism

The concept of transculture took shape in Russia over the past decade and should be clearly distinguished from multiculturalism, a specifically American phenomenon with which it nonetheless shares certain features.

The transcultural project emerged in a totalitarian society, that had been isolated for seventy years from other cultural worlds. These conditions determined the twofold goal of transcultural activity: first, to challenge the one-dimensionality of official culture and second, to ascend to a genuine totality that embraces a variety of modes of cultural thought.

For example, if I live at the end of the twentieth century, how can I acquire the experiences of an Italian of the fourteenth century, or an ancient Greek, or of one of the first Christians? If I am a middle-aged man, I would like to participate somehow in the spontaneous play of children and also to partake of the wisdom of the elderly. If I am an engineer, I cannot realize my full human potential without participating in some artistic, musical, or literary activities. Because the cultural reality in the Soviet Union was so poor, it actually stimulated the imaginative search for alternatives beyond the borders of one country and one century, one age and one profession.

Many representatives of the young Russian intelligentsia had three or four highly differentiated facets to their professional profile. For example, a particular man might be a mathematician by training, while earning a living as a janitor and devoting himself primarily to writing poetry. The same person might sing in a church choir and practice martial arts. To participate in several cultures, some of which originally excluded one another, became the fundamental tenet of transcultural existence. By simultaneously reading books about the Gnostics and about the Gulag, one could attempt to reconcile these experiences within his or her own existence, which might not prove to be so very difficult, when the world is viewed broadly as one big prison.

The multicultural approach, which was the topic of ardent discussion when I first arrived in America, entails a similar impulse to unite different cultures while recognizing their multiplicity. Indeed, transcultural and multicultural tendencies seem to have much in common; they reject ideological canons: totalitarian communism, in the case of the former Soviet Union, and Eurocentrism and white male dominance in the West. They also share a keen interest in those "exotic" cultures that were closed for the Soviet people by the Iron Curtain, and those that were viewed in the West as "oppressed minorities."

This search took very different trajectories in the two societies, however, proceeding in essentially opposite directions. For example, the Eurocentrist approach, which seemed so boring and oppressive to American multiculturists, was highly attractive to Soviet transculturists, who had long been denied the right to be Europeans themselves. A few incidents on the level of personal experience may serve to illustrate this point. I was surprised on one occasion when a friend of mine, a Finnish businessman and writer, went to a Moscow record store to buy many albums of Azerbaijani music, not only for himself, but also as gifts for Western friends who shared his interest. No self-respecting Muscovite would think of buying such albums, since this music was considered provincial and of minor aesthetic value. A similar recollection arises from my first trip abroad, to Hungary in 1984. I was overjoyed at the chance to view *Apocalypse Now,* a film with a tremendous underground reputation in the Soviet Union. But when I tried to convey my enthusiasm to an American traveler with whom I had become friendly, I was surprised to find him more interested in what he deemed a better offer: to attend a performance of the Cuban circus! Thus my prejudice, common among Soviet citizens, against Cuban and Azerbaijani products, as being second-rate to all "Western" products, was definitively revealed.

Of course, these are only surface differences concerning the substance of Russian and American interests. Deeper differences between transcultural-ism and multiculturalism may be found on the level of their ultimate spir-itual goals and structural disparities.

In the United States, the traditional emphasis that is placed on the rights and dignity of individuals naturally produces recognition of a variety of cultures proceeding from different nationalities, races, genders, ages, and so forth. Since the individual is the ultimate minority, it is logical that the individualistic and pluralistic tendencies in America support a multiplicity of separate and distinct minority cultures.

On the other hand, the Russian philosophical tradition places a premium on wholeness, which has played a number of cruel tricks on the events of Russian history and spawned a political totalitarianism that ironically tried to envelop all of life into a single ideological principle. This consequence determined the specific boundaries of Soviet transculture in its attempt to attain a free multidimensional totality opposed to totalitarianism. Thus, the notion of transculture differs from American ideas with their acceptance of many separate and distinct cultures that may exist side by side without taking the slightest interest in one another.

Though the maxim of multiculturalism could be "to accept and value difference," the result of such differentiation is sometimes similar to com-plete *in*difference in practice. It is instructive to see how pluralism, when pushed to the extreme, may turn into its opposite. The paradox of equality for all people, heterosexuals and homosexuals, healthy and handicapped, can lead to an erasure of the fundamental differences between them. There are two kinds of indifference: one is totalitarian, which suppresses everyone who tries to be distinct, and the other is tolerant, accepting everyone who is distinct, as if all people were essentially the same.

Pluralism as such, "self-complacent" pluralism, which recognizes that everyone has morals and customs of his own, tends to make us indifferent and dulls the charms of differentiation. If everything is equal, self-suffi-cient, or justified in and of itself, then we lose compassion or attraction for those who are different from us. According to the logic of total equality, why should the able-bodied pity handicapped, or "differently abled" persons? Pity is seen as insulting and humiliating for them. But such an understanding of "difference" is close to indifference. The compassion of healthy people toward handicapped people, on which many scenes in the Gospels are built, is indispensable for any culture. To imagine those sufferers whom Christ healed as "differently abled" or the dead whom he resurrected as "differently alive" is not only blasphemous but also tasteless—lacking in flavor, neither hot nor cold.

All genuine feeling develops between people because they are deeply different from each other: between a man and a woman, a healthy and a handicapped person, a child and an adult. The greater the difference, the stronger our emotions tend to be. Generally speaking, the theme of emotionality has been vastly underestimated in the last thirty years, roughly since existentialism was ousted from the Western philosophical scene. But now we have entered a new, poststructural epoch when emotions should regain their place in the philosophy of differences, because emotions are the lifeblood of difference.

The richness of culture will be lost if all existing cultures are treated as self-sufficient and perfect in their own way. A more fruitful approach calls on each group to take account of its own *in*sufficiency. A man may feel a deficiency in that he cannot give birth to children, cannot feel what a woman feels; he would like to remain who he is, but also become those he is not. No one can embrace everything in this existence, so everyone lacks something. Perhaps the most effective way to feel difference is to embrace the feeling of one's own incompleteness.

I view culture as a form of compensation for our being incomplete entities. No human is a full entity, so all of us are called to restore, through our cultural perceptions and occupations, the full totality that nature does not give us. I am a middle-aged white male, but at the same time I would like to be black or female or adolescent. These experiences may be acquired through books, theater, painting, cinema as compensations for my being so specific. There are many ways of self-identification within culture that nature cannot provide, so that culture becomes the infinity of self-redefinition, self-compensation. By way of culture one has a chance to become everyone, as if a magic wand allows us to identify with woman, child, or a member of a different race and nation.

At the same time, we must recall that natural cultures have a tendency to become mere extensions of inborn human qualities, as revealed in the very terms, "racial," "national," and "sexual" differences in culture. To find one's own cultural identity means merely to be faithful to one's nature, one's origins. Transcultural pursuits should aim to understand and overcome the limitations of one's inborn culture, that is, those secondary, "cultivated" deficiencies and restrictions where one's cultural self is imprisoned. I would name such a project "creative pluralism," because it does not limit itself to the simple recognition of other cultures' integrity, but goes so far as to consider them all necessary for one another's further development.

Ethnic and sexual minorities both in the United States and in contemporary Russia are anxious to promote their own values and to have opportunities to succeed on a national scale. This multicultural tendency is quite justified but needs to be supplemented by a transcultural perspective. Multiculturalism proceeds from the assumption that every ethnic, sexual, or class culture is important and perfect in itself, while transculture proceeds from the assumption that every particular culture is incomplete and requires interaction with other cultures.

Here I would like to consider the work of Merab Mamardashvili (1930–1990), a major Russian philosopher of Georgian origin, who spent his last years in Tbilisi, where he suffered through the delights of Georgian cultural and political nationalism exacerbated by the downfall of the Soviet empire. Mamardashvili sympathizes with multiculturalism as a mode of liberation from a monolithic cultural canon, but objects to the glorification of ethnic diversity for its own sake. Parroting a typical argument: "Each culture is valuable in itself. People should be allowed to live within their cultures," Mamardashvili objects that "the defense of autonomous customs sometimes proves to be a denial of the right to freedom and to another world. It seems as if a decision were taken for them: you live in such an original way, that it is quite cultural to live as you do, so go on and live this way. But did anyone ask me personally? What if I were a Peruvian, or I don't know who. . . . Perhaps I am suffocating within the fully autonomous customs of my complex and developed culture?"[19]

Thus, what needs to be preserved, in Mamardashvili's view, is the right to live beyond one's culture, on the borders of cultures, to take "a step transcending one's own surrounding, native culture and milieu not for the sake of anything else. Not for the sake of any other culture, but for the sake of nothing. Transcendence into nothing. Generally speaking, such an act is truly the living, pulsating center of the entire human universe. This is a primordial metaphysical act." By metaphysics, in its primary essence, Mamardashvili understands the movement beyond any physical determinance and liberation from any social and cultural identity: "This understandable, noble aspiration to defend those who are oppressed by some kind of culture-centrism, for example Eurocentrism or any other—this aspiration forgets and makes us forget that there exists a metaphysics of freedom and thought that is not peculiar to us alone. This is a kind of reverse racism."[20] This type of racism is reductionism, not only the reduction of diversity of cultures to one privileged canon, but also the reduction of a diversity of personalities to their native, "genetic" culture. To transcend the limits of one's native culture does not constitute betrayal, because the limits of any culture are too narrow for the full range of human potentials. From this standpoint, transculture does not mean adding yet another culture to the existing array; it is rather a special mode of existence spanning cultural boundaries, a transcendence into "no culture," which indicates how, ultimately, the human exceeds all cultural definitions.

Moreover, the essence of a given culture may be penetrated from the viewpoint of another, foreign culture better than from its own inner perspective. In the words of Mikhail Bakhtin, "only in the eyes of an alien culture, does another culture open itself in a fuller and deeper way."[21] As Bakhtin points out, a human cannot fully visualize even his own face—only others can see his real appearance from their location beyond those personal boundaries. In the same way, antiquity did not know the same antiquity that is known to us today. The ancient Greeks had not the slightest idea of what is most significant about them: that they were *ancient*. The essence of "male" culture may be more deeply perceived by females; the essence of "white" culture may be more deeply perceived by blacks, and vice versa. "Being beyond" (that is, in the position of *vnenakhodimost'*, as mentioned above) is an advantageous situation for understanding. One can never understand oneself from within, without taking another's point of view into full account, even if this "otherness" is only fixed in one's own consciousness.

Let me expand on the example of relations between the sexes. Multiculturalism stresses the specific patterns of feminist writing as opposed to traditionally male-dominated literature, while transculturalism emphasizes the feminine ideas and moods in writing by males. Such outstanding Russian thinkers as Vasily Rozanov in his *People of the Moonlight* (1913), Nikolai Berdiaev in *The Meaning of the Creative Act* (1916), and Daniil Andreev in *The Rose of the World* (1950–58), underscore the notion that creativity overcomes the opposition of the sexes, making men more feminine and women more masculine. According to Andreev, perhaps the pre-eminent intellectual influence in contemporary Russia:

In the spheres of the highest creativity, something occurs which is opposite to what we see in the physical world. There the woman is the fertilizing principle while man is the principle of shaping and incarnation. *The Divine Comedy* is the product of two authors and could not appear without both Beatrice and Dante. If we could penetrate the depths of the creative process of the majority of great artists, we would become certain that it was through a woman that the spiritual seed of the immortal creations was thrown into the depth of their [artists'] unconscious, into the hiding-place of their creativity.[22]

From the multicultural point of view, a male writer is a representative of a specifically male culture, whereas a female writer should express a specifically feminine viewpoint. The category of difference becomes primarily a capacity for self-identity; everyone has his or her permanent nature and character, dependent upon being born as a woman or man, black or white, and so on. Multiculturalism supposes that these inborn differences determine specific cultural roles for each individual. Transculture, on the other hand, maintains that cultural development transforms the individual's nature by providing those characteristics that were lacking in his or her original, natural state. Personality is capable of transcending the distinction between sexes and thus is viewed as a microcosm of various cultural types. In Daniil Andreev's view, "not only woman, but man too, must be feminine" (124).

Andreev further predicts that "there will be a cycle of epochs when the feminine component of humanity will manifest itself with unprecedented strength, balancing the previous dominance of masculine forces in a perfect harmony" (125). While multiculturalism defends gender differences against the power of a single male canon, transculture aspires to "all-unity" (*vseedinstvo*), or "androgynism," rather than any type of specialization. In the West, the struggle against sexism is considered to be the transition from forced cultural integration to creative differentiation and equality. In Russia, it is the transition from the narrow-minded splintering of culture to its future spiritual synthesis.

Providing equal opportunities for each race and sex is only the political and legal aspect of culture. The spiritual aspect means helping each sex and race to feel that they exist in the context of other cultures, to help every individual identify not only with his or her own social, national, and sexual group but also with representatives of other groups. The ideal of difference means to be different not only from others, but also from one's own self, to outgrow one's identity as a natural being and to become an integral personality that can include the qualities and possibilities of other people's experience. At the bottom of our souls we want to belong to all cultures and share all possible experiences; this makes every person a potentially transcultural being who is not only immersed in one culture, but tries to counteract it through contact with others.

The discussions of "difference," which have been so popular in academia, remain superficial if they fail to include its crucial aspect: the differences within an integral personality that can embrace "otherness," by occupying the standpoint of different cultures. For a culturologist this means being a representative of other cultures within his or her native culture and being a representative of the native culture within the others. No sooner does the process of differentiation penetrate the intimate self of an individual, than it turns into a process of integration with the other. A guiding principle of such self-differentiation is formulated by Homi K. Bhabha: "Cultural difference marks the establishment of new forms of meaning, and strategies of identification, through processes of negotiation where no discursive authority can be established without revealing the difference of itself."[23] I would like to add that this "difference from itself," not simply "the difference of one from another," is the starting point of cultural integration.

American universities have indeed succeeded in conceiving ever newer alternative and multicultural readings of classical and modern texts. In the next phase it will be essential to integrate all of these alternatives in a broader cultural model capable of appealing not only to specific minorities but to the universal potentials of human understanding. Thus, multicultural differentiation may finally lead to the experience of a new, expanded creative totality which is transculture.

PART IV METHODOLOGY

CHAPTER 10 · Theory and Fantasy

From Structure to the Continuum

In emphasizing the nonaxiomatic character of scholarship in the human-ities, one may cast doubt on principles that until recently were considered axioms themselves. We are accustomed to consider Marxism a "science of the universal laws of the development of nature, society and thought."[1] Nonetheless, the question arises, Is it right to transpose "universal law" into such particular areas of cognitive functioning as theory of verse, tropes, or plot? We can recall attempts to create a "Marxist biology," which led ge-netics into extinction. Does this mean that academician Lysenko created "the wrong" Marxist biology, or that academician Marr worked out "the wrong" Marxist linguistics, but nonetheless the task itself deserves another try?[2] Such a proposition can scarcely live up to the criteria of scholarly enterprise.

The search for a single and unerring methodology usually leads to theo-retical stagnation, insofar as it excludes the vital interaction of various com-peting, mutually supplementary methods, each of which may work well enough in its own sphere, on its own level of the object of study. Literature is the art of the word; thus linguistic methods are applied to it. Literature is the creation of fantasy, the result of a creative process; thus psychological meth-ods are applied to it. The same may be said of sociological, phenomenologi-cal, or semiotic methods, but only with reference to their combined totality can we evoke the whole essence of the object being studied. All methods are good except those that declare war on each other. Like any object, literature does not exist in isolation; rather, it is enmeshed in a complex system of spiritual and material connections that embrace all levels of global exis-tence: the psychosphere, the ideosphere, semiosphere, noosphere, sociosphere. After all, it is well known that the whole is present in each of its parts. This means that we may obtain knowledge of any object by means of any method we choose, but no one method holds the privilege of shutting out or subordinating others to itself.

It follows that methods and concepts, worked out in the process of studying literature may also be applied to cognitive processes involving various other spheres of reality. The very specificity of literature, the boundaries dividing it from nonliterature—these are dynamic features of the object; theory finds itself confronting an unstable phenomenon and renews its attempts at mastery largely by shifting its own boundaries. Certain features of literature—plot, genre, metaphor—may also be found in the events of reality itself. This suggests the possibility of using methods and categories derived from the study of literature to investigate many types of historical collisions, scientific conceptions and paradoxes, ideological clichés, the genres of speech behavior and social communication and, no doubt, other areas as well. If literature is an entire world unto itself, then the reverse is also true: all the world is literature; the small may be found in the large and the large in the small. If sociological, psychological, and linguistic methods may be used to conduct research in literature, then the methods of literary studies may fruitfully illuminate social conditions, the struggles of differing worldviews and the inner world of the individual.

The compelling interest of the cognitive process consists precisely in this: its ability to reveal the interconnections and interpenetrations of varied phenomena. The essence of one proves to be the "envelope" of another. This premise authorizes us to study the "literary" beyond the bounds of literature, the "social" beyond the bounds of society, the "psychological" beyond the bounds of the individual. The object of literary studies may, in fact, be all the world, while literature, in turn, may be effectively investigated by any discipline. This cognitive principle may be characterized as the mobile interrelation of object and method. Methods, concepts, and categories arising in the process of studying a certain object can evolve into a supradiscipline, extending over many narrowly object-bound areas of study, in order to produce a transaesthetics, transpoetics, transpsychology, translinguistics, etc. The object of a transpoetics, for example, would include those properties and components of a literary work—imagery, tropes, stylistic figures, rhymes—that are also found outside of literary works, in the very structure of creation. A historical event may be analyzed as a paraphrase, metaphor, hyperbole, or parody of some other event; for example, one might apply these literary terms to the relationship between the French and Russian Revolutions, or between Stalin and Brezhnev as cult figures. From this we can see that it is incorrect to lock up any one area of knowledge either behind the theories and methods developed within it or behind those that may be brought to it from outside. Literature should not be studied only from the standpoint of literary studies and certainly not only from that of sociological, economic, or psychological studies.

Over the past twenty years, *Voprosy literatury* (Issues in Literature)[3] has printed all types of articles under its rubric "Theory: Problems and Reflections." These include such approaches as historiography, culturology, concrete questions of poetics—everything but strict literary theory. And thank God for this, inasmuch as nothing other than scholastic mental exercises on the topics of "methodology, style, mode, genre, plot and story" could be expected from the "tried and true" procedures of theory, properly so-called.[4] But literary theory only stays alive by virtue of its ventures beyond the limits of both theory and literature in and of themselves, through its forays into history, psychology, etiquette and practices of everyday life, language, myth, the fates of culture: it is here, in connection with other layers and levels of reality, that the traditional categories of literary study have truly functioned by addressing real problems. Now, however, it appears to me that the time has come for a return effect of this multiply interpreted reality on the theory of literature. Theory has attempted to escape from stagnation by moving away from itself, from that "theoretical" and "literary" nature, within whose framework it had ceased to expect the slightest movement. Now the necessity is clear for a decisive renewal or even rebirth of theory: by becoming something different it can return to itself, like a seed that cannot be reborn unless it falls to the earth and dies.

How can literary theory renew itself? It seems that this is too narrow a cognitive area to contain sources for renewal within its own borders.[5] Literary theory is actually a bridge hung between two enormous substantive areas: literature and philosophy. A revitalization must take place on the bridge itself as a result of radical change and parallel adjustments on either of the adjoining sides. The theory of literature is essentially an area of mutual coordination, the creative meeting of, or collision between generalizing thought and the artistic word.

In many cases—such as those of Aristotle, Hegel, and Heidegger—literary theory has emerged as the child of a larger philosophical system, as one of the points of application of a general theory that aims to be all-embracing. The most recent such theory was structuralism, which has occasioned so much bitterness and misunderstanding in our country.[6] Today it is obvious that even though structuralism may be surpassed, it cannot be passed over. One must experience the logic of the specific historical movement that led to structuralism; one must trust in this movement and go beyond it. The next step requires us to discover the insurmountable divergence between the presumed structure of a phenomenon and its actual, "sliding" meaning, to reveal the nonstructured spaces in the object, by subjecting it to strict structural analysis. This extension of structuralism beyond its proper limits has been called "deconstruction." It might also be called simply a self-ironic structuralism, since any object, particularly one so integral and unpredicated as a work of art, may well laugh at attempts to equate its ultimate significance with a structure, just as a living body laughs at death in the form of the skeleton contained within itself.

Nonetheless, deconstruction, with its theoretical irony, is only the first stage of trans-structural research, the goal of which must be to display not only the limitations of structuralism, but also to find a cognitive means of describing this sliding remainder, wherein the uniqueness and meaning of the object is contained.

Destructuring the nature of the object reveals not chaos, but the highest form of suprastructural order, so that to regard structuralism from an ironic standpoint becomes an affirmation of the new positive value of a method that might be called "continualism." This would be a practice devoted to studying phenomena in terms of their interlocking traits. The totality of such continuities forms a continuum on which all points are at once distinct and yet inseparable from each other.[7] Continualism does not divide phenomena into discrete elements, because it is free of obsolete conceptions of the nature of elements as final, essential particles or logical atoms. It looks instead for wavelike manifestations that overflow into one another. It studies culture not as a collection of significant oppositions, but as a totality of many fields of meaning, whose borders pass through the "difference from itself" of each cultural manifestation. Therefore, these borders cannot be objectified in themselves; they "sink" in the flux of interchange. The researcher traces a phenomenon across all possible realms of the intellectual universe, translating it from one language into another, from one system into the next, thereby revealing its suprasystematic properties, its belonging to the Process itself. Realms exist, but without established boundaries; various phenomena exist, but without structurally manifest differences or differentiating signs that can acquire their own self-sufficient being in semiotic analysis.

In the process of "rasterizing"[8] any given realm of objects, we transform its depiction (or description) into a set of tiny points by overlaying them with a logical fretwork of oppositions that allows us to obtain a conventionalized scheme approaching actuality to an undetermined extent: a selective scan of the continuum. It may well be time, however, to replace "elementism" and its rasterization of tiny points with a method of "wandering blips" or a "play of highlights," that crosses from one field into the next, illuminating now one portion of the whole, now another. Thus at any given moment of cognitive inquiry, the mathematical "highlight" may fall on literature, while the poetical one falls on the star chart, and the astronomical one falls on the genetic code, and so on. Perhaps the most difficult challenge is to investigate that which is different without trading it in for "differences," those abstract, primary qualities, extracted from the continuum at the price of its painful disruption, of cutting it apart. Difference is ultimately but the illusory objectification, a hypostatization of the different, or, as Hegel said, an "abstraction from the center."

Structuralism is a particular kind of atomism appropriate to the humanities, despite the fact that fluctuation and fuzziness are basic principles of spiritual culture; as the Gospel states, "The wind blows where it will [in Russian translation, "The spirit breathes where it wills"], and you hear the sound of it, but you do not know whence it comes or whither it goes, so it is with everyone who is born of the Spirit" (John 3:8). Similarly, in defining one spiritual phenomenon, we find ourselves moving into the undefined realm of another. Neither identity nor difference can be distinguished in pure form, separated from phenomena themselves, which are often identical in part and partly different. Only by following the phenomenon through its uninterrupted, self-propelling course of activity can we grasp its fluctuating meaning, comprehend the different, without objectifying it in differences. A method of "contamination," of "free-floating contexts" can aid in this procedure: in order to describe any object we apply concepts borrowed from various fields of culture to create (admittedly) strange categories, in which physical terms alternate and act in tandem with musical ones, theological with aesthetic ones. Each phenomenon passes in succession through all areas, as if, free of boundaries, it floats upon the tide of being, requiring of our cognitive powers not a graph of plotted points in space, but something more like a painting. Rather than a composition in tiny dots, we see fluid shapes, colorful smears on the canvas of creation. Continualism is more akin to oil painting than to the graphic drawing of structuralism. Rather than the dual pairs of binary oppositions interrelating according to black-and-white principles of contrast, it works with the multiple options of a full palette.

It goes without saying that all of this is merely the tentative preliminary stage of probable methodological developments. Only one thing is currently clear: the time for purely nihilistic reaction against structuralism (or its deconstructive counterpart) has passed; now a constructive reaction is required, one that will take into account the new theoretical potentials that structuralism created, but that lead beyond its borders and allow us to move on.

Manifesto: Theory and Fantasy

On the practical side of our theoretical question, we must consider the need of literature itself for an appropriate mode of inquiry. Any theory is the alter-being of its object, the sphere of its growing self-awareness and the possibility of its creative transformation. Literary study is born at the moment when verbal art emerges from the state of self-identity, when folklore becomes literature. This impulse of self-propulsion originates with literature and determines the dynamics and shifts of literary theories, each of which outlines the nearest zone of development for the literature of its own time. Literary study is not simply the academic discipline that studies literature. It is the path of *literary development through self-awareness.*

When literature is stagnant, it has no need of theory, and the type of theory that holds sway at such times has no need for the development of literature. It is satisfied with an ideal object that may have been formed centuries before and that it preserves like a museum piece against any attempts by would-be inheritors to touch this object and draw it into renewed action. No science can create a new theory on the basis of data gathered a century or half-century before. Nonetheless, the better part of all contemporary theoretical constructs in our field is still worked out on the material of that literature which was known to Belinsky or Ovsianiko-Kulikovsky[9] and which was reflected in their systems of generalization. It is understandable that theory which is oriented exclusively toward the literature of the past, or toward the most traditional trends in the literature of our time is doomed to reiterate old theories.

There is an acute lack in our day of theorists and thinkers who participate actively in the literary process, as did Andrei Bely, Viacheslav Ivanov, Victor Shklovsky, and Iury Tynianov in Russia, and André Breton, Jean-Paul Sartre, Roland Barthes, and Theodore Adorno in western Europe. Our literary theory is but weakly connected to literary practice, as science in general is to production, and herein lies the reason for their mutually reinforcing helplessness and backwardness. Theory is effective, however, when it does not simply generalize, but also anticipates, illuminates the past anew from the vantage point of the present, while consciously testing the possibilities of the future. In our criticism, the cognitive status of such forms as the artistic-literary manifesto, credo, program, or project has not yet been precisely defined; clearly, however, these are expressions of the most authentic and originary literary *theory*, theory that has turned its face toward the future, that has been created according to the laws of imagination. Literature has a need for such forward-looking theories that outstrip the comfortable norms of the present tense. These are the active yeasts of the artistic process.

It is unfair to assess the forward-looking influence of recent theory on literature as twentieth-century "modernist wiles," or a mark of aesthetic disintegration. Theory is not only description and analysis, but also prophecy and prognosis. Only the unfortunate peculiarities of the past few decades of Soviet literature and literary studies can explain the fact that we understand theory primarily in the form of monographs and textbooks, whereas the manifesto is the first word in the renewal of literary theory, and the monograph is very nearly the last. If we were to make a selection of the most brilliant works that have become classics in the history of aesthetics and literary studies, we would find in them characteristics of both the manifesto and the treatise, interconnecting different facets of theoretical consciousness. Boileau's "The Poetic Art" and Lessing's "Laocoon," the articles and fragments of the Schlegel brothers and Shelley's "Defense of Poetry," Belinsky's "Literary Daydreams" and Chernyshevsky's "The Aesthetic Relations of Art to Reality," all proclaim new principles of artistic thought that reveal previously unknown properties and patterns of literature as a whole. The most general theoretical questions are posed from within artistic practice as an inspiration and inquiry into its own future. "What literature is" depends upon what it is *becoming* and what it *can* become, because being includes becoming as reality includes possibility.

This is why imagination is perhaps the most essential talent of the theorist, particularly of those who deal with the arts. In the aesthetic disciplines, theoretical imagination is called upon to clear a path for artistic imagination; the theorist must not fall behind art, but should surpass it, or, more precisely, should develop the possibilities of creative fantasy beyond the bounds of art, in the realm of experimental generalizations and "insane" hypotheses, which are just as inspirational to the artist, as artistic productions are to the thinker and researcher. Artistic and theoretical fantasy support and animate each other, forming an integral unity of self-developing culture in dialogue with itself.

In the Russian tradition a certain prejudice, stemming from the Middle Ages and from the negative experience of the Soviet decades, has developed against fantasy, both as an individual gift and as a dimension of culture. Fantasy has been seen as something akin to delirium, or the machinations of demonic powers, inflaming the human mind with empty notions. Such a view is oversuspicious of the spiritual nature of the human being; it attempts to cut off one of our most beneficent abilities—to imagine, to foresee, to discern the unseen and create the unheard-of. Scarcely any other talent has offered such prodigious increase, making great return to the creator throughout the course of development of humankind, in all works of art, craft, and science. Imagination is another world, one that germinates deep in the heart of this world, or, to quote Dostoevsky, that great realist-fantast, it "lives and is alive only through the feeling of its contact with other mysterious worlds." It is the seed of those worlds, sown "on this earth."[10]

And in our present situation, it is just as necessary to affirm the social status of imagination, which creates the future, as it has been to support the already socially recognized status of memory, which preserves the past. It would be destructive to set these abilities in opposition to each other, to erase one by means of the other, since it is only in conjunction that they can provide for the regal dignity of the human spirit, its freedom from the caprice of the moment in power and fashion, and its openness to the sum total of all past and future times. It took a good deal of courage, at a specific point in Soviet history, for example, to rise to the defense of memory, because our past had been wiped out in the name of a future wrongly conceived. But there is a danger that we will fail to master this lesson and, under the banner of a reversed value system, will march against the openness of the future, this time in the name of a narrowly nationalistic past, burying the priceless talent of imagination in the soil of tradition.

This psychological disposition is understandable; for too long we dealt with only one kind of imagination: a degenerated, abstract social utopia. Now, badly burned on this hot, sweetened milk, we find ourselves blowing even on pure, refreshing water. But we must realize that imagination is one of the greatest liberating forces that moves humankind in a forward direction; only when—as train cars are attached to a locomotive—archaic instincts, such as the thirst for power or for universal leveling, are harnessed to imagination does it turn into utopianism. Then it limits itself to the assurance of one unchanging and absolutely "correct" picture of the future. Utopianism is suicide of the imagination: even as it summons masses of people to remake the world, it turns them into gravediggers of their own future.

The time has now come to purify imagination of the elements of crude and malevolent utopianism, to return fantasy to its free and proper element—the medium of creativity, not that of coercion. It is time to understand that imagination is a divine gift and a national treasure, whose loss would be as irredeemable as the destruction of natural resources. To the complex of aesthetic disciplines, including literary studies, belongs an important role in the work of cleansing the imagination and strengthening its authority in society. It is, after all, in works of art that we find imagination in its purest sources, unsullied by the interference of power-seeking or mercenary forces. A nation deprived of its imagination, loses its ability to create the future, to answer its own aspirations. Gradually, it drops out of the circle of history.

To help theory develop a taste for diversity and variety, to help it appreciate competition among diverse conceptual and terminological systems, means to open it to the world of imagination, that world which is contained within theory itself, and which resonates in such joyful and kindred harmony with the creative world of art. In order for inventiveness to be reflected in theory, theory must itself be transformed by inventiveness.

Since the time sixty years ago when our humiliated humanities had to defend their right to invent fantasies in polemics with the leaders of the Left Front of Art, who advocated "unadorned fact," our situation has improved but little.[11] The only difference is that "reliance on fact" has been replaced by "faithfulness to tradition." All that is demanded of theory is that it conform to the given facts or traditions, while no one seems to ask what it can add to these by way of justifying its own irreducible existence. However, in our time, an "extravagant inventiveness"[12] is not simply the allowable self-indulgence of powerless academicians in the imprecise sciences. It is a categorical imperative on its own right, one that pervades the new theories of cognition even as regards the most precise natural sciences. History shows that numerous ideas that renewed the scientific picture of the world in their time arose not in consonance with the facts that were then known (not even to mention traditions), but rather in sharp conflict with them. Paul Feyerabend, a leading contemporary scientific methodologist, has formulated a rule of "counterinduction," which recommends "the invention and elaboration of hypotheses inconsistent with a point of view that is highly confirmed and generally accepted."[13]

All of this strongly suggests that fantasy, which tends to depart from facts rather than unite with them, has an independent value for theoretical pursuits. Concepts, categories, and terms constitute the raw material of creative imagination, just as colors do in painting or words in poetry. The aim of theory is to *multiply ideal existences,* which would then intersect in part with existing facts, while also departing from them to form a multidimensional space of potential worlds. In the same way, the degrees of human freedom multiply with our "extra-locatedness" in relation to the world around us.[14] Theory should correlate with fact according to a principle of supplementarity, by proposing alternatives to one-sided facticity, grafting the possible onto the already present. By virtue of its very existence, such theory turns the possible into the real. As it departs from known fact, theory becomes a fact itself, a fact as yet unknown; in conjunction with other such facts it stimulates the creation of new theories.

> Knowledge so conceived is not a series of self-consistent theories that converges towards an ideal view; it is not a gradual approach to the truth. It is rather an ever increasing ocean of *mutually incompatible (and perhaps even incommensurable) alternatives,* each single theory, each fairy tale, each myth that is part of the collection forcing the others into greater articulation and all of them contributing, via this process of competition, to the development of our consciousness.[15]

The above is true for literary theory and the arts more than for any other area, because the intrinsic patterns of the artistic object itself, which theory seeks to refract and unfold, demand the generation of conceptual systems in accordance with the principles of creative fantasy. In this sense, art theory can lead the movement of scientific consciousness to become the art of generating theories.

It might seem as if the proposed principle of unrestricted multiplication, "proliferation," as Feyerabend says, of alternative ideas and theories annuls the possibility of their correlative evaluation: "each is fine in its own way," so to speak. But this is not the case. One of the criteria that should be advanced to the forefront of cognitive theory is not the conformity of the idea to external facts but its degree of nonconformity to the customary understanding of facts. In other words, an idea proves fertile to the degree that it is able to *amaze.* The most amazing ideas are not at all those that arbitrarily distort facts, nor are they those that monosemantically correspond to them. Instead they are ideas that join with facts in a tense connection of attraction and repulsion, affirming and refuting them simultaneously, making them both clearer and yet more enigmatic. The probability of utterance of such ideas is minimal; hence their richness is maximal. Not unlike orthogonal planes, such theories may intersect with the plane of fact along a single line, while extending beyond the facts in other directions.

Aristotle defined wonder as the starting point of the cognitive process. "For it is owing to their wonder that men both now begin and at first began to philosophize . . . a man who is puzzled and wonders thinks himself ignorant."[16] Are we to suppose that as cognitive consciousness runs its course the original impulse of wonder is exhausted and erased, so that in the end we earn the right to say, "All is now clear in the light of reason, nothing remains at which to wonder"? No, the authentic process of cognition is not like this. Its movement runs from one unexpected event to another, so that amazement becomes a self-generating process: one secret is clarified, but behind this clarity there opens a still deeper secret. The *result* of cognitive processes should also make us wonder, not merely the starting point. Thanks to the triumphant development of science in the twentieth century, the world appears much more wondrous and enigmatic today than it did one hundred years ago, when everything within it seemed obvious, explainable, and somewhat boring.

Unfortunately, the scholarly disciplines in Russia, particularly the humanities, are still held captive to old cognitive paradigms that take correctness and noncontradiction as their points of orientation. The bitter paradox lies in the fact that our scholarly disciplines, not excluding literary studies, have avoided giving full consideration and implementation to all the available facts pertaining to their topics. We have not yet even approached the boundaries of positivism, whereas contemporary scientific methodology already demands that we cross it, rejecting the principles of verification and falsification in favor of alternativity. The old practice leads to a massive accumulation of tautologies and truisms, to which the most honest reaction can only be boredom. An unconscious feeling of boredom is the incorruptible witness to the vacuousness of numerous theoretical works in which "tried and true" methodologies prevent rather than aid the expression of scholarly creativity. The ideas such scholarship seeks to embody may be quite correct and noncontradictory; yet precisely for that reason they fail to interact with facts, but lie upon them like a dead weight. This is true particularly of such authoritative ideas as "moral obligation," "social responsibility," "historical causation," etc. These are applied without analysis to an enormous number of facts (actions, works), depriving them of the last vestiges of originality or inner secrecy, while giving well-known answers to questions that have not even been asked. The authoritarianism of such ideas in the realm of methodology actually undercuts their authority in the ethical and social realm.

This is why the criterion of "wonderment—boredom" would seem to be more radical and productive for the evaluation of ideas and theses, offering greater promise for the renewal of our theorizing than does the traditional logical criterion "truth—falsehood." One may insist forever on the truth of some idea, deduce it from the common mass of facts or traditions, raise it to the level of dogma or absolutes, but if it does not expand the boundaries of our established understandings, if it does not bring the mind to a state of astonishment, then it lacks the quality of living truth. This should not serve to enshrine the merely novel undeservedly, if we keep in mind that old truths uttered hundreds or thousands of years ago are still able to amaze, if we have the desire to ponder them. The problem is that we have confused truth with correctness and made of it the dull, automatically deducible conclusion of an infallible methodology, while attaching the label of "falseness" to any idea that diverges from the facts in its attempt to interact with them freely.

In order to reflect the world truly, an idea must *strike the imagination*.[17] The world, after all, holds no fewer riddles than the imagination holds solutions; it would be naive to suppose that reality is poorer and flatter than our boldest inventions. That which is, in truth, the Truth cannot fail to amaze. In considering the various methods of literary study, we must not neglect the main criterion: Does the theory before us render the world of literature more wondrous and mysterious than it seemed to us before? Does it augment our knowledge of this world with the sanctity of the unknown?

The Social Value of New Ideas

A new rubric is necessary in humanistic studies because the standard genre of the scholarly article (or review, or review article), as it is accepted in the journals, and the exposition of a new idea are quite different things.[18] Articles frequently contain no new ideas whatsoever, or else their ideas are presented in such an expansive manner as to obscure the degree of actual innovation. The result is a kind of scholarly folklore, involving a migration of motifs without any real creative productivity: the means of synonymous expression in any language are virtually endless, and a single idea can be embodied in dozens of different ways by preying on its elusiveness, its lack of theoretical definiteness. Many ideas lack definite authors, and many authors lack definite ideas. These factors produce a mechanism of intellectual blockage. It is necessary to create a more flexible system of preservation and dissemination of ideas, one that could also fit the criteria of continualism, in that it would reflect the uninterrupted process of producing new knowledge, the uninterruptedness of cognitive reality itself.

One could justly point out that the evaluation of original ideas already takes place within the public forum of the dissertation defense, but these activities can go on for years, while the idea accrues often unnecessary, officially "accountable" supporting material, in which its essence, its original mental impulse, is likely to drown. In addition, experience shows that the most innovative ideas are to be found on the points of cusp between various fields, so that they have difficulty "passing muster" with specialized scientific committees and are subsequently lost to that larger science for which they were intended. A mass-circulation journal could be of substantial help in correcting this situation, by offering new life to those good ideas that are currently foundering and by giving initial impulse to further innovations through a Bank of New Ideas. A truly new idea seldom fits into ready-made spheres of knowledge; rather, it wrenches itself away from the well-known nomenclature of dissertation topics and scientific specialization to create its own sphere. It requires a kind of "savings bank" for preservation, one that will be sensitive to intellectual values, not blocked in by compartmentalization. Regardless of the form in which an idea presents itself—be it a conclusion based on empirical data, the formulation of a question, a hypothetical proposition, a theory, fantasy, paradox, pronouncement, or project—it possesses the independent value of a new shift in established systems of concepts. A Bank of New Ideas and Terms would take on the task of registering the totality of such shifts, making it the most substantial information system for any given branch of knowledge.

The problem of creating information banks is currently under intense consideration in many scientific areas and has been supported by appropriate initiatives in the journals *Technology for the Young, Chemistry and Life,* and others. Meanwhile, the human sciences remain in a difficult situation that demands prompt resolution, since the very criteria for identifying and evaluating ideas are far from clear, yet are virtually never discussed; at least, such is the case in literary studies. For these reasons I wish to share the experience of the Bank of New Ideas and Terms, which was founded under the auspices of "Image and Thought," a research seminar focusing on art and scholarship, that originated in Moscow in 1986. The goal of this bank was to foster the development of new methods of thinking in all areas of contemporary culture, to provide the conditions for formulating, shaping, and disseminating original ideas, moving at the junctures of different disciplines and types of social consciousness. This bank accepts for preservation ideas that show a significant degree of innovation, uniqueness, and potential for productive impact on the cultural and intellectual development of society. Discussion and registration of ideas is conducted by experts within the group, representing several different professions. A system of parameters has been worked out for the evaluation of ideas, including the following:

1. Unexpectedness, the capacity to amaze, to disrupt theoretical paradigms and established patterns of thought.

2. Originality, innovativeness, the extent to which the idea differs from others previously put forth in its field.

3. Verifiability, the extent to which the idea is convincing in the light of available facts as well as its logical development from the foundations it proposes.

4. Expressiveness and aesthetic properties of the idea, the inner harmony of its components and levels of argumentation, the proportionality of deductive and inductive elements, its plasticity and clarity, accessibility to intellectual contemplation and compatibility with the laws of imagination.

5. Globality and expansiveness, the volume of material embraced and interpreted by the idea, the range of its repercussions in the given discipline and its major theoretical generalizations.

6. Productivity, the heuristic potential of the idea to influence intellectual development in areas beyond its own basic material and disciplinary boundaries.

7. Realizability, the practical measure of the idea, as applied to the concrete conditions of its development, the possibility of its actualization on various levels of reality.

Such are the principles employed in this group for addressing new ideas. With further refinement they could serve as a basis for a more extensive storehouse of literary ideas and concepts. The press is certainly a vital link in the interconnection of ideas and society, and a rubric of this kind could take on the responsibility and honor of playing a role that neither a discussion group nor an academic institute is able to fulfill. The scholarly press should provide a channel for connecting society with the work of its most powerful intellects; any obstacles or delays in this channel lead to both the intellectual impoverishment of society itself and the deterioration of the social function of intellect. Ultimately, this can bring about a broadly anti-intellectual attitude in the social sector, as well as an antisocietal attitude in the intellectual sector, as witnessed by the Soviet era. Ideally, however, the scholarly press can hold up a mirror to intellect, or a screen for the projection of its ongoing work, open for public view and commentary, and for the consistent stimulation and intensification of social consciousness.[19] Nothing unites one mind with another in so perceptive and valuable a way as does the flash of a new idea. The effectiveness of the scholarly press should rightfully consist in its rapid dissemination of new ideas throughout the arena of public consciousness, without any introductions, conclusions, equivocations, or emendations—just the concentrated essence of innovation. Some of the new concepts may well prove fallacious, but the same rule should apply in the sphere of cognition that applies in jurisprudence: it is better to voice ten fallacious ideas than to silence a single valid one. Actually, it is likely that there are no fallacious ideas, just more and less productive ones. In the realm of ideas nothing is impossible. As Goethe said, to live in an idea means to treat the impossible as if it were possible.

It should be obvious, at any rate, that any new notion stands in need of public discussion and may be accepted or rejected only after this process has taken place, not before. A society that deprives itself of the influx and circulation of new ideas is condemned to stagnation and deterioration.

Appendix: Toward a Concept of the "Kenotype"

The terminological and conceptual apparatus of the humanities in the late Soviet period fell behind the development of contemporary culture in general, due to a long-standing lack of renovation. Thus arises the appeal of new terminological formations, one of which I would like to share with the reader.[20]

The term "kenotype" is formed from the ancient Greek words *kainos*, meaning "new," and *typos,* meaning "form" or "imprint." "Kenotype," then, is literally a "new form"; in the system of culturological concepts it should stand beside "archetype," to which it offers a specific contrastive meaning.

Carl Jung used the term "archetype" to refer to the generalized patterns of images that form the world of human representations in recurrent motifs, passing through the history of all culture. Since archetypes are rooted in the collective unconscious, they may be conceived through the psychic activity of any individual, be it in the form of dreams, artworks, the ancient monuments of religious activity, or the contemporary images of commercial advertising. Such archetypes as the "innocent babe," the "unheeded prophet," the "philosopher's stone," and many others that also have their source in the primitive darkness of the unconscious, are repeated in numerous works of cultural creation.

Along with the notion of the archetype, art and literary theorists often use the concept of "type" to represent concrete historical tendencies of any kind that are generalized in artistic works. In this sense the images of Chatsky, Onegin, Chichikov, and Oblomov are called typical,[21] insofar as they reflect some of the most characteristic traits of their respective epochs, nationality, and specific social level. If archetypal refers to the lowest, prehistoric, atemporal layer of the "collective soul," then typical indicates the imprint of history, in its socially conditioned and concretely meaningful expressions. However, the archetypal and the typical do not exhaust the contents of cultural forms and artistic images, considered as a set of utterly general categories. There remains the possibility that universality may neither be given a priori, nor limited by history, but rather derived from the final significance of history, from the superhistorical condition of the world, in which unfold patterns, formulas, and models unknown to the prehistoric unconscious. In contrast to "archetype," these new forms of spiritual creativity, which pervade all cultures of the Modern Age and are especially prevalent in the twentieth century, can be called *kenotypes*. A kenotype may be defined as a cognitive, creative structure, reflecting a new crystallization of some broadly human experience, occurring in concrete historical circumstances, but not reducible to them, and appearing as the first embodiment of a potential or future development. If, in the case of archetype, the general precedes the concrete, as a preestablished form precedes materialization, and if in a type the two coexist, then in the case of kenotype, the general is a final perspective of the concrete, which arises from history only to outgrow it, touching the borders of eternity. Everything that can come into being has its metaimage in the future, since it prophesies or gives a warning about something. This storehouse of metaimages is far richer than the strongbox of first images, where the ancient unconscious is contained. The openness of history is given to humankind as a birthplace for superhistorical content, where the permanent can obtain its "surplus value," and where its image can not only be preserved, but even grow in time.

For example, the magic mountain in Thomas Mann's novel by the same name is an archetypal image, connected to ancient representations of the dwelling place of gods, including Olympus and Horselberg (the mountain where Tannhäuser spent seven years in captivity to Venus).[22] The tuberculosis sanatorium located on its summit, however, is a kenotypal image, in which Mann develops the crystallization of a historically new conceptual system, represented in his conjectures on "the coming of a new humanity tempered in the crucible of profound knowledge of sickness and death." Such images as a "joli bourgeois au petit endroit humide," as Clavdia Chauchat calls Hans Castorp, or the lung X-ray that he requests of her rather than an ordinary photograph—these are not simply socially characteristic details, nor "formulas given from antiquity" (as Mann defined archetypes); instead, they are kenotypal images, rendering a new cultural semantic that Castorp formulates as "the brilliant principle of disease."

In his essays on Nietzsche and Dostoevsky, Mann emphasizes the historical appearance of "disease" as a cultural phenomenon with a universal meaning, capable of organizing mankind's spiritual life in a new way. For instance, Mann writes of Nietzsche that "It was precisely his illness that became the source of those inspiring impulses, which proved so creative and at times so destructive for an entire epoch."[23] In *The Magic Mountain,* Mann's artfully selected physiological details—the tubercular process as a sickening of the tissues supplying air to the organism, those finest and most "disembodied" of substances—provide continual recourse to an artistic metaphysics of the spirit. Mann's kenotypal depictions are born of a concrete cultural and historical situation: the creative achievement of those "afflicted seers," Dostoevsky and Nietzsche, in the atmosphere of refined disintegration known as fin de siècle or decadence in art and literature. The experience of the First World War expanded this situation into a great variety of meanings, not limited to the framework of a single epoch; the topic of lung disease acquired an eschatological aspect. The kenotypes of the sanitorium and the X-ray, for all their obvious universality, can in no way be projected onto the originary levels of the "collective unconscious," nor do they have analogues in ancient mythology.

Kenotypal formations may be found not only in the sphere of art and literature, but also among the events of contemporary technology and everyday life and culture, where their meaning extends beyond the bounds of a single instance and of contemporaneity itself. A subway system is kenotypal, composed of interconnected underground crypts and containing, not the quiet of the grave, but the bustle and movement of living people by the millions. The kenotypicality of any phenomenon reveals itself in the obvious volume of symbolic values, the abundance of metaphors and analogies that directly accompany it through the process of its social assimilation. For example, cancer is often interpreted as a sickness of the social organism, expressed in the degraded simplification and homogenization of its structures.

One and the same cultural phenomenon may manifest layers of both archetypal and kenotypal significance. So it is with a shoreline that divides the two elements, land and sea: this space is deeply archetypal, as numerous poetic and literary works attest. But the usage of this same physical space for rest and recuperation under the influence of all the natural elements present here—sun, water, and sand—represents a different metaphysical significance: the *beach,* which is a kenotype originating in our era. Consider, "On the shore of desert waves he stood, full of great thoughts." Or "Longed for border of my soul! How often on your shores have I wandered, quiet as the fog, tormented by a secret notion."[24] Pushkin's unfailing intuition informs these lines: the shore is a place for both the lawgiver and mutineer. Precisely on this boundary line begins a surge toward the boundless, the "great thought" and "secret notion" that stretch beyond the bounds of the accessible. On the shore may be seen the figure of a guardian, protecting the borders of the elements, or that of an infractor, plotting to transcend them; here they stand erect or wander along. On the beach, however, everything refers to the horizontal dimension; it is a place not for standing, but for lying, in surrender to an unfocused peace of mind, a lazy repose. If the shore decisively divides the elements into "either . . . or," the beach brings everything together into "both this . . . and that." In the latter instance the borderline of being is transformed into the being and way of life of the borderline itself, the place of rest and contentment where all the elements are tame and loving, as they play around the human center. Could this be the future to which mankind is hurrying with the same haste as it hurries to the beach when summer comes, regaining in these densely populated spaces of the earth a long-lost paradise? Could this be the ultimate task of a self-deified humanity: the transformation of all the earth into an endless beach, an outpouring of golden sand? The kenotype of the beach contains an ominous warning against the degradation of our dream of a return to paradise, a place of eternal bliss.

According to a widespread understanding of archetypes, everything new is but a phenomenological covering for those "primary essences," whose content remains unchanged over the ages. But actually, the essence may be as new as the phenomenon. Time not only varies our original archetypes, it fulfills a more fundamental task as well: the creation of new types, both those that represent generalizations of their epoch, and those that acquire supertemporal significance. Kenotypicality is the potential for universalizing a new historical experience; it is a perspective that addresses not the beginning but the potential end of time, as a vast and growing source of meaning.

To designate these emerging dimensions of the culture of a new era we need a new, prospective terminology that will not hark back to prehistoric phases and forms of consciousness, but will look forward. In the meantime, such terms as "mythologeme," and "archetype" pervade our thinking about contemporary culture, distorting essential matters: the superhistorical and universal orientation that is increasing in contemporary consciousness is not in the least an archaic, prepersonal model, and a retrospective terminology is inappropriate to describe it.

Introducing the concept of the kenotype does not contradict Jung's theory of the unconscious, which allows for the capacity to undergo drastic metamorphoses in anticipation of historical changes. According to Jung, the unconscious is able to create new conceptions; it is historically mobile and productive. In our day it is particularly important to distinguish its conservative, self-protective layers—those that relate to the sphere of archetypes—from its dynamic, creative layers, which are even now producing new kenotypes. The proposed term is intended to remedy not a flaw in Jungian theory, but a flaw in its conventional articulation.

CONCLUSION · A Future after the Future

The paradoxes of postmodernism, as presented in this book, shaped its two interconnected goals: first, to trace the postmodern horizons of contemporary Russian culture; and second, to delineate the movement of contemporary culture beyond the horizon of postmodernism itself.

As mentioned in the Preface the profound tendencies toward irony and complete reversal characteristic of Russian culture allow it to at once embrace postmodernism and reveal its limits in a single act of crowning and dethroning. In Russia, postmodernism is perceived as a parodic unmasking of centuries of logocentrism in Russian culture, of captivity to the word and the ideological principle. But this profound parody parodies itself as it gives rise to ever new enactments and unmaskings, whose ultimate victim turns out to be postmodernism itself.

While the first two parts of this book emphasize the postmodern tendencies of Russian culture, the last two indicate the possibilities for moving beyond the postmodern paradigm. Essayism is a transgeneric mode of writing, the lyrical museum is a trans-semiotic realm of substantiality, culturology is a theoretical emergence into the space of transculture, and, finally, continualism is a transdisciplinary approach in methodology. Common to all four of these "trans-" movements is the overcoming of contingent sign systems, of national and temporal limitations and of the splintering of culture into narrow disciplines. This does not entail a return to the pre-essayistic, presemiotic, predisciplinary or precultural wholeness of myth, things, knowledge, or nature as such; rather, it is the building of a complex, self-reflexive whole beyond postmodernism's playful pluralism.

Parts III and IV address the prospects of a new whole, one that is not exclusive, but presupposes a wealth of difference. Essayism, the lyrical museum, continualism, and transculture are all experiments in the building

of an antitotalitarian totality that includes the postmodern play of differences and simultaneously creates a realm that differs from and is beyond the
province of play itself. Play becomes impossible in a space where there is
nothing but play; for this reason play creates another sphere, which it differentiates and protects from itself. In like manner, difference unfurls its
omnipresence, creating something that differs from difference itself: a possibility of wholeness that I have indicated by the prefix "trans-" in reference
to space and "proto-" in reference to time. Difference cannot be itself unless
it presupposes that which differs from it, namely, unity. The creation of that
which differs from differing is the measure of maturity of difference itself.
The postmodern principle of difference presupposes, to the extent of its
realization, a new wholeness beyond variety in styles, genres, and cultures.
As such new unities are constructed from the sphere of difference itself,
postmodernism crosses over to the next phase of cultural movement. Pluralism of disciplines, semiotic codes, and cultures enters into a new, nontotalitarian whole, where difference acts in mature form, that is, by differing from itself. It no longer opposes itself to wholeness, but rather creates
wholes from itself, from the free play of self-differentiation.

A multiplicity of genres and types of writing opens the prospects of essayism as an integral verbal expression; a multiplicity of verbal descriptions
opens the prospects of approaching the "extra-verbal" singularity of a thing;
a multiplicity of disciplines opens the prospects of overlapping methodologies, such as "transpoetics" or "translinguistics," so that any of them can be
applied to each other's objects; a multiplicity of cultures opens the prospects of entering the space of transculture. The child's play of difference
destroys idols by tearing them down to fragments and quotations; the mature play of difference hears the silence within speech, senses a thing amid
its descriptions, and contemplates the purity of the future amid its failed
projections.

The future is the least popular of all categories in contemporary theory in
the humanities. It is almost considered shameful to speak about the future,
as if it had sullied itself through collusion with "occupationists of the future," those utopianists and totalitarians who used force against the present
in the future's name.

But now is precisely the time to admit that the future, after all, is not to
blame. It deceived all of those who attempted to subdue it. Reaching beyond
the horizon of all utopian proscriptions, it shines anew in all its purity.
Now, after all the utopias and anti-utopias of this century, we obtain, per-

haps for the first time in history, a chance to feel the full depth and decep-tiveness of its purity. This is not the purity of a tabula rasa, where anything one wants may be written, and any grandiose project may be realized. It is rather the purity of an eraser that wipes the clear lines of projects off a chalkboard, transforming someone's plan into a vague blot: a fading pun or pastiche, the remnants of an evaporated outline. Before us opens an image of the future as a great irony that will never allow itself to be objectified and subjected to analysis.

Poststructuralist theories often employ "language" and the "unconscious" as representatives of the radical other. But these still possess a certain struc-ture that can be deciphered in neuroses and metaphors. Only the future is a minus-structure, with its unmitigated meaningfulness in the absence of any definite meaning. In searching for something radically different, maximally nontransparent, we approach the future. It lacks transparency because it is open, and, although it is dark, it obscures nothing.

And then we must consider, why it is that the future's own proclivities—hiding itself, slipping away, evading nomination and manifestations of itself—have been displaced by postmodernism onto the past and present. The impossibility of origin has been revealed in the past, and the impos-sibility of presence has been revealed in the present, the impossibility of truth—everywhere. But all of these impossibilities are known to us from our interactions with the future.

Postmodernism is essentially a reaction to utopianism, the intellectual disease of obsession with the future that infected the latter half of the nine-teenth century and the first half of the twentieth. The future was thought to be definite, attainable, and realizable; in other words, it was given the at-tributes of the past. Postmodernism, with its aversion to utopias, inverted the signs and reached for the past, but in so doing, gave it the attributes of the future: indeterminateness, incomprehensibility, polysemy, and the ironic play of possibilities. The phases of time have been castled. But this postmodern replacement of the future by the past is in no way better than the avant-garde replacement of the past by the future. In revealing the inde-terminateness of meaning in the classical texts of the past, deconstruction reveals itself to be the mirror image of avant-garde constructivism, which posited rigid and absolute meanings in an as yet unconstituted future.

The game of past and future played by postmodernism and avant-gardism is winding down without a winner. This is especially clear in Russia, where postcommunism is rapidly moving into the past, on the very heels of com-munism. There is a need to go beyond the confines of both utopia and its resonating parodies. The "postcommunist epoch" can count only a few years to its name, having already deeply bogged down in the protoplasm of some new, unknown social system. We come out once again into the stage of a "pre-future," but this time with the awareness that it is utterly unknown. The "communist future" remains in the past, but this only means that the future has been cleansed of yet another specter, or idol, and such cleansing, or demythologization, of time is the proper function of the future. At present, the future is again advancing on Russia, not with an exclamation mark this time, but rather with a question, to which there is not and cannot be a known answer.

Postmodernism announced an "end to time," but any end serves to open at least a crack in time for what is to come after and, thus, indicates the self-irony of finality, which turns into yet another beginning. The state of beginning, or origination, is the irony of an end annulled by endlessness, or infinity. But it is as difficult to speak about infinity as it is to speak about an end: it is nowhere to be found except in positing a new beginning. One can only speak about that beginning which reveals infinity negatively, as the semblance and impossibility of finality. To conceive of "beginning" and "end," as necessarily symmetrical and correlative, is to distort the asymmetrical nature of time. Time belongs to the condition of uncompletedness, the preeminence of beginnings over ends. As an example, let us consider literary genres. The tragedy, comedy, novel, and essay all have more or less definite historical beginnings, but their ends are nowhere to be seen. They remain hidden beyond the horizon. All that we know about these genres is but the prototype of their potential future, their "protogenre." A beginning thus understood as leading to an open future and manifesting possibilities for continuation and an impossibility of ending can be designated as "proto."

In affirming the category of uncompletedness, Bakhtin noted with regret, "What we foreground is the *ready-made* and *finalized.* Even in antiquity we single out what is ready-made and finalized, and not what has originated and is developing. We do not study literature's preliterary embryos."[1] Elsewhere, Bakhtin opposes two approaches—"completing" and "initiating," or in contemporary terminology, "post" and "proto"—to the question of "genre as a definite (essentially, petrified) whole, and [of] embryonic genres (thematic and linguistic), with a still undeveloped compositional skeleton, so to speak, the 'first signs' of a genre."[2] Moreover, it is not a matter of studying the first signs of already formed and well-known genres, but of studying originary phenomena as such, in the early stages of their formation, when the fate of the genre still belongs to the future, or rather, to one possible future.

The prefix "proto-," which I propose to use in designating the next, now ripened shift in post-postmodern culture, is a radical transition from finality to initiation as a mode of thinking. In subjecting everything to irony, postmodernism was insufficiently ironic in relation to itself, for only time alone is real irony, in that it never rests on its laurels. In ridding itself of time, postmodernism rids itself of the only possibility for obtaining distance from itself, and, in the end, it becomes just as flat as the utopias it once mocked. The only subject irony has not yet outdone is the future. I refer once again to Bakhtin, who wrote of the impossibility of completing history from within history, and of the future as a laughing disclosure of attempts to stop the unstoppable:

> Nothing conclusive has yet taken place in the world, the ultimate word of the world and about the world has not yet been spoken, the world is open and free, everything is still in the future and will always be in the future.

But this is, after all, also the *purifying* sense of ambivalent laughter.[3]

Essentially, postmodernism, with its rejection of utopias, *was* the last great utopia, precisely because it situated itself after everything; it concluded everything with itself. Where utopias once stood, striving toward the future, laying down a fast track for themselves through bloody revolutions, postmodernism established itself as an all-accepting, already realized utopia. Its similarity with socialist realism is evident in that it proclaims itself as the all-embracing cultural space, the last receptacle of everything that ever unfolded and took shape within history. True, in its time, socialist realism proclaimed itself as something absolutely new, and for that very reason, was obliged to recognize its belonging to history. But postmodernism overcame even this ultimate weakness by announcing its own radically derivative and simulative nature and, therefore, its authentically unsurpassable finality. Postmodernism rejected utopia, rejected a historicity that pushed off from the past in striving toward the future, but then it took over the place of utopia itself. In a sense, postmodernism is more utopian than all previous utopias as it falls in line with the mode of suprahistory, not then and later, but here and now. Previous utopias were more or less oriented toward the future, while postmodernism, in its repulsion of the future, is a utopia of the eternal present, of endlessly playful self-repetition. It is the last utopia, which, having frozen up in comprehensive, "infinite" finality, became "postmodernity."

In defining the further prospects of postmodernism and its transition to the "proto" model, it is well to pause on one moment in the history of this concept that often eludes the attention of researchers. In Lyotard's original projection, postmodernism appeared as an attempt to return from modernism's finalistic, teleological pretensions to an originary, unstable "embryonic state," evident in the initial modernist experiments.

> A work can become modern only if it is first postmodern. Postmodernism thus understood is not modernism at its end but in the nascent state, and this state is constant. . . . The postmodern would be that which, in the modern, puts forward the unpresentable in presentation itself . . . , that which searches for new presentations, not in order to enjoy them but in order to impart a stronger sense of the unpresentable. . . . The artist and the writer, then, are working without rules in order to formulate the rules of what *will have been done*. . . . *Post modern* would have to be understood according to the paradox of the future (*post*) anterior (*modo*).[4]

In 1979, Lyotard thought of postmodernism as a return to the sources of modernism, to the play of pure experimentation that preceded utopian and totalitarian seriousness, with their claims of remaking the world.

But just five years later, Fredric Jameson advanced an entirely different postmodern orientation: toward completeness in the mode of the past, which, indeed, is more appropriate to the meaning of the prefix "post-": "For with the collapse of the high-modernist ideology of style . . . the producers of culture have nowhere to turn but to the past: the imitation of dead styles, speech through all the masks and voices stored up in the imaginary museum of a now global culture."[5] In 1984, the year that Lyotard's book was translated into English, Jameson noted in his preface the gap between Lyotard's understanding of the phenomenon and the reality of this cultural epoch:

> This very commitment to the experimental and the new, however, determine an aesthetic that is far more closely related to the traditional ideologies of high modernism proper than to current postmodernisms. . . . Thus, although he has polemically endorsed the slogan of a "postmodernism" and has been involved in the defence of some of its more controversial production, Lyotard is in reality quite unwilling to posit a postmodernist stage radically different from the period of high modernism. . . . [Lyotard] has characterized postmodernism, not as that which follows modernism and its particular legitimation crisis, but

rather as a cyclical moment that returns before the emergence of ever *new* modernisms in the stricter sense. . . . [H]is commitment to cultural and formal innovation still valorizes culture and its powers in much the same spirit in which the Western avant-garde has done so since the fin de siècle.[6]

Who is right in this dispute? Obviously, the postmodernism known to us is closer to Jameson's characterization, but the subsequent evolution of postmodernism approaches the boundary of "what will have been done" described by Lyotard, and earlier, by Bakhtin. The idea of "the last," "the completed" is exhausted before our eyes. The very concept of "postmodernism" is beginning to sound more and more absurd. How long after modernism will we continue to use it as our privileged reference point? Are we not now also located in postantiquity, post-Renaissance, postbaroque, postrealism? And since the epoch immediately preceding us is postmodernism, haven't we already entered post-postmodernism, or even post-post-post- . . . ? Instead of such a proliferation of posts, I would suggest defining the current epoch in terms of "proto-."

As its prefixes accumulate, this post-post-post- . . . modernism reveals the properties of time within itself; once again it stands before the future, and in so doing, passes beyond its own limits. As more and more "posts" are layered atop one another, each of them becomes only a "proto-," a predecessor of something that comes next. "Before the next" is a more appropriate definition of uncertainty than "after the last." If what we mean by postmodernism is the play of indeterminate meanings, why shouldn't we use the future as the model of such uncertainty rather than the already-determined past? The "not-yet" contains many possibilities absent in the "already."

Does this sound like a new kind of utopianism? Utopianism imposes a certainty on the future and presents it as an obligation and necessity rather than a possibility. The same was true of the futurist artists of the 1910s and 1920s as well as the so-called futurologists, whose specialty in the 1960s and 1970s was "scientific" prediction of the future, proceeding from deterministic concepts. Proto-, as it is emerging on the boundary of post-, is not proto-*something*, it is *proto* in itself, which, for the sake of playful convention, might also be called "proteism," incorporating a reference to the Greek god, Proteus, whose dominion is the seething sea and who personifies possibility in his polymorphousness. Utopianists have taught us to fear the future that they represent as an inevitable paradise. In order to overcome utopianism, it is not enough to be anti-utopianist or even postutopianist;

one has to restore one's love of the future, not as a promised State, but as a state of promise, as expectation without determination.

Lyotard's formula, "what will have been done" assumes something finished in the future as a point of departure for further events, the supposition of a future after the future. His definition of postmodernism as the "future anterior," or a future located in the past, in relation to another, approaching future, might be shifted to reveal that we are not so much addressing this future in the past, as the one it precedes.

The epoch that comes "after the future" does not simply abolish the future, but opens it anew. Only the future conceived as already attained and under control is abolished, and it is after just such a dead, objectified future—be it called communism, industrialism, or avant-gardism—that we now find ourselves living. At the same time, the future is now being de-objectified. Here opens such a future as cannot be embodied and built, which always turns up "after" and, by its silence, dissolves the meanings of the preceding layers.

It seems that Jameson and Lyotard are both right; only after our experience (and exhaustion) of Jameson's postmodern paradigm that is "turned to the past" can we elaborate upon Lyotard's paradigm of postmodernism as an emerging "nascence" without fear that this will send us back in time to repetitions of avant-garde and utopian delusions and disenchantments. Jameson's postmodernism, which, like pastiche, is consciously derivative and quotational, broke the ground for Lyotard's, with its new return to the "nascent state," the "original after the derivative," but this time, with the mediating experience of quotationalism.

The mode of "protodiscourse" is neither avant-garde self-expression nor postmodern quotationism. Rather, it is a kind of self-quotation by which an individual enters the process of self-differentiation, whereby his discourse is absolutely original and derivative at the same time. Such originality is not a personal pretension and not a form of aggression toward others, but a conscious inevitability: each is doomed to be first in saying something, and simultaneously, each is free to relate his utterance to a preexisting source. As a result, I speak as if I were quoting myself. The distinction between me and the other passes through myself and can never be fixed rigorously and objectively. The other is located within me, and I speak in his name. This is a "derivative originality," in which originality itself is produced as a quotation from some possible source contained in the speaker's consciousness, but not equivalent to his own selfhood.

Dmitry Prigov, the conceptualist poet mentioned more than once in these pages, calls such indivisible combinations as derivativeness, or quotation-alism, paired with originality a "shimmering aesthetic." The reader will never know in advance if the author is original or citational, sincere or parodic in his pronouncements because the degree of his self-identification changes from line to line, from word to word.

> In our times postmodernist consciousness is superseded by a strictly conceptual virtual distance of the author from the text. . . . Taking the place of the conceptual, a shimmering relationship between the author and the text has developed, in which it is very hard to define (not only for the reader but for the author, too) the degree of sincerity in the immersion into the text and the purity and distance of the withdrawal from it. I.e., the fundamental content becomes the drama between the author and the text, his flickering between the text and a position out-side of it."[7]

Prigov finds "shimmering aesthetics" to be a new, advanced stage of concep-tualism, even referring to it as "postconceptualism," since the parody and pastiche that are traditionally associated with conceptualism are enriched with a "new sincerity." This kind of sincerity is postconceptual in that it never clearly distinguishes itself from the simulation of sincerity. In other words, "shimmering aesthetics" presupposes a tension between the origi-nal and citational modes of expression. Early conceptualism was "hard," whereas later permutations have become "soft" since there has been a move-ment from a strict preoccupation with ideological codes and their alienat-ing, ironic reproductions to a much more lyrical and authentic engagement of the author with the text. If previously, in "classic" conceptualism, any claim of sincerity was only a mask or a citation, now citation becomes a hidden, humble form of sincerity. Thus, a mode of "self-citation" arises where the authenticity of the text is neither asserted nor abolished but re-mains "shimmering."[8]

This relocation of accents onto authenticity, sincerity, and innovation reflects a deep fracture in postmodern consciousness. Not long ago, it was thought that nothing could be said for the first time, but now it is clear that, on the contrary, nothing can be said that will not become new at the moment it is uttered. Even Borges's Pierre Menard, who copies out entire chapters of Don Quixote word for word, emerges not as a postmodern hero, but as one of the approaching epoch, when none can help but be primal, even in literally repeating another's text. The same text written in the twentieth century has a wholly different meaning than it had as written in the seventeenth. "Cervantes' text and Menard's are verbally identical, but the second is almost infinitely richer."[9] Newness manifests itself contrary to intention and accompanied by the consciousness of its own inevitability; this is its profound distinction from avant-garde innovation, self-enraptured and aggressive. This is the cross of the new, rather than its banner. We cannot but be first and speak first, not because this is praiseworthy, but because it is unavoidable.[10]

And so, even as it changes orientation from the past to the future and from repetition to the new, the approaching epoch takes on the experience of postmodernism, where newness is no longer a free ground for titanic whims but becomes a mechanism of the inevitable. In contrast to avant-garde and utopian projects, directed toward the future solely for the sake of its remaking, the time of "proto-" points up the inevitability and uncertainty of the future, as a factor not unlike Freud's unconscious, Lacan's language, or Foucault's episteme. The future is truly "stepping up to us," as one says in Russian (*nastupaet*), which means that we "fall back" before it, although we have no way of telling, who it is we fall back before (*otstupaem*). The future lacks all substance; it is a mechanism of pure negativity that nonetheless acquires positivity in us and through us. It is the ultimate horizon of all otherness; it is the most "other" we can ever encounter or experience: a language without grammar, a subconscious without dreams, pure nothingness that inevitably becomes all, while remaining nothing again and again.[11]

The very concept of "the other" undergoes a change. In the postmodern view, it conveyed a hint of reproductivity: if the "other" speaks in us, then there is nothing left but to repeat others. The property of "being other" was attributed to a separate, alien person, even though I might well be this "other" myself. But to be other means to be new, to differ from others and from oneself. It now seems strange that, for postmodernism, otherness or alterity entailed a postulate of unavoidable *repetition* (to be "like others"), rather than a postulate of unavoidable *newness* (to be "other").

This rehabilitation of the new implies that culture repossesses all the things "forbidden" by the postmodern fashion: originality, history, metaphysics, and even utopia. But these have lost the totalitarian pretensions that once made us suspect them of "master thinking," desirous of establishing a new "crystal palace" or Gulag Archipelago.[12] The future is not written down from utopian dictation; rather, it wipes away rigid strokes and creates a proto-utopia, one of many possible sketches of futuricity. The state of proto- does not foretell the future, nor does it proscribe, although it does soften the present, giving any text the quality of a rough draft, of uncompletedness, and a certain rawness. The future emerges as a soft form of negativity, as a vagueness within any sign, or diffuseness of any meaning.

The traditional concept of proto- itself changes its meaning. Formerly it was used to designate that which came before something already formed and known. When the Renaissance came to appear complete, as it receded into the past, only then could its early stages receive the name of proto-Renaissance. Thus, from the standpoint of a prepared and realized future, the past was renamed and came to appear as a step leading to a preordained ending. Such was the trick of determinism when it prescribed the past by means of its own future, thereby creating the illusion that the future is foreseen by the past.

I am speaking of a version of proto- that has nothing to do with determinism or teleology. It is not posed to the past from an already established future, nor does it define the future from the perspective of the past. Proto- is a new, noncoercive attitude toward the future, in the modality of "maybe," rather than of "must be" or "will be." So originality, after being killed off by postmodernism, is reborn as a project that does not assume its own realization, but lives on in the genre of "a project." Proto- is the epoch of ever-changing projects, whose realization becomes not a transfiguration of reality, but the simple fact of their proposal. So many mocked, forgotten, and already impossible modes of consciousness embodied in utopian and metaphysical projects will discover their potential just as soon as they are understood precisely as potentials lacking any dictates of obligatory existence.

Contemporary Russian culture is defined less and less by its relation to the communist past. Rather, this is the protostage of some as yet unknown cultural formation, whose name, thus far, can only be guessed. Can there be a field of the humanities that aims to study protophenomena, a science of newly uttered names? After all, at the moment of its emergence, we cannot say the protophenomenon of *what* this will turn out to be. Ancient and medieval tales of love were termed prenovelistic, or protonovelistic, only when the genre of the novel and its accompanying theory were well formed. But how can we name the sustained piercing shriek with which poet Dmitry Prigov accompanies his recitations of poetry, consisting otherwise, by half, of quotations from classical sources? How can we name the painstakingly handwritten tags artist Ilya Kabakov so abundantly attaches to his paintings, albums, and installations? What are we to call these nonnovels, non-paintings, and nonpoems, which exist for the time being without a genre? Here is where we can avail ourselves of the designation "proto-": "proto-shrieks" and "protoinscriptions" do not suppose a ready-made terminology, since they themselves gradually overgrow into the terms for possible genres of the future.

NOTES

Preface

1 K. Skalkovsky, ed., *Materialy dlia fiziologii russkogo obshchestva: Malen'kaia khrestomatiia dlia vzroslykh* [Materials for a physiology of Russian society: A small primer for adults] (St. Petersburg: A. S. Suvorin, 1904), 6, 39, 10, 21. Compare Dostoevsky's reference to "the premature exhaustion of the mind and imagination of our society as yet so young but grown so untimely decrepit" (in the public procurator's speech, *The Brothers Karamazov*, trans. David McDuff [London: Penguin Books, 1993], 800).

2 Iury M. Lotman and Boris A. Uspensky, "Binary Models in the Dynamics of Russian Culture (To the End of the 18th Century)," first published 1977. Quoted from Lotman and Uspensky, *The Semiotics of Russian Cultural History*, ed. A. D. Nakhimovsky and A. S. Nakhimovsky (Ithaca: Cornell University Press, 1985), 63.

3 "The basic cultural values (ideological, political, and religious) of medieval Russia were distributed in a bipolar field and divided by a sharp boundary without an axiologically neutral zone. . . . Duality and the absence of a neutral axiological sphere led to a conception of the new not as a continuation, but as a total eschatological change. . . .

"The new does not arise out of a structurally 'unused' reserve, but results from a transformation of the old, a process of turning it inside out. Thus, repeated transformations can in fact lead to the regeneration of archaic forms." Lotman and Uspensky, *Semiotics of Russian Cultural History*, 31, 33.

4 Consider Nikolai Berdiaev's description of the typical time-orientation of Russian culture: "Among us the intelligentsia could not live in the present; it lived in the future and sometimes in the past" (from *The Russian Idea* [Hudson, N.Y.: Lindisfarne Press, 1992], 43). When these two time frames, "in the future" and "in the past," come together, the result is a strange leapfrog effect whereby we find ourselves "on the eve of the past" or "after the future."

5 Thomas Mann, *Doctor Faustus*, in *Gesammelte Werke* (Berlin, 1955), 6:263.

Introduction

1   See Victor Erlich, *Russian Formalism: History. Doctrine* (The Hague: Mouton, 1965), especially chap. 11, "Marxism Versus Formalism."

2   V. N. Voloshinov, *Marxism and the Philosophy of Language,* trans. Ladislav Matejka and I. R. Titunik (Cambridge: Harvard University Press, 1973), especially chap. 1: "signs can arise only in interindividual territory" (12). See also Michael Holquist, ed., *The Dialogic Imagination: 4 Essays by M. M. Bakhtin* (Austin: University of Texas Press, 1981), "Epic and Novel," especially 13–15.

3   "System of systems" is a description coined in Iury Tynianov and Roman Jakobson's 1929 essay "Problems in the Study of Literature and Language," available in translation in Ladislav Matejka and Krystyna Pomorska, eds., *Readings in Russian Poetics: Formalist and Structuralist Views* (Ann Arbor: Michigan Slavic Publications, 1978).

4   Mikhail Epstein, "Kul'turologiia: zadachi i vozmozhnosti (k otkrytiiu Laboratorii sovremennoi kul'tury)" [Culturology: tasks and potentials (for the opening of the Laboratory of Contemporary Culture)], lecture presented in Moscow, 26 March 1988. Some of these remarks were later published in Mikhail Epstein, "Govorit' na iazyke vsekh kul'tur" [To speak the language of all cultures], *Nauka i zhizn',* no. 1 (1990): 100–103. Portions of this speech are reproduced in Chapter 9 of the present volume.

5   Nikolai Berdiaev, *Russkaia ideia* [The Russian idea] (Paris: YMCA Press, 1946), 195.

6   M. M. Bakhtin and P. N. Medvedev, *The Formal Method in Literary Scholarship,* trans. Albert Wehrle (Cambridge: Harvard University Press, 1985), 3.

7   Ellen Berry, Kent Johnson, and Anesa Miller-Pogacar, "Postcommunist Postmodernism—An Interview With Mikhail Epstein," in *Common Knowledge* 2, 3 (1993): 110.

8   See Chapter 9 of this volume, "Culture—Culturology—Transculture."

9   Mikhail Epstein, personal letter to Anesa Miller-Pogacar, 23 July 1992.

10   For example, while Fredric Jameson seldom comments on the "Second World" per se, he indicates that incomplete modernization should preclude postmodern development as a cultural phenomenon. See "Postmodernism and Utopia," *Boston Institute of Contemporary Art Publications* (March 1988): 12–13. See also Frederic Jameson, chap. 10, "Secondary Elaborations," in *Postmodernism, or, the Cultural Logic of Late Capitalism* (Durham: Duke University Press, 1991), 297–418, especially 314 and 381.

11   Helena Goscilo, Introduction to *Glasnost: An Anthology of Literature Under Gorbachev,* coedited with Byron Lindsey (Ann Arbor: Ardis, 1990), xxxi–xlv.

12   Mikhail Bakhtin, *Problems of Dostoevsky's Poetics,* trans. Caryl Emerson (Minneapolis: University of Minnesota Press, 1984), 81.

13   Mikhail Epstein, personal letter to Anesa Miller-Pogacar, 23 July 1992.

14   Bakhtin's 1970 interview with the journal *Novyi mir* is devoted to this topic. See "Response to a Question from *Novy mir,*" in Mikhail Bakhtin, *Speech Genres*

and Other Late Essays, ed. Caryl Emerson and Michael Holquist, trans. Vern McGee (Austin: University of Texas Press, 1986).

15   Mikhail Epstein, personal interview with Anesa Miller-Pogacar, 3 May, 1990.

1 · New Currents in Russian Poetry

This study, published in Mikhail Epstein, *Paradoksy novizny* [Paradoxes of the new] (Moscow, Sovetskii pisatel', 1988), is a revision of two earlier articles that first appeared in *Voprosy literatury* [Issues in Literature], no. 5, (1986), and *Oktiabr'* [October], no. 4, (1988). Portions of the translation by Anesa Miller-Pogacar appeared in Kent Johnson and Stephen Ashby, eds. *Third Wave: The New Russian Poetry* (Ann Arbor: University of Michigan Press, 1992). In the present version, the original text has been slightly abridged and revised by the author.

1   Thus, for the symbolists, "rose" means the blossoming of the Eternal Feminine; for the acmeists, "rose" is simply a flower, neither more nor less. Mandelshtam wrote in the manifesto "Utro akmeizma" [The dawn of acmeism], "A = A: what a beautiful poetic theme." Osip Mandelshtam, *Collected Works,* 3 vols. (New York: beautiful poetic theme." Osip Mandelstam, *Collected Works,* 3 vols. (New York: Inter-Language Literary Associates, 1971), 2:324.

2   The year 1956 was the height of Khrushchev's thaw, when the Twentieth Communist Party Congress acknowledged and repudiated certain crimes of the Stalin era. A.M.-P.

3   Elsewhere, Epstein has written of the distinctiveness of the new generation as follows: "The new poetry arouses in the reader a feeling of aesthetic unease, a loss of orientation. There are many complaints of secret coding, extreme complexity. . . . This is not a matter, however, of a complexity in the language, but rather of the fundamental absence of any stable center, which used to be identified with the lyric 'I.' All complexities could be cleared up in correlation with the centered system of self-reference: 'I am thus-and-so. . . . I see the world as so-and-so.' No matter how demonically terrifying or cynically demoralized, fantastically cruel or naively dull-witted (as in the poetry of the early years of this century, the 20s, the Oberiuty and others), reference to the poetic 'I' nonetheless gave readers the happy chance of transforming themselves, of moving aside their own 'I' in favor of another's. But now there is no one with whom to identify. Poetry ceases to be a mirror for the self-infatuated ego; there remains only a murky blot of banalities, left over from his final rocklike structure that leads the gaze away, not back to the self. A poetry of Structure has come to replace the poetry of the self, because at a decisive breaking point in poetic history, the 'I' revealed its unreliability, inauthenticity, it traitorously evaded all responsibility, so that responsibility was taken up by structure: social structures, sign structures, atomic and genetic structures." Quoted from Epstein's "Kak trup v pustyne ia lezhal" [I lay like a corpse in the desert], in *Den' poezii, 1988* [Day of poetry, 1988] (Moscow: Sovetskii pisatel', 1988). An English translation by John High has appeared as "Like a Corpse I Lay in the Desert," *Five Fingers Review,* nos. 8–9 (1990): 162–167. A.M.-P.

4   An untranslatable pun on the Russian *lesa*, which means both forests and scaffolding. A.M.-P.

5   The Oberiu, or Oberiuty, was a Leningrad group active in experimental art from 1927 to 1930; members included Daniil Kharms, Alexander Vvedensky, Nikolai Zabolotsky, Konstantin Vaginov, Nikolai Oleinikov and others. Their work was theatrical, iconoclastic, and in some cases futuristic, involving experiments with trans-sense language and nonobjectivity. A.M.-P.

6   Peter Konchalovsky (1876–1956) was a well-known painter of landscapes and still lifes. A.M.-P.

7   *Resultant* is a mathematical term referring to a single vector that represents the sum of forces or velocities of two or more vectors. A.M.-P.

8   *Literatura endinogo potoka,* a "single stream of literature," was a fashionable slogan of the 1930s, when Stalinist aesthetics attempted to unite all "progressive" literature of the past and present on the bases of "realism" and being "for the people."

9   This statement dates to 1983. A.M.-P.

10 *Vysokomalokhudozhestvennyi* is a descriptor borrowed from Mikhail Zoshchenko (1895–1958), best known as the author of numerous satiric and humorous feuilletons and short stories. A.M.-P.

11 Kaluga is a provincial city on the Oka River in central Russia. In this poem Prigov conceptualizes the typical motifs of grassroots mentality, which extols "modest," "nongarish" beauty of the "quiet" Russian province and its humble inhabitants.

12 See notes 5 and 10. A.M.-P.

13 NEPmen were entrepreneurs of the early Soviet period when small-scale capitalistic ventures were allowed under Lenin's New Economic Policy, 1921–28. A.M.-P.

14 Lebiadkin is a character in Dostoevsky's *The Possessed* (1872), a buffoon who pens trite and pompous verse; the "cannibaless Ellochka" appears in *The Twelve Chairs* (1928), a humorous novel by Ilya Ilf and Evgeny Petrov (pen names of Ilya Fainzilberg and Evgeny Kataev). A.M.-P.

15 In Russian *iazyk* means both "tongue" and "language." A.M.-P.

16 Quoted from the translation by Gerald Janecek in Johnson and Ashby, *Third Wave,* 142. A.M.-P.

17 A reference to the whitewashing of reality through official proclamation in the Stalin and Brezhnev eras, falsification of production quotas, etc. See also Chapter 6. A.M.-P.

18 A technique of rendering dialectical and vernacular speech characteristics in Russian literature. A.M.-P.

19 Epstein alludes here to the three styles codified in Lomonosov's eighteenth-century poetic theory (high, middle, and low). A.M.-P.

20 A typical pejorative term of the Soviet era, "hooliganism" (*khuliganstvo*) has been used to describe all manner of undesirable social behavior, from assault to swearing. A.M.-P.

21 This refers to one of Pushkin's best-known short poems, "The Prophet," which describes poetic inspiration in terms of a profound religious experience. Epstein

has also emphasized the themes of mortality and dehumanization, predominant in postcommunist culture, in relation to this work by Pushkin as well as to contemporary poetry; he writes: "Re-reading Pushkin's 'The Prophet' with today's vision, the inevitable *dying* of the human hero strikes us for the first time. He is given a snake's bite in place of a tongue, a burning coal in place of a heart—all his humanness is sundered and put to death. What is this monster that lay in in the desert . . . ! It was a prophet, with all in readiness to answer the Lord's call: 'I lay like a corpse in the desert . . .' Contemporary poetry sometimes reminds us of a corpse which has already lost the traits of the living and the human—here and there protrude some kind of sharp fangs, membranes, angular bodies. But try to feel it: all of this unimaginable aggregate is ready to rise up and announce the truth with one word from above. . . . The seraph has already completed the down and dirty work of preparing a new superhuman organism for life. And people who see in it only an inhuman monster or an assortment of mechanical parts—they don't know that from these alone will they hear the thought and will of God. We live in an unknown and perhaps very brief pause, before: 'And God's own voice was heard to me . . .' All we can do now is to wait and listen, so as not to miss the voice in the wilderness where a prophet in his loneliness, appears to be a corpse." From "Kak trup v pustyne ia lezhal"; see note 3. A.M.-P.

22 Another reference to Pushkin's "The Prophet." A.M.-P.

23 Despite the similarity of their prefixes, "metarealism" has little in common with "surrealism," in that it is concerned not with the subconscious, but with a super-consciousness; it does not intoxicate, but sobers creative reason. "Surrealistic images are like the images induced by opium" (A. Breton's, "Surrealist Manifesto"). The surrealists were repelled by soberly plebeian, reasonable bourgeois reality and brought into it the whimsy of intoxicating dreams. Metarealism is repelled by the monstrous senselessness, the drunken haze and fogginess that has covered the historical horizon of the Soviet epoch; for that reason, it calls in every way possible for an awakening, for an emergence from the hypnotic drunkenness of this single reality into a multidimensional perception of the world.

24 Fëdor Tiutchev (1803–73) was one of the greatest nineteenth-century Russian poets and an originator of philosophical lyricism. A.M.-P.

25 See full translation of this poem earlier in this chapter. A.M.-P.

26 In his article "Chto takoe metabola? O 'tret'em' trope" [What is metabole? On the 'third' trope], Epstein defines metabole as a type of mediation between the two tropes conventionally called metaphor and metonymy: "From the poetic and stylistic standpoints, it seems helpful to designate as 'metabole' the kind of trope which reveals the very process—the intermediate steps—of transfering meaning, the hidden foundation on which the closeness and likening of objects takes place . . . [and] from which emerges the fullness of their encompassed and assimilated reality." (*Stilistika i poetika* [Stylistics and poetics], [Moscow, 1989], 75, 76, 77.) Thus, for Epstein, metabole completes a triad of tropes including metaphor and metonymy. If metaphor is a transfer of meaning through similarity, and metonymy is its transfer through contiguity, then metabole functions through an inner commonality. A.M.-P.

27 It is curious that polemics between metarealists and conceptualists reproduce the logical essence of the long-past and irreconcilable argument between realism and nominalism (whose moderate version at one time was also called "conceptualism") in medieval philosophy. This conflict centered on the question, Do general ideas (such as "love," "the good," "beauty") have the fullness of reality, or are they limited to the sphere of words (nomination) and concepts? This conflict proved difficult to resolve by logical means and continues to be resolved variously in contemporary poetic practice: one side of an idea merges with reality, while the other separates from it. The striving for complete merging reaches its limit in metarealism; and in conceptualism, the striving for complete separation.

28 "Kenotype" (from ancient Greek, *kainos,* "new") differs from archetype in that it offers a figurative formula, or generalized schematic eidos, of a historically new phenomenon, such as "metro," "beach," or "newspaper." For more detail, see Chapter 10, "Appendix."

2 · Avant-Garde Art and Religion

An earlier version of this article appeared in *Novyi mir* [New world], no. 12 (1989). The full Russian text is published in Mikhail Epstein, *Vera i obraz. Religioznoe bessoznatel'noe v russkoi kul'ture 20-go veka* [Faith and image: The religious subconscious in twentieth-century Russian culture] (Tenafly, N.J.: Hermitage Publishers, 1994).

1 Pierre Cabanne, *Dialogues with Marcel Duchamp* (New York: Viking Press, 1971), 107, 7.

2 V. Vanslov, "Modernizm: krizis burzhuaznogo iskusstva" [Modernism: The crisis of bourgeois art], in *Modernizm: analiz i kritika osnovnykh napravlenii* [Modernism: Analysis and criticism of its main trends] (Moscow: Iskusstvo, 1980), 19.

3 Maxim Gorky, "V. I. Lenin," *Polnoe sobranie sochinenii. Khudozhestvennye proizvedeniia v 25 tomakh* (Moscow: Nauka, 1974), 20: 30.

4 James H. Billington writes as follows of the phenomenon of holy foolery (*iurodstvo*) in his *The Icon and the Axe* (New York: Vintage, 1970): "The rise of prophesy in fifteenth- and early sixteenth-century Muscovy is evidenced in the growth of extreme forms of Christian spirituality, such as . . . 'folly for Christ's sake' . . . holy fools became revered for their asceticism and prophetic utterances as 'men of God' " (59). A.M.-P.

5 D. S. Likhachev, A. M. Panchenko, N. V. Ponyrko, *Smekh v Drevnei Rusi* [Laughter in Old Russia] (Leningrad: Nauka, 1984), 80. Further citations to this work appear in the text.

6 "Dyr bul shchil ubeshchur" is a famous poetic line in "trans-sense" or "transrational language" by the futurist poet Alexei Kruchenykh (1886–1968). A.M.-P.

7 Vladimir Mayakovsky, "The Cloud in Trousers," quoted from the translation by Max Hayward and George Reavey in *The Bedbug and Selected Poetry,* ed. Patricia Blake (Bloomington: Indiana University Press, 1975), 107–9. A.M.-P.

8 Mayakovsky, "The Cloud in Trousers," 85. A.M.-P.

9 Mayakovsky, "The Cloud in Trousers," 83. A.M.-P.

10 Velimir Khlebnikov (1885–1922) was a leading poet of the Russian futurist movement. A.M.-P.

11 This is a line from the poem "Ia slovo pozabyl, chto ia khotel skazat' " [I forgot the word I wanted to say] (1920) by acmeist poet Osip Mandelshtam (1891–1938). A.M.-P.

12 Nikolai Berdiaev, from the public lecture "The Crisis of Art," delivered in Moscow, 1 November 1917. Nikolai Alexandrovich Berdiaev (1874–1948) was a former social democrat from Kiev who turned away from Marxism to become a religious philosopher. His work is now associated with Christian existentialism. Some of Berdiaev's ideas are based on the mystical teachings of Jacob Boehme. See also Chapter 6 and Chapter 9. A.M.-P.

13 See Vladimir Lossky, *The Mystical Theology of the Eastern Church* (Crestwood, N.J.: St. Vladimir's Seminary Press, 1976), 23–43.

14 The interrelations of soc-art (socialist art) and conceptualism are not easily defined. Initially it was thought that "soc-art," the movement begun by Russian émigré artists V. Komar and A. Melamid, was a more suitable name for Russian "conceptualism." But gradually the advantages of the latter term came to light. First, it offered a deeper, more radical link with an entire system of thinking and culture: "concept," "conception," "conceptualism," indeed, a current in medieval philosophy opposed, along with "nominalism," to realism. Second, and more important, it offered freedom from any particular social construct and appropriateness to ideological consciousness as such, regardless of what type of ideology one might profess.

15 See Ilya Kabakov, *Ten Characters* (New York: ICA and Ronald Feldman Fine Arts [1989]).

16 Lev Rubinshtein, "A Little Nighttime Serenade," quoted from the translation by Gerald J. Janecek in *Third Wave: The New Russian Poetry*, ed. Kent Johnson and Stephen M. Ashby (Ann Arbor: University of Michigan Press, 1992), 139. A.M.-P.

17 Work by the conceptual poets was first published in Russia in the annuals *Poeziia* [Poetry] (Moscow: Molodaia gvardiia, 1989, no. 52) and *Zerkala* [Mirrors] (Moscow: Moskovskii rabochii, 1989). See also Chapter 1 and Chapter 3.

18 Perhaps this aesthetic of backwardness and intentional repetition should be called not "avant-garde" but "arrière-garde"? See Chapter 3.

19 Lev Rubinshtein, "A Little Nighttime Serenade," in *Third Wave: The New Russian Poetry*, 141. A.M.-P.

20 Quoted from the translation by Colm Luibheid in "The Mystical Theology," *Pseudo-Dionysius. The Complete Works* (New York: Paulist Press, 1987), 141. A.M.-P.

21 Pseudo-Dionysius, "The Mystical Theology," 138.

22 Pseudo-Dionysius, "The Mystical Theology," 139.

23 Both segments are from *Eugene Onegin: A Novel in Verse*, quoted from the translation by Vladimir Nabokov (Princeton University Press, Bollingen Series 72, 1975), 104. A.M.-P.

24   The relation of conceptualism to Russia's intermediary position between West and East is discussed in detail in Chapter 6, section 3.

25   Consider Berdiaev's comment: "Such a feeling of having no basis is perhaps a national Russian trait. It is a mistake to regard as national only loyalty to conservative basic principles." From Nikolai Berdiaev, *The Russian Idea,* trans. R. M. French (Hudson, N.Y.: Lindisfarne Press, 1992), 44.

26   These quotations are from Pushkin's *The Bronze Horseman,* Gogol's *Dead Souls,* and Dostoevsky's *The Adolescent.* See also Chapter 6. A.M.-P.

3 · After the Future

This article appeared in Russian in the journal *Znamia* [Banner], no. 1 (1991). The translation, by Gene Kuperman, was first published in the *South Atlantic Quarterly* 90, no. 2 (Spring 1991). The present version has been edited and revised in consultation with the author.

1   In his *Notes from Underground,* Dostoevsky presents a fictionalized polemic with Nikolai Chernyshevsky's visions of the rational betterment of human nature, symbolized by a utopian Crystal Palace. See also Conclusion, n. 12. A.M.-P.

2   This is a reference to the poem "Ia slovo pozabyl, chto ia khotel skazat' " [I forgot the word I wanted to say] (1920) by Osip Mandelshtam.

3   This is a reference to Dostoevsky's story "Bobok" (1873), in which the nonsense word "bobok" was to be a call for people to shed their clothes and inhibitions. Epstein explains that the phonetically similar "sovok" was used as a pejorative nickname, combining connotations of the words "Soviet" and *sova,* Russian for "owl." A.M.-P.

4   In the early days of the Soviet Union it was often questioned whether the capitalist world economy would allow socialism to develop in only one country. Popular jokes and sayings have developed a variety of puns on this idea. A.M.-P.

5   The island of Patmos, located near Greece in the Aegean Sea, is thought to be the place where the Apostle John wrote the Apocalypse.

6   Listed are the names of widely read contemporary novelists. A.M.-P.

7   The "superfluous person" is a term used widely in discussions of Russian literature and cultural life to refer to the position of socially privileged, usually young, men who, despite their often idealistic inclinations, found few avenues for applying themselves in any positive way in Russian society and tended to give in to amoralism or ennui. Alienated from their own social milieu, they nonetheless avoided joining oppositional movements such as Decembrism. Popular use of the term seems to originate with the publication of Ivan Turgenev's "Diary of a Superfluous Man" in 1850. A.M.-P.

8   Evgeny Onegin, protagonist of Pushkin's verse novel of the same name (1833), and Pechorin, Lermontov's *Hero Of Our Time* (1840), were among the prominent "superfluous men" of nineteenth-century literature. In the twentieth century, the type continued in Kavalerov, protagonist of Iury Olesha's *Envy* (1927), and Odoevtsev, of Andrei Bitov's *Pushkin House* (1978). A.M.-P.

9   Kalinych is a character in Ivan Turgenev's *Notes of a Hunter* (1852), which has

been called a "Russian *Uncle Tom's Cabin,*" by virtue of its frank descriptions of peasants' lives. Nikolai Leskov's "Enchanted Pilgrim" (1873) is a tale of the misadventures of a runaway serf. Vasily Shukshin began publishing stories about odd and often humorous characters of rural origins in 1963. A.M.-P.

10 On Alexander Herzen, see Chapter 6, note 2. A.M.-P.

11 Epstein explains that the older, somewhat endearing oddball (*chudak*) evolves into "the kind of *chudak* that begins with the letter 'm.'" In Russian, *mudak* is derived from a slang term for "testicle" and refers to a person who is dull, stupid, or narrow-minded. A.M.-P.

12 A more detailed discussion of the poetic styles mentioned here and below may be found in Chapter 1. A.M.-P.

13 On Vladimir Soloviev, see Chapter 9, note 10. A.M.-P.

14 See Chapter 2, note 6. A.M.-P.

15 The Russian word *iazyk* means both language and tongue. Gene Kuperman, (trans).

16 Hence, another possible name for this literary current: "presentism," as suggested in Chapter 1.

4 · Relativistic Patterns in Totalitarian Thinking

This chapter was first published as part of a larger study entitled *Relativistic Patterns in Totalitarian Thinking: An Inquiry into the Language of Soviet Ideology,* under the editorship of Peggy McInerny, issued as Occasional Paper No. 243 of the Kennan Institute For Advanced Russian Studies, a division of the Woodrow Wilson International Center For Scholars (Washington, D.C., 1991).

1 Bernard Susser, *The Grammar of Modern Ideology* (London: Routledge and Kegan Paul, 1988), 3.

2 *Arkhiv Marksa i Engelsa,* (Moscow, 1935), 4:99.

3 The concept and term "ideolinguistics" were proposed in the author's article "Sposoby vozdeistviia ideologicheskogo vyskazyvaniia," in *Obraz dvadtsatogo veka* (Moscow: Institut nauchnoi informatsii po obshchestvennym naukam, 1988), 167–216. See also Mikhail Epshtein, "Otsenochnost' v leksicheskoi sisteme iazyka," *Iazyk sovremennoi publitsistiki* (Moscow: Goskomizdat, 1989), 28–47.

Of course I cannot claim to have discovered this field; my task here is to clarify its specific boundaries. Among recent works elaborating upon various aspects of ideolinguistics, one should mention the following, listed in chronological order of their publication: Theodor Pelster, *Die politische Rede im Westen und Osten Deutschlands* (Dusseldorf, 1966); Claus Mueller, *The Dialectics of Language: A Study in the Political Sociology of Language* (New York, 1970); Colin H. Good, *Die deutsche Sprache und die Kommunistishe Ideologie* (Frankfurt, 1975); Dominique Labbé, *Le Discours Communiste* (Paris: Presses de la Fondation Nationale des Sciences Politiques, 1977); Roger Fowler et al., *Language and Control* (London: Routledge and Kegan Paul, 1979); Gunther Kress and Robert Hodge, *Language as Ideology* (London: Routledge and Kegan Paul, 1979); Paul E. Cor-

coran, *Political Language and Rhetoric* (St. Lucia, Australia: University of Queensland Press, 1979); Dwight Bolinger, *Language, the Loaded Weapon* (London: Longman, 1980); O. Reboul, *Langage et Idéologie* (Paris: P.U.F., 1980); *Essais sur le Discours Soviétique: Sémiologie, Linguistique, Analyse Discoursive,* 3 (Université de Grenoble, 1981); Maurice Cranston and Peter Mair, eds., *Langage et Politique* (Language and Politics) (Brussels, 1982); Michael J. Shapiro, ed., *Language and Politics* (New York: New York University Press, 1984); Patrick Seriot, *Analyse du Discours Politique Soviétique* (Paris: Institut d'études Slaves, 1985); Françoise Thom, *La Langue de Bois* (Paris: Julliard, 1987) [English translation: *Newspeak: The Language of Soviet Ideology,* trans. Ken Connelly (London: Claridge Press, 1989)]; Ruth Wodak, ed., *Language, Power, and Ideology: Studies in Political Discourse* (Philadelphia: John Benjamins, 1989).

While some works in this field have been published in the USSR, the majority of Soviet texts are, in my opinion, excessively influenced by "Marxist-Leninist Ideology" and too engaged in the dispute with "bourgeois ideology" to offer objective investigation. See: Iu. V. Kovalenko, *Iazyk i Ideologiia: Filologicheskie etiudy,* Vypusk I (Rostov on the Don, 1974); T. B. Kriuchkova, *Iazyk i ideologiia: K voprosu ob otrazhenii ideologii v iazyke* (Leningrad, 1976); *Iazyk i ideologiia: Kritika idealisticheskikh kontseptsii funktsionirovaniia i razvitiia iazyka* (Kiev, 1981); *Funktsionirovanie iazyka kak sredstva ideologicheskogo vozdeistviia* (Krasnodar: Kubanskii gosudarstvennyi universitet, 1988).

The weakness of Soviet literature on this topic is offset by works published abroad by Russian émigrés, including L. Rzevskii, *Iazyk i Totalitarizm* (Munich, 1951); Andrei i Tatiana Fesenko, *Russkii iazyk pri Sovetakh* (New York: Rausen Bros., 1955); Roman Redlikh, *Stalinshchina kak dukhovnyi fenomen,* Part 2: *Sovetskii iazyk* (Frankfurt am Main: Possev, 1971); Ilya Zemtsov, *Sovetskii politicheskii iazyk* (London: Overseas Publications, 1985) [English translation: *Manipulation of a Language; The Lexicon of Soviet Political Terms* (Hero Books, 1984)]; Ilya Zemtsov, *Real'nost' i grani perestroiki: Spravochnik* (London: Overseas Publications, 1989).

4 See a review of various theories regarding the relationship between ideology and language in Mikhail Epstein, *Relativistic Patterns in Totalitarian Thinking,* ed. Peggy McInerny, 5–12.

5 Raymond Aron, *The Opium of the Intellectuals* (New York: Doubleday, 1957), 236.

6 Daniel Bell, *The End of Ideology: On the Exhaustion of Political Ideas in the Fifties* (Cambridge: Harvard University Press, 1988), 400.

7 *Encyclopaedia Britannica,* 30 vols. (Chicago: Encyclopaedia Britannica, 1976), 9:194.

8 *Great Soviet Encyclopaedia,* ed. A. M. Prokhorov (New York: Macmillan, 1973), 10:120.

9 S. I. Hayakawa cites several good examples of latent judgments that express the opposite ideological bias: "To many people, the word 'communist' has both the informative connotation of 'one who believes in communism' and the affective connotation of 'one whose ideals and purposes are altogether repellent.'

Words . . . applying to believers in philosophies of which one disapproves ('athe-ist,' 'radical,' 'heretic,' 'materialist,' 'fundamentalist') likewise often commu-nicate simultaneously a fact and a judgment on that fact. Such words may be called 'loaded'—that is, their affective connotations may strongly shape people's thoughts." S. I. Hayakawa and Alan R. Hayakawa, *Language in Thought and Action,* 5th ed. (San Diego: Harcourt Brace Jovanovich, 1990), 48.

10 In the selection of examples, the following dictionaries proved helpful: *Slovar' sinonimov russkogo iazyka,* 2 vols. (Leningrad: Nauka, 1970); Z. E. Aleksan-drova, *Slovar' sinonimov russkogo iazyka* (Moscow: Sovetskaia entsiklopediia, 1969), M. R. Lvov, *Slovar' antonimov russkogo iazyka* (Moscow: Russkii iazyk, 1984); G. P. Poliakova, G. Ia. Solganik, *Chastotnyi slovar' iazyka gazet* (Moscow: Moscow State University Press, 1971).

11 The term "conversive," as used in semantics, refers to the opposite roles of the participants in the same interaction: when *A* "*wins,*" *B* "*loses;*" if *A* "*sells,*" *B* "*buys.*" Pragmatic, or evaluative, conversives refer to the opposing attitudes of the participants to the same phenomenon: what *A* views as "dreams," *B* views as "ravings" (*mechty-bredni*).

12 A. S. Makarenko, *Sochineniia* (Moscow, 1958), 7:13.

13 This does not preclude the Western press from using the techniques of evalua-tive conversion; after all, the laws of ideological thinking are everywhere identi-cal, although they may have different weight in different cultures. "During the Boer War, the Boers were described in the British press as 'sneaking and skulking behind rocks and bushes.' The British forces, when they finally learned from the Boers how to employ tactics suitable to warfare on the South African veldt, were described as 'cleverly taking advantage of cover.' " Hayakawa and Hayakawa, *Language in Thought and Action,* 46.

14 The analogy of "money" and "ideas" is examined in more detail in the conclu-sion to this chapter.

15 The title of Vsevolod Vishnevsky's dramatic play that became a symbol of the necessity of suffering in order to achieve the final triumph of communism.

16 Substitutives are not synonyms in a strict linguistic sense and they may be sub-stituted for each other only on the abstract level of ideological consciousness. Synonymy is a relationship between words, substitution, between ideologemes.

17 In traditional logic, the tetradic structure is generally known as the "logical square." Since antiquity, the logical square has represented the relationship be-tween four types of propositions: affirmative and negative, universal and par-ticular.

The French philosopher and logician R. Blanché points out that "[t]he tradi-tional theory on quantification follows a binary pattern. First, it distinguishes the universal from the particular. Then dividing this first dichotomy with a second, establishes both positive and negative forms for each of these terms. The result is a total of four quantitative concepts." Blanché immediately follows this assertion with his principal qualification: "But common language, whose stan-dard usage continues to be employed, has only three terms at its disposal: all, none, and some; the particular concept lacks the duality known by the universal concepts." R. Blanché, *Les Structures Intellectuelles* (Paris: Librairie Philosophique J. Vrin, 1966), 35.

Indeed, the majority of ordinary words expressing "particular" concepts, such as "tree" or "cup," are devoid of any duality. Ideologemes are easily organized within tetradic structures because they express judgments or propositions more so than do other words.

For a general review and bibliography of the "logical" and "semiotic" square, see Oswald Ducrot and Tzvetan Todorov, *Encyclopedic Dictionary of the Sciences of Language* (Baltimore: Johns Hopkins University Press, 1979), 114–17; A. J. Greimas and J. Courtes, *Semiotics and Language: An Analytical Dictionary* (Bloomington: Indiana University Press, 1982), 309–11; and "The Logic of Propositions" in *Encyclopedia of Philosophy* (New York: Macmillan, 1972), 5:35–36, 45.

18　Here, as in some other cases, I have not listed the exact American equivalent of a Russian tetrad or dyad, which would be impossible, but a roughly similar lexical pattern that should make sense to an American reader.

19　Thucydides, *History of the Peloponnesian War,* chap. 9, in *Great Books of the Western World* (Encyclopaedia Britannica, 1952), 6:437.

20　Yeltsin apparently realizes this himself: "Yeltsin speculates that Gorbachev kept him around for political balance. With the prickly, impetuous Yeltsin to his left, the conservative Ligachev to his right, Gorbachev himself seemed the omniscient centrist." Bill Keller, "Boris Yeltsin Taking Power," *New York Times Magazine,* 23 September 1990, 81.

21　The terms "Left" and "Right" are used here in their conventional Soviet meaning which differs from Western usage. When "the Left," i.e., Bolsheviks, became the ruling party of the USSR, the followers of official Soviet doctrine came to be called "right." Thus Trotsky is "left" and Bukharin is "right" in a traditional, Western sense, whereas Yeltsin, a proponent of market economy, is called "left" only because of his opposition to official politics. In the essence of their views, Ligachev is closer to Trotsky, while Yeltsin is closer to Bukharin. In the post-Soviet period, the traditional designation of orthodox communists as "left" and followers of market model as "right" is gradually being restored.

22　George Orwell's "doublethink" is an appropriate intuitive description of this tetradic model: "To hold simultaneously two opinions which cancelled out, knowing them to be contradictory and believing in both of them, to use logic against logic." Orwell, *1984* (New York: New American Library, 1983), 32.

23　Niccolò Machiavelli, *The Prince,* in *Great Books of the Western World* (Encyclopaedia Britannica, 1952), 23:32.

24　V. I. Lenin, *Polnoe sobranie sochinenii,* 55 vols., 5th ed. (Moscow: Politizdat), 30:152.

25　Lenin, *Polnoe sobranie sochinenii,* 30:39; compare 30:20–21.

26　Karl Marx and Friedrich Engels, *Collected Works* (New York: International Publishers, 1976), 5:5.

27　The Soviet worldview is characterized by extreme materialism in theory and extreme idealism in practice. We could even say that Soviet Marxism's overstated materialism is nothing but an ideological phantom, in the postmodern sense of the word. Such "hypermaterialism" is a sort of simulacrum, the product of pure mentality. The self-serving raison d'être for such countless Soviet simulacra as hyperunity, hyperlabor, hyperparty, hyperpeople, hyperpower, and hyperfuture does not differ much from that of Western media. If in the West visual simulacra bring great profit, in the Soviet Union ideological simulacra have long brought great power. For more information on the concepts of "simulacrum" and "hyper" phenomena, see Jean Baudrillard, *Simulations* (New York: Semiotexte, 1983).

28   J. V. Stalin, *Works* (Moscow: Foreign Languages Publishing House, 1956), 12:189.

29   I. V. Stalin, *Sochineniia* (Moscow: Politizdat, 1951), 13:601–2.

30   Karl Marx and Friedrich Engels, *Sochineniia*, 50 vols., 2d ed. (Moscow: Politizdat), 35:131–32.

31   M. S. Gorbachev, *Ob osnovnykh napravleniiakh vnutrennei i vneshnei politiki SSSR* (On the main directions of the U.S.S.R.'s domestic and foreign policy) (Moscow: Polizdat, 1989), 30–31.

32   A semantic function may be defined as "an abstract, typical meaning which, like grammatical meaning, is expressed by a rather large amount of words." Iu. D. Apresian, *Leksicheskaia semantika* (Moscow: Nauka, 1974), 45.

The theoretical approach to semantic functions was elaborated in the late sixties and early seventies by a group of Soviet linguists: Igor Melchuk, Aleksandr Zholkovsky, and Iury Apresian. An example of semantic function is "Magn," which means "very," "to a high degree," and is expressed in different contexts by such words as "jet" (jet-black hair, jet-black eyes), "pitch" (darkness), "deathly" (silence), "pouring" (rain), and so on (*zhguchii briunet, kromeshnaia t'ma, grobovoe molchanie, prolivnoi dozhd'*). I. A. Melchuk described approximately forty such functions in his book *Opyt teorii lingvisticheskikh modelei "Smysl—Tekst"* [Experiment in the theory of linguistic models "meaning—text"] (Moscow: Nauka, 1974).

Deeper analysis has shown the difficulty of describing ordinary language in terms of semantic functions. On the one hand, the number of such functions cannot be limited to specific logical groups; on the other hand, the lexical variety and richness of ordinary language does not yield to functional classification, no matter how many functions are introduced.

Ideological language, however, is more appropriately described in terms of abstract, typical meanings than is ordinary language. All ideological words are divided into "positive" and "negative"; this considerably facilitates their functional description. Ideological language is also devoid of specific words with narrow meanings that resist any generalization, such as "strawberries," "auburn," "to lisp." Thus, the functional approach may prove to be much more applicable to the sphere of pragmatics than to the sphere of semantics, the field from which it originally emerged.

33   In Soviet ideological language, "naturalism," "empiricism," and "positivism" generally refer to the adherence to scientific facts regardless of Party doctrine and a "class approach."

34 There are a number of popular Soviet ideologemes with the same negative meaning for which exact American equivalents cannot be found: *sobstvennichestvo,
khishchnichestvo, priobretatel'stvo, potrebitel'stvo, veshchizm.* All of them refer
to the "bourgeois" vice of "consumerism."

35 See the discussion of dualistic models of Russian history in the Preface.

36 An informative review of Russian modes of address and their changes in the
Soviet era may be found in Bernard Comrie and Gerald Stone, *The Russian
Language since the Revolution* (Oxford: Oxford University Press, 1978), chap. 7,
172–99. Unfortunately, the authors do not dwell on the Party and Komsomol
"ideolects" of speech etiquette.

37 For the sake of clarity, "full name" here refers to an individual's formal forename
and patronymic.

38 Once again we see the untranslatable meaning of Soviet ideological terms,
whose connotative meanings are far more specific and "predetermined" than
those of their American English equivalents. For example, we are forced to use
the same English verb, "proclaim," for two different Russian verbs, *provozglashat'* and *proklamirovat',* even though the first Russian verb is positive (to
proclaim truth, freedom) and the second, extremely negative (to proclaim something false, illusory, unrealizable).

39 Engels, letter to Mehring, 14 July 1893.

40 Herbert Marcuse, *Soviet Marxism: A Critical Analysis* (Harmondsworth: Penguin Books, 1971), 16–17.

41 For a critical discussion of this issue, see the chapter entitled "Basis and Superstructure—Reality and Ideology," in Marcuse, *Soviet Marxism,* 106–7.

42 Louis Althusser, *Lenin and Philosophy and Other Essays* (New York: Monthly
Review Press, 1971), 160–62.

43 The role of ideas in a communist society and the formation of a postcommunist
ideological environment as well as the concept of "ideosophy," as the postideological totality of consciousness, are explored in Mikhail Epstein, *Novoe Sek-
tantstvo* [New sectarianism: The varieties of religious-philosophical consciousness in Russia, the 1970s–1980s] (Holyoke, Mass.: New England Publishing,
1993). See especially the section "Komediia idei" [Comedy of ideas], 152–68.

5 · Labor of Lust

An early Russian version of this study was published in *Syntaksis,* no. 25 (1989).
Sections 1 and 2 were translated from the Russian by Andrew Wachtel; parts of
section 3 were first presented at the conference "The Occult in Russian and Soviet
Culture," at Fordham University, New York, June 1991. An English version appeared
in *Common Knowledge* 1, 3(1992).

1 *"Est' blud truda i on u nas v krovi."* A literal translation of this passage would
read, "there's a whoring after labor, and it's in our blood." From the poem "Mid-
night in Moscow. A sumptuous Buddhist summer" (1932). *Complete Poetry of
O. E. Mandelstam,* trans. B. Raffel and A. Burago (Albany: State University of
New York Press, 1973), 212.

2   Andrei Platonov, *The Foundation Pit*, trans. Thomas P. Whitney (Ann Arbor: Ardis, 1973), 34.

3   Maxim Gorky, *Meshchane* [Philistines], from *Polnoe sobranie sochinenii* (Moscow: Nauka, 1970), 7:40. Characteristically, Gorky was the first to proclaim, in the mid-1920s, labor as the main, comprehensive theme of Soviet literature.

4   Vladimir Mayakovsky, "At the Top of My Voice," quoted from the translation by Max Hayward and George Reavey in *The Bedbug and Selected Poetry*, ed. Patricia Blake (Bloomington: Indiana University Press, 1975), 223–25.

5   Maxim Gorky, *My Universities*, from *Collected Works*, 10 vols. (Moscow: Progress Publishers), 7:402–3.

6   Vladimir Mayakovsky, "Letter from Paris to Comrade Kostrov on the Nature of Love," in *The Bedbug and Selected Poetry*, 213.

7   Cited in Grigory Brovman, *Trud. Geroi. Literatura. Ocherki i razmyshleniia o russkoi sovetskoi khudozhestvennoi proze* (Moscow: Khudozhestvennaia literatura, 1974), 146.

8   Brovman, *Trud. Geroi. Literatura*, 148.

9   Platonov, *The Foundation Pit*, 36.

10 Mikhail Sholokhov, *Sobranie sochinenii* [Collected works], 8 vols. (Moscow: Pravda Publishing House, 1962), 7:45.

11 Sholokhov, *Sobranie sochinenii*, 6:62.

12 V. I. Lenin, "Political report to the Central Committee of 2 December 1919," *Complete Works*, 39:360.

13 From "Retribution" by Aleksandr Blok.

14 Karl Marx and Frederick Engels, *Selected Works* (Moscow: Progress Publishers, 1970), 50.

15 The goddess of love, who has "the sensuality of Astarte" and "Aphrodites' infatuated regard for beauty," reveals to Vera Pavlovna: "Think of those burning cheeks and shining eyes you saw in the dance hall, think of the comings in and goings out. It was I who called them away, for I dwell in the room of every maid and man where curtained doors and sumptuous carpets keep the silence and my secret inviolable. . . . Mine, I tell you, all is mine. Labor lends its strength and vigour to my enjoyment, revelry the making-ready and restful afterglow. I am the end and all in life." Nikolai Chernyshevsky, *What Is to Be Done? Tales of New People. A Novel* (Moscow: Raduga Publishers, 1983), ch. 4, xvi, 10, 408.

16 Herbert Marcuse, *Eros and Civilization: A Philosophical Inquiry into Freud* (New York: Vintage Books, 1962), 197.

17 G. P. Fedotov, *The Russian Religious Mind* (New York, 1960), 1:362.

18 Nikolai Berdiaev, *The Russian Idea*, trans. R. M. French (Boston, 1962), 6.

19 Joanna Hubbs, *Mother Russia: The Feminine Myth in Russian Culture* (Bloomington: Indiana University Press, 1988).

20 For Lenin the most authoritative source is Engels's formulation, which also deduces materialist teachings from the worship of nature: "Those who assumed that a spirit existed before nature constituted the idealistic camp. But those who considered nature the primary element formed various schools of materialism. At first the expressions 'idealism' and 'materialism' implied nothing else." From

Karl Marx and Friedrich Engels, *Sochineniia,* 2d ed. (Moscow: Politizdat, 1961), 21:283.

21   A letter to Maxim Gorky, 13 or 14 November 1913. V. I. Lenin, "On Religion" (Moscow: Progress Publishers, 1969), 39.

22   This possibility was stipulated by Freud, for example, in "Totem and Taboo": "The son's efforts to put himself in the place of the father-god became even more obvious. The introduction of agriculture increased the son's importance in the patriarchal family. He ventured upon new demonstrations of his incestuous libido, which found symbolic satisfaction in his cultivation of Mother Earth" (*The Freud Reader,* ed. Peter Gay [New York: W. W. Norton, 1989], 507).

23   Friedrich Engels, *Ludwig Feuerbach,* as cited in Joseph Stalin, *Dialectical and Historical Materialism,* in his *Selected Writings* (New York: International Publishers, 1942), 412.

24   Stalin, *Dialectical and Historical Materialism,* 421.

25   Gastev cited in I. R. Shafarevich, *Russofobiia* [Russophobia] (Moscow: Tovarishchestvo russkikh khudozhnikov, 1991), 119.

26   Maxim Gorky, *Mother* (part 2, chap. 3), *Sobranie sochinenii* [Collected works], 18 vols. (Moscow: Gosudarstvennoe izdatel'stvo khudozhestvennoi literatury, 1960), 4:161–63.

27   Gorky, *Mother,* 398.

28   Maxim Gorky, "O. M. M. Prishvine" [On M. M. Prishvin], in Prishvin's book *Zhen' shen'* [Ginseng] (Moscow, 1937), 650.

29   Lenin, *Sochineniia* [Works] 4th ed. (Moscow: Politizdat, 1952), 14:117.

30   *Russian-English Dictionary of Winged Words* (Moscow: Russkii iazyk, 1988), 126. This maxim was advanced by Michurin in 1934, as if to confirm Mandelshtam's metaphor of labor-lust, fashioned in 1932.

31   Gachev derives the name of this complex from that of the Persian epic hero of the *Shah-nama* by the Firdousi (941–1020). As Russian examples of filocide, he cites Ilya Muromets, hero of the well-known cycle of *bylinas,* and Gogol's epic character Taras Bulba, both of whom murder their own sons. In Russian history, the best-known tsars, Ivan the Terrible and Peter the Great, committed filocide, as, in a sense, did Stalin, since he refused to exchange prisoners in order to gain his son Yakov's release from the Nazis, thereby condemning him to death. See Georgy Gachev, "Natsional'nye obrazy mira," *Voprosy literatury,* no. 10 (1987). English translation forthcoming in *Re-Entering the Sign: Articulating New Russian Culture,* ed. Ellen Berry and Anesa Miller-Pogacar (Ann Arbor: University of Michigan Press).

32   See Boris Paramonov, "Chevengur i okrestnosti," *Kontinent* (Paris) 54 (1987): 333–72.

6 · The Origins and Meaning of Russian Postmodernism

Portions of this chapter were first presented at the Modern Language Association Conference, San Francisco, December 1991.

1   Viacheslav Kuritsyn, "Postmodernizm: novaia pervobytnaia kul'tura," [Post-modernism: New primitive culture] *Novyi mir* [New world], no. 2 (1992): 227, 232. An English translation is forthcoming in *Re-Entering the Sign: Articulating New Russian Culture,* ed. Ellen Berry and Anesa Miller-Pogacar (Ann Arbor: University of Michigan Press).

2   A conference on literary postmodernism was held at the Gorky Literary Institute (Moscow) in April 1991; a roundtable on philosophical postmodernism was organized by *Voprosy filosofii,* the leading Moscow journal in the field (the proceedings are published in no. 3, (1993): 8– 16).

3   Marquis de Custine, *Nikolaevskaia Rossiia* (Moscow: Izdatel'stvo politicheskoi literatury, 1990), 94, 155–56.

4   Alexander Ivanovich Herzen (1812–70) was a prominent writer and publicist who founded and edited the liberal socioliterary journal, *The Pole Star* and its affiliated newspaper, *The Bell.* The latter was a leading organ in the debate over serfdom and land reform; it was printed abroad to avoid the tsarist censors and smuggled into Russia between 1857 and 1867. A.M.-P.

5   K. Skalkovsky, ed., *Materialy dlia fiziologii russkogo obshchestva. Malen'kaia khrestomatiia dlia vzroslykh. Mneniia russkikh o samikh sebe* (Saint Petersburg: A. S. Suvorin's Press, 1904), 106.

6   Is it not this "nominativity," this pure concern with names, that gives rise to the sinister power of the *nomenklatura,* that is, those people selected by no one and by no means meriting their stature, but who are named "secretary," "director," or "instructor" and have received power by virtue of these names?

7   On contemporary Russian conceptualism, see Chapter 1.

8   Fëdor Dostoevsky, *Notes from Underground,* quoted from the translation by Michael Katz for the Norton Critical Edition (Norton: New York and London, 1989), 5. A.M.-P.

9   Fëdor Dostoevsky, *A Raw Youth,* part I, chap. 8. Dostoevsky has several varia-tions on the theme of this vision, which affected him deeply, for example, in *A Weak Heart* (1848), in *Petersburg Dreams in Verse and in Prose* (1861), and in the sketches for *The Diary of a Writer* (1873).

10 Voluntary unpaid work on days off, originally on Saturdays. A.M.-P.

11 Dmitry Prigov, "Reagan's Image in Soviet Literature," quoted from the transla-tion by Andrew Wachtel in *Third Wave: The New Russian Poetry,* ed. Kent Johnson and Stephen Ashby (Ann Arbor: University of Michigan Press, 1992), 105. A.M.-P.

12 Jean Baudrillard, "The Precession of Simulacra," *Semiotexte* (New York, 1983), 2.

13 Dummy villages erected, according to foreigners, by the order of Prince Potem-kin along the route he was to take with Catherine II after the annexation of the Crimea, 1783. This expression is used allusively of something done for show, an ostentatious display designed to disguise an unsatisfactory state of affairs, a pretense that all is well, etc. See *Russian-English Dictionary of Winged Words* (Moscow: Russky iazyk, 1988), 162.

14 A key term in the Hindu traditions of India, roughly denoting the world of

sensuous phenomena, or cosmic illusion preventing one from attaining the perception of the Absolute.

15   Of course, this opposition of East and West rarely appears in a pure form, being supplemented by an internal opposition in the form of nonorthodox, "heretical" movements. But the tendency is of just this type. Albert Schweitzer concludes: "Both in Indian and European thought the affirmation and negation of the world and of life coexist side by side; however, in the Indian thought, the latter predominates, in European thought, the former." Quoted from *Vostok-Zapad* [East-West], (Moscow: Nauka, 1988), 214.

16   Ilya Kabakov, "On the Subject of 'the Void,' " in *Zhizn' mukh. Das Leben der Fliegen Kölnischer Kunstverein* (Cologne: Edition Cantz, 1992), 233.

17   I do not attribute any evaluative meaning to the terms "simulacrum" and "simulation." A "simulacrum" is neither better nor worse than that what it simulates; its nature is simply different.

18   Ilya Kabakov, "Kontseptualizm v Rossii" [Conceptualism in Russia], in *Zhizn' mukh*, 247, 249.

19   Dmitri Prigov, "Forty-ninth Alphabet Poem," in *Third Wave. The New Russian Poetry*, ed. Johnson and Ashby, A.M.-P.

20   Dmitri Prigov, "What more is there to say?" in *Third Wave: The New Russian Poetry*, ed. Johnson and Ashby, 102. We find a similar assumption on the part of the youngest of this generation of conceptualists, Pavel Peppershtein (born 1966): "The problem of self-expression through poetry never particularly concerned me; I was more interested in exposing certain 'poses' of culture and the methods of its self-reading." In *Third Wave: The New Russian Poetry*, 192.

21   It is curious that Prigov managed to transform his own name into a literary concept. The usage of a patronymic in Russian is required in official situations or in addressing elder people, but Prigov always introduced himself as "Dmitry Aleksandrovich" and addressed others in the same "official" manner. What would sound natural in the mouth of an official or a polite academician, acquired an additional "parodic" intonation in relation to such an "underground" figure as Prigov was. Prigov's self-representation as "Dmitry Aleksandrovich" is an example of how everyday communication can be conceptualized and transferred to the level of metalanguage.

22   Abram Tertz (Andrei Siniavsky), *On Socialist Realism* (New York: Pantheon Books, 1960), 90–91. For Siniavsky himself, the self-contradiction of socialist realism was something to be resolved by moving in the direction of *conscious* and *deliberate* classicism, which is not far from the conceptualists' intentional exploitation of socialist realist technique. On the one hand, Siniavsky still believed at that time (the late 1950s) in the fruitfulness of a "pure" artistic direction and identified himself as a modernist and as a representative of phantasmagoric art. On the other hand, while insisting on the self-conscious development of Soviet classicism and proposing that Stalin's death would be surrounded with religious miracles and that his relics would cure men possessed by demons (92), Siniavsky was the first critic to anticipate Soviet conceptualism, that is, the second stage of postmodernism.

23 *Literaturnyi entsiklopedicheskii slovar'* [Encyclopedic dictionary of literature]
    (Moscow: Sovetskaia entsiklopediia, 1987), 416.

24 Socialist realism was inclined to oppose itself very sharply and vehemently to
    avant-gardism. A recent treatment of their interrelationship, found in Boris
    Groys's valuable and provocative *The Total Art of Stalinism,* argues a contrary
    position, presenting the art of Stalin's epoch as the triumph of the avant-gardist
    project. Socialist realism is, from this point of view, "both reflected and consum-
    mated avant-garde demiurgism" (*The Total Art of Stalinism: Avant-garde, Aes-
    thetic Dictatorship, and Beyond,* trans. Charles Rougle [Princeton: Princeton
    University Press, 1992], 72). In contrast, Groys identifies socialist realism with
    postmodernism, claiming that "beginning with the Stalin years, at least, official
    Soviet culture, Soviet art, and Soviet ideology become eclectic, citational, 'post-
    modern'" (108). Groys is absolutely right to point to the affinity of socialist
    realism with both utopian avant-gardism and postmodernism, but it is important
    not to conflate these two aspects, as in his statement: "The utopianism of Soviet
    ideology consists, as it were, in its postmodernity" (108).

    I would suggest that socialist realism is neither avant-gardist nor postmodern-
    ist but represents a lengthy transition between the two epochs. By the fact of its
    realization in Stalin's time, the utopian project of the avant-garde ceases to be
    utopian and avant-gardist and gradually enters a postutopian—hence postmod-
    ernist—dimension. The messianic and transcendental ideas that the avant-garde
    opposes to existing reality, socialist realism presents as inherent to an already
    transformed, "new" reality, which postmodernism comes to interpret as ideolog-
    ical simulation and "hyperreality." In this context, the entire phenomenon of
    totalitarianism can be viewed as one mode of transition from avant-gardist pu-
    rity of style to postmodernist playful eclecticism. Early modernism's emphasis
    on the experimental sterility of aesthetic form is as serious as postmodernism's
    emphasis on eclecticism is playful. But why can't omnivorous eclecticism be
    combined with an imperative of seriousness in one cultural paradigm? This is
    where totalitarianism locates itself: as the intermediate link between modernism
    and postmodernism, attempting to embrace the diversity of styles and forms and
    to subject them to one unifying and compulsory design. Serious purity, serious
    eclecticism, playful eclecticism: these three stages may be identified as avant-
    gardism, socialist realism, and postmodernism, respectively.

    In the West, a similarly transitional status can be ascribed to so-called high
    modernism, which also attempts to supersede the experimental reductiveness of
    early modernism (the avant-garde) by bringing together a diversity of styles, but
    with a sense of their tragic incommensurability. Both high modernism and so-
    cialist realism may be qualified as two synchronically developing (1930s–
    1950s) forms of "serious eclecticism," with their principal divergence occurring
    in the realm of pathos. That is to say that seriousness can have two aesthetical
    modes: heroic/optimistic or tragic/pessimistic. The first is based on the value of
    comprehensive and aggressive collectivism, the second on the value of individu-
    ality, which strives in vain to embrace the universal while remaining aware of
    the inevitability of existential alienation. There is a certain affinity between such

major figures of Soviet and Western literature of the 1930s as Sholokhov and Faulkner, Platonov and Hemingway, Gorky and Thomas Mann. It is worth noting that representatives of high modernism were much better received by Soviet critics than were the early modernists (avant-gardists). What united Soviet writers with high modernists, in spite of their principal ideological distinctions, was the aesthetics of eclecticism, treated in the most serious and ethically responsible manner. For Soviet critics, the typical term used to assimilate high modernists into the ranks of "progressive" literature was "humanism," presupposing that all of these writers, Soviet and Western, were concerned not with the purity of stylistic devices—like the avant-gardists—but with the fate of humanity and its spiritual survival in the age of alienation. Certainly this hypothesis of "serious eclecticism" as a common quality of socialist realism and high modernism, and as a transitional stage between the serious purity of the avant-garde and the playful pastiche of postmodernism, requires a detailed elaboration that would lead us beyond the scope of this book.

25   Poet Andrei Voznesensky (1933–) and prose writer Vassily Aksyonov (1932–) were leaders of the 1960s generation and were associated with the youth theme in post-Stalinist literature. They had affinities with the futurist and abstractionist trends of the early avant-garde. They have been compared with writers of the American Beat generation. A.M.-P.

26   Tom Wolfe, "Stalking the Billion-Footed Beast: A Literary Manifesto for the New Social Novel," *Harper's Magazine,* November 1989, 50.

27   Wolfe, "Stalking the Billion-Footed Beast," 49.

28   Andrei Alexandrovich Zhdanov was a powerful Communist Party functionary from 1934 through 1948. His postwar denunciation of poet Anna Akhmatova and satirist Mikhail Zoshchenko for the alleged lack of social values in their works signaled a return to pervasive Party control of the cultural sphere, after the comparative freedom of the war years. A.M.-P.

29   *Doklad t. Zhdanova o zhurnalakh "Zvezda" i "Leningrad." Sokrashchennaia i obobshchennaia stenogramma dokladov t. Zhdanova na sobranii partiinogo aktiva i na sobranii pisatelei v Leningrade, OGIZ: Gosudarstvennoe izdatel'stvo politicheskoi literatury* [Comrade Zhdanov's report on the journals *Star* and *Leningrad,* a shortened and summarized stenogram of the report presented at the meeting of party activists and at the meeting of writers in Leningrad, State Publishing House of political literature] (Moscow, 1946), 12, 16–17.

30   Wolfe, "Stalking the Billion-Footed Beast," 49.

31   These issues are discussed at length in my article "Tom Wolfe and Social(ist) Realism," *Common Knowledge* [Oxford University Press] 1, no. 2 (1992): 147–60.

7 · At the Crossroads of Image and Concept

First published in *Voprosy literatury,* no. 7, (1987); this study was subsequently included in Epstein, *Paradoksy novizny.*

1   The first edition of Montaigne's *Essays* came out in the year 1580. See the pro-

ceedings of the international colloquium on this book and its significance for contemporary culture in *Montaigne et ses essais, 1580–1980* (Actes du Congrès du Bordeaux, Paris, 1983).

2   *Dictionary of World Literary Terms,* ed. J. T. Shipley (London, 1970), 106; A. F. Scott, *Current Literary Terms: A Concise Dictionary of Their Origin and Use* (Macmillan: London, 1965), 98. The distinctiveness of essay among literary genres can be paradoxically defined through its nondefinition: "Even more than most literary forms, the essay defies strict definition." John Gross, Introduction to *The Oxford Book of Essays,* chosen and edited by John Gross (Oxford: Oxford University Press, 1992), xix.

3   *The Complete Works of Montaigne,* trans. Donald M. Frame (Stanford: Stanford University Press, 1957), Book 2: chap. 8, 278. All quotations from Montaigne have been selected from this edition; subsequent citations are included in the text.

4   Seneca, *Lettres à Lucilius,* 1.3.3. Texte établi par François Préchac. (Paris: Société d'édition Belles Lettres, 1956), 1:8.

5   Mikhail Bakhtin, *Voprosy literatury i estetiki* (Moscow, 1975), 457, 480.

6   Quoted from Charles Lamb (1775–1834), *The Essays of Elia and the Last Essays of Elia* (London: Oxford University Press, 1946), 157, 191, 264. A.M.-P.

7   Mikhail Bakhtin, *Voprosy literatury i estetiki,* 476.

8   See the interesting observations on this subject by O. Vainshtein in her essay "Dlia chego i dlia kogo pisat' essay?" [For what and for whom does one write an essay?] *Literaturnaia ucheba* [Literary education], no. 2 (1985): 215–17.

9   The ambivalence of the Russian term for "essay" (*opyt*) offers a synthesis of the meanings "experience," which embraces the past, and "experiment," which tests the future—a kind of "experimence."

10   *Filosofskii entsiklopedicheskii slovar'* [Encyclopedic dictionary of philosophy] (Moscow, 1983), 377, entry on "mythology."

11   "Thought-image" is my translation for the author's term *mysleobraz.* A.M.-P.

12   S. A. Tokarev and E. M. Meletinsky, "Mifologiia," in *Mify narodov mira* [Myths of the peoples of the world] (Moscow, 1980), 1:13.

13   The author makes an untranslatable pun on the Russian words for "doubt," *somnenie,* and "opinion," *mnenie,* in which the prefix *so-* corresponds to the English "co-," or "along with." A.M.-P.

14   For details see Claude Lévi-Strauss, *Structural Anthropology* (Garden City, N.Y.: Anchor Books, 1967), translated from the French edition of 1958 by Claire Jacobson and Brooke Grundfest Schoepf. A.M.-P.

15   Quoted from Ivan Morris's translation from the Japanese, in *The Pillow Book of Sei Shonagon,* (New York: Columbia University Press, 1967), 1:69. Morris writes in his introduction that Sei Shonagon was a lady-in-waiting to Empress Sadako at the end of the tenth century A.D. and is considered to be "among the greatest writers of prose in the long history of Japanese literature" (xiii). A.M.-P.

16   J. Thomas Rimer writes in *Modern Japanese Fiction and Its Traditions* (Princeton: Princeton University Press, 1978) that the Japanese genre known as *zuihitsu* is an artistic essay whose name literally means "following the brush," (77). A.M.-P.

17   It is precisely this orientation in the essay toward the peculiar and often whimsical ways of the author himself that distinguishes this genre from ethnography proper (such works as Gleb Uspensky's [1843–1902] "Nravy Rasteriaevoi ulitsy" [The ways of Rasteriaeva Street]), in which the regulative function of myth has been lost: custom is taken as something frozen, belonging to objective reality, rather than as an expression of the magical will of the collective or the moral will of personality.

18   Tsvetaeva's essay (1932) is entitled in Russian "Zhivoe o zhivom." All quotations are from Marina Tsevetaeva, *Sochineniia* (Moscow, 1980), 2:190–92. A.M.-P.

19   Olga M. Freidenberg, "Obraz i poniatie" [Image and concept], *Mif i literatura antichnosti* [Myth and the literature of antiquity] (Moscow, 1978), 189, 188.

20   Mikhail Bakhtin, *Voprosy literatury i estetiki*, 450, 451.

21   The physiological sketches produced by Russian writers of the 1840s are considered an important phase in the development of realistic prose. These short, loosely structured works described living conditions of the lower classes, usually in an urban setting. A.M.-P.

22   *Joseph und seine Brüder.* In Thomas Mann, *Schriften und Reden zur Literatur, Kunst und Philosophie* (Frankfurt am Main: Fischer Bücherei, 1968), 2:384.

23   Robert Musil's *The Man Without Qualities* was first published in part in 1930. We quote from Eithne Wilkins and Ernst Kaiser's translation of 1954 as printed in the Picador edition (London: Pan Books, 1979), chap. 62, "The earth too, but Ulrich in particular, pays homage to the Utopian idea of Essayism" (29). A.M.-P.

24   Quoted from *Iunost'* [Youth], no. 6 (1982): 98.

25   Iury Olesha, *Ni dnia bez strochki. Iz zapisnykh knizhek* (Moscow: Sovetskii pisatel', 1965), 10 and 11.

26   The most graphic indication of this is imprinted in those experiments that graft philosophy into the genre of the diary, where the fleeting prattle of the moment barges shamelessly into meditations on eternity, and the petty shards of private life sink into the flesh of the contemplated life, wounding and scarring it, as in Vasily Rozanov's *Fallen Leaves* and *Solitude*.

27   Husserl, "Filosofiia kak strogaia nauka," in *Logos* (St. Petersburg, 1911), Book 1, 27.

28   *Husserliana: Gesammelte Werke* (Haag, 1950–79), 6:465.

29   Consider Losev's remarkable admission as to the integrative orientation of his creative scholarly work: "What is dear to me? The combination of strict systematicness with artistic, figurative vision." Quoted from *Voprosy literatury*, no. 10 (1985): 216.

   Particular notice should be taken of the work of Georgy Gachev, executed in an utterly original genre known as "life-thoughts," which profoundly renew the panoramic intellectual quest of the entire twentieth century. Perhaps never before has essayistic consciousness constructed such multileveled thought-images, descending to the very heart of the everyday while simultaneously soaring to the heights of pure speculation. See especially his *Natsional'nye obrazy mira* [National images of the world] (Moscow, Sovetskii pisatel', 1987).

30   Thomas Mann, *Schriften und Reden*, 1:384.

31 Ibid., 389, 390.

32 See Charles Lamb, *The Essays of Elia and the Last Essays of Elia* (London: Oxford University Press, 1946). A.M.-P.

8 · Thing and Word

An early version of this essay was presented at the 1984 Vipper Conference and included in its proceedings under the title *Veshch' v iskusstve* [Thing in art] (Moscow, 1986); subsequently revised and expanded, it appeared in Epstein, *Paradoksy novizny.*

1 The Kremlin Armory and Diamond Fund contain treasures of antique military equipment and the tsarist crown jewels. A.M.-P.

2 Epstein speaks of the indivisibility of human beings and their things in terms of *cheloveshchnaia obshchnost'*—"human-thing commonality"—which allows things to obtain a "forehead" (*chelo*) from a person (*chelovek*) while offering material extensions to the human body. A.M.-P.

.3 I proposed the project of creating such a discipline in the article "Realogiia—nauka o veshchakh" [Realogy—the science of things], *Dekorativnoe iskusstvo SSSR* [Decorative art of the USSR], no. 6 (1985): 21–22, 44. See also the following interesting discussions of the proposed project and the general problematics of "realogy," published in various issues of the same journal: V. Aronov, "Veshch' v aspekte iskusstvoznaniia" [Things from the perspectives of art studies], no. 11 (1985); L. Annenkova, " 'Realogiia' i smysl veshchi" ["Realogy" and the meaning of a thing], no. 10 (1986); and N. Voronov, "Na poroge 'veshchevedeniia' " [On the threshold of "thing studies"], no. 10 (1986).

4 Distinctions in usage between the Russian *veshch'* and *predmet* are indicated in the *Slovar' sochetaemosti slov russkogo iazyka* [Dictionary of Russian word combinations] (Moscow: Russkii iazyk, 1983), 53, 423.

5 In Russian only the complements "object" and "thing" differentiate these statements; the verbs are identical: *On sdelal khoroshii predmet* and *On sdelal khoroshuiu veshch'*. It is not possible to retain the identity of phrasing in English without straining acceptable usage. A.M.-P.

6 See V. V. Kolesov, "Drevnerusskaia veshch'" [The thing in Old Russia], in *Kul'turnoe nasledie Drevnei Rusi* [Cultural heritage of Old Russia] (Leningrad: Nauka, 1976), 260–64.

7 Antimaterialism originates at precisely the same time as "thingism" (mass production and consumer fetishism) and suffers from the same limitations. One of the earliest and best examples of the contemporary view of this problem can be found in Mayakovsky's tragedy "Vladimir Mayakovsky" (1913):

> Old man with cats: In the land of cities they became the masters
>> and now come creeping to crush us, soulless hordes of things.
>> . . . There, you see!
>> I wasn't wrong when I foresaw an enemy in their embraces!
> Man with a long face: But maybe things should be loved?
>> Maybe things have a different kind of soul?

This is exactly the point: not to reject things, complaining of their "soulless-ness," but to assume that they have their own, a "different" kind of soul, which requires a response and must be comprehended through love. Antimaterialism takes up the torch from materialism and hurls these things, already alienated from man, even farther into the zone of nonbeing and the accursed, thus eth-ically justifying the results achieved by commercial fetishism. But the task should be to draw closer to them, assimilating them even in their basic alien quality. The colder, more random, more "industrial" a product may be, the greater internal care is needed for it to compose itself as a thing, as an ontological fact; this orphanhood of the majority of things in contemporary life should in-spire neither malice nor apathy, but a sense of kinship, a willingness to adopt, to make up for their initial rootlessness.

8   It may well have been Rilke who sensed earlier and more deeply than anyone else the new demands placed on human creativity by the crisis in the traditional assimilation and succession of things. He wrote: "For our grandfathers there still were 'a home,' 'a well,' a familiar tower, and simply their own dress or coat; almost everything was a vessel from which they were drawing something human and into which they invested and stored something human. . . . Animated things, participating in our lives, disappear and cannot be replaced. *Perhaps we are the last ones to know such things.* We have a responsibility not only for keeping their memory (this would be too little and unreliable) and their human and divine (as in domestic deities) worth. . . . Our goal is to accept this transient perishable earth with such depth, such passion, and such suffering that its essence would 'invisibly' resurrect in us once again." R. M. Rilke, "Letter to V. von Gulevich, 13. XI. 1925," *Vorpsvede. Auguste Rodin. Letters. Poems* (Moscow: Iskusstvo, 1971), 305. "Vorpsvede" is the name of a group of German landscape painters in the late nineteenth and early twentieth centuries. Rilke devoted a long essay to them.

9   Quoted from Thomas P. Whitney's translation of Andrei Platonov, *Kotlovan: The Foundation Pit,* bilingual edition (Ann Arbor: Ardis, 1973), 8. A.M.-P.

10   Platonov, *The Foundation Pit,* 32 (translation corrected).

11   In substantiating realogy as a field of knowledge one could use Rickert's ideas on the construction of "individualizing" sciences, which (in distinction from the "generalizing" ones) deal with the meaning of singular phenomena; see Heinrich Rickert, *The Philosophy of History* (St. Petersburg, 1908), 19 passim. Not only history, as the study of meaning in single-instance events on the axis of time, but a new X discipline should be included in such sciences to study the unique formations of meaning on the axes of space. What we have tentatively called "realogy" is such a science of things, as the formational units of space, the borders of its meaningful divisions, through which are manifest its axiological fullness and the cultural significance of the metrics of nature (not unlike the understanding of history as a revelation of axiological fullness in time, in the meaningful units of events).

According to contemporary conceptions in the humanities, things endow space with the properties of a text. "In space, things illuminate a particular paradigm which they themselves represent, and their ordering represents a syntagma, that is, a kind of text"; V. N. Toporov, "Space and Text," in *Text: Semantics and Structure,* ed. T. V. Tsivian (Moscow: Nauka, 1983), 279–80. Thus, realogy is the science of *realized* space—that is, space that has been divided and filled with things—space and its textual properties, which are recoded in linguistic texts in the genre of "verbjects." The lyrical museum is a space that speaks in two languages simultaneously: the language of things and of words, thereby revealing the limits and potentials of their intertranslatability.

12   The general idea for such a division of space belongs to the linguist Alexei Mikheev. A feasible, concrete design for a lyrical exposition has been proposed by artist Francisco Infante. What follows is a related literary-conceptual project.

13   These may be compared with the experiments of other authors, participants in a proposed exhibition: V. V. Aristov and A. V. Mikheev, "Text descriptions of things as exhibits for a 'lyrical museum,'" in *The "Thing" in Art: Conference Proceedings, 1984* (Moscow: Sovetskii pisatel', 1986), 324–31.

14   Quoted from *The Complete Works of Montaigne,* trans. Donald M. Frame (Stanford: Stanford University Press, 1957), 298. A.M.-P.

15   In Russian, "language" and "tongue" are expressed by the same word: *iazyk.* A.M.-P.

9 · Culture–Culturology–Transculture

The greater part of this chapter was presented as a lecture at the official opening of the Laboratory of Contemporary Culture in Moscow, on 26 March 1988, with the intention of offering a program for the laboratory's future work (see the Introduction for additional information). The lecture was published in abridged form in *Nauka i zhizn'* [Science and life], no. 1 (1990): 100–103. Additional material contained in the present essay was developed in conversation with Anesa Miller-Pogacar at the Woodrow Wilson International Center for Scholars, 10 January 1991.

1   See the more extensive discussion of the concept "proto" in the Conclusion.

2   The type of knowledge that incorporates an awareness of the wholeness of the world cannot be limited to any one single scientific, artistic, or philosophical field but rather should emerge as an experiment in shaping a transcultural consciousness capable of overcoming the boundaries that divide specific disciplines.

3   Oswald Spengler, "Causality and Fate," in *The Decline of the West,* vol. 1, introduction, section 12.

4   Aleksandr Nikolaevich Radishchev (1749–1802) is best known as the author of a travelogue describing his observations of rural poverty and conjectures on the possibilities for social reform, entitled *A Journey From Petersburg to Moscow,* for which he was sentenced to ten years of Siberian exile. Gavrila Romanovich Derzhavin (1743–1816) was well known in his lifetime as both a statesman and a poet. He came to be considered the greatest writer of lyrics and odes of the era of Catherine the Great. A.M.-P.

5   "Decembrism" refers to a short-lived conspiratorial movement that ended tragically for its primarily young, aristocratic participants following their attempted

demonstration of protest against serfdom and other tsarist policies in December 1825. Five leaders of a diverse group centered among officers of the military were executed as a result of the conspiracy, and many more were sent into exile. On the "superfluous man," see Chapter 3. A.M.-P.

6   A similar definition of culture is proposed by the contemporary Russian philosopher Vladimir Bibler, who writes "Culture may be defined as a form of self-determination, self-preconditioning (and the possibility of reconsidering) of human activity, will, consciousness, thinking, and fate, ... as the form of concentration in an individual fate, in the present, of all past and future times" (Bibler, *Ot naukoucheniia—k logike kul'tury. Dva filosofskikh vvedeniia v dvadtsat' pervyi vek* [From the logic of science to the logic of culture: Two philosophical introductions to the twenty-first century] [Moscow: Politizdat, 1991], 304).

7   Osip Mandelshtam, *Slovo i kul'tura* [Word and culture] (Moscow, 1987), 42–43.

8   Mikhail Bakhtin, *Speech Genres and Other Late Essays,* trans. Vern W. McGee, ed. Caryl Emerson and Michael Holquist (Austin: University of Texas Press, 1986), 2.

9   Bibler, *Ot naukoucheniia—k logike kul'tury,* 286, 289.

10 Vladimir Soloviev (1853–1900) was a philosopher and poet who strongly influenced both the symbolist movement in Russian literature and Orthodox religious thought of the early twentieth century.

Petr Yakovlevich Chaadaev (1794–1856) was a social philosopher and independent scholar who came to be considered a leading thinker of the "Westernizing" bent, in that he sharply criticized what he deemed the isolationism and narrowness of native Russian traditions, while expressing admiration for Western European ways. Although none of his critical works could be published during his lifetime, Chaadaev's thought survived as an inspiration to such poets as Pushkin and Mandelshtam.

Alexei Stepanovich Khomiakov (1804–60) devoted himself to the areas of historical philosophy, theology, and creative writing. Ostensibly an ideological opponent of Chaadaev, Khomiakov became a leader of the Slavophile movement, which sought the roots of Russian culture in traditional beliefs and practices; nonetheless, the two men are said to have had profound personal respect for one another. Certain of Khomiakov's ideas were later extrapolated in Soloviev's work as well as among the symbolists.

The reference to "a thousand or two thousand years separating us from the ... turning points of our own and world culture" indicates the Christianization of Kievan Rus in 988 A.D. (see further mention in Chapter 6) and the dawn of Christianity, respectively. A.M.-P.

11 Saint Serafim of Sarov (1760–1833) taught that the goal of Christian life is to search for the Holy Spirit (*stiazhanie Dukha Sviatogo*). He is considered to be the greatest spiritual patron of Russia, and a number of churches, restored in the postcommunist period, are dedicated to him.

12 On Vladimir Soloviev, see note 10 above.

Dmitry Sergeevich Merezhkovsky (1865–1941) was a writer and religious philosopher associated with the early phases of the Russian symbolist movement.

On Nikolai Berdiaev see Chapter 2, especially note 12, and also Chapter 6. A.M.-P.

13 The German thinker Johann Herder was probably the first (as early as 1784–91) to insist on the principle of plurality of cultures, in his *Ideas on the Philosophy of History of Mankind*. It was not until the early twentieth century, however, that this usage was established in European languages. See Raymond Williams, *Keywords: A Vocabulary of Culture and Society* (New York: Oxford University Press, 1976), 79.

14 This example is taken from the first issue of the magazine *Dar. Kul'tura Rossii* (1992), which is sponsored by the current Russian government and intended to present the most characteristic aspects of contemporary Russian culture.

15 Pushkin's phrase refers to the violent excesses and poor leadership typical of Russian peasant and national rebellions, such as those instigated by Stenka Razin between 1670 and 1671 and by Emelian Pugachev between 1773 and 1775. The combination of these men's names with the suffix *-shchina* yields a term meaning, roughly, "the Razin or Pugachev syndrome," which is here extended to the names of Lenin and Stalin as well. A.M.-P.

16 See, for example, Sri Aurobindo, *SAVITRI: A Legend and a Symbol* (Pondicherry, India: Sri Aurobindo Ashram Press, 1950–51).

17 "In order to understand, it is immensely important for the person who understands to be located outside the object of his or her creative understanding—in time, in space, in culture." Bakhtin, *Speech Genres and Other Late Essays*, 7.

18 In Bibler's definition, "culture is a communication of actual and/or potential cultures" (*Ot naukoucheniia—k logike kul'tury*, 298). I prefer to avoid the vicious circle that Bibler deliberately and permanently emphasizes in his works, incorporating the concept of culture in the very definition of culture and producing a kind of tautology. This exemplifies his "logic of paradox," but it must be clear, that "culture" in the left and right parts of his definition belong to different logical types, and what arises through the "communication of cultures" is a new, "meta" level of cultural existence that I call "transculture."

19 Merab Mamardashvili, "Drugoe nebo" [Another sky], in his *Kak ia ponimaiu filosofiiu* [How I understand philosophy] (Moscow: "Kul'tura" imprint, Progress Publishers, 1992), 335, 337.

20 Mamardashvili, "Drugoe nebo," 336.

21 Bakhtin, *Speech Genres and Other Late Essays*, 7.

22 Daniil Andreev, *Roza Mira. Metafilosofiia istorii* [The rose of the world: A metaphilosophy of history] (Moscow: Prometei, 1991), 123.

23 Bhabha, Homi K. "DissemiNation: Time, Narrative, and the Margins of the Modern Nation," in Homi K. Bhabha, ed., *Nation and Narration* (London: Routledge, 1990), 313.

10 · Theory and Fantasy

A version of this article first appeared in *Voprosy literatury*, no. 12 (1987). The appendix was first published in Epstein, *Paradoksy novizny*.

1 *Filosofskii entsiklopedicheskii slovar'* [Encyclopedic dictionary of philosophy] (Moscow, 1983), 344.

2 Trofim Denisovich Lysenko (1898–1976) was a director of the USSR Academy of Sciences Institute of Genetics, and Nikolai Iakovlevich Marr (1865–1934) was a leading Soviet linguist. During the Stalin era, these men advanced new theoretical approaches in their respective fields in an attempt to introduce Marxist methods and perspectives, much of which was later renounced and abandoned. A.M.-P.

3 *Voprosy literatury* [Issues in literature] is a prominent academic journal, published jointly by the Gorky Institute of World Literature in Moscow and the (former) Union of Soviet Writers since 1957. A.M.-P.

4 The methods of Soviet Marxist scholarship had degenerated by the 1970s and 1980s into a pure scholasticism that could not be criticized in official publications. Scholars tended to avoid theoretical topics that had to be justified on Marxist-Leninist grounds. Thus literary theory became the province of ideologues and dogmatists, while creative thinkers gave the appearance of having nothing to do with theory as they worked in such applied areas as poetics or the typology of cultures in which Marxist methodology was not strictly required.

5 Talent in the area of pure literary theory is extremely rare, if, indeed, it is possible at all. Exceptions to this rule would seem to serve as its affirmation; for example, only under the intense pressure of historical conditions did Mikhail Bakhtin's enormous talent accommodate itself primarily to this sphere, which artificially narrowed and restricted his intellectual diapason.

6 The Soviet approach to structuralism and semiotics, as practiced from the 1950s through the 1980s primarily by two loosely affiliated groups known as the Moscow-Tartu School, suffered consistent disparagement in the orthodox Marxist press throughout the Brezhnev era. A.M.-P.

7 History itself may be seen as such a continuum, thereby returning historicism to our discussion, on the generalized level of continualism, which may apply to time, space, and meaning alike. I find the most stimulating and fundamental contribution to the methodology of continualism in the works of contemporary Russian scientist and scholar Vasily Nalimov (b. 1910): *In the Labyrinths of Language: A Mathematician's Journey* (1981), *Realms of the Unconscious: The Enchanted Frontier* (1982), *Space, Time, and Life: The Probabilistic Pathways of Evolution* (1985), all edited by Robert G. Colodny and published in Philadelphia by ISI Press. Proceeding from the mathematical apparatus of the theory of probability, Nalimov comes to the interpretation of meaning as a "wavelike" continuity that cannot fit any "discrete" concept.

8 This term is coined from "raster," the optical fretwork used to transform points of light into an image; this consists of an alternation between transparent and opaque (or absorbent and nonabsorbent) elements.

9 Vissarion Belinsky (1811–48) has been called the first professional literary critic in Russian history. He established a method of discussing both the moral—or in most cases, sociopolitical—and artistic merits of literary works. Ovsianiko-

Kulikovsky (1853–1920), a follower of Alexander Potebnia's psychological linguistics, studied literary images as evidence of personality types from the standpoint of cultural history. A.M.-P.

10   *The Brothers Karamazov,* quoted from the translation by David Magarshak (New York: Penguin Books, 1982), 377. A.M.-P.

11   The Left Front of Art, known in Russian by the acronym LEF, was an affiliation of experimental artists, poets, and critics, active between approximately 1922 and 1928. Among the better-known participants and associates of the group were the futurist poets Vladimir Mayakovsky, Nikolai Aseev, and Aleksei Kruchenykh, and the formalistically inclined theorists Victor Shklovsky, Boris Eikhenbaum, and Osip Brik. The group published a journal entitled *LEF* between 1922 and 1925. A.M.-P.

12   The expression of philosopher Valentin Asmus, who in the 1920s argued against LEF's theories of "unadorned fact." "As in nature, a plant is forced to put out tens of thousands of seeds, a fish to spawn tens and hundreds of thousands of eggs so that in the end only a few new trees and fish may grow up, so too should inventiveness 'play' as it creates thousands of perhaps predominantly strange and fantastical variants of ideal or potential being, in order that as a result of this 'play' one or two tasks for theoretical thinking could be solved." From *Voprosy teorii i istorii estetiki* (Moscow: Iskusstvo, 1968), 33. Not coincidentally, it was at approximately the same time that the most consistent philosophical apology for imagination ever conceived in the history of Russian thought appeared in Ia. E. Golosovker's *Imaginativnyi absoliut* [The imaginative absolute] (first nonpublished version, 1928–36). This work proposed the task of "building a gnoseology of the imagination, in order to open the eyes of thinkers and touch the conscience of science with regard to the role of imagination in culture"; quoted from Ia. E. Golosovker, *Logika mifa* [The Logic of myth] (Moscow: Nauka, 1987), 153. The "conscience of science" is an apt target, since nowhere else is imagination put to such clandestine use, almost unwillingly, and with such contrived disdain, as in the natural sciences.

13   Paul Feyerabend, *Against Method: Outline of an Anarchistic Theory of Knowledge* (London: New Left Books, 1975), 47.

14   The term *vnenakhodimost',* known to American readers primarily from the work of Mikhail Bakhtin, is usually rendered in English as "transgredience" or "extralocality." This transcendent positionality of subjective consciousness vis-à-vis its surroundings has been explained as follows: "I go out to the other in order to come back with a self. I 'live into' an other's consciousness. . . . I render the other complete by the additions I make to her from my position of being both inside and outside her." From Katerina Clark and Michael Holquist, *Mikhail Bakhtin* (Cambridge: Harvard University Press, 1984), 78–79. A.M.-P.

15   Feyerabend, *Against Method,* 30.

16   Aristotle, *Metaphysics,* Book 1, chap. 2, in *A New Aristotle Reader,* ed. J. L. Ackrill (Princeton: Princeton University Press, 1987), 258.

17   In Russian the words "reflect," "strike," and "imagination" all contain the same root: *otrazhat', porazhat',* and *voobrazhat'.* A.M.-P.

18   The appeal for a "new rubric" was originally addressed to the editors of *Issues in Literature;* see note 3 above. A.M.-P.

19   For a more detailed discussion of this point, see M. N. Epstein, "Operativnost' pechati kak spedstvo intensifikatsii i integratsii nauchnogo myshleniia" [Functionality of the press as a means for intensification and integration of scientific thought], in *Uskorenie i perestroika v sisteme nauchno-tekhnicheskoi informatsii SSSR* [Acceleration and perestroika in the system of scientific and technical information of the USSR] (Moscow, 1987).

20   The following explication of the concept of kenotypes was submitted to the Bank of New Ideas and Terms described in this chapter. As a new term proposed for use throughout the humanitarian disciplines, Epstein's notion of kenotype was discussed by participants in the bank and has since been adopted by a number of scholars. A.M.-P.

21   Listed are the names of heroes from the following works: Griboedov's *Woe From Wit* (1824), Pushkin's *Eugene Onegin* (1833), Gogol's *Dead Souls* (1842), and Goncharov's *Oblomov* (1859). A.M.-P.

22   Rhineland mythology includes a tale of "Venus and the good Knight Tannhäuser" who enjoyed a liaison on an enchanted mountain. A.M.-P.

23   Thomas Mann, "Nietzsche's Philosophie im Lichte unserer Erfahrung," in *Schriften und Reden Zur Literatur, Kunst und Philosophie,* ed. Hans Burgen (Frankfurt am Main: Fischer Bucherei, 1968) 3:24.

24   These are lines from Pushkin's poems *The Bronze Horseman* and "To the Sea," respectively. A.M.-P.

Conclusion: A Future after the Future

1   Mikhail Bakhtin, *Speech Genres and Other Late Essays,* trans. Vern W. McGee, ed. Caryl Emerson and Michael Holquist (Austin: University of Texas Press, 1986), 139.

2   Mikhail Bakhtin, *Literaturno-kriticheskie stat'i* [Literary critical articles] (Moscow: Khudozhestvennaia literatura, 1986), 513.

3   Mikhail Bakhtin, *Problems of Dostoevsky's Poetics,* ed. and trans. Caryl Emerson (Minneapolis: University of Minnesota Press, 1984), 166.

4   Jean-François Lyotard, *The Postmodern Condition: A Report on Knowledge* (originally published in French in 1979), trans. Geoff Bennington and Brian Massumi (Minneapolis: University of Minnesota Press, 1984), 79, 81.

5   Fredric Jameson, "Postmodernism, or The Cultural Logic of Late Capitalism," *New Left Review* (Oxford: Alden Press), no. 146 (June 1984): 65.

6   Fredric Jameson, Foreword to Jean-François Lyotard, *The Postmodern Condition: A Report on Knowledge,* xvi.

7   Dmitry Prigov, "What More is There to Say," in Kent Johnson and Stephen M. Ashby, eds., *Third Wave: The New Russian Poetry* (Ann Arbor: University of Michigan Press, 1992), 102.

8   A major representative of "new sincerity" in contemporary Russian prose is Venedikt Erofeev (1938–90), the author of the short novel *Moskva—Petushki*

[Moscow to the end of the line]. For the analysis of "new sentimentality" and "counterirony" in his works, see my article "Posle karnavala, ili vechnyi Venichka" [After the carnival, or eternal Venichka], *Zolotoi vek* [The Golden Age] (Moscow), no. 4 (1993): 84–92.

In Russian cinema, a manifestation of "new sincerity" can be found in Dmitry Meskhiev's *Over Dark Water* (1992), which presents stereotypical situations from the lives of the generation of the sixties (the cult of male friendship, the dignity of suicide, etc.) and thus can be viewed as a parody of films of that time, such as those of Marlen Khutsiev. However, the parodic element is counterbalanced by a strong lyrical and nostalgic empathy that creates the field of "the shimmering aesthetic." One of the last utterances of the protagonist, who appears to his son after his death, is "what is more beautiful than trivial effects?" And this is not only the ethical conclusion of his life, but also the aesthetic formula of "new sincerity." If "hard" conceptualism demonstrated the stereotypical character of emotion, then "soft" conceptualism, which transcends the postmodernist paradigm, consciously reveals the emotional power and authenticity of stereotypes.

9   Jorge Luis Borges, "Pierre Menard: Author of the Quixote," in his *Labyrinths* (New York: Modern Library, 1983), 42.

10 This, again, invokes Bakhtin's legacy, which, according to his well-known investigators, presupposes the inevitability of innovation. "Indeed, some of Bakhtin's models demonstrate that freedom is, paradoxically, inevitable: 'We live in freedom by necessity,' as W. H. Auden wrote." Gary Saul Morson and Caryl Emerson, *Mikhail Bakhtin: Creation of a Prosaics* (Stanford: Stanford University Press, 1990), 38.

11 Russian culture is known for its special devotion to "futurocentrism," which is perhaps another form of "logocentrism" (the archetype of the "second coming": Logos arrives from the future). This utopian bias, however, has found a strong opposition in such "prophetic" Russian thinkers as Herzen, Tolstoy, Dostoevsky, and Berdiaev, who rejected "the sacrifice of the present for the sake of the future" as a sort of revolutionary idolatry. It is remarkable that their *negation of future* as a predictable and attainable reality helped to formulate the conception of *future as negation*. According to an outstanding Russian philosopher S. L. Frank (1877–1950), "We know about the future decisively nothing. The future is always a great X of our life—unknown, impenetrable mystery." S. L. Frank, *Nepostizhimoe* [Incomprehensible] (Paris, 1939), 35. This presupposes a new, algebraic rather than arithmetic approach to future as "unknown quality." For more detail on the utopian and anti-utopian conceptions of the future in Russian thought, see George Kline " 'Present,' 'Past,' and 'Future' as Categoreal Terms, and the 'Fallacy of the Actual Future,'" *Review of Metaphysics* 40 (1986): 215–35.

12 "Crystal palace" is a name given to a building designed by Sir Joseph Paxton and displayed at the Great Exhibition of London in 1851. Nikolai Chernyshevsky made this edifice a symbol of the attainment of human happiness through rational social organization in his programmatic novel *What Is to Be Done?* (1863)

Fedor Dostoevsky responded with speculations on the failures of rationalism in *Winter Notes on Summer Impressions* (1863) and *Notes From Underground* (1864).

"Gulag Archipelago" refers to the Soviet system of penal camps and prisons and serves as the title of Alexander Solzhenitsyn's documentary work on this topic published in 1973. A.M.-P.

INDEX OF NAMES

INDEX OF SUBJECTS